Stories of the Law

Stories of the Law

*Narrative Discourse and the Construction
of Authority in the Mishnah*

MOSHE SIMON-SHOSHAN

Oxford University Press is a department of the University of Oxford.
It furthers the University's objective of excellence
in research, scholarship, and education by publishing worldwide.

Oxford   New York
Auckland   Cape Town   Dares Salaam   Hong Kong   Karachi
Kuala Lumpur   Madrid   Melbourne   Mexico City   Nairobi
New Delhi   Shanghai   Taipei   Toronto

With offices in
Argentina   Austria   Brazil   Chile   Czech Republic   France   Greece
Guatemala   Hungary   Italy   Japan   Poland   Portugal   Singapore
South Korea   Switzerland   Thailand   Turkey   Ukraine   Vietnam

Oxford is a registered trade mark of Oxford University Press in the UK and
certain other countries.

Published in the United States of America by
Oxford University Press
198 Madison Avenue, New York, NY 10016

© Oxford University Press 2012

First issued as an Oxford University Press paperback, 2013.

All rights reserved. No part of this publication may be reproduced,
stored in a retrieval system, or transmitted, in any form or by any means,
without the prior permission in writing of Oxford University Press, or as expressly
permitted by law, by license, or under terms agreed with the appropriate reproduction
rights organization. Inquiries concerning reproduction outside the scope of the above
should be sent to the Rights Department, Oxford University Press, at the address above.

You must not circulate this work in any other form
and you must impose this same condition on any acquirer.

Library of Congress Cataloging-in-Publication Data
Simon-Shoshan, Moshe, 1970–
Stories of the law : narrative discourse and the construction of
authority in the Mishnah / Moshe Simon-Shoshan.
p. cm.
Includes bibliographical references.
ISBN 978-0-19-977373-2 (hardcover :alk. paper); 978-0-19-935638-6 (pbk).
1. Narration in rabbinical literature.   2. Mishnah—Criticism, Narrative.   3. Jewish law
in literature.   I. Title.
BM496.9.N37S56 2012
296.1'27406—dc23
2011029887

To my wife,
Bracha
ישא ברכה מאת ה'
and my children:
Zvi Aryeh Chaim, Tova Shlomit, and Batsheva Zipporah
די לא יפסוק ודי לא יבטול מפתגמי אורייתא

CONTENTS

Acknowledgments ix
Preface for Nonspecialists in Rabbinic Literature xiii
Notes on Texts, Translations, and Transcriptions xv

1. Introduction 1

PART ONE   NARRATIVITY IN THE MISHNAH

2. Stories, Narratives, and Narrativity 15
3. A Typology of Mishnaic Forms 23
4. Mishnaic Topography 59
5. The Mishnah in Comparative Context 73

PART TWO   THE MISHNAIC STORY

6. Transmission, Redaction, and Rhetoric 95
7. Exempla: Who Is a Rabbi? 130
8. Case Stories: Repetition and Renewal 167
9. Etiological Stories: Original Nightmares 194

10. Conclusion 220

Appendix: List of Stories in the Mishnah 232
Notes 234

Bibliography   263
Citation Index: Mishnah, Tosefta, Yerushalmi, and Bavli   275
Subject Index   277

ACKNOWLEDGMENTS

"Were it not for Thy Torah..."
—Psalms 119:92

This book is in many ways the culmination of a journey that has consumed much of the past twenty or so years of my life. As such, each stop along the way needs to be noted for its contribution to the text in front of you.

The first steps of this voyage were taken in the month of Elul 5748—August 1988, when I first arrived in Alon Shvut to begin what would ultimately become more than three years of study at Yeshivat Har Etzion. It was there that I was initiated into the analytic study of Talmudic texts, gaining knowledge and skills crucial to the writing of the book. It was also there that I began the intensive study of traditional Hebrew narratives, in this case those of the Bible, both on my own and with teachers including, most notably, R. Mordechai Breuer z"l. Later, at the yeshiva's Herzog Teachers Institute (now College) I gained my earliest introduction to the critical study of rabbinic texts and of Semitic languages. Most importantly, it was at Yeshivat Har Etzion that I was inspired to embark on a life committed to the study and teaching of traditional Jewish texts.

My next stop was Princeton University, where I received my undergraduate education. Here I was taught the methods and theory of literary analysis and of humanistic studies in general. The tools and ideas that I learned there are evidenced on every page of this book. In particular I was privileged to work with several outstanding scholars in that time. In my junior year, under the tutelage of Ilana Pardes and Andrew H. Plaks, I began my first efforts at narrative analysis of biblical texts. During the summer before my senior year in college I received an NEH summer grant and worked under the supervision of Moshe Bernstein of Yeshiva University. I was fortunate to have my senior year coincide with Robert Alter's residency as a visiting professor at Princeton. Professor Alter's supervision of my senior thesis helped me to produce my first extended work of literary scholarship and taught me much about the crafts of reading and writing.

Following graduation, I returned to Israel, to the Hebrew University, where I began the philological and historical study of rabbinic literature in earnest. During that time, I was blessed to work with Jonah Fraenkel on a one-on-one basis. He supervised my first forays into the world of rabbinic stories.

I continued my studies in biblical and rabbinic literature at the University of Pennsylvania. The doctoral dissertation that I wrote there under David Stern is the basis of this book. On repeated occasions, both during the writing of the dissertation and subsequent to it, David challenged me to push my work beyond well-charted territory and conventional conclusions. The book is far richer as a result.

I physically wrote my dissertation largely in the Brandeis University library during my sojourn in Boston. At Brandeis, the Judaica librarians, Jim Rosenblum and Nancy Zibman, welcomed me warmly and greatly assisted my work. While in Boston, I also benefited from the rich scholarly community there, especially from Sacvan Bercovitch and Bernard Septimus.

In writing this book, I extensively revised and expanded my dissertation. This would not have been possible if not for the two years I spend as a Krietman Fellow at Ben-Gurion University, where I was hosted by Tamar Alexander and the department of Hebrew literature.

My editor Cynthia Read and the entire staff at Oxford University Press have been a pleasure to work with and have been models of professionalism.

Many individuals contributed to this book through their expertise, by reading and commenting on segments of the manuscripts or in other ways. The following is a partial list of these people: Elizabeth Alexander, Maria DiBattista, Caryl Emerson, Yoel Finkelman, Shamma Friedman, Shalom Holtz, Adina Moshavi, David Prebor, David Rothstein, Jeffrey Rubenstein, Avi Schmidman, Sasha Stern, and Suzanne Stone. My mother, Naomi Goldstein, and my brother, Jeremy Rosenbaum Simon, deserve special mention for their unflagging support and willingness to read and edit chapters on short notice. Similarly, in addition to their technical contributions, Ishay Rosen-Zvi, Beth Berkowitz, and Steven Fraade all expressed consistent enthusiasm for this project, which was a source of constant encouragement to me over the years.

I would like to acknowledge Harvard University Press for granting the rights to reproduce the first line of Emily Dickenson's poem number 1129 at the head of chapter 6 of the book. Similarly, the last line of W. B. Yeats' "Among School Children," which appears at the head of chapter seven is reprinted with the permission of Scribner, a division of Simon & Schuster, Inc., from *The Collected Works of W. B. Yeats, Volume I: The Poems, Revised by W. B. Yeats*. Copyright © 1928 by The Macmillan Company, renewed 1956 by Georgie Yeats. All rights reserved. Electronic rights to this text were granted by A P Watt Ltd. literary agents on behalf of Gráinne Yeats. Parts of chapter 6 first appeared in *Diné Israel* 24 (2007) under the title "Halakhic Mimesis: Rhetorical and Redactional Strategies in Tannaitic Narrative." They are reproduced with permission.

Aharon, aharon, I would like to thank my wife, Bracha. Her support during the entire period in which this book was conceived and written in its various incarnations was absolutely crucial to me. She further painstakingly edited the entire final manuscript and suggested and helped design the charts that accompany chapter 3. It is to her and to the three children she has given us, Zvi, Tova, and Batsheva, that this book is dedicated.

Beit Shemesh, Israel
Rosh Chodesh Adar II 5771

PREFACE FOR NONSPECIALISTS IN RABBINIC LITERATURE

It is my hope that this book will also be of interest to readers other than scholars and students of rabbinic literature, especially people interested in the study of narrative, legal theory, and other humanistic disciplines. This preface provides such prospective readers with a brief introduction to the Mishnah and related works so that they will understand the terms and concepts whose meanings are otherwise assumed in the body of the book.

The Mishnah is one of several works that we attribute to "the rabbis." When used in this context, the terms "rabbi" and "rabbis" refer to the individuals whose teachings would become the dominant religious force among Jews in the Land of Israel and Mesopotamia and ultimately in the entire Jewish world. They contributed to, compiled, and edited the major legal, exegetical, and general religious texts recognized as the basis of most forms of Judaism to this day. For our purposes, we might define the rabbinic period as covering roughly the first half of the first millennium CE.

The Mishnah is the foundational text of rabbinic law. It was completed around the year 200 CE in the Galilee region of the Land of Israel. Tradition attributes its editorship to R. Judah Hanasi (the Patriarch). Most of the rabbinic authorities cited in the Mishnah were active in the period from the destruction of Jerusalem and its Temple by the Romans in the year 70 CE (which is referred to by the rabbis and in this book simply as "the Destruction") and the completion of the Mishnah some one hundred and thirty years later. These rabbis are collectively known as the Tannaim.

The Mishnah is divided into six "orders" or *sedarim* (singular *seder*) which break down the corpus of Mishnaic law into broad categories. This book focuses on the *seder* entitled *Mo'ed*, which deals with laws and rituals connected to the holidays. Each *seder* is further broken down into tractates. Each tractate deals with an individual subtopic related to the concerns of the *seder* in which it is found. Most of the tractates in *Mo'ed* treat an individual holiday.

Tractates are further broken down into chapters, which in turn are divided into sections. Each of these sections is known individually as a "mishnah." To avoid confusion between these individual units and the work as a whole, I refer to these units as "paragraphs."

Not all of the legal traditions of the Tannaim were included in the Mishnah. Teachings that are formulated in Mishnaic style but not included in the Mishnah are called *baraitot* (singular *baraita*). The largest collection of such texts in our possession is known as the Tosefta. It was compiled not long after the Mishnah and is divided into a nearly identical set of *sedarim* and tractates.

In the centuries following its publication, the Mishnah became the central text of study in the rabbinic circles and academies of both the Land of Israel and Mesopotamia. Each of these rabbinic communities produced a work known as a "talmud," which was a summation of their studies of the Mishnah. In this book I refer to the Palestinian Talmud and Babylonian Talmud by their traditional Hebrew names, the Yerushalmi and the Bavli, respectively. The Talmuds present glosses and in-depth discussions of the Mishnah. In the process, they present and discuss *baraitot* that parallel the Mishnah's discussions. Thus, despite their later provenance, the Talmuds are an important source of the teachings of the Tannaim that are either absent or recorded in a different manner by the Mishnah and Tosefta. The rabbis of the Talmudic period are known as Amoraim.

NOTES ON TEXTS, TRANSLATIONS, AND TRANSCRIPTIONS

All quotations of the Mishnah in this book are based on the Kaufmann manuscript of the Mishnah as it has been transcribed in the Accordance database. It has been checked against a facsimile of the original manuscript.

Potentially significant variants have been noted from the printed text, the Parma manuscript of the Mishnah and genizah fragments. All manuscript work has been based on the facsimiles on the website of the Jewish National and University Library website (http://jnul.huji.ac.il/dl/talmud/).

Translations of the Mishnah are based on those found in the Soncino translation of the Talmud. I have made alterations to this translation as I have seen fit. Unless otherwise noted, citations of individual tractates refer to sources in the Mishnah.

Quotations of the Tosefta are based on the text of the Lieberman edition (Jewish Theological Seminary of America, 1992). Translations are my own.

Yerushalmi quotations are based on the Leiden manuscript as it has been transcribed in the Academy of the Hebrew Language edition of the Yerushalmi, edited by Yaakov Sussman (Jerusalem, 2001). Translations are my own.

The manuscripts on which individual quotations of Bavli texts are based are identified in the endnotes. Translations are based on the Soncino translation.

Standard commentaries on the Mishnah are referred to by their common names. Unless otherwise noted, such citations refer to the comments on the relevant passage in the Mishnah. Maimonides' commentary is cited from Yosef Kafah's translation (Jerusalem, 1967). Rashi is cited from the standard printing of the Talmud. Bertinoro, *Tiferet Yisrael*, and other traditional rabbinic commentaries are cited from a reprint of the Vilna edition of the Mishnah (Vilna, 1908–10). "Kehati" refers to the Mishnah commentary of Pinhas Kehati, *Mishnayot mevo'arot* (Jerusalem, 1967–68).

Transliterations from Hebrew follow the "general purpose style" found on pages 28 and 79 of *The SBL Handbook of Style* (Peabody, MA, 1999).

1

Introduction

> "No one can ever believe this Narrative, in the reading, more than I believed it in the writing."
>
> Charles Dickens, preface to the 1876 "Charles Dickens" edition of *David Copperfield*

The Mishnah all but begins with a story. The first tractate of the Mishnah, *Berakhot*, opens with a discussion of the appropriate time to say the evening Shema prayer. After a brief discussion of the progression of the night from dusk to dawn, the Mishnah relates:

> Once it happened
> that [Rabban Gamliel's] sons came home [late] from a wedding feast.
> They said to him,
> "We have not recited the [evening] Shema."
> He said to them,
> "If the dawn has not yet come,
> you are still bound to recite the [evening] Shema."

I have loved this tale ever since I first studied it as a child. I pictured R. Gamliel's sons stumbling through the backdoor of their house in the wee hours of the morning, hoping not to disturb their sleeping family. To their surprise, they find their father at the kitchen table in his dressing gown, deep in study. The sight of their father reminds them that the festivities have distracted them from their obligation to accept the yoke of heaven through the recitation of the Shema. Their father looks up from his book with a mixture of concern and rebuke. He informs them that it is still possible to rectify their lax behavior, provided the night has not yet ended.

This story embodies two of the most fundamental tensions of the human condition: between fathers and sons, and between Apollonian order and Dionysian exuberance. In the end, order is restored. The sons return to the house of their father and fulfill their obligations to their Father in Heaven. Yet the law requires that these young men rejoice in front of their friends' brides no less than it requires them to proclaim their allegiances to the One True God by reciting the Shema. There will be other late nights which might not end with all obligations fulfilled.¹

But what is this story, and scores of others like it, doing in the Mishnah, a work of law? The story does communicate R. Gamliel's position that one may recite the evening Shema throughout the night. However, this cannot be the story's primary function within the Mishnah's discourse. Right before the Mishnah tells this story, it delineates, in concise apodictic terms, the range of positions regarding the latest time to recite the Shema:

Until the end of the first watch.
These are the words of R. Eliezer
The sages say:
Until midnight.
Rabban Gamliel says:
Until the dawn comes up.

By the time the reader² gets to the story, he or she already knows R. Gamliel's position. In general, laws that the rabbis transmit through stories could just as well be formulated as more abstract legal rulings or principles. What then drives these jurists to become storytellers? What role do stories such as this play in the Mishnah and in classical halakhic discourse in general?

Between Halakhah and Aggadah

Despite the plethora of stories scattered throughout the Mishnah, the Tosefta, and the legal sections of the Talmuds, the question of the nature and function of stories within these classical legal texts has received scant attention from scholars both ancient and modern. The marginal status of these stories is tied up with the history of the interpretation of rabbinic literature. The oldest and most fundamental generic distinction in the study of rabbinic literature is that between halakhah and aggadah. "Halakhah" refers to the body of rabbinic ritual, civil, and criminal law, which is rooted in the biblical texts and the traditions and practices of Second Temple Judaism.³ "Aggadah" has traditionally been defined in negative terms. It refers to all rabbinic discussions that are not halakhic in nature. This includes interpretations and expansions of nonlegal biblical texts, accounts of post biblical events, theological discussions, ethical maxims, and medical advice.⁴

This distinction between halakhah and aggadah goes back to the rabbinic sources themselves. By the early Middle Ages, differentiating between aggadic and halakhic texts became crucial to virtually any consideration of the nature, status, and authority of Talmudic and Midrashic literature. Virtually all of the great medieval theorists took it as axiomatic that aggadic texts possess a different theological and metaphysical status than halakhic texts and that their study demands a distinct set of hermeneutic tools.[5]

The Geonim, the religious leaders of Babylonian Jewry in the early medieval period, were the first to put forward a systematic theory of halakhah and aggadah.[6] For the Geonim, aggadic texts lacked the binding authority of halakhic sources. They were "mere approximations...many of which are untrue."[7] However, with the rise of Maimonidian rationalism and kabbalistic mysticism as two of the dominant systems of thought in medieval Judaism, aggadah began to acquire a more positive image. It was now understood as a metaphorical or allegorical vehicle for teaching difficult and even esoteric ideas. Aggadah thus acquired independent value as the transmitter of core ethical and metaphysical teachings of the rabbinic tradition.[8]

Stories do not have a clear place within this scheme. Across cultures, narratives tend to challenge categorizations between "high" and "low," and between specialized and more popular forms of literature. Rabbinic stories, individually and as a group, play just such a role within rabbinic literature, cutting across this distinction between halakhah and aggadah.

When I use the terms "rabbinic" or "sage" stories, I refer specifically to stories which recount the deeds of individual rabbis. Sage stories can be distinguished from other narrative genres created and transmitted by the rabbis, such as expansions of biblical narratives and parables.[9] However, individually and as group, they cannot easily be defined as either halakhah or aggadah.

Certainly some rabbinic stories belong more to the category of halakhah, while others are more aggadic in nature. At one end of the spectrum of rabbinic stories are the brief anecdotes like the one at the beginning of the Mishnah noted earlier. Although their exact role and contribution to halakhic discourse is not always easy to determine, these stories appear in halakhic contexts and convey halakhic data. Yet, as we have seen in the case of the first story in the Mishnah, these stories can convey broader, non-halakhic themes as well.

At the other end are the relatively lengthy stories, especially those found in the Babylonian Talmud. These stories present a much greater degree of mimetic detail and character development than their more concise cousins. They frequently include tales of miraculous deeds and divine interventions involving rabbinic heroes. Such stories are normally categorized as aggadic in nature. They focus on human, moral, and metaphysical concerns rather than on strictly halakhic issues.

Yet even these stories are often rooted in halakhic discourse. A prime example is "the story of the oven of Akhnai,"one of the longest and most celebrated stories in all of rabbinic literature.[10] It tells of a violent conflict between R. Eliezer and the rabbinic establishment led by R. Joshua and R. Gamliel. It is filled with human suffering, desperate prayers, and spectacular miracles. It even includes a couple of cameo appearances by God himself.

For all its drama and wonder, this story emerges out of the most mundane of halakhic discussions. It comes in the context of the Talmud's wide-ranging discussion of the Mishnaic laws of fair practices in the marketplace. The story further grows from a dispute regarding an extremely technical aspect of halakhah, the question of the susceptibility to ritual impurity of a particular model of segmented oven. Like the simple halakhic stories of the Mishnah, this story also presents a legal dispute in a narrative form. Further, the account opens with the citation of the Mishnah in *Kelim* (5:10) which presents the dispute between R. Eliezer and the rabbis on this matter, and cryptically notes, "This is the oven of Akhnai." The entire story might be seen as a gloss and expansion of this Mishnah.

The story as a whole does not deal extensively with technical aspects of halakhah. Nevertheless, it is deeply concerned with issues that might be defined as "meta-halakhic" or jurisprudential: How are halakhic disputes to be resolved? What is the relative weight of different claims to legal authority? How do we balance the needs of the many against the needs of the few? Stories such as this play a potentially crucial role in halakhic discourse as they work through the fundamental principles upon which halakhah is decided and enforced.

Abraham Maimonides

The problem of classifying rabbinic stories is illustrated in the work of Abraham Maimonides (1186–1237), son of the great Moses Maimonides. R. Abraham was one of the few medieval thinkers to recognize narrative as an independent category of rabbinic literature and is perhaps the only such writer to identify the halakhic story as a distinct genre. In the final section of his "Discourse on the Dicta of the Sages," a treatise devoted to explicating his father's approach to aggadic texts, R. Abraham presents a taxonomy of the types of stories that are found in rabbinic literature. The first of these categories is the didactic narrative, a nonfictional story whose purpose is to teach a lesson of some sort. R. Abraham further breaks this group into a series of subgenres.

The first subgenre is "the story that teaches a lesson with regard to the law." R. Abraham's main example of such a story is the account in Mishnah *Sukkah* 2:7 of the sages' visit to R. Yohanan b. Hahoroni. The narrative dramatizes the dispute between the houses of Hillel and Shammai regarding the need to sit with one's entire body within the sukkah, the booth in which one is required to dwell during the Sukkot holiday.[11] Like the story about R. Gamliel and his sons, it presents a rabbinic ruling with regard to a real situation.

R. Abraham's decision to describe this group of stories in the middle of a treatise on aggadah calls attention to their liminal status. By definition, these stories are halakhic in nature and in content. Yet they are stories, which R. Abraham sees as an essentially aggadic form. They therefore need to be discussed and classified in the context of a work on aggadic literature. Halakhic stories thus straddle the fence between halakhah and aggadah.

If we read further, we find that R. Abraham's third subgenre of didactic stories is those that teach a theological point. R. Abraham cites as his main example yet another Mishnaic story, the story of Honi Hame'agel and his miraculous prayer for rain in *Ta'anit* 3:8. For R. Abraham, the point of the story is to teach that God responds to the prayers of the righteous.[12] Yet Moses Maimonides himself, in his commentary on this Mishnah, states that the purpose of this story is precisely to teach a halakhic lesson. According to him the story is part and parcel of the Mishnah's halakhic discussion about the propriety of praying for the cessation of excessive rain. In Maimonides' reading, Honi prays for the rain to stop and is rebuked by R. Simeon ben Shetah for his behavior. We thus learn that such prayers are inappropriate. In contrast, R. Abraham's younger contemporary and fellow rationalist interpreter of aggadah, R. Hillel of Verona, places this story among accounts of "miracles and wonders."[13] The latter interpretation places the story ever further toward the aggadic end of the spectrum. Again and again, rabbinic stories defy simple classification as either halakhic or aggadic.

History and Its Discontents

With the waning of the Middle Ages, a new approach to rabbinic stories emerged that offered to break the deadlock between aggadah and halakhah. Scholars who were open to Western humanistic approaches began to look at these stories with a historian's eye. The trend began with R. Azariah dei Rossi in the sixteenth century,[14] but did not really gather steam until the emergence of the Jewish Enlightenment movement and the rise of the *Wissenschaft des Judentums* approach in the nineteenth century. In the twentieth century, the historical approach to rabbinic stories would be championed by leading Israeli scholars such as Gedaliah Alon and Ephraim. E. Urbach.[15] Though these scholars employed a wide range of methodologies and approaches, they were united in their assumption that rabbinic stories function to record actual events and circumstances in the individual and collective lives of the rabbis. As Joshua Levinson explains:

> While scholars recognized that these stories contained patently unhistorical portions and that different rabbinic compilations sometimes presented varied or even contradictory versions of the same event, they nevertheless assumed that the account preserved an historical kernel of a "real" occurrence. The task of the historian was to separate the embellishments from the historical core, to identify the most reliable version, and to produce a sound biography or history.[16]

By focusing on the essential story-ness of rabbinic stories, namely the fact that they report events from the past, the historical approach succeeded in uniting all rabbinic stories under a single methodological framework. The opposition between halakhah and aggadah was no longer relevant to the reading of rabbinic stories. All that mattered was the human and material reality to which the stories give us access.

Starting in the late 1960s, an emerging scholarly consensus began to challenge the validity of the historical approach. In the United States, this reassessment is most associated with the work of Jacob Neusner and his students.[17] Neusner argued that all the historical caution and care in the world will not suffice to derive reliable data about historical events from rabbinic stories. These stories come down to us as part of rabbinic works that were edited a long time—in many cases centuries—after the events described in the stories purportedly took place. There is no reason to believe that the authors of these stories had access to any reliable information about the events they describe. Furthermore, "the story is something other than history. Those who read this material as history misread the purpose of the storyteller."[18] In Neusner's view, rabbinic stories are highly fictionalized, if not entirely fictional, accounts whose purpose is to convey rabbinic ideology. If these texts can teach us history, it can only be the history of the ideas and mentalities of their authors, not of the deeds of their protagonists. As such, an entirely different set of tools is needed to interpret them.

Jonah Fraenkel and the Literary Approach

At about the same time that Neusner was formulating his attacks on traditional historical criticism, in Jerusalem a very different scholar, Jonah Fraenkel, was developing a systematic alternative to these methods.[19] Fraenkel argued that rabbinic stories must first and foremost be treated as literary works. In order to gain the tools necessary to analyze the texts, the scholar of rabbinic stories must turn to the theories and methodologies that have been developed and practiced in academic departments of literature. Fraenkel developed a method of formal analysis and "close reading" akin to the practices of the New Critics whose methods dominated the Anglo-American critical scene in the mid-twentieth century.[20]

For Fraenkel, as for the New Critics, the literary text is a closed hermeneutic structure in which artistic form and ideological content are inexorably intertwined.[21] Fraenkel's studies of rabbinic stories almost invariably involve the selection of individual stories from within the entire corpus of rabbinic literature. Having isolated a story, he then subjects it to literary analysis. Generally speaking, Fraenkel will group together several disparate stories that he perceives as being structurally or thematically connected and present them in a single study.

Fraenkel's pathbreaking work demonstrated the richness and complexity of rabbinic narrative art. In particular, Fraenkel illuminated the rabbinic storytellers' penchant for irony and ambiguity and for portraying the tragic nature of the human condition. He found for the rabbinic story a place of honor within the canon of Hebrew literary art.

For all the originality of Fraenkel's approach, his work also reflects a fundamental return to traditional methods of interpretation. Fraenkel unequivocally defines the stories that he analyzes as "aggadic." This is evidenced by the titles of his two books devoted to these stories, both of which declare the subject at hand to be the "aggadic narrative." Fraenkel identifies aggadic texts as having inherent "literary" qualities. His work rests on his sharp distinction between "historical" and "literary" texts.[22] Historical works "reflect a conscious desire to preserve the past," whereas literary works "aspire to educate the public."[23] Fraenkel places the rabbinic stories that he studies, namely, the aggadic ones, squarely in the "literary-didactic" genre. As such, these stories are best studied using the tools of general literary criticism rather than those of positivist historical scholarship.[24]

Fraenkel admits that the majority of texts which we would identify as "rabbinic stories" are decidedly halakhic and nonliterary in nature. He describes a complex interplay between the "aggadic" and the "halakhic" story and between aggadah and halakhah in general. Ultimately, however, he maintains a strict generic and methodological distinction between the two categories.[25] Literary analysis is reserved only for stories that belong to the former group.

Fraenkel thus bifurcates the world of rabbinic stories on the basis of a threefold dichotomy. On the one hand there are aggadic, literary, and fictional stories. On the other, there are halakhic, nonliterary, and/or historical stories. We have already discussed the problem with neatly dividing rabbinic stories into halakhic and aggadic camps. Fraenkel's assumption that some texts can be privileged as inherently "literary" is also problematic. The notion of "literariness" was central to the argument of many mid-twentieth century critics. With the rise of deconstruction, the New Historicism, and other forms of cultural studies in the later decades of the twentieth century, this assumption would come under serious challenge.[26] Literariness is currently seen as a socially constructed category that reflects a text's place within a given culture rather than the essential qualities of the text. Contemporary critics tend to seek out not specialized hermeneutics but methods that will allow them to consider a culture and its products in all of their variety.

Finally, Fraenkel's notion that rabbinic stories are inherently fictional[27] also bears reexamination. In halakhic discourse, the claim that a given text accurately represents "the way things really were" is crucial to its rhetorical efficacy and metaphysical legitimacy. Halakhic transmission rests on the claim that it accurately transmits the authoritative teachings of previous generations of scholars. Since rabbinic story-telling and halakhic transmission are so inexorably intertwined it follows that rabbinic stories also claim to relate not fictions, but actual events in which historical figures spoke the words and performed the deeds recorded.

This does not mean that these stories are necessarily useful sources for contemporary historians. The authors and editors of rabbinic literature had very different criteria for determining "what really happened" than do modern historians. Many rabbinic stories do not contain even a kernel of recoverable historical information. Nevertheless, from the perspective of the authors, editors, and original audience of rabbinic stories, these stories transmit not only spiritual or moral truth but also concrete historical information. They are, or at least purport to be, deeply rooted in historical and material reality. This fact is crucial to understanding the genre of rabbinic stories.

A host of scholars have followed in Fraenkel's wake in the study of rabbinic stories.[28] These scholars have advanced Fraenkel's work, often attempting to respond to the weaknesses in his method by incorporating recent developments in literary, historical, and Talmudic studies. Most notably for our purposes, Jeffery Rubenstein, Shulamit Valler, and Barry Wimpfheimer have placed great emphasis on the importance of understanding the halakhic context of rabbinic stories.[29] However, even these scholars frame their discussion in terms of a fundamental dichotomy between narrative and halakhah. In their work, there is an inevitable tension which results from the coexistence and interaction of narrative discourse and halakhic texts and rulings.[30]

Central Thesis of the Book

In sum, halakhah and narrative have been consistently viewed by scholars as being in some way opposed to one another. As a result, halakhic stories have been marginalized by scholars throughout history. In fact, halakhic stories are a central genre within the world of classical rabbinic literature. They serve as a primary tool for the transmission of halakhic rulings and principles. Yet they also serve as the bridge which unites the worlds of halakhah and aggadah. Finally, it is within the space of halakhic stories that the rabbis most energetically construct and critique their notions about halakhah as a wider process and system and their commitment and concerns regarding the necessity of an elite rabbinic class in order to insure the continued transmission and observance of the law.

In order to be fruitfully analyzed, these stories need to be considered both as halakhah and as aggadah, and they need to be approached using literary, historical, and other academic methods as necessary. The reader must always bear in mind that these stories purport to transmit not only moral and legal truths but historical truths as well. Furthermore, a full understanding of this phenomenon cannot be achieved by cherry-picking stories of interest and analyzing them independent of their contexts. Rather, rabbinic stories must be systematically studied as integral parts of the larger works in which they appear.

Narrative before the Law

In recent decades many American legal and literary scholars have adopted a dichotomy between "law" and "narrative" that in many ways parallels their Judaic studies colleagues' tendency to view rabbinic narratives as a form of aggadah as opposed to halakhah. Perhaps the dominant voice in this discussion has been that of Robert Cover, especially in his essay "Nomos and Narrative."[31] For Cover, narrative and law are two fully distinct, though interrelated, realms. In his view, laws can exist only in the context of the stories which define their origin and authority. Though subsequent scholars have suggested various other understandings of the relationship between law and narrative, they have tended to accept Cover's basic premise that law and narrative represent two fundamentally different and even mutually exclusive modes of discourse.[32] This approach to the study of law and narrative has recently been vigorously challenged by Peter Brooks.[33] Brooks's arguments in many ways parallel my own position regarding the place of narrative in classical halakhic texts. He faults earlier scholars for their failure "to recognize the pervasive presence of narrative throughout the law."[34] Brooks calls for the systematic application of the tools of narrative analysis to legal texts and proceedings.

Placed in the context of Brooks's work, this book can thus be seen as part of a wider effort to promote a more holistic approach to the question of law and narrative in addition to its agendas relating to the narrower field of rabbinic literature. The title of the book is meant to capture the complexity of this relationship between law and stories. *Stories of the Law* can be understood simply as "stories *about* the law." Such stories are distinct from the law, though they may make a decisive impact on the law from the outside. On the other hand, the title can also refer to "stories that are *part of* the law." That is, they derive from legal texts and sources. These stories are not external to the law but a part of its warp and woof. This dual nature of the relationship between law and narrative underlies much of the book.

Plan of the Book

This book aims to demonstrate these claims about legal stories through a study of the role of narrative and stories in the Mishnah and its halakhic discourse. As the most fundamental text of rabbinic law, the Mishnah represents the ideal starting point for the investigation of the relationship between stories and halakhic texts. The book focuses on *Seder Mo'ed*, the second major division of the Mishnah, which deals with the laws and rituals regarding holidays. We will examine a large selection of stories from *Mo'ed* and analyze numerous chapters and extended segments of the Mishnah in their entirety. I argue that stories are an integral part of the Mishnah's halakhic discourse. They serve not only to present individual cases and rulings but also to convey fundamental rabbinic teachings about the nature of halakhah and the individuals to whom it has been entrusted.

My choice of *Mo'ed* was ultimately arbitrary, motivated in part by the relative accessibility of the material to the non-specialist reader. Nonetheless, this choice inevitably engenders a selection bias of its own. There can be no doubt that *Mo'ed* contains many of the most developed stories in the Mishnah. As a result, this study may exaggerate the literary interest of Mishnaic stories. Also, a study of another segment of the Mishnah would likely reveal many more stories that do not fit into the generic categorizations that I propose. Such a study would possibly lead to the definition of more genres of Mishnaic stories. Moreover, the genre that I have dubbed "etiological stories" appears to be overrepresented in *Mo'ed* and would probably be less prominent in a study of another selection or of the entire Mishnah. Nevertheless, I feel confident that *Mo'ed* is sufficiently representative of the Mishnah as a whole to serve as a basis for an understanding of the place of narratives and stories throughout the Mishnah.

This book has two parts. The first part deals with the place of stories and other narratives within the wider discourse of the Mishnah. Part 2 of the book focuses on the Mishnaic story itself.

In chapter 2 we begin by defining the terms "story" and "narrative." These terms do not lend themselves to a precise or absolute definition. They need to be understood in terms of the broader concept of "narrativity." Narrativity refers to a set of characteristics possessed in some degree by a wide range of texts. "Narratives" and "stories" refer to different classes of texts that possess a certain set level of narrativity.

In chapter 3, I apply these concepts and terms to the range of literary forms through which the Mishnah formulates its law. The Mishnah regularly juxtaposes texts with greatly varying degrees of narrativity. Mishnaic narratives and stories are thus part of a continuum of forms found in the Mishnah. They represent an integral part of its discourse.

Chapters 4 and 5 explore the implications of the Mishnah's use of narrativity. In chapter 4, I demonstrate how looking at the Mishnah through the lens of narrativity yields an entirely new perspective on the nature of the Mishnah as a literary text and as a legal document. As opposed to traditional source-critical approaches or more contemporary formalist readings of the Mishnah, I argue that the Mishnah needs to be viewed as a "dialogic" text whose meaning emerges from the tension between its various forms and viewpoints.

In chapter 5, I compare the role of narrative and narrativity in the Mishnah to its role in other ancient legal texts. I examine legal texts from ancient Mesopotamia, the Bible, Qumran, and the Roman legal corpus. This will allow us to appreciate both the Mishnah's distinctive features and its relationship to the cultures from which it emerged.

Chapter 6 opens Part 2 of the book, which focuses on the Mishnaic story itself. It lays out the basic methodological issues that bear on the study of Mishnaic stories. This includes questions regarding the transmission and redaction of the Mishnah and ways of evaluating the rhetorical strategies used by the Mishnaic storytellers.

The final chapters of the book each focus on one of the three genres of Mishnaic stories that I identify: the exemplum, the case story, and the etiological story. My argument is that these stories do not simply transmit individual rulings but also participate in a larger dialog regarding the nature and extent of rabbinic authority. Exempla relate to the notion of rabbis as embodiments of halakhah in their daily lives. Case and etiological stories deal with the rabbis' roles as interpreters of the law and as legislators, respectively. Each of these chapters explores the way in which a particular genre both reinforces and problematizes the rabbis' claims to normative authority. In addition, in these chapters I further examine the various possible relationships between law and narrative that exist in the Mishnah.

Previous Scholarship on Halakhic Stories

My work did not come into being in a vacuum. Two leading scholars of the previous generation, E. Z. Melammed and Arnold Goldberg, already wrote preliminary studies of the Mishnaic story.[35] Similarly, Catherine Hezser initiated the systematic study of the rabbinic story, through her thorough work on the stories in Yerushalmi *Neziqin*.[36] As I have already noted, several scholars have also recently drawn attention to the relationship between rabbinic stories and their legal contexts.

Another important approach is reflected in the work of Daniel Boyarin and his students. Starting with his book *Carnal Israel*, Boyarin has sought to study rabbinic literature using the tools of the New Historicism. Boyarin integrates the methods of literary scholars, historians, and social scientists. He sees halakhah and aggadah as a part of a single discursive network and is sensitive to the complex interrelations between the two.[37] Among Boyarin's students, Charlotte Fonrobert's understanding of the role of stories within halakhic discourse anticipates some of my own conclusions.[38] Two other scholars whose work on the relationship between narrative and halakhah from a cultural studies perspective has influenced my own are Beth Berkowitz and Ishay Rosen-Zvi.[39]

My work is distinguished from these scholars' by its concern with issues of genre and modes of discourse. Boyarin and his followers generally produce thematic studies. Formal issues such as the nature and role of narrative tend to be of secondary concern for these scholars. Though I deal extensively with issues of power relationships and authority, both political and spiritual, I focus first and foremost on the problem of narrative and stories in the Mishnah. Discussions of ideological and historical issues grow out of this primary focus.

Since the tractate *Berakhot* is not in *Seder Moʻed*, I will not have the opportunity to further discuss the story with which we opened this chapter. It is my hope that, having read this book, readers will have acquired the tools to arrive at their own conclusions about the story and the many others like it throughout the Mishnah.

PART ONE

NARRATIVITY IN THE MISHNAH

2

Stories, Narratives, and Narrativity

> "I have a story," I said, after a while.
> "A story?"
> "Yes."
> "Of what use is a story? I'm hungry."
> "It's a story about food."
> "Words have no calories."
> "Seek food where food is to be found." ...
> "Let's hear your story," he said, panting.
> "Once upon a time there was a banana and it grew. It grew until it was large, firm, yellow and fragrant. Then it fell to the ground and someone came upon it and ate it."
> He stopped rowing. "What a beautiful story."
> "Thank you."
> "I have tears in my eyes."
> "I have another element," I said.
> "What is it?"
> "The banana fell to the ground and someone came upon it and ate it—and afterwards that person *felt better*."
> "It takes the breath away!" he exclaimed.
> "Thank you."
> A pause.
> "But you don't have any bananas?"
> "No."
>
> Yann Martel, *Life of Pi*

Narrative is perhaps the most ubiquitous and multifarious of all literary forms. Stories, be they epic poems or modern novels, hold prominent places in the literary canons of virtually every culture. Yet storytelling is hardly the sole preserve of the belles lettres. Narratives are also an important feature of many other forms of discourse, including the study of law, medicine, history, and philosophy. The linguist and narrative theorist William Labov went so far as to argue that "narratives are privileged forms of discourse which play a central role in almost every conversation."[1] We all tell stories in our day-to-day speech. Small children learn this craft as part of the normal process of language acquisition. Indeed, the potential for creating stories may well be one of the fundamental, universal characteristics of language.² A definition of the terms "narrative" and "story" must take into account the fact that these forms are often enmeshed with other linguistic structures and modes of discourse. On the other hand, such a definition must also allow for the richness and complexity of more developed, "literary" narratives.

Narrativity

In order to encompass this wide range of narrative forms, I will first focus on the broader category of "narrativity." Narrativity refers to a collection of textual attributes. All texts exist along a continuum of greater or lesser narrativity depending on the number and prominence of the narrative attributes they contain. When we refer to a text as a "narrative" or a "story," we mean that it contains a certain critical mass of narrativity. However, the precise line between "narratives" and "non-narratives" is inherently arbitrary. The distinction between the terms "narrative" and "story" is similarly a question of convention. I use the terms "narrative" and "story" to demarcate two critical points along the continuum of narrativity based on the criteria set out below.

Narrativity emerges from the confluence of two distinct elements in a text which I call "dynamism" and "specificity." "Dynamism" refers to the fact that narratives are fundamentally about transition, transformation, and change. "Specificity" indicates that narratives are rooted in the particular, focusing on individual characters and unique events, and occur at demarcated points in time and space. Narrativity thus inheres in texts to the extent that they describe change and transition while at the same time focusing on the concrete, the specific, and the time-bound.

Dynamism: E. M. Forster's Minimal Narrative

In their definitions of narrative, literary theorists overwhelmingly tend to focus on dynamism at the expense of specificity. For example, E. M. Forster, in his classic work *Aspects of the Novel*, suggests the following sentence as an example of a minimal story:

"The king died and then the queen died of grief."[3]

In his analysis of this text, Forster focuses exclusively on its dynamic aspects. For him, the salient qualities that make this text a story are that it is a "narrative of events arranged in their time sequence...the emphasis falling on causality."[4] This statement succinctly encapsulates all of the formal traits that collectively define the minimum requirements for dynamism in a narrative or story.

First, Forster presumes that the constituent elements of narratives are "events."[5] For a text to be dynamic, something has to happen. Narratives are first and foremost the representation of happenings. Events are thus the fundamental building blocks of narratives. To be sure, it is not always a simple matter to break down a story into discrete events.[6] However, in relatively simple narratives such as those found in the Mishnah, a definition of "event" is possible. In such narratives, each time a narrative presents a verb that describes some action of change of state we have a representation of a narrative event. The complete event is represented by the entire clause in which the verb appears.[7] Thus, in the case of Forster's story, we have two events each centered on the verb "died." The first event is "the king died." The second is "the queen died of grief."

Returning to Forster's statement that a narrative consists of "events arranged in their time sequence," the next operative word in this phrase is "time." The dynamic nature of narratives demands that they portray the passage of time. This is done through the representation of at least two events in sequence. This creates the illusion of a seamless continuum of time moving inexorably forward. In the case of the death of the king and queen, the reader does not merely experience two discrete events. Rather, through the phrase "and then," the reader follows the passage of time from the death of the king through the death of the queen.

Finally, we come to the element of narrative which Forster calls "causality." Forster argues that the sentence "The king died and then the queen died" is not, despite its narrative elements, a narrative. In order to transform this text into a narrative, we must add the final clause, "of grief." True dynamism requires not only that the events follow each other sequentially but also that they be inherently interrelated. It is not sufficient that the death of the queen chronologically follows that of the king. The queen's death must follow from that of the king. This is what Forster and others call the need for "causality" in a narrative.[8] The term "causality" suggests a degree of inevitability and determinism that does not necessarily reflect the contingent manner in which narrative events often unfold. A better formulation of this requirement is presented by Binder and Weisberg, who state that a narrative must present "one event as standing in some relation of significance to a later event such that one is made meaningful by the other."[9] Taking my cue from these scholars, I will refer to the *interrelationship* of events in a narrative rather than using the more problematic term "causality."

The Narrative Potential of Stative Verbs

In light of this notion of the interrelationship between events, we can further fine-tune our definition of a narrative event. Clearly, any dynamic verb can constitute the core of a narrative event. But what about stative verbs such as "to be"? In general, stative clauses cannot be considered narrative events. For instance: "The king died. His kingdom was near the sea" is certainly not a narrative. It lacks two of the requirements of dynamism listed above. First, the two clauses are not in sequence. Presumably the kingdom was by the sea before, during, and after the king's death. Furthermore, there is no inherent interconnection between the two clauses. There is no reason to believe that the king's death was related to his kingdom's location or vice versa. Generally speaking, stative clauses represent relatively timeless and unchanging states of being that have no place in the dynamic sequence of a narrative. However, this is not always the case. As a general rule, whenever a "being" verb can be replaced with a "becoming" verb without any significant change of meaning, the clause in question can be considered a "stative event" in a narrative. Take the following example:

> The king died and then the queen was very sad.

The second clause in this case also involves the stative verb "was." However, "the queen was very sad" could be rephrased as "the queen became very sad." The clause describes a transition from one state (not being very sad) into another (being very sad). Furthermore, this transition is a direct result of the previous event. This text contains two sequential interconnected events and hence is a full-fledged narrative.

The Definition of "Narrative"

The general characteristic of narratives as dynamic texts thus translates into three minimal requirements for narratives: (1) narratives are representations of events; (2) narratives present two or more events in sequence; (3) these events must be inherently interrelated in such a way as to portray some change in the world represented by the text. Given the centrality of dynamism to the traditional definitions of narrative, I will term any text which displays the above three features a "narrative."

Specificity

Something, however, is missing. These dynamic attributes do not fully express our intuitions about what makes Forster's text a story. To illustrate the problem, let us look at a similar model text:

> Kings die, and then their queens die of grief

This text meets the requirements to qualify as a "narrative" that was presented above. It too presents two interrelated events in sequence. However, I think most readers would agree that this text is in some way less of a story than Forster's. This is because it lacks "specificity." Our new text purports to describe a general phenomenon which applies to any number of monarchs and their consorts in different times and places. Forster's text, in contrast, contains a minimal level of specificity. We know neither the names of the king and queen, nor where they ruled. But we know that the story tells of one and only one king and one and only one queen. Similarly, while we do not know when this story happened, we know that it happened "once upon a time," that is, once and only once and at a specific point in the past.

More extensive narratives tend to provide even more specificity. This tendency reaches its height in the tradition of the modern novel, in which the characters and their motives, as well as the setting and background of the story, are described in rich and precise detail. It is therefore hardly surprising that critics tend to identify specificity as a distinguishing feature of modern realistic fiction, rather than as a fundamental aspect of narrativity.[10] However, the fact that we intuitively differentiate between Forster's example and my more general text demonstrates that specificity is something that we associate even with some of the simplest of narrative texts.

Unlike the need for dynamism, which is emphasized in one form or another by virtually all narrative theorists, the need for specificity has generally been minimized or even ignored by most students of narrative. Gerald Prince and Wendy Steiner are among the few narrative theorists who emphasize the need for specificity in narrative.[11] I am aware of only one writer who presents a definition of narrative that focuses on specificity almost to the exclusion of dynamism; G. A. Gaballa writes, "A story is a specific event carried out by particular characters in a particular place."[12]

It is hardly a coincidence that both Steiner and Gaballa are interested in narrative expressed through painting. Steiner emphasizes that, as an essentially atemporal medium, painting can possess only limited dynamism. The flip side of this is the clichéd observation that a picture is worth a thousand words. It is precisely a painting's ability to simultaneously present a vast number of details that makes it especially suited to the expression of specificity, even beyond that of written texts.

The notion that a still life or landscape painting might possess narrativity might seem to stretch the normal uses of the word "narrative" and "story" beyond recognition. It is precisely my intent to provoke the reader to rethink conventional understandings of these terms. A text may meet the minimum requirements to be considered a narrative on the basis of dynamism alone. However, ultimately narrative is about more than action and change. It is also about representing and engaging the particular and unique aspects of individuals, objects, and situations.

Our primary concern, however, is not with paintings but with the way in which texts express specificity through language. One of the most important aspects of these expressions relates to the choice of grammatical tense. Numerous critics have pointed out that the past tense, or more specifically the preterit, is the primary tense for storytelling.[13] Events in stories must happen once and only once at a definable point in time. Only the past tense can fully provide the sort of concreteness and specificity necessary for stories.

Another way of further defining the need for specificity is that a story must recount events using verbs in the *realis* mood.[14] That is, the events described by them are represented as having been realized in the material world. The reality portrayed by realis verbs may be fictional, nonfictional, or some combination of the two. The important thing is that the reader is called upon to imagine an actual situation, event, or story.[15] Realis accounts are to be distinguished from *irrealis* accounts, which "are verbalizations of experience that is unrealized either because it is predicated on taking place in the future or because it is in some sense hypothetical."[16] This dichotomy between realis and irrealis texts will be important in distinguishing between stories and other narrative forms in the Mishnah.

The Definition of "Story"

We are now ready to present our definition of a "story":

> A story is any representation of a sequence of at least two interrelated events that occurred once and only once in the past.[17]

Any texts that possess all of these characteristics will be termed a "story." Stories belong to the wider category of narrative. Any sequence of two interrelated events, even if it lacks specificity, will be termed a "narrative." Texts that possess some combination of narrative attributes but do not meet the requirements to be termed a "story" or a "narrative" will be referred to as "possessing narrativity."

Some may argue that one cannot attribute narrativity to a text that describes no action purely on the basis of its specificity. I acknowledge the primacy of dynamism, by granting texts that reach a certain threshold of dynamism the title of "narrative" while not offering equivalent status to texts that contain a critical mass of specificity. Ultimately, however, I am arguing for a fundamental reconception of the nature of narrative and narrativity. Specificity is ultimately an independent and constituent element of the human endeavor we call "storytelling" and must have a place in any effort to define and describe the products of that endeavor.

Narrativity and the Novel

Until now, my discussion of narrativity focused on the minimal requirements for stories and narratives. The continuum of narrativity, however, extends well beyond the starting points for narratives and stories. More developed stories such as modern novels will present much more complex chains of interrelated events than the minimal two-event narrative sequence above. They will also contain details that go beyond the simple fixing of the story in a specific time and place. Moreover, complex narratives tend to incorporate texts that in and of themselves possess little to no narrativity. Two of the greatest novels of the nineteenth century, *Pride and Prejudice* and *Anna Karenina*, both famously open with decidedly non-narrative declarations:

> It is a truth universally acknowledged, that a single man in possession of a good fortune, must be in want of a wife.

and

> Happy families are all alike. All unhappy families are unhappy in their own way.[18]

These passages both purport to declare universal truths about human family life. They lack both dynamism and specificity. However, by integrating them into their stories about specific individuals and the events that occur to them in the context of their particular attempts at family life, Austen and Tolstoy make these opening declarations into crucial parts of their narrative texts.

Dialog

There are many other characteristics of texts, which, though they are not among the defining elements of narratives and stories, can be said to enhance a text's narrativity. The presence of character and dialog are examples of such narrativity-enhancing characteristics. Character and dialog are the most common ways in which narratives express both their dynamism and their specificity. Human beings are finite and unique, and they are given to action. Human and human-like characters are thus common features of stories. The most specifically human form of action is speech. Speech allows a person to express his or her individual thoughts and feelings and hence is most conducive to displaying the unique facets of a character. Speech is also a primary means by which people interact with each other. Dialog thus often plays an important role both in generating dynamic interaction between characters and in portraying the specific and particular attributes of individual characters.

Reported dialog in and of itself represents a borderline case in the classification of narratives and stories. Speech acts are the most ephemeral of actions. By themselves, they make no physical mark on the world around them. It is not always easy to attribute dynamism to a chain of utterances. Along similar lines, it is often difficult to establish whether a given reported statement or dialog represents an actual onetime event or the repeated expression of an individual's sentiments.

Consider the following exchange:

> The king said, "I like E. M. Forster."
> "So do I," said the queen.

We have here a pair of past-tense events arranged in sequence. The second event is a response to the first. Nevertheless, nothing changes over the course of this exchange. So far as we can tell, only the preexisting opinions of the king and queen are revealed. Without further context, we don't even know if the characters learned anything from the exchange or if they were already aware of each other's opinions. Given this lack of change, we also cannot be sure that this dialog occurred only once. Since their opinions appear to be static, this conversation could have occurred many times in the course of the king and queen's relationship. Given its potentially static and general nature, it is difficult to classify this text as having sufficient dynamism and specificity to be considered a narrative or a story.

The narrativity of this dialog could be boosted if we were to assign to it a specific time and place. For example, if it were introduced with the phrase, "On or about December 1910, at Bloomsbury Castle, the King said..." We can now be assured that this dialog occurred at a specific time and place in the past and has sufficient specificity to be deemed a story. Still, it is unclear whether the dialog itself chronicles sufficient change to warrant being called a narrative.

Other dialogs contain a stronger dynamic element and can be classified as narratives. Let us look at another literary discussion between the king and queen:

> The king said, "I like E. M. Forster."
> The queen said, "Did you know that Forster wrote a book called *Two Cheers for Democracy*?"
> "I don't like Forster anymore," said the king.

This dialog results in a significant change in the state of mind of the king. First, he learns that Forster wrote a book that in some way praises democracy. Then, as a result of this knowledge, he revises his opinion of Forster. Given this change, this dialog implicitly happened only once in the king's life. Dialogs in which one of the speakers either makes a significant discovery or changes his or her opinion in the course of the conversation are sufficiently dynamic and specific to be considered stories.

Conclusion

The categories and definitions of "narrativity," "dynamism," "specificity," "narrative," and "story" create a precise yet flexible framework in which texts can be classified and compared in terms of their place within the broader category of narrative discourse. Most importantly for our purposes, they will provide us with the tools to analyze the place of narrative discourse in the Mishnah.

3

A Typology of Mishnaic Forms

> "The Hebrews and the Chinese codified every conceivable human eventuality; it is written in the *Mishnah* that a tailor is not to go out into the street carrying a needle once the Sabbath twilight has set in."
>
> Jorge Luis Borges, *"The Zahir"*

Having established criteria for defining narratives and stories as well as for measuring the relative level of narrativity of any given text, we are now ready to embark on the first stage of our study of narrative and narrativity in the Mishnah: charting the range of literary forms in the Mishnah along the axes of narrativity. Viewed from the narrative perspective, the Mishnah contains a remarkably wide range of texts, from those that possess little if any narrativity to fully formed stories.

This is by far the most technical of the chapters in this book. For readers who lack the interest or background to read the chapter in its entirety, reading the summary of the chapter that follows, as well as looking at the charts on pages 26 and 27 which summarize this chapter's major conclusions in visual format, will suffice.

Chapter Summary and Graphic Representations of Mishnaic Forms, Their Relationships, and Their Relative Levels of Narrativity

In this chapter we study three basic varieties of Mishnaic texts: irrealis texts, realis texts, and speech acts. Irrealis texts are those that present hypothetical situations or actions. Since stories must be realis texts, which refer to an actual event in the past, irrealis texts are inherently limited in their narrativity. At most they can be narratives, representing a hypothetical sequence of actions. This category in turn divides into two subcategories: apodictic and casuistic formulations. Apodictic formulations state the law in an absolute manner, such as: "It is prohibited to do X" or "Y must be done." They generally contain only a single verb, and hence are generally not narratives. Their exact level of narrativity depends on a variety of factors, primarily the specificity and dynamism reflected in the verb forms used in the individual statement.

Casuistic statements are "if…then…" statements that establish the law in a given situation. By definition they consist of two parts, the description of the case and the ruling. These two parts almost always constitute two interconnected events and are therefore narratives. Once again, the exact level of narrativity will depend on the verb forms used and other factors.

The next general category of texts to be examined is realis texts. These texts possess an inherently high degree of specificity since they refer to a specific event in the past. Not all realis texts, however, refer to a onetime event or events. Some of these texts describe events that happened multiple times in the past. These texts have a lower degree of specificity than those which portray an event that happened once and only once in the past. These texts also vary with regard to dynamism. Some of them present only a single event and hence have a limited degree of dynamism. Others present a chain of interrelated events. When a realis text presents a chain of interrelated events that happened only once in the past, we have a story.

All of the stories that emerge out of these types of realis statements fall into the general class of the ma'aseh (pl. ma'asim). Ma'asim are stories that involve an event in the past that is the focus of halakhic interpretation or development. These types of stories each fall into one of three genres: exempla, case stories, and etiological stories.

The final category of texts that we shall examine is speech acts. Speech acts are special types of realis texts. Rather than describing the way in which the law applies to various categories of individuals, objects, and situations in the world, speech acts describe the transmission of law among the rabbis in the house of study. In their simplest form they consist of a report that "Rabbi X said" a certain statement. These statements have limited narrativity because they do not describe an individual action or specific quotation but rather a statement that was presumably repeated many times by the rabbi in question. The form "Rabbi X said" has greater narrativity because it seems to report an actual instance in which the rabbi said the words in question. Speech acts gain more specificity when they are presented in the form of dynamic dialogs. Finally, speech acts form the core of actual stories. The genre of stories that center on speech acts will be called "beit midrash stories" because they generally describe events that occur within the beit midrash, the rabbinic house of study and deliberation.

In the final section of this chapter we will see how these different forms come together in the Mishnah through an examination of the first chapter of *Shabbat*. We will see how in a single chapter, a wide ranges of forms with differing degrees of narrativity are deployed.

Most of the examples in this chapter are drawn from the tractate *Shabbat*. Unless otherwise noted, all references are to *Shabbat*. In a few instances, where no example of a given Mishnaic form is to be found in *Shabbat*, I shall cite examples from *Pesahim*, and in one instance each from *Rosh Hashanah* and *'Eruvin*. My goal is not to present an exhaustive catalog of all of the literary forms that are found in the Mishnah. I do not discuss several important Mishnaic forms, including rhetorical questions, exegesis,[1] and lists. I intend only to present the forms that mark key points along the continuum of narrativity in the Mishnah. I shall begin with those forms that possess the lowest degree of narrativity and then move along the continuum all the way to stories.

On the following pages are a pair of charts (Charts 3.1 and 3.2) presenting the various linguistic and literary features identified in this chapter in a way that will make it easier for the reader to understand their interrelationships. For technical reasons it was necessary to break up the chart into two parts. Together the two charts cover the three main categories of Mishnaic texts that I identified: irrealis texts, realis texts, and speech acts.

These charts seek to represent two different sets of relationships between the various Mishnaic forms. First is the hierarchal relationship between categories of forms and their subcategories. Each of the three main types of texts is represented by a tree which illustrates the relationship between the broader and the narrower categories. Thus, in the first chart, "irrealis texts" divides into "apodictic formulations" and "casuistic formulations." "Apodictic formulations" in turn breaks down into "verbal clauses" and "nonverbal clauses," and so on.

The chart also maps the various forms' relative levels of narrativity. The further down on the page that a form appears, the greater the narrativity. The page is further broken down into zones labeled "low narrativity statements," "narratives," and, in the case of the second chart, "stories." The reader can thus tell whether or not each form qualifies as a narrative or a story, as well as the relative level of each form when compared to another.

Irrealis Texts

We can now begin our catalogue of Mishnaic forms. The majority of halakhic formulations in the Mishnah are irrealis in nature. This means that they refer to potential or hypothetical situations rather than real events. Though irrealis texts cannot be stories, they may contain significant degrees of narrativity and, in some cases, be classified as narratives. The irrealis texts of the Mishnah fall into two general categories: apodictic and casuistic. These categories further break down into numerous subcategories based on grammatical and stylistic characteristics which impact on statements' narrativity. Having considered these various categories of irrealis statements, I will also consider the effect on narrativity of juxtaposing multiple statements against each other.

Apodictic Formulations

Apodictic formulations are the fundamental building blocks of all halakhic exposition in the Mishnah. They state the halakhah with regard to a given object, person, situation, or action. These statements generally contain at most a single verb and hence, at best, a single narrative event. As such, their potential narrativity is limited. Apodictic statements may be divided into two subcategories: nonverbal and verbal clauses.

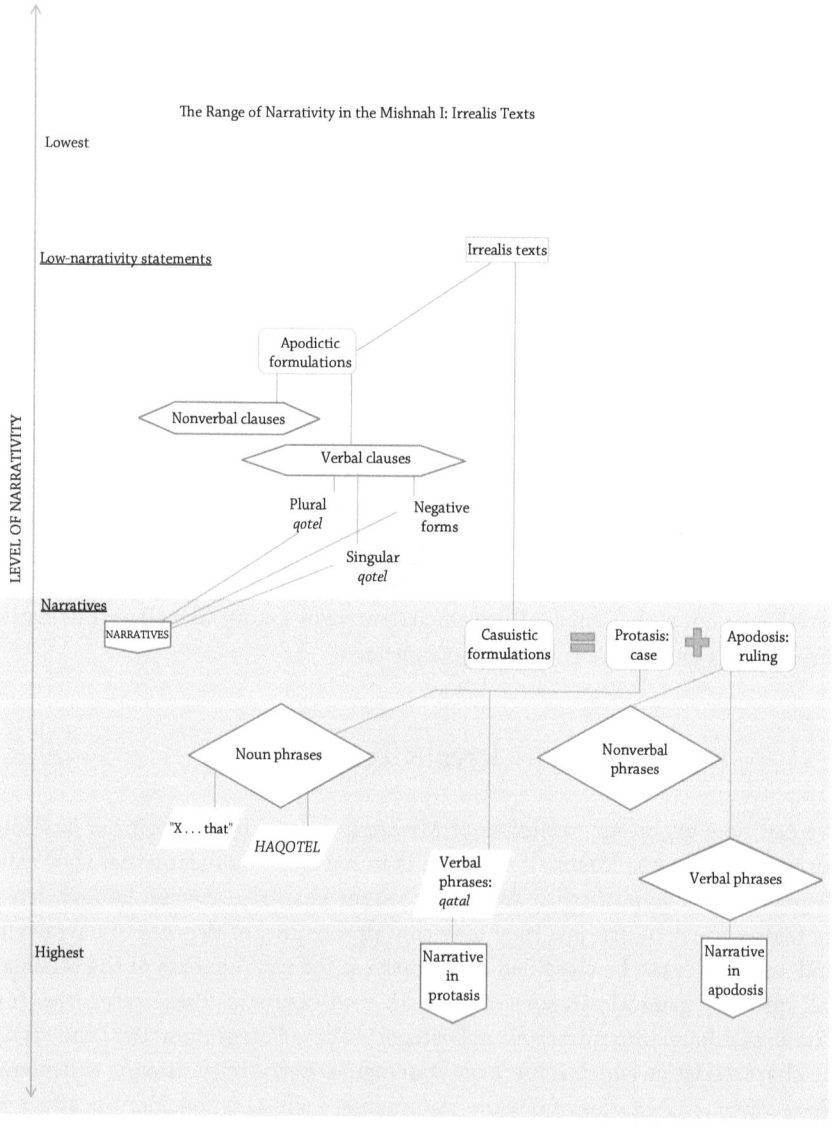

Chart 3.1

A Typology of Mishnaic Forms

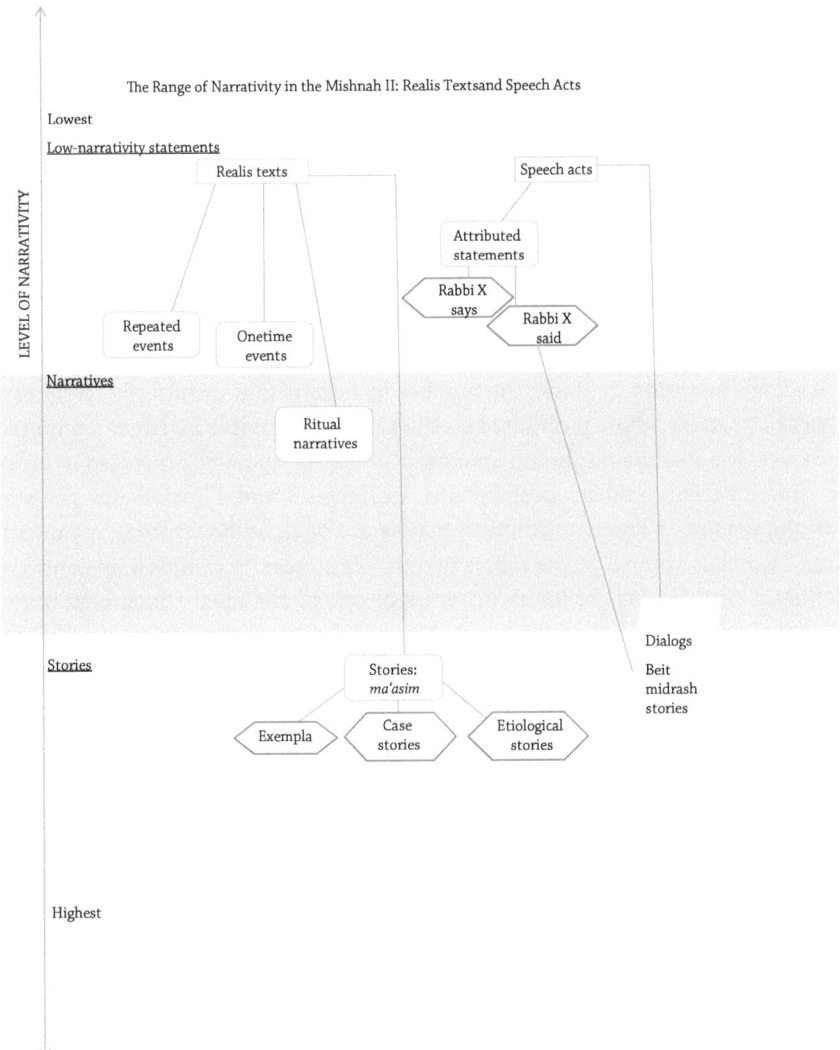

Chart 3.2

Nonverbal Clauses

In Hebrew, the present tense of the verb "to be" is implied through the juxtaposition of a subject and a predicate.[2] This creates the possibility of a clause which lacks a verb. Such nonverbal clauses possess little, if any, dynamism. They tend to describe a durative attribute of a subject rather than an action. They may, however, possess varying degrees of specificity. The following examples illustrate the range of specificity found in nonverbal clauses:

1) אֲבוֹת מְלָאכוֹת אַרְבָּעִים חָסֵר אֶחָת

2) שִׁעוּר הַמְלַבֵּן וְהַמְנַפֵּץ[3] הַצּוֹבֵעַ וְהַטּוֹוֶה

3) כָּל יִשְׂרָאֵ' בְּנֵי מְלָכִים[4]
4) כָּל קֶשֶׁר שֶׁאֵינוּ שֶׁלְקַיָּימָא אֵין חַיָּיבִים עָלָיו

כַּפּוֹל שִׁעוּרוֹ כִּמְלוֹא רוֹחַב הַסִּיט

1. The primary labors are forty less one (7:2).
2. The standard of one who bleaches, hackles, dyes, or spins [wool] is a full double *sit* (13:4).
3. All Israel are royal children (14:4).
4. Any knot that is not permanent entails no culpability (15:2).

Each of these examples represents a different type of nonverbal clause. Example 1 is an enumeration. It states the number of actions that fit into the larger category of primary labors prohibited on the Sabbath. Example 2 defines a required measure. It notes the minimum amount of wool that must be processed in order to violate various Sabbath prohibitions. Examples 3 and 4 both define the status of a person or object. Example 3 makes use of an ad hoc status, "royal children," which is applied by the rabbis in only a few cases.[5] Example 4, in contrast, defines a certain class of knots in terms of one of the most fundamental distinctions in halakhah, liable/exempt. Most of the nonverbal clauses in *Shabbat* establish the status of people, objects, and actions in terms of this opposition or in terms of basic halakhic distinctions such as prohibited/permitted or pure/impure.

From the perspective of dynamism, none of these statements possesses any narrativity. They describe permanent states that are beyond the reach of change and causality. However, when it comes to the question of specificity, there is a disparity between the levels of narrativity found in the different examples. Only example 2 refers to relatively concrete and specific actions: bleaching, hackling, dying, and spinning. The other examples refer only to general categories which encompass a wider range of objects, actions, or individuals. Example 2 thus possesses a higher level of narrativity relative to the other examples.

Even the Mishnah's use of general categories reflects a certain degree of narrativity relative to the legal formulations found elsewhere in rabbinic literature and other legal texts. Building on the work of Benjamin De Vries and Ephraim E. Urbach,[6] Leib Moscovitz emphasizes the tendency of the Tannaim to avoid abstract concepts in their legal formulations. "Abstract concepts...may be defined as notions which are intangible and incapable of mental visualization."[7] They are "concerned with metaphysical concepts such as causation and potentiality [rather] than with mundane, physical concepts such as doors and spoons."[8] In his survey of the legal generalizations of the Tannaim, Moscovitz finds that they generally "reflect conceptualization at a very low level, both in terms of the scope and the degree of abstraction of these generalizations."[9] "Explicit Tannaitic generalizations...do not explicitly mention abstract metaphysical entities such as change, intention, and transience; such statements speak of objects and items familiar from everyday life."[10] According to Moscovitz, true conceptual formulation does not emerge in halakhic thinking until after the Tannaitic period. Even the most generalized of Tannaitic statements contain a certain degree of relative specificity.

The examples cited above bear out Moscovitz's conclusions. Examples 3 and 4 both present categories that simply organize people or things that are familiar to everyday life. Example 3 places all Jews into a single legal category, whereas example 4 notes the halakhic properties of non-permanent knots. Example 1, on the other hand, speaks of primary categories of Sabbath labor. Certainly, one cannot visualize "primary categories of Sabbath labor" the way in which one can visualize the category of "Israel" or "non-permanent knots." However, even the relatively abstract concept of "primary categories of Sabbath labor" breaks down into a set of very specific individual actions as enumerated in the rest of the Mishnah. This tendency in the Mishnah's style means that even the most general statements in the Mishnah possess a relative degree of specificity and concreteness, and hence of narrativity.

Verbal Clauses: Verb Forms

Verbal clauses represent the bulk of the apodictic statements in the Mishnah. These clauses require, allow, or forbid a particular action. The fact that they focus on actions means that verbal clauses contain a certain degree of inherent dynamism. However, since they generally contain only one action verb, they tend to represent a single event. We might think of verbal clauses as narrative fragments awaiting another interconnected event to make them into full-scale narratives.

Whereas the level of dynamism is fairly standard among apodictic statements, the level of specificity varies significantly. This is due in part to the range of grammatical and syntactic forms taken on by apodictic statements. Fundamentally, there are two basic variants of the prescriptive statement as it appears in the simple form: the standard, plural *qotel* form and the less frequent, singular *qotel* form.[11] Additionally, other factors can also affect the narrativity of active statements, including word order and negations.

Standard Form: Plural *Qotel*

Most apodictic statements are formulated using the plural *qotel* form. For example:

1) מַצִּילִים מְזוֹן שָׁלוֹשׁ סְעוּדוֹת
2) קוֹשְׁרִים דְּלִי בְּפַסִיקְיָא
3) בְּנֵי מְלָכִים סָכִים עַל גַּבֵּי מַכּוֹתֵיהֶם שֶׁמֶן וֶוֶרֶד[12]

1. [We] may save food for three meals (16:2).[13]
2. [We] may tie a bucket [over a well] with a strap (15:2).
3. Royal children may anoint their wounds with rose oil (14:4).

The use of the plural *qotel* as a modal in apodictic statements has been widely discussed by scholars of Mishnaic Hebrew.[14] The modal use of *qotel* is striking both because *qotel* is normally a participle and because the usual form of the modal in Mishnaic Hebrew is *yiqtol*. Sharvit argues that the common denominator of the various uses of *qotel* in Mishnaic Hebrew is that they are "not past."[15] *Qotel* is thus fundamentally opposed to the paradigmatic narrative tense, the preterit. Furthermore, Azar suggests that all the uses of *qotel* can be related in some way to the present.[16] Segal more moderately states that *qotel* is most frequently used to represent actions performed in the present.[17] As a result, even when used in a modal context, *qotel* inevitably carries with it some of the overtones of the present tense. This further reduces the narrativity of *qotel* verbs in prescriptive statements. As Dwight Bolinger argues:

> We might call the simple present tense the BASE TENSE, to which all other tenses are oriented, but which is itself oriented to nothing, expressing merely the FACT OF PROCESS. The simple present has no confines, but all other tenses are confined in some way. It is timeless not in the sense of "eternal" but of "non-committal about time."[18]

The unrestricted temporal nature of the present tense makes it inherently unsuitable to narrative. The tense lacks temporal specificity. The use of the *qotel* in verbal clauses thus reduces their overall narrativity.

The standard form of the verbal clause makes use of the plural form. This further reduces its narrativity. The use of the plural emphasizes the fact that the Mishnah is not talking about an actual onetime action but a potential action that may be executed countless times by countless individuals.[19]

Despite these common factors regulating the level of narrativity present in active apodictic statements, there exists a significant range of specificity within this class of statements. The above examples are arranged in increasing order of specificity. Example 1 is the least specific. The subject of the sentence remains unspecified. Any and all people, or at least all Jews, can fill in this slot. Similarly, the direct object of the sentence refers to a broad category, "food enough for three meals." Example 2 similarly lacks a defined subject. However, the objects of the sentence are more clearly presented: a bucket and belt. The student can much more easily envision the situation described here. In example 3, we finally have a named subject: "kings' children." The reader does not imagine generic people but rather people of a certain social class, who likely dress a certain way and live in a particular setting. Similarly, the activity under discussion, anointing wounds with rose oil, is also described quite vividly. The reader has little trouble imagining this entire scene.

Singular Form
Apodictic statements can also make use of the singular *qotel* form. The singular is more specific than the plural. Its use encourages the reader to envision

a single iteration of the hypothetical event described. The singular form also creates possibilities for further specificity, as the following examples illustrate.

1) נוֹתֵן שֶׁמֶן בַּתְּחִלָּה לְתוֹךְ הַמַּיִם אוֹ לְתוֹךְ הַמֶּלַח

2) נוֹטֵל אָדָם קוּרְנָס לְפַצֵּעַ בּוֹ אֱגוֹזִים

3) הַקִּיטֵּעַ יוֹצֵא בְּקַב שֶׁלּוֹ

1. [1] puts oil first into the water or into the salt (14:2).
2. A man may take a hammer to split nuts (17:2).
3. A stump-legged person may go forth with his wooden stump (6:8).

Example one, like most of the plural statements examined above, has no explicitly stated subject. In example 2, however, the subject is specified through the use of the word *adam* ("one," "a person"). In singular proscriptive statements, the subject is often represented through the use of general terms like "he" or "one," or, in cases where gender is significant, "a man"/"a woman." Though these terms are not at all specific, the presence of a singular noun holding the place of the subject encourages the student to envision an individual person engaging in the activity at hand. Finally, in example 3, the subject is not a generic person but a cripple. Like the example of the aristocrats anointing themselves with oil, this text presents us with a relatively detailed picture. In this case, it is that of a cripple going out on the Sabbath on his wooden stump.

Negative Statements

The Mishnah does not speak only of what one may or must do. It frequently speaks of activities that are prohibited by the halakhah. For example:

1) אֵין נוֹתְנִין אֶת הַפַּת לַתַּנּוּר עִם חֲשֵׁיכָה

2) לֹא יֵצֵא הַחַיָּט בְּמַחֲטוֹ סָמוּךְ לַחֲשֵׁיכָה

1. [We] may not put bread into an oven just before nightfall (1:10).
2. A tailor may not go out with his needle near nightfall (1:3).

These two examples illustrate the basic forms of the negative statement. Example 1 illustrates the plural *qotel* form, which uses the word *'ayn*. Example 2 illustrates the singular *yiqtol* form which makes use of the word *lo*.[20] This is the first form that we have seen that makes use of the standard *yiqtol* to express the modal. I have previously argued for the relative lack of narrativity of the *qotel*. In some ways, the *yiqtol* form possesses even less narrativity than the *qotel*. Mishor argues that the "characteristic quality [of the *qotel*] is its concrete and descriptive expression of facts."[21] In this respect, *qotel* implies a significant degree of specificity. When used as a modal, Mishor argues, *qotel* serves to state the existence of a norm rather than describe a potential action. The use of *yiqtol*, in contrast, implies the modal proper. It prescribes potential action rather than merely describing a norm. Verbs expressed in the *yiqtol* form lack the concreteness and specificity of verbs expressed in *qotel*.

Generally speaking, statements that prohibit actions are less dynamic than those that prescribe or permit activities. However, the narrative potential of "negative events" should not be unduly downplayed. A negative event can take its place in a chain of events that constitute a narrative. In many narrative contexts, the fact that a character does not act is just as significant as the fact that he or she does act. Furthermore, negative statements tend to conjure up the image of the action that they prohibit. When reading example 1, the reader is not likely to envision a cold empty oven on the Sabbath eve. Rather, he or she is far more likely to envision the prohibited action, placing bread in the oven. Similarly, in example 2, the student almost inevitably pictures a tailor walking down the street with a needle in his lapel. From the perspective of the reader's response, these passages convey the representation of action, not inaction.

Other Factors: Word Order
Several factors other than verb form may potentially impact the narrativity of an apodictic statement. The first of these is word order, as the following examples illustrate:

1) כָּל כִּתְבֵי הַקֹּדֶשׁ מַצִּילִין אוֹתָן מִפְּנֵי הַדְּלֵיקָה
2) כָּל הַכֵּלִים נִטָּלִים בַּשַּׁבָּת וְדַלְתוֹתֵיהֶם עִמָּהֶן
3) מֵלְיָיר הַגָּרוּף שׁוֹתִין מִמֶּנּוּ בַשַּׁבָּת
אַנְטִיכֵי אַף עַל פִּי גְרוּפָה[22] אֵין שׁוֹתִין מִמֶּנָּה

1. All sacred writings may be saved from a fire (16:1).
2. All utensils may be handled on the Sabbath and their doors with them (17:1).
3. [If] a *muliar* is cleared of its coals, one may drink from it on the Sabbath. But as to an *antiki*,[23] even if its coals have been cleared, one may not drink from it (3:4).

In these cases, the direct object is placed at the beginning of the sentence. This draws the student's attention toward the object and away from the action that may or may not be done to it. Though these sentences technically describe an action, they primarily focus on the status of the object at hand. They thus have a stative aspect to them. They are less dynamic than sentences that place greater emphasis on the predicate.[24]

Adverbial Phrases
Some apodictic statements contain adverbial phrases that increase their narrativity. By specifying the time, place, and/or motivation of a given action, one

can increase a statement's specificity. Arguably, all of the statements in *Shabbat* have a heightened level of specificity since they are virtually all set on the Sabbath. Some fix the actions they describe in time and space with even more precision:

שְׁלוֹשָׁה דְבָרִים²⁵ צָרִיךְ אָדָם לוֹמַר בְּתוֹךְ בֵּיתוֹ
עֶרֶב שַׁבָּת²⁶ עִם חֲשֵׁיכָה
עִשַּׂרְתֶּן
עֵירַבְתֶּן
הַדְלִיקוּ אֶת הַנֵּר

Three things must a man say in his house,
On the eve of the Sabbath just before night:
Have you rendered tithes?
Have you prepared the *'eruv*?²⁷
Kindle the lamp (2:7).

Here we are given the exact time (Friday at twilight) and the exact place (a person's home) where the event takes place. This Mishnah even implicitly conjures up the last-minute preparations for the Sabbath that the person is directing.

This passage also places a line of dialog into the mouth of its subject. This dialog is merely a simple stereotyped statement. However, the fact that actants in Mishnaic texts have the potential to engage in speech acts establishes the possibility of more complex and expressive speeches such as those found in more sophisticated Mishnaic narratives and stories.

Another common element of stories is the description of the thoughts and feelings of characters. Such depictions are not a defining characteristic of all stories. However, the fact that a narrator describes the inner experience as well as the external traits and actions of a character increases the narrative's specificity. The halakhah is often concerned with inner states as well as external behavior. Hence, the Mishnah often describes the thoughts and intentions of individuals. For example:

1) קוֹשְׁרִים לִפְנֵי בְהֵמָה בִּשְׁבִיל שֶׁלּ ֹא תֵצֵא
2) שׁוֹבֵר אָדָם אֶת הֶחָבִית לֶ ֹאֱכֹל מִמֶּנָּה גְרוֹגָרוֹת

1. [We] may tie [a rope] in front of an animal, that it should not go out (15:2).
2. One may break open a cask in order to eat dried figs thereof (22:3).

The Mishnah here states possible motivations that lie behind various potential actions. In addition to meeting the halakhic necessity of discussing these motives, these descriptions represent a higher level of detail in the Mishnah's presentation of individuals and their actions. The descriptions are both more specific and more dynamic. Rather than describing a single action in a vacuum, the Mishnah presents actions which are preceded by thoughts and intentions and which anticipate events that will happen after the action. While only one event is actually described, these statements suggest a whole chain of events.

Narratives
Occasionally, apodictic statements present a series of interconnected events. For example:

לֹא יִקּוֹב אָדם שְׁפוֹפָרֶת שֶׁלַּבֵּיצָה וִימַלְּאֶנָּה שֶׁמֶן וְיִתְּנֶינָה עַל פִּי הַנֵּר בִּשְׁבִיל שֶׁתְּהֵא מְנַטֶּפֶת.

A man may not pierce an eggshell, fill it with oil, and place it over the mouth of a lamp, in order that it should drip (2:4).

In cases such as this, the apodictic statement constitutes a complete narrative. We might call this example a negative narrative since it describes an event that is not supposed to happen. In order for this text to be turned into a story, it would have to read something like this: "Once there was a person who pierced an egg shell, filled it with oil, and placed it at the mouth of the candle so that it would drip." The narrative would then recount a onetime series of events that happened in the past, rather than merely a chain of possible actions.

Casuistic Formulation

Casuistic formulation consists of two parts. The first, called the protasis, consists of a hypothetical case or situation. The second half, the apodosis, contains a ruling on the case, formulated in a manner similar to an apodictic statement. Casuistic formulations tend to have greater narrativity than apodictic statements. The two halves of casuistic formulations generally each present a single narrative event. Taken as a whole, the casuistic formulation almost invariably presents two interrelated events. Hence, they are almost always narratives.

Protasis: Hypothetical Cases

I shall start by analyzing the various forms of hypothetical cases, independent of the rulings that follow them. I will then consider the compound formulation as a unit.

Noun Phrases
Many protases are not independent clauses but noun phrases. By definition, noun phrases focus on the object and not the action, and are of limited narrativity. The noun phrases come in two basic forms: "X...that" and *haqotel*.

"X...THAT"
In this form, the phrase begins with a regular noun which is subsequently modified. As we have seen in the case of apodictic statements, the placement of the noun at the beginning of the clause or phrase draws the reader's attention away from the action and toward the object of the action. For example:

תַּנּוּר שֶׁהִיסִיקוּהוּ[28] בַּקַּשׁ אוֹ בַגְּבָבָה

> An oven that was heated with stubble or rakings (3:2)

Here the reader focuses on the oven and not on the act of adding fuel. Thus, though an action is implicitly described here, the phrase remains relatively undynamic. In some cases, the noun clause lacks a verb altogether:

מָעוֹת שֶׁעַל הַכָּר

> Money that is on a cushion (21:2)

This case involves a fact rather than an action: there are coins on a cushion. As far as the case is concerned, it does not matter how or when the coins were placed on the pillow. They may have been resting there since creation. Hence the case itself presents complete stasis.

HAQOTEL

In many situations, the Mishnah makes use of the *haqotel* form to describe hypothetical cases:

1) הַמַּכֶּה בַקּוּרְנָס עַל הַסַּדָּן
2) הַכּוֹתֵב שְׁתֵּי אוֹתוֹת בְּהֶעְלֵם אֶחָד

1. One who beats with the sledge hammer on the anvil at the time of his work (12:1)
2. One who writes two letters in one state of unawareness (12:4)

The *haqotel* form is in reality a noun, not a verb form. Nevertheless, these are nouns that are defined by a particular action.[29] Indeed, these phrases are often translated into English by transposing them into simple descriptions of actions, as in the translations presented above.[30] Such translations capture the fact that the fundamental intent of the *haqotel* form is to present a dynamic event and not a state. The *haqotel* form thus places an action at the center of the reader's attention. In this sense, it possesses a higher level of dynamism and narrativity than the "X...that" form.

Qatal Clauses

In other situations, the protasis takes the form of a clause containing a verb in the *qatal* form:

1) נָפְלָה דְלֵיקָה בְּלֵילֵי שַׁבָּת
2) עָשָׂה[31] כֶּבֶשׁ לֵירֵד בּוֹ

1. [If] a fire broke out on a Sabbath night (16:2)
2. [If a gentile] made a stairway to descend by it (16:8)

As Azar explains, the *qatal* form "refers to an action which happened in the absolute and specific past which is understood as a onetime event.... This past is the 'narrative' or 'preterit' past which is completely removed from the time of the speaker."[32] *Qatal* is thus "the narrative tense par excellence," and is one of the defining features of stories in the Mishnah.[33] In the above cases, however, *qatal* is used to express a hypothetical case. As Segal explains, this usage of *qatal* is meant to portray these hypothetical actions "*as if* they already happened in the past."[34] Indeed, these hypothetical cases are formally indistinguishable from narrative events found in actual stories. Only the context allows the student to know these are meant to be hypothetical and not actual events. While the use of *qatal* does not change the irrealis nature of these hypothetical cases, it does encourage the student to think of these hypothetical cases *as if* they were actual events set in the past. As a result, these texts have a significantly higher degree of narrativity than the other types of formulations that we have examined thus far.

Narratives

Some hypothetical cases depict a series of interrelated actions, as the following examples illustrate:

1) פָּשַׁט הֶעָנִי אֶת יָדוֹ לִפְנִים וְנָתַן לְתוֹךְ יָדוֹ שֶׁלְּבַעַל הַבַּיִת
2) צְבִי שֶׁנִּכְנַס לַבַּיִת נָעַל[35] אֶחָד בְּפָנָיו

1. [If] the poor man stretched his hand within and places [an article] into the hand of the master of the house (1:1)
2. A deer that entered a house and one person shut [the door] before it (13:6)

These hypothetical narratives are remarkably close to actual stories. Example 1 could in fact be mistaken for a story if one were unaware of its context, which directs us to read the verb as hypothetical rather than a past event. Example 2, in contrast, calls attention to its hypothetical nature only through the word "that," which is represented by a one-letter prefix in the Hebrew. It is only this one letter that denies this hypothetical text the potential to be a story recounting a real event in the past.

Apodosis: Rulings

The second clause of the compound formulation is a ruling in the form of an apodictic statement. The combination of the first and second clause generally creates a narrative structure. However, the level of narrativity varies with the nature of the prescriptive clause. In order to evaluate the impact of the apodosis on the entire casuistic formulation, we will quote both the hypothetic case and the ruling, separated by a "slash" in each citation.

Nonverbal Clauses
When the ruling is formulated as a nonverbal clause, the overall level of narrativity of the casuistic formulation is lowest:

1) הַמּוֹצִיא עֵצִים / כְּדֵי לְבַשֵּׁל בֵּיצָה קַלָּה
2) צְבִי שֶׁנִּכְנַס לַבַּיִת וְנָעַל[36] אֶחָד בְּפָנָיו / חַיָּב

1. [In a case of] one who carries out wood / [the standard for culpability is] as much as is required for boiling a light egg (9:5).
2. [In a case of] a deer that enters a house and one person shuts [the door] before it / [The person] is culpable (13:6).

In example 1, the apodosis sets a minimum halakhic requirement. This case does not constitute a narrative because the two clauses do not occur in succession. Both refer to the same event, the transportation of some wood outside. There is not sufficient dynamism to make this statement a narrative. Example 2 does constitute a rudimentary narrative. In and of itself, the second clause lacks dynamism because it simply establishes the status of the person as culpable. Yet, when placed after the first clause, the second clause is transformed from a designation of an unchanging status to an account of a person's transformation from one status to another as a result of his actions. This meets the minimum threshold of dynamism that we have set for narratives.

Verbal Clauses
Cases where both the protasis and the apodosis of the casuistic formulation contain verbs and each portrays an active event are the most common and obvious examples of narrative forms in casuistic formulations. For example:

1) נָפְלָה דְּלֵיקָה בְּלֵילֵי שַׁבָּת / מַצִּילִים מְזוֹן שָׁלוֹשׁ סְעוּדוֹת
2) עָשָׂה[73] כֶּבֶשׁ לֵירֵד בּוֹ / יֵרֵד[38] אַחֲרָיו ישראל

1. [If] a fire broke out on a Sabbath night / food for three meals may be saved (16:2).
2. [If a gentile] made a stairway to descend by it / an Israelite may descend after him (16:8).

As both of these cases illustrate, statements of this sort by definition contain a simple progression of two interrelated events. First the fire breaks out and then the people save the food. First the gentile makes a gangway and then the Israelite comes down after him. Once again, these narratives are easily converted into stories simply by changing the verbs to past tense. Casuistic narratives are distinguished by the fact that the two events occur in different tenses and aspects. The first clause uses the *qatal* in a hypothetical manner, whereas the second clause utilizes either the *yiqtol* or the *qotel* form in a modal sense.

Example 2 is our first case of the use of the *yiqtol* form that is not preceded by the negative word *lo*. Whereas in apodictic statements *yiqtol* is used only in negative statements using the word *lo*, in casuistic formulations *yiqtol* may be used in positive prescriptive statements as well.[39] I have no explanation for this discrepancy.

Narrative in the Ruling
Occasionally, the ruling of a casuistic statement constitutes a narrative in and of itself:

1) מָעוֹת שֶׁעַל הַכַּר / נוֹעֵר אֶת הַכַּר וְהֵן נוֹפְלוֹת
2) אִם לָא שָׁחַק מֵעֶרֶב שַׁבָּת / לוֹעֵס בְּשִׁינָּיו וְנוֹתֵן[40]

1. Money that is on a cushion / one tilts it on a side and it falls off (21:2).
2. If one did not crush [the cumin] on the eve of the Sabbath / one must chew [it] with his teeth and apply [it to the wound] (19:2).

In these cases, the apodosis contains two discrete interrelated events. In example 1, the narrative is contained entirely in the apodosis, since the protasis, as we have already explained, does not constitute a narrative event. In example 2, the protasis is a negative event: the failure to crush cumin to be used in a circumcision before the Sabbath. In this case, the two clauses come together to form a narrative chain made up of three events: the failure to grind the cumin on the eve of Sabbath, the chewing, and the application on the Sabbath.

Multiple Paths

We have now analyzed the basic irrealis forms that the Mishnah uses to present halakhah and have evaluated their relative narrativity. There is still one more important factor which impacts the level of narrativity of the Mishnah's irrealis statements: the Mishnah's tendency to juxtapose and interweave multiple variants of the same case. The first paragraph in *Shabbat* is a particularly rich example of this technique. To facilitate a better understanding of this complex passage, I have broken it down into sections preceded by headings.

A Typology of Mishnaic Forms

Opening Summary Statement
יְצִיאוֹת הַשַּׁבָּת שְׁתַּיִם שֶׁהֵן אַרְבַּע בִּפְנִים
וּשְׁתַּיִם שֶׁהֵן אַרְבַּע בַּחוּץ
כֵּיצַד הֶעָנִי עוֹמֵד בַּחוּץ וּבַעַל הַבַּיִת בִּפְנִים

Part A
Cases
1) פָּשַׁט הֶעָנִי אֶת יָדוֹ לִפְנִים וְנָתַן לְתוֹךְ יָדוֹ שֶׁלְּבַעַל הַבַּיִת
2) אוֹ שֶׁנָּטַל מִתּוֹכָהּ וְהוֹצִיא

Ruling
הֶעָנִי חַיָּב וּבַעַל הַבַּיִת פָּטוּר

Part B
Cases
1) פָּשַׁט בַּעַל הַבַּיִת אֶת יָדוֹ לַחוּץ וְנָתַן לְתוֹךְ יָדוֹ שֶׁלֶּעָנִי
2) אוֹ שֶׁנָּטַל מִתּוֹכָהּ וְהִכְנִיס

Ruling
בַּעַל הַבַּיִת חַיָּב וְהֶעָנִי פָּטוּר

Part C
Cases
1) פָּשַׁט הֶעָנִי אֶת יָדוֹ לִפְנִים וְנָטַל בַּעַל הַבַּיִת מִתּוֹכָהּ
2) אוֹ שֶׁנָּתַן לְתוֹכָהּ וְהוֹצִיא

Ruling
שְׁנֵיהֶם פְּטוּרִים

Part D
Cases
1) פָּשַׁט בַּעַל הַבַּיִת אֶת יָדוֹ לַחוּץ וְנָטַל הֶעָנִי מִתּוֹכָהּ
2) אוֹ שֶׁנָּתַן לְתוֹכָהּ וְהִכְנִיס

Ruling
שְׁנֵיהֶם פְּטוּרִין

Opening Summary Statement
The carryings out of the Sabbath are two, which are four within, and two, which are four without.
How so? The poor man stands without and the master of the house within.

Part A

Cases

1. If the poor man stretches his hand within and places [an article] into the hand of the master of the house, or
2. If he takes [an article] from it and carries it out,

Ruling

The poor man is liable, and the master of the house is exempt.

Part B

Cases

1. If the master of the house stretches his hand without and places [an object] in the poor man's hand, or
2. Takes [an object] therefrom and carries it in,

Ruling

The master is liable, while the poor man is exempt.

Part C

Cases

1. If the poor man stretches his hand within and the master takes [an object] from it, or
2. Places [an object] therein and he carries it out,

Ruling

Both are exempt.

Part D

Cases

1. If the master stretches his hand without and the poor man takes [an object] from it, or
2. Places [an article] therein and he carries it inside,

Ruling

Both are exempt.

The Mishnah presents a total of eight different scenarios. All of them are based on the same premise: a poor person stands outside of a house while the householder is inside the house. Something is passed from one to the other. The cases are grouped into four sets (A–D) of two (1–2). Each set contains a "case" section which presents two alternative situations. A single ruling that pertains to both cases follows. This paragraph thus presents two distinct methods for linking together disparate narratives. The first is the grouping together of narratives that share a single premise even though they may result in differing halakhic outcomes. The second is the coupling of two different cases that share a similar outcome into a single casuistic formulation.

The very next paragraph displays two more techniques for interweaving different cases:

ל״א יִכָּנֵס לֹא לַמֶּרְחָץ וְלֹ[41]א לַבּוּרְסְקִי וְלֹ[42]א לֶאֱכֹל וְלֹא לָדִין וְאִם הִתְחִילוּ / אֵין מַפְסִיקִין

> He may not enter the baths nor a tannery, nor eat, nor engage in a lawsuit, yet if they began / they need not break off (1:2).

Here, an individual event is divided into multiple possibilities. This apodictic statement has a single implied subject, "a man," and a single predicate, "enter." However, it has multiple alternative direct objects: a bathhouse, a tannery, etc. The account thus forks into different directions. Furthermore, the apodictic statement is followed by a casuistic formulation: "If they began / they need not break off." This section deals with a post facto case in which the initial principle of not undertaking various activities on Friday afternoon is violated. It rules that once such actions are started, one need not desist from them. Simple prescriptive statements in the Mishnah are often followed in this way by casuistic formulations that present related possibilities.

By presenting narratives and events that mirror each other and emerge from one another, the Mishnah calls attention to the fact that these events are merely theoretical constructs that can be easily manipulated for heuristic purposes. The Mishnah thereby emphasizes the irrealis nature of these texts and reduces their level of narrativity.

Jorge Louis Borges imagined an extreme version of such a bifurcated narrative in his story "The Garden of Forking Paths."[43] Borges envisions a novel that presents all of the possible paths that the plot could take. Chatman calls such texts "antistories":

> If the classical narrative is a network (or "enchainment") of kernels affording avenues of choice, only one of which is possible, the antistory may be defined as an attack on this convention which treats all choices as equally valid.... What they call into question precisely in narrative logic, that one thing leads to one and only one other, the second to the third and so on to the finale.[44]

The presence of texts in the Mishnah that share some characteristics with such "antistories" calls our attention to one of the fundamentally antinarrative characteristics of halakhah or any system of law or norms. Whereas narratives seek to present a single chain of events, the halakhah seeks to encompass all possibilities, potentialities, and eventualities. The all-inclusive nature of law stands in opposition to the specific nature of narrative.

Realis Texts

We will now move on to those texts in the Mishnah that are rooted in reality. These are texts that tell of events that are portrayed as having actually happened in the past.

Repeated Events

The Mishnah occasionally records the regular practices of individuals or communities that are deemed to be of normative significance. The morphological hallmark of the repeated event is the use of the *haya + qotel* form to express the iterative past,[45] as in the following cases:

1) אוֹ' רַבָּן שִׁמְעוֹן בֶּן גַּמְלִיאֵ'
נוֹהֲגִין הָיוּ בֵית אַבָּא שֶׁהָיוּ[46] נוֹתְנִין
כְּלֵי לָבָן שֶׁלָּהֶן לְכוֹבֵס נָכְרִי
שְׁלֹשֶׁת יָמִים קוֹדֶם לַשַּׁבָּת
2) פָּרָתוֹ שֶׁל ר' אֶלְעָזָר בֶּן עֲזַרְיָה
הָיְתָה יוֹצֵא בִרְצוּעָה שֶׁבֵּין קַרְנֶיהָ

1. R. Simeon ben Gamliel, said:
   It was the practice in my father's house to give
   white garments to a gentile launderer
   three days before the Sabbath (1:9).
2. R. Eleazar ben Azariah's cow
   used to go out with a strap between its horns (5:4).

These accounts are fundamentally similar to certain types of Mishnaic stories. Like these stories, repeated events draw on the deeds of individuals and groups as a source for normative behavior. However, repeated events are not stories, because they lack key elements of both dynamism and specificity. They tell of a single event that occurred multiple times in the past. Though the repetitive nature of the actions described in these texts may reduce their level of narrativity, it may actually increase their value as halakhic sources. The fact that it is reported that a certain rabbi did an action repeatedly, as opposed to only once, decreases the possibility that the rabbi's actions were misreported or misunderstood. Once again, halakhic concerns can lead the Mishnah to favor a formulation that has less rather than more narrativity.

Ritual Narrative

Ritual narratives are among the most prominent narrative forms in the Mishnah. These texts record the sequence of events in legal, cultic, and other rituals. Most frequently, they describe the cultic rituals that took place in the Temple. There are no examples of this phenomenon in *Shabbat*. I present here a passage from *Pesahim* 5:5–7:

(5) הַפֶּסַח נִשְׁחַט בְּשָׁלוֹשׁ כִּתִּים
שֶׁנֶּ׳
וְשָׁחֲטוּ א׳תוֹ כ׳ל קְהַל עֲדַת יִשְׂרָ׳אֵ
בֵּין הָעַרְבָּיִם⁴⁷
קָהָל וְעֵדָה וְיִשְׂרָ׳אֵ
נִכְנְסָה כַּת הָרִאשׁוֹנָה וְנִתְמַלַּת הָעֲזָרָה
נָעֲלוּ דַלְתוֹת הָעֲזָרָה
תָּקְעוּ וְהֵרִיעוּ וְתָקְעוּ
הַכֹּהֲנִים עוֹמְדִים שׁוּרוֹת שׁוּרוֹת וּבִידֵיהֶם בַּזִּיכֵי כֶסֶף וּבַזִּיכֵי זָהָב
שׁוּרָה שֶׁכּוּלָּהּ כֶּסֶף כֶּסֶף
וְשׁוּרָה שֶׁכּוּלָּהּ זָהָב זָהָב וְלֹ׳א הָיוּ מְעוֹרָבִים
וְלֹ׳א הָיָה לַבַּזִּיכִין שׁוּלַיִים
שֶׁמָּא יַנִּיחוּם וְיִקְרַשׁ הַדָּם
(6) שָׁחַט יִשְׂרָ׳ וְקִיבֵּל הַכֹּ׳הֵן
נוֹתְנוֹ לַחֲבֵירוֹ וַחֲבֵירוֹ לַחֲבֵירוֹ
מְקַבֵּל אֶת הַמָּלֵא וּמַחֲזִיר אֶת הָרֵיקָם
כֹּ׳הֵן הַקָּרוֹב אֵצֶל הַמִּזְבֵּחַ זוֹרְקוֹ זְרִיקָה אַחַת כְּנֶגֶד הַיְסוֹד
(7) יָצָאת כַּת הָרִאשׁוֹנָה וְנִכְנְסָה שְׁנִיָּה
יָצָאת שְׁנִיָּה וְנִכְנְסָה שְׁלִישִׁית
כְּמַעֲשֵׂה הָרִאשׁוֹנָה כֵּן מַעֲשֵׂה שְׁנִיָּה וּשְׁלִישִׁית
קָרְאוּ אֶת הַ⁴⁸הַלֵּל
אִם גָּמְרוּ שָׁנוּ וְאִם שָׁנוּ שִׁילֵּשׁוּ
אַפְעַל פִּי שֶׁלֹ׳א שִׁילְּשׁוּ וּ⁴⁹מִימֵיהֶם
ר׳ יְהוּדָה אוֹ׳ מִיָּמָיו שֶׁלְּכַת הַשְּׁלִישִׁית לֹ׳א הִגִּיעָה
לְאָהַבְתִּי כִּי יִשְׁמַע ה׳ מִפְּנֵי שֶׁעַמָּהּ מְעוּטָטִים.

6) The Passover offering is slaughtered in three divisions,
   for it is said,
   "And the whole assembly of the congregation of Israel shall slaughter it
   at twilight" [Ex. 12:6]
   [i.e.,] "assembly," "congregation," and "Israel."
   The first division entered, the temple court was filled,
   they closed the doors of the temple court.
   They sounded a *teki'ah*, a *teru'ah*, and a *teki'ah*.
   The priests stood in rows, and in their hands were basins of silver and of gold;
   a silver row which was entirely of silver,
   and a gold row which was entirely of gold;
   they were not mixed.
   The basins had no [flat] bottoms,

lest they put them down and the blood become congealed.
The Israelite killed [the lamb], and the priest caught [the blood];
he handed it to his colleague and his colleague [passed it on] to his colleague;
and he received the full [basin] and gave back the empty one.
The priest nearest the altar sprinkled it once over against the base [or the altar].
The first division [then] went out and the second entered;
the second went out and the third entered.
As the manner of the first [group], so was the manner of the second and the third.
They recited the Hallel;
if they finished it they repeated, and if they repeated, they recited it a third time,
though they never did recite it a third time.
R. Judah said: The third division never reached
"I love that the Lord should hear..." [Psalms 116:1] because the people for it were few.

Conceptually and linguistically, ritual narratives emerge from two of the forms that we have already discussed, apodictic statements and repeated events. The text above comes in the context of a series of apodictic statements and hypothetical cases dealing with the paschal sacrifice. In one sense, the ritual narrative is merely a stringing together of apodictic statements that supply instructions for a complex task. In this sense, they are irrealis, not realis, narratives. On the other hand, this description of the paschal sacrifice contains details that are almost certainly not meant to be normative. The passage ends with a discussion that is unquestionably realis in nature: it discusses the number of times the Hallel prayer was actually repeated by the Levites on Passover night during the period before the destruction of the Temple. In this way, ritual narratives are more like a chain of repeated events than of prescriptive statements. They report the way the Temple cult was actually practiced rather than explaining how it should be practiced.

This tension between the prescriptive and descriptive nature of ritual narratives is reflected in the two different verb forms that alternatively predominate in these texts. As Yohanan Breuer has demonstrated, ritual narratives use either the *qotel* or the *qatal* as their primary verb form.[50] The use of the *qotel* corresponds to the prescriptive aspect of the ritual narrative. In this respect, the ritual narrative may be viewed as nothing more than a stringing together of apodictic statements.[51] The use of *qatal*, in contrast, as in the case above, suggests the descriptive aspect of the ritual narrative. It implies an event that actually happened. In using *qatal* to report a repeated action, these ritual narratives attain a level of specificity that goes beyond that of the repeated action.[52] The more usual form for expressing the iterative past is the auxiliary *haya* + *qotel*. *Qatal* is usually reserved for the simple past. It is as if the reader is being encouraged to envision a single iteration of the ritual rather than focusing on the fact that the event recurred on a regular basis for generations. These ritual narratives might thus be seen as pseudostories, which very closely approximate the experience of an actual story.

Onetime Events

On rare occasions, the Mishnah reports an individual onetime event that happened in the past. An example of this phenomenon appears later on in the Mishnah's discussion of the paschal sacrifice, *Pesahim* 7:2:

אֵין צוֹלִין אֶת הַפֶּסַח ל'א בְשִׁפּוּד וְל'א בָאַסְכָּלָה
ר' צָדוֹק אוֹמ'[53]
מַעֲשֶׂה בְרַבָּן גַּמְלִיאֵל שֶׁאָמַ' לְטָבִי עַבְדּוֹ
צֵא וּצְלֵה לָנוּ אֶת הַפֶּסַח עַל הָאַסְכָּלָה

One may not roast the Passover offering on either a [metal] spit or grill.
R. Zadok said,
It once happened that R. Gamliel said to his servant Tevi,
"Go out and roast us the Passover offering on the grill."

Here we have a quotation from R. Gamliel. Unlike most other statements quoted in his name, this statement is rooted in time and place. It takes place at a particular time (a certain Passover eve) and place (Jerusalem) and is addressed to a single individual (Tevi). It thus possesses more than the requisite specificity to make it a story. What this text lacks is dynamism. It presents only a single event and therefore does not qualify as a narrative, let alone a story. Nevertheless, the student can easily reconstruct the events leading up to and following this event. This passage comes in the midst of the Mishnah's account of the rituals of Passover eve. On the basis of this account, the student can easily fill in R. Gamliel's activities before and after he tells Tevi to roast the paschal sacrifice.

The way in which realis and irrealis methods of presenting halakhah are juxtaposed in this passage is also worthy of note. There is a dispute as to whether it is permissible to roast the paschal sacrifice on a grill. The first opinion, that it is prohibited, is presented in the form of an apodictic statement. The second opinion, that of R. Gamliel, is presented through a recounting of one of his deeds. We shall investigate this aspect of the text further in chapter 4.

Stories: *Ma'asim*

In order to understand the place of stories among the forms used by the Mishnah to formulate laws, we first must examine the Mishnah's use of the term *ma'aseh* as a technical term for introducing and describing certain types of texts.[54]

The term *ma'aseh* announces the intrusion of real life events into the largely theoretical and hypothetical discourse of the Mishnah. It introduces an event that happened in the past which has halakhic implications or ramifications of one sort or another. This can be a repeated or onetime event or an event that takes place as part of series of interconnected events, i.e., part of a story.

However, the term *ma'aseh* has a special relationship with Mishnaic stories in particular. There are three distinct usages of the term *ma'aseh* in the Mishnah, which I term the exempla, the case story, and the etiological story. As these names suggest, in the second two groupings the *ma'aseh* by definition comes in the context of a story. Exempla as well are often formulated as stories. These three types of *ma'aseh* thus also define the three major genres of Mishnaic stories. Collectively, such stories represent a significant majority of the stories in the Mishnah.

Exempla

Exempla are *ma'asim* which portray the acts of individual rabbis or of groups of people who are considered to be righteous and knowledgeable in the law.[55] Their actions can be taken as precedents for proper halakhic behavior. Exempla are the only type of *ma'aseh* that does not inevitably come in the context of stories. Rather, as demonstrated by the following examples, they can possess at least three different degrees of narrativity:

1) מַעֲשֶׂה בְשׁוּק שֶׁלַּפַּטָּמִים שֶׁהָיָה בִּירוּשָׁלַיִם
שֶׁהָיוּ נוֹעֲלִין וּמַנִּיחִין
אֶת הַמַּפְתֵּחַ בַּחַלּוֹן שֶׁעַל גַּבֵּי הַפֶּתַח
2) מַעֲשֶׂה בְרַבָּן גַּמְלִיאֵל שֶׁאָמַ' לְטָבִי עַבְדּוֹ
צֵא וּצְלֵה לָנוּ אֶת הַפֶּסַח עַל הָאַסְכָּלָה
3) עָשָׂה[56] כֶּבֶשׁ לֵירֵד בּוֹ, יֵרֵד[57] אַחֲרָיו ישרא'
וְאִם בִּשְׁבִיל ישרא' אָסוּר
מַעֲשֶׂה בְרַבָּן גַּמְלִיא' וְהַזְּקֵנִים
שֶׁהָיוּ בָאִין בִּסְפִינָה
וְ[58]עָשָׂה גוֹי כֶּבֶשׁ לֵירֵד בּוֹ[59]
וְיָרְדוּ בּוֹ זְקֵנִים

1. It happened at the butchers market in Jerusalem
    that they would lock [their shops] and leave
    the key in a window above the door ('Eruvin 10:8).
2. It once happened that R. Gamliel said to his servant Tevi,
    "Go out and roast us the Passover offering on the grill" (Pesahim 7:2).
3. If a gentile makes a stairway to descend by it,
    an Israelite may descend after him;
    but if on the Israelites' account, it is forbidden.
    It once happened that R. Gamliel and the elders

were traveling on a ship,
when a gentile made a stairway for going down,
and R. Gamliel and the elders descended by it (*Shabbat* 16:8).

Example 1 is a repeated event. It tells of the actions of a large and loosely defined group of people, those who frequented the cattle market of Jerusalem. As we have seen previously, example 2 is a onetime event. Finally, example 3 is a story. The *ma'aseh* proper is the fact that R. Gamliel and the elders descended down the ramp. However, in order for this event to have any halakhic significance, it must be placed in the context of story. This establishes that the ramp in question was in fact built by a gentile on the Sabbath.

Exempla are, in a sense, the realis cousins of apodictic statements. Just as an apodictic statement requires, allows, or forbids a particular hypothetical action, an exemplum portrays actual actions whose implication is that that class of action is either required, allowed, or, in some cases, forbidden. Similarly, since they generally focus on only a single action, they are not by definition narratives, which require a minimum of two actions. Exempla thus do not have a common narrative structure in the conventional sense. Their defining "structure" consists of the presence of an individual narrative event that presents a rabbi acting in a manner that has halakhic significance. However, many exempla do present a chain of interrelated events and hence do qualify as stories. As such, exempla can and should be considered a genre of rabbinic stories.

Case Stories

Case stories involve a *ma'aseh* which is an event or practice whose halakhic status is in some way ambiguous. A rabbi or rabbis then responds to the *ma'aseh*, generally by issuing a ruling. For example:

מַעֲשֶׂה שֶׁעָשׂוּ אַנְשֵׁי טְבֶרְיָה
הֵבִיאוּ סִילוֹן שֶׁלַּצּוֹנִין לְתוֹךְ אַמָּה שֶׁלַּחַמִּין
אָמְרוּ לָהֶם חֲכָמִין
אִם שַׁבָּת[60] כְּחַמִּין שֶׁהוּחַמּוּ בַשַּׁבָּת
אֲסוּרִים בִּרְחִיצָה וּבִשְׁתִיָּה
אִם בְּיוֹם טוֹב, כְּחַמִּין שֶׁהוּחַמּוּ בְּיוֹם טוֹב
אֲסוּרִין בִּרְחִיצָה וּמוּתָּרִין בִּשְׁתִיָּה

It happened that the people of Tiberias
placed a cold water pipe into a channel of hot water.
The sages said to them:
"On Shabbat, water heated thus is like any other water heated on Shabbat—
it is forbidden to use it for washing or drinking.
On festivals, it is like any other water heated on festivals—
it is forbidden to use it for washing but permitted for drinking" (3:4).

Case stories draw on the pattern of the casuistic formulation. However, instead of presenting a hypothetical case and a general ruling, they present an actual case followed by a ruling issued specifically for that case.[61] They transform the narrative pattern of the casuistic formulation into a full-fledged story. Case stories are thus defined by a minimal narrative form:

A) an event or situation whose halakhic status is not immediately obvious (the ma'aseh)
B) a rabbi or rabbis' evaluation of the case.[62]

Since case stories consist of an actual case followed by an actual ruling, as such they fit our definition of "story" as consisting of a sequence of two interrelated onetime events.

Etiological Stories

While most ma'asim appear either in the context of exempla or case stories, on one occasion[63] the term is used in the context of a third genre, the etiological story. Etiological stories relate the origins of a rabbinic enactment. Generally speaking, etiological stories have a terminology of their own which does not involve the use of the term ma'aseh. The following passage in *Rosh Hashanah* 2:1–2 contains two examples of fairly conventional etiological stories:

בָּרִאשׁוֹנָה הָיוּ מְקַבְּלִים
עֵדוּת הַחוֹדֶשׁ מִכָּל אָדָם
מִשֶּׁקִּלְקְלוּ הַמִּינִים,[64]
הִתְקִינוּ
שֶׁלֹּא יְהוּ מְקַבְּלִים אֶלָּא מִן הַמַּכִּירִים

בָּרִאשׁוֹנָה הָיוּ מַשִּׂיאִים מַשּׂוּאוֹת
מִשֶּׁקִּלְקְלוּ הַכּוּתִים
הִתְקִינוּ שֶׁיְּהוּ שְׁלוּחִים יוֹצְאִין

Originally, they received
testimony of the new moon was from anyone.
When the sectarians became corrupted,
it was ordained
that testimony should be received only from persons known [to the court].

Originally, they used to light beacons.
When the Cutheans became corrupted,
it was ordained
that messengers should go forth.

These stories usually open with the phrase *barishonah*, "originally." This is followed by a description of particular ritual or law as it was previously practiced.

The next section opens with "when." This introduces an event or series of events that made the previous practice no longer feasible. Finally, the term *tiqnu*, "they enacted," or "it was ordained," introduces a rabbinic enactment that involves a new practice meant to compensate for the disruption of the old one. In one instance, Yoma 2:1–2, the term *ma'aseh* is substituted for "when." In this case, the *ma'aseh* is an event which caused the cessation of a particular practice and necessitated the rabbinic enactment of a pattern of behavior. This use of *ma'aseh* could be dismissed as an exception that proves the rule that the term *ma'aseh* always comes in the context of an exemplum or a case story. However, even in this case, the use of the word conforms to our general definition of Mishnaic *ma'asim* as realis events that have ramifications for future halakhic practice. This suggests that there is indeed an inherent link between the central event in the etiological story and the other forms associated with *ma'asim*. I therefore believe that, on the basis on Yoma 2:1–2, it is legitimate to consider the etiological story as one of three genres that are connected to the *ma'aseh*.[65]

Ma'asim: Summary

The term *ma'aseh* describes an event that happened in the past which has halakhic implications. The nature of the relationship between the event and the halakhic process varies. The event itself may be a legal precedent; it may be the occasion for a ruling which potentially has broader halakhic implications; or it may signal a crisis that necessitates a rabbinic reform in the law.

These possibilities correspond to three distinct Mishnaic narrative forms: the exempla, the case story, and the etiological story. Despite their differences, each of these genres deals with instances in which halakhic discourse comes into dialog or confrontation with material historical events from beyond the realm of the rabbinic study hall. Though the term *ma'aseh* does not always appear in these texts, I argue that the term might also be used to refer to texts that belong to this set of genres. Hence the term *ma'aseh* in this book refers either to individual events in the past with historical ramifications or to a text which is a member of one of the three genres that we have designated: the exempla, the case story, and the etiological story.

Speech Acts

Thus far, we have considered only one set of verbs in the Mishnah: those that describe the potential or actual fulfillment or violation, of the halakhic norms that are the Mishnah's central focus. We have traced the full range of narrativity of clauses containing such verbs from non-narrative to stories. There remains, however, another large body of actions described in the Mishnah that also have the potential to be narrative events. These are the phrases that describe not the performance or violation of the law but its transmission. In an oral culture such as that of the Mishnah, this is done primarily through speech acts. Most frequently, this involves the use of the root '-m-r, "say," which is by far the most common verb in the Mishnah.[66] The way in which the Mishnah describes the transmission of individual laws has the potential to enhance or reduce the narrativity of individual Mishnaic passages. While I will not present a full study of this aspect of the Mishnah's narrativity, a brief survey is certainly in order.

Attributed Statements

Most statements in the Mishnah are anonymous. Considered as the product of a speech act, these statements emerge as possessing little narrativity. The speech act itself is implied rather than explicitly stated. The act is not in any way fixed in time or space. It is as if the statement represents a universal truth that transcends time and place. Frequently though, the Mishnah cites a statement in the name of a particular rabbi using the verbal the root '-m-r. This raises the level of narrativity of the statement. Now the statement is linked to a single individual who lived at a certain time and in a certain place. These attributions are generally made using one of two formulations: "Rabbi X says" and "Rabbi X said."

"Rabbi X Says"

The phrase "Rabbi X says," using the *qotel* form *'omer*, possesses a relatively low level of narrativity. As we have already discussed, the present tense is a fundamentally non-narrative form. The phrase "Rabbi X says" does not imply a specific statement made by a rabbi at a given time. Rather, it informs us of a position held by a particular rabbi. We can talk about this position in the present tense because, even though the rabbi himself has long since passed on, his halakhic position is essentially timeless.

Often, the Mishnah juxtaposes two opposing statements, each introduced by "Rabbi X says." This creates the illusion of a dialog. Such "debates" have relatively low levels of narrativity. In addition to the fact that the statements are formulated in the atemporal *qotel* form, the two statements are neither truly sequential nor interconnected. The order of the statements could be reversed or they could be presented independently without affecting their meanings.

"Rabbi X Said"

The introductory phrase "Rabbi X said," significantly heightens the narrativity of the passage in question. When the Mishnah makes use of the *qatal* form *'amar*, it implies that the statement that follows was made at a specific point in the past. Not all uses of *'amar* necessarily imply the simple past. Generally, though, *'amar* is used to introduce statements that directly relate to the preceding statement in the Mishnah. The term introduces questions, rejections, supporting arguments, and proofs of other rabbis' positions. It also introduces stories and dialogs within stories. *'Amar* thus precedes statements that have a high degree of specificity and are dynamically linked to their contexts.[67]

Dialogs

Occasionally the Mishnah presents dialogs between two rabbis. Generally, these texts serve to expound the underlying logic of the opposing halakhic positions.

An example of such a dialog is found in *Pesahim* 6:5:

הַפֶּסַח שֶׁשְּׁחָטוֹ שֶׁלֹּא לִשְׁמוֹ בַּשַּׁבָּת
חַיָּיב עָלָיו חַטָּאת
וּשְׁאָר כָּל הַזְּבָחִים שֶׁשְּׁחָטָן לְשֵׁם הַפֶּסַח
אִם אֵינָן רְאוּיִים הֵן[68]
ר' אֱלִיעֶזֶר מְחַיֵּיב חַטָּאת
ר' יְהוֹשֻׁעַ פּוֹטֵר
אָמַ' ר' אֱלִיעֶזֶר
מָה אִם הַפֶּסַח שֶׁהוּא מוּתָּר לִשְׁמוֹ
כְּשֶׁשִּׁינָּה אֶת שְׁמוֹ חַיָּיב,
זְבָחִים שֶׁהֵם אֲסוּרִים לִשְׁמָן
כְּשֶׁשִּׁינָּה אֶת שְׁמָן אֵינוּ דִין שֶׁיְּהֵא חַיָּיב
אָמַ' לוֹ ר' יְהוֹשֻׁעַ
לֹא
אִם[69] אָמַרְתָּה בַּפֶּסַח שֶׁשִּׁינָּהוּ בְדָבָר אָסוּר
תֹּ'אמַר בִּזְבָחִים שֶׁשִּׁינָּן בְּדָבָר מוּתָּר
אָמַ' לוֹ ר' אֱלִיעֶ'
אֵמוּרֵי צִיבּוּר יוֹכִיחוּ[70]
שֶׁהֵן מוּתָּרִין לִשְׁמָן
וְהַשּׁוֹחֵט לִשְׁמָן חַיָּיב
אָמַ' לוֹ ר' יְהוֹשֻׁעַ
לֹא
אִם אָמַרְתָּה בָּאֵמוּרֵי צִיבּוּר שֶׁיֵּשׁ לָהֶם קִצְבָה
תֹּ'אמַר בַּפֶּסַח שֶׁאֵין לוֹ קִצְבָה.

If the Passover was slaughtered for a different purpose on the Sabbath,
[the slaughterer] is liable to a sin offering on its account.
While all other sacrifices, which he slaughtered as a Passover,
if they are not eligible, he is culpable;
while if they are eligible,
R. Eliezer rules him liable to a sin offering
and R. Joshua rules him not culpable.
R. Eliezer said to him,

"If the Passover, which is permitted for its own purpose,
yet when he changes its purpose he is culpable;
then [other] sacrifices, which are forbidden [even] for their own purpose,
if he changes their purpose is it not logical that he is culpable?"
R. Joshua said,
"Not so.
If you say [thus] of the Passover, where he changed it for that which is forbidden;
will you say [the same] of sacrifices where he changed them for that which is permitted?"
Said R. Eliezer to him:
"Let the public sacrifices prove it,
which are permitted for their own sake,
yet he who slaughters [other sacrifices] in their name is culpable."
Said R. Joshua to him,
"Not so.
If you say [thus] of public sacrifices, [that is] because they have a limit;
will you say [the same] of the Passover, which has no limit?"

The first part of this passage sets the stage for R. Eliezer and R. Joshua's debate concerning the status of the person who sacrifices an animal on the Sabbath as a Paschal sacrifice even though it had previously been designated as a regular sacrifice. R. Eliezer rules that such a person is liable to a sin offering, while R. Joshua rules that the person is not liable. In the remainder of the passage, the two rabbis engage in a debate in which R. Eliezer presents two arguments for his position. Following each argument, R. Joshua explains why he rejects R. Eliezer's claim.

Based on the criteria offered in the previous story, dialogs such as this are at best marginal stories. No significant change occurs as a result of the conversation. Each rabbi leaves the encounter holding the same opinion as before. Nevertheless, it could be argued that the fact that R. Eliezer learns of R. Joshua's arguments and still maintains his position suggests enough dynamism to push this text over the threshold in to the category of story. If, however, one of the interlocutors convinced the other to change his position, this would clearly constitute a story. While there are no examples of this in *Seder Moʻed*, several dialogs recorded elsewhere in the Mishnah record such a transformation. Notably, there are a number of debates between the schools of Hillel and Shammai that conclude with the narrator stating that in response to house of Shammai's arguments, "The school of Hillel, changing their view, ruled in agreement with [the position of] the school of Shammai."[71] Such dialogs can be considered stories.

"Beit Midrash" Stories

The Mishnah's representation of the activities of transmitting halakhah thus generates stories that are beyond the realm of the *maʻaseh*. Unlike *maʻasim* which deal with the rabbinic response to events that occurred in the "outside world," these are stories that emerge from within the closed discourse of the rabbinic study hall, the beit midrash. These stories portray how it is that the rabbis transmit teaching as well as how they conduct and resolve disputes. Not all of these stories involve dialogs. One example of such a story is found in *Shabbat* 1:4.

אֵילוּ מֵהֲלָכוֹת שֶׁאָמְרוּ בַּעֲלִיַּית
חֲנִינָה בֶן חִזְקִיָּה בֶן גַּרוֹן[72] שֶׁעָלוּ לְבַקְּרוֹ
נִימְנוּ[73]
וְרָבוּ בֵּית שַׁמַּי עַל בֵּית הִילֵּל
שְׁמוֹנָה עָשָׂר דָּבָר גָּזְרוּ בוֹ בַיּוֹם

> And these are of the rulings which they stated in the upper chamber of
> Hananiah ben Hezekiah ben Garon when they went up to visit him.
> They took a count,
> and the school of Shammai outnumbered the school of Hillel;
> and on that day they enacted eighteen measures.

This story tells of a meeting in which a series of disputes were resolved in favor of the school of Shammai. The story focuses on the internal deliberations of the rabbis who secluded themselves in an upper chamber. Though the essential activities here, "took a count, and...outnumbered," are undertaken through speech acts, there is no reported speech here. This represents a different genre of beit midrash stories from the dialogs that we just saw. It portrays not the open discussion of the beit midrash but rather the way in which the rabbis closed off discussion by ruling in favor on a particular position.

Ma'asim and Beit Midrash Stories

Narrativity appears along two intersecting trajectories in the Mishnah. On the one hand, the Mishnah seeks to categorize and regulate a huge range of objects and actions from the world at large. This includes both hypothetical irrealis formulations as well as realis statements that refer to concrete events. These provide the Mishnah with the bulk of its narrativity: from its generalized principles and categorizations to hypothetical situations and cases to the class of realis texts and stories that I am calling *ma'asim*. On the other hand, the Mishnah also regularly refers to individual rabbis and their activities in the beit midrash, transmitting and discussing these cases and rulings. This presents another continuum of specificity and dynamism, ranging from simple attributions to dialogs and beit midrash stories.

These two strains of narrativity become particularly interrelated in *ma'asim*. Though *ma'asim* deal with events from the outside world, they inevitably also relate to the world of the beit midrash. In case and etiological stories and often exempla as well, the stories focus on a rabbinic speech act through which of a rabbi or rabbis attempt to integrate problematic or unexpected events from the outside world into the strictures of the halakhah. More developed *ma'asim* also contain dialogs between rabbis. The *ma'aseh* thus embraces the full spectrum of narrativity found in the Mishnah.

The Range of Narrativity in the Mishnah: A Case Study of *Shabbat* 1

Now that we have laid out the range of forms that appear in the Mishnah, the next step is to understand how these forms interact with each other within individual Mishnaic passages. We have already seen a few examples of how the Mishnah interweaves various types of simple apodictic statements, casuistic forms, and realis texts, including stories, into an integrated halakhic work. Now we will embark on a more systematic investigation of this phenomenon.

The vast majority of the Mishnah is made up of various forms of the simple active prescriptive statement and the compound formulation. Stative prescriptive statements on the one hand and realis forms, including stories, on the other are relatively rare. Furthermore, individual sections of the Mishnah tend primarily to make use of only one type of active prescriptive statement or compound formulation. For example, *Shabbat* 10–12 makes overwhelming use of the compound form, with the hypothetical case formulated in the *haqotel* conjugation. However, almost invariably, a range of other forms are interspersed with this dominant form.

The first chapter of *Shabbat* is a good example of the way the Mishnah presents a wide range of forms against the backdrop of single, dominant form. In Chart 3.3 you will find the complete text and translation of the chapter broken down into sections and subsections that I have designated using capital letters. In the final column, each subsection is described in terms of the categories for classifying different Mishnaic statements that have been laid out in this chapter.

This chapter represents a discrete literary unit. With the exception of the opening paragraph, the entire chapter deals with activities that are prohibited before the Sabbath lest they lead to a violation on the Sabbath itself.[74]

The dominant form in this chapter is the negative apodictic statement. Much of the chapter follows a very specific format and its variant, which in the chart is designated as formula A and A'. Formula A repeats itself four times in paragraphs 5–8. Each of these paragraphs follows the pattern: "The school of Shammai says it is forbidden to X except in order to Y. The school of Hillel permits." Formula A' appears twice in paragraph 10. In both of these cases, no tradents are cited. The basic pattern of "It is forbidden to X except in order to Y" remains.

apodictic, nonverbal	The carryings out of the Sabbath are two which are four within, and two which are four without.	יציאות השבת שתים שהן ארבע בפנים ושתים שהן ארבע בחוץ	1A
rhetorical question	How so?	כיצד?	1B
multiple paths, causistic formulations, *qatal* form, narrative in protasis.	The poor man stands without and the master of the house within:	העני עומד בחוץ ובעל הבית בפנים	1C
	If the poor man stretches his hand within and places [an article] into the hand of the master of the house, or if he takes [an article] from it and carries it out, the poor man is liable, and the master of the house is exempt.	פשט העני את ידו לפנים ונתן לתוך ידו של בעל הבית או שנטל מתוכה והוציא העני חייב ובעל הבית פטור	
	If the master of the house stretches his hand without and places [an object] in the poor man's hand, or takes [an object] therefrom and carries it in. the master is liable, while the poor man is exempt.	פשט בעל הבית את ידו לחוץ ונתן לתוך ידו של עני או שנטל מתוכה והכניס בעל הבית חייב והעני פטור	
	If the poor man stretches his hand within and the master takes [an object] from it, or places [an object] therein and he carries it out, both are exempt;	פשט העני את ידו לפנים ונטל בעל הבית מתוכה או שנתן לתוכה והוציא שניהם פטורים	
	if the master stretches his hand within or places [an article] therein and he carries it inside, both are exempt.	פשט בעל הבית את ידו לחוץ ונטל העני מתוכה או שנתן לתוכה והכניס שניהם פטורים	
negative apodictic, *yiqtol* form	One must not sit down before a barber near Minḥah until he has prayed	לא ישב אדם לפני הספר סמוך למנחה עד שיתפלל	2A
multiple paths, negative apodictic, *yiqtol* form.	nor may he enter the baths or a tannery, nor to eat nor for a lawsuit.	לא יכנס לא למרחץ ולא לבורסקי ולא לאכול ולא לדין	2B
causistic formulations, *qatal* form, apodictic, *qotel* form	Yet if they began, they need not break off.	ואם התחילו אין מפסיקין	2C
negative apodictic, *ayn' qotlin* form	One must break off for the reading of the Shema, but not for prayer.	מפסיקין לקרות קריאת שמע ואין מפסיקין לתפלה	2D
			2E
multiple paths, negative apodictic, *lo yiqtol* form	A tailor must not go out with his needle near nightfall, lest he forget and go out.	לא יצא החייט במחטו סמוך לחשכה שמא ישכח ויצא	A
motive clause	Nor a scribe with his quill;	ולא הלבלר בקולמוסו	B
negative apodictic, *lo yiqtol* form	And one may not search his garments for vermin.	ולא יפלה את כליו	C
negative apodictic, *lo yiqtol* form	nor read by the light of a lamp.	ולא יקרא לאור הנר	D
negative apodictic, *lo yiqtol* form	In truth, the hazan may see where the children read.	באמת אמרו החזן רואה היכן התינוקות קוראין	E
apodictic, *qotel* form	But he himself must not read.	אבל הוא לא יקרא	F
negative apodictic, *lo yiqtol* form			G
negative apodictic, *lo yiqtol* form	Similarly, a *zab* must not dine together with a *zabah*.	כיוצא בו לא יאכל הזב עם הזבה	H

Chart 3.3

motive clause	as it may lead to sin.	מפני שמביאין לידי עבירה	1
beit midrash story	These are of the halakhot, which they stated in the upper chamber of Hananiah b. Hezekiah b. Garon, when they went up to visit him. They took a count, and house of Shammai out numbered house of Hillel; and on that day they enacted eighteen measures.	אלו מן ההלכות שאמרו בעלית חנניה בן חזקיה בן גרון כשעלו לבקרו נמנו ורבו בית שמאי על בית הלל ובו ביום גזרו שמנה עשר דבר	4
formula A	house of Shammai rules: ink, dyes, and alkaline plants may not be steeped unless they can be dissolved while it is yet day; but house of Hillel permits it.	בית שמאי אומ' אין שורין דיו סמנים וכרשינים, אלא כדי שישורו מבעוד יום ובית הלל מתירין.	5
formula A	house of Shammai rules: bundles of wet flax may not be placed in an oven unless they can begin to steam while it is yet day nor wool in the dyer's kettle, unless it can assume the color [of the dye]; but house of Shammai permits it. house of Hillel rules: snares for wild beasts, fowls, and fish may not be spread unless they can be caught while it is yet day; but house of Hillel permits it.	בית שמאי אומ' אין נותנין אונין של פשתן לתוך התנור אלא כדי שיהבילו מבעוד יום ולא את הצמר ליורה אלא כדי שיקלוט את העין בית הלל מתירין. בית שמאי אומ' אין פורשין מצודות חיה ועופות ודגים אלא כדי שיצודו מבעוד יום ובית הלל מתירין.	6 A B
formula A	house of Shammai rules: one must not sell to a gentile, or help him to load [an ass], or lift up [an article] upon him unless he can reach a nearby place; but house of Hillel/Shammai permits it.	בית שמאי אומ' אין מוכרין לגוי ואין טוענין עמו ואין מגביהין עליו אלא כדי שיגיע למקום קרוב ובית הלל מתירין.	7
formula A	house of Hillel/Shammai rules: Skins must not be given to a tanner nor garments to a gentile washer unless they can be done while it is yet day; but in all these [cases] house of Hillel/Shammai permits [them] before sunset.	בית שמאי אומ' אין נותנין עורות לעבדן ולא כלים לכובס גוי אלא כדי שיעשו מבעוד יום ובכולן בית הלל מתירין עם השמש.	8
			9

speech act, *amar*	R. Simeon b. Gamaliel said:	אָמַר רַבָּן שִׁמְעוֹן בֶּן גַּמְלִיאֵל	A
repeated event	It was the practice in my father's house to give white garments to a gentile washer three days before the Sabbath.	נוֹהֲגִין הָיוּ בֵּית אַבָּא שֶׁהָיוּ נוֹתְנִין כְּלֵי לָבָן לְכוֹבֵס גּוֹי שְׁלֹשֶׁת יָמִים קוֹדֶם לַשַּׁבָּת	B
implied speech act	And both [schools] agree:		C
apodictic, pl. *qotel* form	the beam of the [oil]press and the circular winepress may be laden.	וְשָׁוִין שֶׁטּוֹעֲנִין בְּקוֹרַת בֵּית הַבַּד וּבְעִגּוּלֵי הַגַּת	10
formula A'—multiple paths	Meat, onion[s], and egg[s] may not be roasted unless there is time for them to be [completely] roasted.	אֵין צוֹלִין בָּשָׂר בָּצָל וּבֵיצָה אֶלָּא כְדֵי שֶׁיִּצּוֹלוּ	A
formula A'—multiple paths	Bread may not be put into an oven just before nightfall, nor a cake upon coals, unless there is time for its surface to form a crust.	אֵין נוֹתְנִין אֶת הַפַּת בַּתַּנּוּר עִם חֲשֵׁכָה וְלֹא חֲרָרָה עַל גַּבֵּי גֶחָלִים אֶלָּא כְדֵי שֶׁיִּקְרְמוּ פָנֶיהָ	B
speech act *omer*	R. Eleazar said:	רַבִּי אֶלְעָזָר אוֹמֵר	C
second path for 10B	There must be time for the bottom [surface] thereof to form a crust.	כְּדֵי שֶׁיִּקְרֹם הַתַּחְתּוֹן שֶׁלָּהּ	
apodictic, pl. *qotel* form.	The paschal sacrifice may be lowered into the oven at nightfall;	מְשַׁלְשְׁלִין אֶת הַפֶּסַח בַּתַּנּוּר עִם חֲשֵׁכָה	A
apodictic, pl. *qotel* form, multiple paths	and the fire in the chamber of the hearth may be kindled but in the country, there must be enough time for the fire to hold its greater part.	וּמַאֲחִיזִין אֶת הָאוּר בִּמְדוּרַת בֵּית הַמּוֹקֵד וּבַגְּבוּלִין כְּדֵי שֶׁיֶּאֱחֹז הָאוּר בְּרֻבּוֹ	B	11
speech act *omer*	R. Judah says,	רַבִּי יְהוּדָה אוֹמֵר	C
third path for 11B.	In the case of charcoal, just a little [suffices].	אַף בְּפֶחָמִים כָּל שֶׁהוּא	

Chart 3.3 (Continued)

These passages possess a relatively low level of narrativity. They present a single negative event or a series of alternative negative events using the plural *qotel* form. These are followed by an alternative case in which the stated action or actions are permitted. Finally, a single position is attributed to the school of Hillel, namely that they permit the action which house of Shammai prohibits. The only narrative aspect to these statements is that they refer to an action. However, the action is portrayed in a negative manner and in the present and imperfect tenses. The actions never occur in a series and they are never in the past tense.

Despite its relatively uniform level of narrativity, the chapter also contains peaks and valleys of high and low narrativity. The chapter opens with the lowest possible degree of narrativity. The Mishnah uses an apodictic nonverbal clause, "The carryings out of the Sabbath are two which are four within, and two which are four without," to enumerate the number of possible ways of violating the prohibition of "going out" on the Sabbath. No concrete actions or objects are mentioned, only abstract categories that need to be further defined in the course of the Mishnah's discussions.

In contrast, paragraph 4 contains the only actual story in the chapter, reflecting the highest level of narrativity. It is a beit midrash story that describes the circumstances under which the preceding rulings were made.[75] Only at this point in the chapter does the Mishnah actually refer to an event which happened at particular place, the "upper chamber of Hananiah ben Hezekiah ben Garon," and at a particular time in the past, "when they went up to visit him." The next highest point of narrativity is in 9B, where the Mishnah records a repeated event, which relates the regular practice in R. Gamliel's household with regard to laundering before the Sabbath.

The chapter also contains a range of forms of varying degrees of narrativity including casuistic formulations at 1C, and 2C, speech acts of different forms in the multiple appearances of formula A and A' and in 9A, 10C, and 11C, as well as examples of the phenomenon that we have called "multiple paths" in 1C, 2B, 3A, and 10B. Emphasizing the incompleteness of the basic typology of Mishnaic forms that I have presented is the fact that fact that several lines in the chapter are designated using terms that have not been discussed thus far. Thus I have dubbed 1B a "rhetorical question," 3B and 3I "motive clauses," and 9C an "implied speech act."

To sum up, the first chapter of *Shabbat* integrates a wide range of forms with varying levels of narrativity into a flowing exposition of activities forbidden on the eve of the Sabbath. The Mishnah easily moves back and forth between various forms of the prescriptive statement, between abstract, stative clauses and detailed narratives, and between prescriptive statements, stories, and repeated events. This practice is representative of the way in which the level of narrativity in the Mishnah can fluctuate widely even within a single chapter. In the next chapters we will investigate some of the implications of this phenomenon for our understanding of the Mishnah as a literary, legal, and historical text.

4

Mishnaic Topography

> "Judaic dialectic, unlike the Hegelian, is irreconcilable and hence interminable. Judaism accepted a dialectic, consisting only of thesis and antithesis. The third Hegelian stage, that of reconciliation, is missing."
> Joseph B. Soloveitchik, *"Majesty and Humility"*

Now that we have completed our survey of the forms of narrativity found in the Mishnah, the question remains: what is the significance of this data? How can it help us better understand the nature of the Mishnah and Tannaitic halakhah?

Studying the role of narrativity in the Mishnah allows us to gain a fresh perspective on what I call the "textual topography" of the Mishnah. The concept of textual topography draws on a metaphor comparing written texts to maps. A conventional road map portrays everything as if it exists on a single plane. The only way of charting the spatial relationship between two points on such a map is in two dimensions, by drawing a straight line between the two. As a result, two points that appear to be close to each other on the map may in reality be separated by a considerable distance. For instance, one may be on the top of a mountain and the other at the bottom of an adjacent valley. Similarly, two points that are at a great distance from each other on the map may in fact share the same elevation. These topographic features can only be observed on the map if we superimpose contour lines on it. This allows us to see the terrain in three dimensions and better understand the relationship between the various locales represented on the map.

Similarly, most texts present themselves in a uniform style. Except for chapter and subject headings, words all appear in the same script or font. The only relationship between the words that is evident is two dimensional. The words appear to be meant to be read in sequence as they appear on the page. However, scholars often attempt to impose "contour lines" on texts that they study. They hope to show that when applying linguistic, literary, or historical criteria, a new set of relationships between the different parts of the texts will become apparent.

By reading the text in light of these relationships, new meanings can be uncovered.

Critical Mishnah Scholarship and the Historical Topography of the Mishnah

Critical Mishnah scholarship attempts to chart the Mishnah's topography in historical terms. This line of scholarship began with the work of nineteenth-century German scholars such as Zacharias Frankel in his *Darche Hamishnah* and David Z. Hoffman in his *Hamishnah Harishona*. This approach reached its apex in the mid-twentieth century with the work of Israeli scholars, notably J. N. Epstein, Hanoch Albeck, and Abraham Goldberg.[1] These scholars view the Mishnah as the product of a lengthy process of transmission and redaction. For them, one of the most important activities in the study of the Mishnah is determining the relative age and provenance of each part of the Mishnah. The Mishnah viewed through the eyes of the critical scholar thus has a variegated terrain. There are the low plains of the "early Mishnah" of the Second Temple period and the high peaks of later additions, the last of which were inserted by medieval copyists.[2] Of course, the actual mappings vary greatly from scholar to scholar depending on their understandings of the origins, development, and redaction of the Mishnah. However, they share the same focus on the history of the Mishnaic text and the belief that a historical-topographical map is the key to navigating the Mishnah's complexities.

I fundamentally accept the legitimacy and importance of uncovering the Mishnah's historical strata. However, in practice, such reconstructions tend to be highly speculative. Furthermore, traditional Mishnah critics tend to work on the positivist assumption that tracing the history of a text is equivalent to finding its meaning. Philological and historical work do not absolve the critic of the responsibility to consider the work as a whole as it has come down us.

Neusner's "Flat" Mishnah

Jacob Neusner has suggested a radically different approach to mapping the surface of the Mishnah. Unlike the diachronic methods of the historical critics, Neusner advocates a synchronic approach that focuses on the rhetoric and thematics of the Mishnah rather than its historical development. From Neusner's perspective, there is no need for any sort of topographical map of the Mishnah. The Mishnah is a carefully leveled plane. Whatever minimal variety there is in the Mishnah's forms and ideas belies its essential uniformity. On the rhetorical level, Neusner argues that "the Mishnah manages to say whatever it wants" using "a remarkably limited repertoire of formulary patterns."[3] This creates a regular and homogeneous literary style. Along similar lines, the Mishnah's conceptual content is also fundamentally unified. Despite its wide-ranging technical interests, in Neusner's view, "the Mishnah presents a system, distinctive, whole, fully interacting in all of its parts, capable of making a coherent statement."[4] Moreover, Neusner sees the Mishnah as not simply a legal work but a "philosophical" work, which

> expresses a deeply embedded ontology and methodology of the sacred, specifically of the sacred within the secular, and of capacity for regulation, therefore sanctification, within the ordinary: All things in order, all things then hallowed by God who orders all things.[5]

If you throw a dart into the Mishnah, Neusner believes, no matter where it lands you will find the same rhetorical features and ideological content.[6] There is no need for any markings to signify the special properties of individual points within the Mishnah beyond the basic demarcation of orders, tractates, and various topical subsections. Neusner's flat, synchronic vision of the Mishnah contrasts sharply with the rough terrain of the historical critics' diachronic Mishnah.

Neusner does not entirely reject the possibility or value of approaching the Mishnah from a historical point of view. He has presented his own theory of the development of the Mishnah based on his belief that it is possible to differentiate Mishnaic strata that date to before and after the Bar Kokhba revolt.[7] However, Neusner has written numerous books and articles about the Mishnah without making use of this theory.[8] Ultimately, it seems, he does not see such historical analysis as being necessary for the understanding of the Mishnah. The linguistic, thematic, and ideological unity of the final product eclipses in significance whatever signs of earlier stages of development can be recovered from the Mishnah.[9]

Neusner's two-dimensional mapping of the literary and ideological aspects of the Mishnah is highly problematic. In my cataloging of Mishnaic forms, I have shown that there are far more than a handful of formulations available to the redactors of the Mishnah. Furthermore, these forms are mixed together so that most individual chapters of the Mishnah contain a microcosm of this formal diversity. Similarly, his attempts to reduce the astonishingly diverse range of issues and concerns treated by the Mishnah to a few broad philosophical themes remain unconvincing.[10] Nevertheless, Neusner deserves credit for insisting that Mishnah study not be limited to historical and philological questions. Rather, the critic must engage the Mishnah as a literary and ideological work as well.

Toward a Narrative Topography of the Mishnah

I argue for a third approach, which calls for the mapping of the Mishnah based on levels of narrativity. Like the traditional critical scholars, I seek to divide the Mishnah into various strata. However, my breakdown of the Mishnah is based on literary rather than historical-philological categories. I seek to divide up Mishnaic passages on the basis of their use of different literary forms with varying degrees of narrativity as I classified them in the previous chapter.[11] Such a method reveals a diverse terrain with peaks in the stories and low points in the most general apodictic statements, as well as frequent steep slopes and drops, when texts of high and low narrativity abut each other. Often, as in the case of chapter 1 of *Shabbat*, discussed in the previous chapter, we will observe a flat plane at a set elevation that is punctuated by depressions and protuberances, reflecting the Mishnaic editor's choice of a "baseline" form to which other types of formulations are added. This calls attention to the range of narrativity in a given passage, by giving the reader a standard "sea level" from which he or she can appreciate the high points of the stories and low points of apodictic rules.

The varying degrees of narrativity in the Mishnah reflect the Mishnah's rhetorical and ideological complexities, not necessarily its archaeology. Whatever the history of the text, the ultimate object of study remains the text of the Mishnah as it has come down to us and the meanings that we can wrest from it. The study of the prehistory of the text serves mainly to enrich our readings of the text itself. In this sense, my approach is more similar to that of Neusner, whose project reflects one man's search for meaning in the Mishnaic text as it appears before us.

The mapping of narrativity that I am suggesting demands a new methodology for approaching and interpreting the text of the Mishnah, an approach that can bridge the gap between heterogeneous and homogeneous views of the text. Such a method must engage the Mishnaic text as a whole while still respecting the differences between the multifarious literary forms through which the Mishnah presents its laws.

In pursuit of such a method, I have turned to the work of the twentieth-century Russian philosopher and literary theorist Mikhail Bakhtin. Though Bakhtin was primarily a theorist of the modern novel, several aspects of his thought are particularly well suited to application to the Mishnah and other rabbinic texts. Bakhtin emphasized the study of linguistic form and style as crucial to understanding the ideational content of literary texts. He was particularly interested in the way in which individual texts contain a range of different styles and forms. Bakhtin, however, distinguished himself from his formalist colleagues in maintaining that the most important part of a literary text is its discontinuities, its heterogeneity, and its "unfinalizability." Bakhtin thus expounded a theory of the "heteroglossia" of all linguistic products. In his seminal essay "Discourse in the Novel" he explains that at any given moment in its evolution, language is stratified not only into linguistic dialects in the strict sense of the word (according to linguistic markers, especially phonetic), but also—and for us this is the essential point—into languages that are socio-ideological: languages of social groups, "professional" and "generic" languages, languages of generations and so forth.[12]

Later in the same essay Bakhtin further explains the nature of these "languages" that exist within every text:

> All languages of heteroglossia, whatever the principle underlying them and making each unique, are specific points of view on the world, forms for conceptualizing the world in words, specific worldviews, each characterized by its own objects, meanings, and values. As such, they all may be juxtaposed to one another, mutually supplement one another, contradict one another, and be interrelated dialogically.[13]

For Bakhtin, all language, and especially literary language, is stratified into multiple "dialects," which emerge from different social, linguistic, and individual usages. These dialects each reflect a different worldview. The essential meaning of texts lies not in the sum or synthesis of these positions, but in the "dialogic" interactions between these dialects and their contrasting worldviews. A thorough reading of a literary text leads not to a resolution, but to the perpetuation and enrichment of the tensions and conflicts between the texts' various voices.

The most obvious way in which the Mishnah might be considered a dialogic text is the manner in which it presents conflicting opinions on the same topic. The juxtaposition of opposing opinions quite literally creates a dialog between different voices and different points of view. The Mishnah rarely rules explicitly on these disputes. Rather it leaves an open dialog regarding many of the most basic rulings and principles of halakhah.

However, the Mishnah can be seen as dialogic in a deeper way as well. The various forms used by the Mishnah, with their varying degrees of narrativity, may be understood as representing different Bakhtinian dialects, each with its own distinct point of view. Viewed from this perspective, the Mishnah does not present a single "statement" as in the Neusnerian view, nor does it present a set of independent texts that have been unified to varying extents by a redactor. Rather, the Mishnah presents an open ended dialog between a series of different forms and the worldviews they represent.

Such an approach allows us to find meaning in the Mishnah without positing that we are reconstructing the intent of an individual author or redactor. The meaning of the text lies in the interplay between the various voices in the text, whether they were all shaped and put together by a single creative hand or are the result of a gradual accretion and the work of generations of editors, or, as is most likely the case, some combination of these forces. This meaning is by nature unstable as the interaction between voices within the text generates a range of possible results and not a single unequivocal statement.

Narrative versus apodictic approaches to law

In order to understand the way in which the different "dialects" that I have identified in the Mishnah reflect distinctive ideas and points of view, we must first take a step back and consider the relationship between law and narrative, both in the Mishnah and in legal texts in general.

Much recent scholarship on "law and narrative" going back at least to Robert Cover's classic "Nomos and Narrative"[14] tend to view them as fully distinct and even opposing realms, which, to be sure, nevertheless have the potential to interact with each other.

In fact, however, law and narrative are intersecting realms. Both are means for ordering human actions, human experience, and the human environment. Laws seek to accomplish this goal in the social and political realm, whereas narrative operates in the linguistic and symbolic realm. The overlap between them thus comes when law is expressed in a narrative form. Narrative is one of several choices available to jurists for this job. Narrative structures reality in a way that is both dynamic and specific. The question of narrativity in legal formulations is thus intimately bound up with the extent to which law is a dynamic and specific endeavor or its opposite, a universal and static construct.

We might then suggest two broad opposing conceptions of law. These two conceptions reflect opposite endpoints of a continuum. In reality, legal systems work off a conception of law that stands somewhere between these two paradigms, though they generally favor one approach or the other.

On one side is what we might call an apodictic approach to law. This view sees law as emerging from a hierarchy of unchanging general principles and rules. The law at any given time and in any given circumstance can be derived through an application of these timeless principles to the situation at hand. Law at its essence remains an abstract affair of concepts and principles rather than one of cases and rulings. This view emphasizes the need for law to address all situations at all times. It must embody unchanging principles, providing stability and equality for the society on which it is imposed. Historically, this approach was emphasized in the jurisprudence of the civil law tradition that emerged in Continental Europe in the early modern period. Civil law jurists pursued a rational science of law, influenced by ideas about natural law. Their literary form of choice was the systematic law code, which organized general, apodictic statements of law.[15]

In contrast to this we have what we might call the narrative approach to law. In this view, the essence of law lies in its application to individual cases, not in the systematic formulation of general principles. To be effective, law must be specific, addressing individual circumstances in particular historical and social situations. It also must be dynamic, open to change and subjectivity. The processes of formulation, transmission, and implementation are not external to the law but integral parts of it. This approach to law is reflected in the English common law tradition, especially as it was classically formulated by the jurists of the seventeenth century. Common law, unlike natural law, derives not from universal reason but from specific and idiosyncratic "artificial reason" of the particular lawyers and judges. Law is conceived of as a nonsystematic and discursive process that focuses on concrete judgments that emerge from the particulars of the case rather than from general principles. Common law's preferred form of legal formulation is the narrative account of actual cases rather than the declaration of apodictic principles.[16]

These two approaches to law each suggest a different understanding of the nature of judges and others who apply the law. Apodictic views of law see law as a "thing," a body of norms that exists independently of any individual or community. In such a system a judge is "an authority." Her power derives ultimately from her intellectual mastery of the law and ability to apply it to current situations. Thus, legal academics had particular prominence in the development of the civil law tradition, as their expertise in the law granted them authority.[17] Similarly, such an approach to halakhah roots the authority of individual rabbis in their knowledge and mastery of the law. In such a view, a rabbi's power does not extend beyond his proper understanding and application of the preexistent principles and rules of the halakhah.

In contrast, a narrative view of law see law more as an "activity," which has no existence outside of the individuals and communities that practice it.[18] As such, a decisor's authority ultimately derives not from his knowledge of law but from the fact that he holds an accepted position within the community that endows him with the authority to interpret and apply the law. In this view, a judge is not "an authority" but "in authority."[19] Judges cannot be wrong, because there is no objective standard against which they can be measured. They can only be overruled by a higher court. Thus the English common law system arose not in conjunction with the rise of academic law faculties but with the establishment of a strong, royally backed judiciary.[20] Similarly, in this view, the rabbi's knowledge of the law may be a prerequisite for his authority, but ultimately his power to deliver rulings derives from his divinely or humanly ordained position as an authorized interpreter of the law.

This claim of enhanced power for individual legal decisors under a regime of narratively formulated law contrasts sharply with many conventional accounts of the impact of narrative approaches on a legal system. Numerous contemporary scholars of law and narrative see the two discourses as reflecting divergent social and moral perspectives. In this view, "legal storytelling has the virtue of presenting the lived experience of marginalized groups and individuals in a way that traditional legal discourse does not."[21] In our view it is precisely an apodictic approach to law that has the most egalitarian potential. Such an approach rests on universally applicable rules that are accessible to all. A narrative approach to a law assumes a potentially infinite set of possible narratives, for which there is no objective mechanism for favoring one narrative over the other. Such an approach must rely on the subjective evaluations of the juridical elite, whose rulings are not subject to challenge from the outside.

In reality, any functioning legal system must combine elements of both the apodictic and the narrative approaches. It must balance the need for uniformity against the need to examine the particulars of each individual case. The ways in which these systems strike this balance will of course vary, as we have seen in our discussion of the civil and common law traditions. Our main concern here is not with actual functioning legal systems but with legal texts and the way in which their use of varying degrees of narrativity implies varying approaches to the nature of the laws set forth within them.

In the Mishnah, both of these approaches are represented in the range of literary forms that are intermingled within it. The Mishnah's broad statements of principle suggest a legal system that emerges from a strong system of underlying norms. On the other hand, the Mishnah's stories exemplify a view of law as a series of individual rulings, specific to the time, place, and individuals involved. The range of forms in between, such as the casuistic formulation, reflect different degrees of synthesis of narrative and apodictic approaches. In the Mishnah as a whole, these varying points of view are brought into conflict and dialog with each other.

Most legal systems integrate elements of both of these approaches and make use of a variety of literary forms to record law.[22] However, these literary forms are generally segregated into separate homogenous genres. For example, narrative accounts are found in records of judicial proceedings, whereas apodictic statements are placed in legal codes. What makes the Mishnah distinctive, is the way in which such a broad range of literary forms, and the jurisprudential points of view they represent, are mixed together in a single central legal text. The topography of the Mishnah generates a particularly vigorous conversation on these matters. Taken as a whole, the Mishnah certainly skews toward the narrative end of the spectrum. Even its apodictic statements tend toward the concrete rather than the abstract. However, by regularly juxtaposing forms of differing narrativity, the Mishnah forces the student to constantly reevaluate the status of the laws that are being presented. Are the Mishnah's laws ultimately anchored in its stories, with their real authority emerging from the rulings of specific rabbis in specific cases? Do the Mishnah's laws emerge out of an abstract conceptual framework that is never fully articulated in an explicit manner? Or does the Mishnah's center of gravity lie with the middle ground of forms like the casuistic formulation? Though showing a certain preference for the narrative, the Mishnah never really answers these questions. Rather, its form suggests that its laws exist in a dynamic tension between the idea of law as an abstract system on the one hand and a contingent process on the other.

It is important to emphasize that the relationship between specific legal forms and specific conceptualizations of the nature of law is not as hard and fast as some have suggested.[23] Abstract legal maxims can be seen as merely summing up the trend in earlier case law, rather than as presenting binding rules. Similarly, more narrative formulations of the law may point to a more fundamental legal principle or distinction that underlies them. We certainly see this in the Mishnah. Chains of specific cases in the Mishnah serve to illustrate an unstated general principle or underlying system, while conceptual frameworks presented by the Mishnah at times turn out to be post facto attempts to unify a set of disparate rulings.[24] The Mishnah's dialog on the nature of law is thus not simply a dialog between the various literary forms that appear in it. It is also generated by the at times uneasy relationship between the form that a Mishnaic law takes and the motivations that appear to underlie the ruling. Thus, for example, when a law expressed through a narrative formulation appears in fact to express a deeper principle, a dialog emerges between the surface form, which emphasizes the specificity and dynamism of the law, and the underlying motivation, which suggests that the law emerges from unchanging general principles. This internal dialog in turn enters into dialog with the disparate passages that surround it, which may themselves be similarly in tension with themselves.

The analysis of the Mishnah from a dialogic perspective highlights one of the crucial characteristics of the Mishnah as literary text. The Mishnah is an inherently ambiguous text. It often fails to explain the background or motivations for its rulings. It is frequently possible to construct multiple mutually exclusive conceptual frameworks that explain the Mishnah's rulings. More importantly for our purposes, the relationship between adjacent lines in the Mishnah is often unclear. Frequently, we find two statements in the Mishnah of differing narrativity juxtaposed to one another. The two statements deal with a similar issue, but the intended relationship between the two is unclear. Is one meant to confirm, compliment, or contradict the other? This ambiguity further complicates and enriches the dialog between the voices of Mishnah, as the reader must investigate the multiple possible angles of engagement between the various fragments of the text. The two Talmuds' interpretations of the Mishnah are often helpful in illuminating these ambiguities. The Talmudic authors often seek out multiple and at times extreme interpretations of the Mishnah that illustrate the range of meaning that is latent in these seemingly simple texts.

Mishnaic Dialogism in Action: *Pesahim* 7:1–2 and *Shabbat* 16:8

In order to illustrate this complex dialogic relationship between the literary and conceptual elements of the Mishnah, I will now analyze two different passages in which exempla are juxtaposed with other literary forms. The first of these,

Pesahim 7:1–2, has already been cited in an earlier chapter. We will now consider it in its broader context. The exemplum itself is presented in bold:

כֵּיצַד צוֹלִין אֶת הַפֶּסַח

שִׁפּוּד שֶׁלָּרִימּוֹן[25]

תְּחָבוֹ מִתּוֹךְ פִּיו עַד בֵּית נְקוּבָתוֹ

וְנוֹתֵן אֶת כְּרָעָיו וְאֶת בְּנֵי מֵעָיו לְתוֹכוֹ

דִּבְ׳ רִ׳ מֵאִיר[26]

רִ׳ עֲקִיבָה אוֹ׳

כְּמִין בִּישּׁוּל הוּא זֶה

אֶלָּא תּוֹלָן חוּצָה לוֹ

אֵין צוֹלִין אֶת הַפֶּסַח לֹא בְשִׁפּוּד וְלֹא בְאַסְכָּלָה

רִ׳ צָדוֹק אוֹמִ׳[27]

מַעֲשֶׂה בְּרַבָּן גַּמְלִיאֵל שֶׁאָמַ׳ לְטָבִי עַבְדּוֹ
צֵא וּצְלֵה לָנוּ אֶת הַפֶּסַח עַל הָאַסְכָּלָה

נָגַע בְּחַרְסוֹ שֶׁלַּתַּנּוּר

יִקְלוֹף אֶת מְקוֹמוֹ

נָטַף מֵרֶטְבוֹ עַל הַחֶרֶס וְחָזַר עָלָיו

יִטּוֹל אֶת מְקוֹמוֹ

How is the Passover offering roasted?
A spit of pomegranate wood:
thrust it into its mouth as far as its buttocks,
and place its knees and entrails inside of it.
This is the view of R. Meir.
R. Aqiba said,
This is in the nature of seething.
Rather they are hung outside of it.
One may not roast the Passover offering either on a [metal] spit or grill.
R. Zadok said,
It once happened that R. Gamliel said to his servant Tevi,
"Go out and roast us the Passover offering on the grill."
If [the paschal lamb] touched the earthenware of the oven,
he must pare its place.
If some of its juice dripped onto the earthenware and dripped back onto it,
he must remove its place.

This passage presents a series rulings regarding the appropriate way to roast the paschal sacrifice. Each ruling has a relatively high level of specificity. No larger principle is stated. Yet, these apodictic and casuistic formulations appear to all be based on a single underlying principle: a requirement that the entire sacrifice to be cooked by direct exposure to fire, forbidding any contact with heated liquids or other materials that might aid in the cooking process.[28]

Paragraph 1 focuses on the need to exclude any heated liquid from the cooking process. The chapter opens by prescribing the use of a spit made out of pomegranate wood. Pomegranate wood is particularly dry and it is apparently used because other woods might exude moisture which in turn would "boil" part of the meat. The Mishnah then records a debate between R. Meir and R. Aqiba about the necessity of removing the innards of the animal and roasting them separately. R. Aqiba explicitly states that his reason for prohibiting roasting the animal with its innards inside is that such a procedure would constitute a form of boiling these organs inside the animal. R. Meir apparently did not extend the prohibition against boiling to cooking in the animal's own natural juices.

Paragraph 2 focuses on the prohibition against letting the paschal sacrifice come into contact with other heated materials. Since spits and grills are made of metal,[29] they will conduct heat and in turn cook the meat with which they come into contact. The end of the paragraph deals with situations in which the meat has come into contact with the walls of the earthenware oven or with gravy that has fallen onto the walls of the oven and then dripped back onto the animal. In both cases, the affected meat must be removed, apparently because it has been cooked by means other than the direct heat of a fire.

The introduction of the exemplum into the midst of the passage interrupts and threatens this structure. It presents an incident in which the general principle forbidding roasting with indirect heat was not observed. R. Gamliel instructed his slave to roast his sacrifice on the very type of grill that the Mishnah prohibited in the previous line. The authority of the exemplum is rooted not in a legal principle but in the fact that the individual action depicted actually occurred in the historical Temple and not in merely in a theoretical ruling.[30] More importantly, the action was taken by the great R. Gamliel. His behavior is a source of law in and of itself. It need not necessarily be explained as consistent with a larger system. The exemplum thus not only poses a challenge to the ruling prohibiting spits and grills, it presents an alternative authority structure and methodology for determining the law in this situation.

However, if they are to be of any use as precedents, exempla and other *ma'asim* must always be expanded beyond the specific case to which they refer. Given our reading of the entire passage, it makes sense for us to ask: Why does R. Gamliel allow for the use of grills? Does he reject the principle requiring that the paschal sacrifice be directly roasted? Or does he merely argue about its implementation? Both of these possibilities are considered in the Yerushalmi.[31] Indeed it is even possible, as the Bavli argues,[32] that R. Gamliel did not dispute the prohibition against grills, but that this particular event reflected a special circumstance in which all would agree that the use of the grill was permissible. Our efforts to abstract an underlying rule or principle from R. Gamliel's actions thus reveals the fundamental ambiguity of the relationship between the exemplum and the rulings that surround it. The ambiguity of R. Gamliel's motivations means that we can never finalize the relationship between the exemplum and the Mishnah's other statements. R. Gamliel may reject the Mishnah's fundamental principle, modify it, or perhaps even embrace it.

This passage in the Mishnah demonstrates how a series of relatively specific apodictic and casuistic formulations work together to present an implicit general rule regarding the paschal sacrifice. This set of statements stands in dialogical tension with a onetime narrative event. The dialog between the event and the principle remains unresolved. R. Gamliel's action may challenge the principle or simply limit its application. On the other hand, we might reject the possibility of abstracting any lesson from R. Gamliel's actions. They remain a onetime event whose larger significance is an enigma. All of these possibilities contribute to the dialog between the various parts of this Mishnaic passage.

A similar dynamic can be seen in *Shabbat* 16:8, which includes yet another exemplum involving a R. Gamliel:[33]

נָכְרִי שֶׁהִדְלִיק אֶת הַנֵּר
מִשְׁתַּמֵּשׁ לְאוֹרוֹ יִשְׂרָאֵל
וְאִם בִּשְׁבִיל יִשְׂרָאֵל
אָסוּר
מִלָּא מַיִם לְהַשְׁקוֹת בְּהֶמְתּוֹ
מַשְׁקֶה אַחֲרָיו יִשְׂרָאֵל
וְאִם בִּשְׁבִיל ישרא׳
אָסוּר
עָשָׂה[34] כֶּבֶשׁ לֵירֵד בּוֹ, יֵרֵד[35] אַחֲרָיו ישרא׳
וְאִם בִּשְׁבִיל ישרא׳
אָסוּר
מַעֲשֶׂה בְרַבָּן גַּמְלִיאֵ׳ וְהַזְּקֵנִים
שֶׁהָיוּ בָאִין בִּסְפִינָה
וְ[36]עָשָׂה גוֹי כֶּבֶשׁ לֵירֵד בּוֹ[37]
וְיָרְדוּ בוֹ זְקֵנִים

If a gentile lights a lamp,
an Israelite may make use of its light.
But if [he does it] for the sake of the Israelite,
it is forbidden.
[If] he draws water to give his own animal to drink,
an Israelite may water after him.
But if [he draws it] for the sake of the Israelite,
it is forbidden.
[If] a gentile made a ramp for going down,
an Israelite may descend after them.
But if [he makes it] for the sake of the Israelite,
it is forbidden.
It once happened that R. Gamliel and the elders

were traveling in a ship
when a gentile made a ramp for going down,
and R. Gamliel and the elders descended by it.

Here, too, we find an example of implicit conceptualization. In this case, it is expressed through a series of parallel casuistic formulations. The Mishnah presents three cases of a gentile doing work on the Sabbath: lighting a candle, drawing water for animals, and erecting a gangplank from which to descend from a boat. In each case, it is permitted to benefit from the gentile's labors, unless the work was done with the specific intent of benefiting a Jew. When presented in this sequence, these cases collectively suggest a single principle that underlies all of the rulings: Jews may only benefit from work done by a gentile on the Sabbath in cases in which the work was done for the gentile's own benefit. If the work was done on behalf of a Jew, one may not benefit from it on the Sabbath.

The final case of the gangplank is followed by an exemplum that builds on the previous hypothetical case and gives the irrealis narrative a setting in reality. It tells of a situation in which R. Gamliel and the elders arrived on a boat (on the eve of the Sabbath). The story then repeats verbatim the hypothetical situation, "a gentile made a ramp for going down," and transforms the ruling "An Israelite may descend after him" into the second narrative event of the story, "and R. Gamliel and the elders descended on it." The smooth transition from irrealis narrative to story is aided by the fact that the original hypothetical case already has a relativity high degree of narrativity, due to its use of the *qotel* form. There is thus no need to alter the formulation of the hypothetical statement when assimilating it into the story.

This close relationship between the story and the casuistic formulation that precedes it would seem to suggest that the story emerges from the general principle implicitly presented in the first part of the Mishnah. Though the exemplum presents these actions as having the sanction of R. Gamliel and his comrades, their authority ultimately emanates from the consistent application of a rule that transcends any individual or situation.

The specific nature of this exemplum has apparently been assimilated into the discourse of timeless, abstract legal principles. Yet a careful reading of this paragraph will elicit other, conflicting voices from the text. First of all, on a linguistic and literary level, the integration of this story into the framework of the Mishnah is not as complete as it would first appear. The set of three cases in the Mishnah are presented using a method that I called "multiple paths" in chapter 3. In each instance, the Mishnah first presents a case in which a gentile does work on the Sabbath and then declares it to be permitted for a Jew to benefit from it. This ruling would at first seem to be unqualified. The gentile's intention does not matter; his work may always be benefited from on the Sabbath. However, each case is followed by a second situation in which the gentile does the same work for the benefit of a Jew. In such a case, benefit is prohibited. The second case implicitly limits the first one to situations in which the gentile has not worked for the benefit of a Jew. A story, by its very nature, can tell of only one situation and a single outcome. The exemplum of R. Gamliel on the boat tells only of a case in which benefit from the gentile's labors is permitted. The exemplum itself does not specify the gentile's intentions in building the gangplank. Given the fact that the exemplum is patterned after the casuistic case that precedes it, we might well presume that in this case as well the gentile acted in his own interests. Yet the ambiguity remains. The exemplum can still be read as an opposing voice. The acts of R. Gamliel and his comrades may violate the principle implied in the rest of the paragraph by suggesting that it is permissible to disembark regardless of the gentile's intentions.[38] The story thus resists full assimilation into the theoretical structure of the rest of this paragraph.

More important than this potential ambiguity in the text is the question of the significance of the exemplum in the flow of the passage. If, indeed, the law flows from a principle that has already been established, as I previously posited, what value is there to citing the story at all?[39] The fact that the Mishnah feels the need to relate this story suggests that this story has independent value and does not simply convey a redundant ruling. We might even argue that despite its position at the end of the passage, the exemplum is in fact the basis from which the general principle underlying the previous rulings has been derived. Where it not for R. Gamliel's actions, we would never know that it is permissible to benefit from work done on the Sabbath by a gentile for his own benefit. Ultimately, we cannot know which came first, the principle or the story. By presenting both the casuistic formulations with their underlying principle as well as the exemplum, the Mishnah is balancing apodictic and narrative formulations of, and approaches to, the law. On the one hand, it presents a series of hypothetical cases which collectively imply a broader abstract principle. However, in citing the story, the Mishnah is acknowledging that there is more to the law than abstract rules. Law is also expressed through its concretization and observance in particular situations. Its authority derives from the practice of individual rabbis such as R. Gamliel and his colleagues. The Mishnah leaves these two approaches in tension, juxtaposing them without choosing between them.

The passages from Mishnah *Pesahim* and *Shabbat* which we have just analyzed demonstrate the heterogeneous topography of the Mishnah. In virtually every part of the Mishnah, texts of varying levels of narrativity brush up against each other, overlap, and emerge from one another. The relationship between general principles and specific cases, and between stories, casuistic, and apodictic formulations is never stable. We interpret these different voices in light of each other, but no one voice ever becomes completely dominant. This interaction generates an unfinalizable discourse that debates not only the individual laws under consideration but the very nature of halakhah and the roots of its authority.

5

The Mishnah in Comparative Context

"Nothing in the law is more fascinating than its persistence in looking backward."
    Ken W. Purdy, *"In the Matter of the Assassin Merefirs"*

One of the advantages of analyzing the Mishnah in terms of its narrativity is that it gives us a basis on which to compare it with other legal documents from the ancient world. This endeavor in turn has the potential both to highlight the unique characteristics of the Mishnah as well as to demonstrate how the Mishnah is related to its cultural contexts.

Survey of Ancient Legal Texts

The two most obvious choices for comparison to the Mishnah are the Pentateuch and Roman legal compilations. The Pentateuch, or Torah, was the sole authoritative legal text recognized by the editors of the Mishnah. Indeed, it is the only written legal text with which we can be sure they had direct familiarity. In contrast, it is highly unlikely that any of the rabbis of the Mishnah had direct access to any of the classic works of Roman law. However, rabbinic halakhah emerged in the context of Roman imperial hegemony, more or less contemporaneous with the development of the classical Roman legal tradition. Roman law thus offers an example of how a geographically and chronologically parallel culture formulated its laws.

To the Torah and the Roman texts I will add two more sets of legal texts. The first comprises the legal texts written in cuneiform writing in ancient Mesopotamia and surrounding areas. No study of biblical law can be undertaken without first considering the wider world of ancient Near Eastern law of which it was a part. As such, our consideration of narrativity in biblical law is best prefaced with a similar overview of ancient Near Eastern law. Furthermore, recent scholars have repeatedly established links between the rabbinic and the Mesopostamian scribal traditions.[1] Though the rabbis certainly had no direct knowledge of millennia-old Akkadian and Sumerian sources, it is certainly possible that they were indirectly influenced by these legal traditions.

The other set of sources is the legal texts of the Dead Sea Scrolls, specifically the Damascus Document. Like the Mishnah, the scrolls were written in Hebrew in the Land of Israel and draw on similar biblical texts and postbiblical legal and exegetical traditions as did the rabbis. Though written several centuries before the Mishnah, the Dead Sea Scrolls might be considered the closest thing we have to an example of an alternative development of the Jewish legal tradition during the Greco-Roman period.

What will emerge from this comparative study is that the ancient Near Eastern texts, the Bible, and the Dead Sea Scrolls are all part of a wider tradition in legal writing that we might call the ancient Semitic tradition of legal composition. The Mishnah breaks this tradition and embraces a style that, while distinctive, bears clear similarities to the Roman tradition of legal composition.

Cuneiform Texts

The cuneiform law collections in our possession mostly date from the second millennium BCE and are written in Sumerian, Akkadian (including Assyrian and Babylonian), and Hittite. In contrast to the Mishnah, the cuneiform collections contain an extremely narrow range of narrativity. The laws in these collections are presented only in irrealis forms. The sole exception to this rule is a formulation occasionally found in the Hittite Laws: "Formerly they did such and such, but now he shall do such and such."[2] This formulation roughly corresponds to the Mishnaic etiological story discussed previously. The laws in these collections are overwhelmingly formulated in a casuistic manner.[3] However, apodictic statements do appear sporadically in these texts.[4]

The cuneiform collections generally make use of a standard type of casuistic formulation known as the conditional formulation. Martha Roth typifies this formulation as "If a man (or an ox or a slave, etc.) does such and such then..." This is the only type of casuistic formulation found in the Sumerian law collections (*tukum-bi lú*... etc.), in the Akkadian Code of Hammurabi (*šumma awīum*... etc.), and in the Hittite laws (*takku LÚ-an*...).[5] In contrast, the neo-Babylonian laws make exclusive use of the relative construction "a man who..." (*amēlu ša*), in their formulation of casuistic laws. Only the Laws of Eshnunna, Middle Assyrian laws, and Middle Assyrian palace decrees make use of the relative construct in addition to the predominant conditional formulation.

The choice between relative and conditional clauses has potential ramifications for the level of narrativity found in a given casuistic formulation. Daube writes as follows with regard to relative and conditional clauses in Roman law:

> "If a man does this or that" tells you a story—though of something yet to come. It puts a situation that may arise, and informs you how to meet it. "Whoever does this or[?] that" refers not to a situation but to a category, a person defined by his action.... It is more general, abstract, detached.[6]

According to Daube, the conditional clause possesses greater narrativity than the relative clause. The conditional clause tells a "story"; it invites the reader to imagine a specific event. The relative clause, in contrast, lacks such specificity. Its focus is on static concepts rather than on dynamic events.

In contrast to the Mishnah's wide range of narrativity, the cuneiform law collections as a whole might be characterized as containing a moderate yet consistent level of narrativity. From the point of view of textual topography, these texts might be seen as open plains, with occasional gentle hills and troughs. Most of the law collections make almost exclusive use of either the relative or the conditional variants of the casuistic formulation. Only in a few collections are the two types mixed. On rare occasion, we find apodictic formulations that possess less narrativity than the standard casuistic forms. The cuneiform laws almost never achieve greater narrativity than that of the casuistic forms. With the sole exception of the etiological passages in the Hittite laws, there are no realis formulations of any sort and certainly nothing that reaches the level of a story as we have defined it.

The greatest range of narrativity among the cuneiform law collections is found in the Laws of Eshnunna. The majority of laws in this collection are formulated in the conditional casuistic form. Three more (LE 12, 13, 19) are in the relative form.[7] The Laws of Eshnunna also contain numerous nonverbal apodictic statements that set prices and wages (LE 1–4, 7, 8, 10, 11) as well as four examples of verbal apodictic statements (LE 15, 16, 51, 52). Still, the Laws of Eshnunna do not approach the diversity of narrativity found in the Mishnah.

Whereas the Mishnah brings together a diverse range of forms and genres in a single corpus, ancient Near Eastern writers segregated them into different homogeneous texts. Many of the genres and forms found in the Mishnah that lack parallels in the cuneiform law codes have their equivalents in other genres of cuneiform texts. For example, many of the "judicial" or "courtroom" texts collected by Remko Jas and William W. Hallo bear a basic similarity to the "case stories" of the Mishnah.[8] These are all realis texts that often present the story of a real legal dispute followed by a report of the court's decision. Similarly, we have numerous cuneiform texts that share the Mishnah's concern with ritual and cultic issues.[9] Especially notable in this context are the Ugaritic descriptive ritual texts described by Baruch A. Levine, which, like the Mishnah's ritual narratives, straddle the genres of prescriptive instructions and descriptive accounts.[10]

Though the formulation of the laws in the cuneiform law collections may lack a high level of narrativity, many of the law collections possess an additional feature not found in the Mishnah that significantly increases the overall narrativity of those texts. The Mishnah's laws are presented without any general context. The text of the Mishnah tells us neither who composed these laws nor when, nor under what circumstances. The closest that we come to any such "master narrative" which explains the origins and authority of the laws in the Mishnah is the opening passage of Avot, "Moses received the law from Sinai and transmitted it to Joshua."[11] Ironically, this text opens the only non-legal tractate of the Mishnah. Many of the Mesopotamian law codes, in contrast, provide precisely this type of contextualization for their laws. Shalom Paul speaks of "a manifest dichotomy of frame and corpus, a temporal and personal container, so to speak, encasing traditional and impersonal case law, i.e., prologue-epilogue as against actual laws."[12] The most extensive and well preserved of these is the prologue and epilogue found in the Code of Hammurabi. As Paul summarizes it:

> [The prologue] first recounts Anu's and Enlil's selection of Hammurabi to be king over Babylon. He is charged by these gods to promote the welfare of the people entrusted to his care by "causing justice to shine forth in the land and by destroying the wicked and evil so that the strong might not oppress the weak" (I:32–39). A long list of his principle military, economic, political, social, and cultic achievements then follows, whereupon he declares, "When Marduk commissioned me to guide the people of the land aright, I set forth truth and justice in the language of the land, thereby making the mood of the people happy" (V:14–24)....
>
> The epilogue...commences with a statement that the laws which Hammurabi established were just and equitable.... He later reiterates the religious setting of his promulgation when he states, "I, Hammurabi, am a righteous ruler, one to whom Shamash has granted the eternal truths" (XXVb:95–98). Hammurabi then exhorts all future kings not to alter his laws or remove his reliefs.... The stele concludes with a lengthy catalogue of curses invoking the gods to punish those who fail to comply with his words and disregard his wishes.[13]

Literary frames such as the one that surrounds the Code of Hammurabi have the effect of collectively narrativizing the laws that they encapsulate. They add greater specificity to the laws by locating the moment and place in which they were legislated. They lend dynamism to the laws by placing them in a sequence of historical events. The texts of the frames themselves are generally realis texts and in some cases, such as the prologue to the Code of Hammurabi, full-fledged stories. This phenomenon of encasing enumerations of legal obligations within a historical prologue and an epilogue of curses is found in other cuneiform literary genres as well, especially Hittite treaty documents.[14]

Stories and other realis texts thus play very different roles in the Mishnah and in the ancient Near Eastern law collections. In the Mishnah, such texts increase the level of heterogeneity. They serve to differentiate individual laws by presenting them in forms distinct from each other. In contrast, framing stories and related realis forms in the cuneiform collections are not used to formulate individual laws in the body of the legal text. Rather, such forms create homogenizing master narratives which encompass all of the laws, giving them a single source of authority and point of origin.

The Torah

The problem of the relationship between law and narrative in the Torah is far more complex than it is in the cuneiform law collections.[15] The laws of the Torah are inextricably intertwined with the Torah's sweeping historical narrative. It is impossible to give priority to either the legal or the historical aspects of the Torah. Rather, The Torah can be viewed both as a historical account that has legal texts embedded in it and as a legal text that is supported by historical material. Nevertheless, as scholars of biblical law have repeatedly emphasized, there is a fundamental similarity between the way the laws are embedded in historical narrative in the Torah and the way the prologues and epilogues surround the laws in cuneiform legal and treaty documents.[16] In both cases, the historical sections provide a master narrative in which the authority of the laws or the treaty is rooted.

When it comes to the biblical legal texts themselves, generations of scholars have devoted themselves to comparing and contrasting biblical and cuneiform law from a formal perspective. For our purposes, the most important difference between biblical and cuneiform law is that apodictic legal formulations play a far more prominent role in biblical law collections than in cuneiform ones.[17] In the Torah, casuistic and apodictic legal formulations exist side by side. The Torah's formulations, therefore, present a wider range of narrativity than those of the cuneiform collections, which are largely restricted to casuistic formulations. In contrasting the casuistic and apodictic laws in the Bible, Mackenzie finds two distinct approaches to law, not unlike the dichotomy between narrative and apodictic law that I have argued for in the Mishnah. Casuistic law, he writes, "is strictly pragmatic; that is, it is quite independent, per se, of any religious doctrine or ethical principle. No general principles are appealed to, no axioms laid down.... This is in marked contrast to the categorical and unconditional mode of expression proper to apodictic law."[18]

Despite this wider range of formulations, the Torah's legal texts still present relatively little diversity when compared to the Mishnah. Realis texts, and stories in particular, are almost entirely absent from the Torah's legal sections. There are two important general exceptions to this rule. The first category of exceptions is to be found among the so-called motive clauses of the Torah. These are sentences in which the motivation or reason for a specific law is given. This phenomenon is an important distinguishing trait of biblical law in and of itself, the implications of which have not yet been fully explored.[19] Our concern is with a specific category of motivations for the laws which Sonsino calls "historical experiences."[20] These explanations root various practices and laws in the historical experiences of the people of Israel. Among the most prominent examples of this phenomenon is the explanation for the prohibition against oppressing the stranger, "For you were strangers in the land of Egypt,"[21] and the explanations of various aspects of the Passover ritual, such as: "You shall observe the Feast of Unleavened Bread... in the month of Aviv, for in the month of Aviv you went forth from Egypt."[22] Motive clauses refer to individual historical events or circumstances. Nevertheless, these motive clauses still involve the use of actual stories in the presentation of law. Virtually all of the "historical experiences" motive clauses refer back to the same master narrative of exile and redemption of Egypt that encapsulates and grounds all of biblical law.[23] Whereas the stories attached to individual laws in the Mishnah tend to differentiate those laws, giving them a distinctive narrative context, the motive clauses tend to place individual laws within the wider master narrative that gives structure and meaning to the legal system as a whole.

The only other examples of the Torah's use of story in legal contexts are the following set of incidents: the story of the blasphemer (Lev. 24:10–23), the story of the people who were impure at Passover (Num. 9:6–14), the story of the wood gatherer (Num. 15:32–36), and the story of the daughters of Zelophehad (Num. 27:1–11) and its sequel (Num. 36). All of these narratives are variants of a single biblical "type scene"[24] in which Moses is confronted by an individual or group of individuals whose actions or status pose a legal problem that Moses is unable to resolve on his own, based on previous revelation. Moses turns to God who responds with a ruling for the specific case as well as with new laws meant to cover similar incidents in the future.[25] As in the case and etiological stories of the Mishnah, these biblical narratives present unique circumstances, relatively unconnected to any master narrative, which account for the emergence of a particular law or ruling. These texts are at once stories and legal sources. It is important to note that such stories are exceedingly rare in the Torah. Indeed, they are entirely absent from the books of Exodus and Deuteronomy. Furthermore, with the exception of the story of the blasphemer, they are not integrated into the Torah's major legal collections. Ultimately, these stories remain outliers with regard to the range of methods used by the Torah to present law.

The legal texts of the Torah possess a greater level of heterogeneity than those of the ancient Near East in terms of the range of narrativity displayed and the variety of topics covered. Yet the Torah still does not display the range of narrativity found in the Mishnah. Realis texts in general, and stories in particular, play only a minor role in the Torah's legal formulations. Similarly, the Mishnah generally makes use of stories to increase the heterogeneity of its text by giving distinct identities to individual laws. The Torah, like the ancient Near Eastern law collections, primarily deploys stories as master narratives that serve to unify the diverse law into a cohesive whole.

Dead Sea Scrolls: The Damascus Document

In a recent article, Steven Fraade has initiated a systematic formal comparison of the Mishnah with the legal writings of the Dead Sea sect.[26] Fraade focuses on the Damascus Document, arguing that it is the most suitable text for such an endeavor. He emphasizes that both the Damascus Document and the Mishnah reorganize and reinterpret the laws of the Torah and received traditions in similar manners. They are both texts that are at once diverse in their subject matter yet carefully organized by topic. On the basis of these and other similarities, Fraade goes so far as to declare that the Damascus Document is "an antecedent to the Mishnah."

Yet, as Fraade acknowledges, when we compare the role of narrative and narrativity in the two texts, we find little common ground. The laws of the Damascus Document are largely formulated using apodictic forms of one sort or other, with occasional use of casuistic formulations. Viewed from this perspective, the Damascus Document appears as a photo negative of the Laws of Eshnunna, which relies primarily on casuistic formulators with occasional use of apodictic rulings.

The Damascus Document, like its ancient Near Eastern and biblical predecessors, also has a framing story. The introductory section, known as the Admonition, tells of the origins of the sect and places them in the context of the biblical account of God's covenants with humans. The document concludes with what Fraade understands to be a description of an annual ritual of blessings and curses meant to enact a renewal of the sect's covenant with God. In terms of these details, the structure of the Damascus Document is most similar to biblical and ancient Near Eastern covenant texts, especially the book of Deuteronomy.

Still, the Damascus Document does not display the same clear breakdown between narrative frame and legal body displayed by the cuneiform legal texts and, to a lesser degree, in the Bible. As Fraade notes, "Important statements of law and legal scriptural interpretation are central to the Admonition itself, often interwoven with accounts of the community's origins, its self-understanding with respect to covenantal history, and its derision of adversaries for their legal laxity."[27] This interweaving of law with historical-theological narrative and polemic is perhaps the most distinctive element of the Damascus Document and the Qumran legal documents as a whole, when considered from the perspective of the relationship between law and narrative.

Despite their idiosyncrasies and distinctive features, the cuneiform legal collections, the Torah, and the Damascus Document share a series of common elements which would appear to define a broader legal-literary tradition that was current in the ancient Near East during the first millennia BCE. These texts all make use almost exclusively of apodictic and casuistic forms in formulating laws. They open with a framing story which details the origins of the laws presented in the context of the history of the community on which they are meant to binding. The Mishnah breaks with this tradition. It presents its law through a mixture of a wide array of forms and techniques, and it does not present a framing story to explain the origin and authority of its laws. These characteristics of the Mishnah are unprecedented in Near Eastern legal literature. In order to find legal texts that bear some similarity to the Mishnah in its deployment of narrative and narrativity, we must turn to a body of texts that, while geographically more distant, is chronologically much closer to the Mishnah: the Roman legal tradition.

Roman Law

The principle source of Roman law for modern scholars is known as the *Corpus Iuris Civilis*, which was compiled under the authority of the emperor Justinian. For our purposes, the most significant part of the *Corpus* is the *Digest*. The *Digest*, a collection of juristic writing, was completed in the early 530s CE. It consists of extracts from earlier jurists, most of whom lived three to four centuries earlier, roughly contemporaneous with the production of the Mishnah.[28] Also important is the *Institutes* of Gaius, an introductory work on Roman law which dates from around 160CE. The *Institutes* owes its significance to the fact that it is by far the most complete work of classical Roman law to survive independent of the *Digest*.[29]

Two contemporary scholars have already called attention to the formal similarities between rabbinic and Roman law. Yaakov Elman has compared and contrasted the Mishnah and the *Institutes* of Gaius, while Catherine Hezser has presented a more detailed comparison of the *Digest* and the Yerushalmi.[30] Many of Hezser's conclusions are applicable to a comparison of the Mishnah and the *Digest* as well.

Like the Mishnah, both the *Digest* and the *Institutes* are composed of a mixture of apodictic and casuistic formulations.[31] The apodictic statements include both general principles and specific rules. These texts also make use of stories as an integral part of their presentation of the law. Gaius is fond of telling stories that trace the development of the law. For example, Gaius writes: "Formerly, the patricians used to say that they were not bound by plebian statutes which were made without their authorization. Subsequently, however, the Hortensian act was passed providing that plebian statues should bind the whole people."[32] This genre of story is in many ways comparable to the etiological stories found in the Mishnah.[33] In a similar vein, the *Digest* occasionally presents narrative histories of the legal institutions under consideration.[34] More frequently, the *Digest* presents accounts of actual cases that are quite similar to the Mishnah's case stories. Hezser cites the following example of this genre:

> Someone has rented a ship for shipping three thousand *metretes* of oil and eight thousand *modii* of grain from the province of Cyrene to Aquileia. It happened, however, that the loaded ship was retained in this province for nine months and its cargo confiscated. It has been asked whether he [the owner of the ship] could demand payment of the freight charges agreed upon according to the contract from the one who rented [the ship]. He [Scaevola] answered that he could do so in accordance with the [details] which were stipulated.[35]

There are also other varieties of stories and onetime incidents in the *Digest*, such as the following cautionary note appended to a discussion of the offense of violating the city walls: "Indeed, the tradition is that Romulus's brother Remus was slain on the very ground that he tried to climb over the city wall."[36] We thus find as broad a range of narrativity in these Roman legal texts as we do in the Mishnah. Furthermore, Hezser has shown that these various types of legal texts are woven together into a unified legal exposition, similar to the way they are in the rabbinic texts.[37]

Roman law is also heterogeneous with regard to the sources cited in it. Unlike the biblical and cuneiform legal collections, which speak with a single authoritative voice, the *Digest* is made up of a kaleidoscopic array of citations from earlier legal scholars. These scholars, especially Ulpian, in turn make regular reference to still earlier authorities.[38] Though Gaius speaks with a single, authoritative voice, he, too, refers to earlier authorities with some frequency. Still, there is an important difference between the Mishnah and the Roman sources on this score. Neither Gaius nor the *Digest* regularly juxtaposes opposing opinions in the manner that we find in the Mishnah in virtually every chapter. Ultimately, the Roman sources aim to present a unified view of the law, whereas the Mishnah regularly leaves issues unresolved.[39]

There is an additional narrative element in at least some of the major Roman legal works that is absent from the Mishnah. The second chapter of the *Digest* is entitled "The Origin of Law and of All the Magistracies and the Succession of the Jurists." The *Digest* here cites first a brief introductory remark from Gaius's *Twelve Tables* and then a much longer passage from Pomponius's *Manual*. In it, Pomponius traces the history of Roman law and legal institutions from the founding of Rome until roughly his own day. This text appears to function both in the *Digest* and in its original context in much the same way as the historical introductions that we have seen in cuneiform, biblical, and Qumranic legal texts. It places the subsequent laws into a historical context, explaining their origins and authority. It would seem that Gaius also prefaced his now lost *Twelve Tables* with a similar such passage. Though not universal, the practice of framing a legal work in a master narrative was certainly familiar to the Roman legal writers.

Despite these distinctions, from a formal perspective the Mishnah is clearly much closer to its Roman context than to its Near Eastern predecessors. This is not to suggest that the authors of the Mishnah were directly influenced by Roman legal writings. There is no evidence that the rabbis had access to any of these works. Indeed, the Roman work to which the Mishnah is most similar, the *Digest*, was compiled centuries after the Mishnah. While it is possible that the editors of the Mishnah had indirect knowledge of the work of the Roman jurists, more likely the similarities between the Mishnah and Roman legal texts are the result of the parallel development of two legal cultures that operated in the context of similar historical and cultural forces.[40] These two bodies of work might best be viewed as products of a common experience of life in the Mediterranean world during the centuries around the turn of the Common Era.

If we take this comparison of Roman and Mishnaic law to its logical conclusion, it would follow that the Roman law codes can also be read as dialogic texts that engage in a discourse about the very nature of law. Such a conclusion ultimately awaits a thorough formal examination of these works, which is beyond the scope of this book or the expertise of its author. However, such a reading is bolstered by the fact that at least one scholar of Roman law, Peter Stein, has identified two conflicting tendencies in Roman jurisprudence that roughly correspond to the tension between narrative and non-narrative conceptions of law that we have discerned in the Mishnah.

Traditionally, scholars have viewed the classical period of Roman jurisprudence (27 BCE–284 CE) as a period in which the approach to law had many things in common with what I have described as a narrative conception of law. As Fritz Schulz wrote of this period:

> Abstract formulations of principle occur chiefly in the elementary works. Even in them the task of defining basic concepts is shirked. Questions of detail were what really interested the classical lawyer, and the method they applied to them remained at bottom casuistical.... Even in the more theoretical works, such as Julian's and Marcellus' *Digesta*, case law is dominant, and no attempt is made to translate abstract principles.[41]

Stein rejects this interpretation. He demonstrates that running through classical Roman jurisprudence is an opposing tendency as well. Stein argues that *regulae*, concise, generalized, juristic rules, played an important role in the writings of the classical jurists. The formulation of these rules goes back to the preclassical Republican period when Roman jurists and other writers, among them Cicero, came under the influence of Aristotelian notions of science and knowledge. "Cicero makes it clear that he and his contemporaries took it for granted that the civil law was a complete and coherent body of principles and...[that] it could be discovered and set forth definitively like geometry or music."[42]

In the late classical and postclassical periods, the *regulae* achieved increasing prominence and authority. This trend culminated in the concluding title of Justinian's *Digest* [50.17], which consists of a list of *regulae* selected and edited so that each one constitutes "a succinct statement having a broad general application."[43]

Unlike in rabbinic literature, in Roman jurisprudence the tension between narrative and non-narrative forms of law is not merely implied by the juxtaposition of varying legal formulations. Roman legal theorists explicitly debated the relative merits of the two approaches to law. In the classical period, there were two opposing schools of thought as to the nature and authority of the *regulae* as opposed to case law. As Stein explains:

> Some jurists, following the lead of Laebo, recognized that the formulation of such rules was more than a neutral statement of fact. By his choice of terms the jurist who formulated the rule made a positive contribution of his own. He could bring into the open the underlying principle of the rule, which may previously have been unexpressed. Once it was stated, the rule applied to all cases, which came within the principle, unless an exception was proved to have been recognized in practice. Other jurists, led by Sabinus, argued that, whether it was called a *regula* or a *definitio*, a juristic rule was merely a reflection of the actual state of law but had no normative force. The contrast between these two views remained latent throughout the classical period.[44]

Among the most prominent adherents of Laebo's belief in the importance of rules was Gaius, who conceived "of the law as a body of *regulae*" that ought to fit together in a systematic manner.[45] Perhaps the most famous expression of Sabinius's view is the oft-quoted formulation of Javolenus, the leader of the Sabinian school at the end of the first century CE. He declared that "every definition in civil law is dangerous, for it is rare for the possibility not to exist of its being overthrown."[46]

It is possible that the heterogeneous nature of Roman legal texts in part reflects this unresolved debate among Roman jurists. The fact that Roman jurists explicitly formulated these competing viewpoints increases the plausibility of my claim that there is a confrontation between narrative and apodictic conceptions of law underlying Mishnaic discourse. The rabbis of second-century Palestine were almost certainly unaware of the jurisprudential debates that were going on in Rome at the time. Furthermore, I do not claim that the editors of the Mishnah were necessarily consciously aware of the conceptual implications of the stylistic choices they made in formulating the Mishnah. However, the fact that similar debates about the nature of law did take place in the classical Mediterranean world means that I am not necessarily imposing on the Mishnah and its editors anachronistic categories based on modern Western jurisprudence. The categories I use were part of the wider conceptual world in which the rabbis operated.

Master Narratives: Framing Stories and Anecdotes

One of the differences between the various legal texts that we have seen is the way in which they deploy stories in the context of presenting law. The Mishnah is the only tradition that we have seen that does not make use of a "framing story," an introductory narrative which establishes the origins and history of the laws presented. On the other hand, the Mishnah, along with the Roman sources, is distinguished by its use of "anecdotes," brief stories relating to individual laws which are integrated into the text. Contemporary critical scholarship tends to view anecdotes as inherently opposed to all master narratives, arguing that "any *petit recit* would puncture the historical *grand recit* into which it is inserted."[47] In subsequent chapters I will examine ways in which the Mishnah's anecdotes do in fact play a subversive role. First, however, it is important to understand how both framing stories and anecdotes can function in legal texts to construct and define legal authority and legal community by establishing master narratives.

Most of the discussion in recent decades about the relationship between law and narrative has focused on the role of framing stories in defining the nature of the law.[48] Most prominent among these voices is that of Robert Cover, who declared at the beginning of his seminal essay "Nomos and Narrative":

> No set of legal institutions or prescription exists apart from the narratives that locate it and give it meaning. For every constitution there is an epic, for each Decalogue a scripture. Once understood in the context of the narratives that give it meaning, law becomes not merely a system of rules to be observed, but a world in which we live.[49]

Framing stories place the law and the community that practices it within a historical continuum. They tell a master narrative that intertwines the origins of the law, the community, and its authority structure, generally tracing them to some heroic event or encounter with the divine. For example, as Martha Roth explains with regard to the narratives that surround the ancient Near Eastern legal collections:

> These frames establish a political context for the compositions, relating the series of laws to the role of the king as the divinely authorized guardian and administrator of justice... the prologue and epilogue outline the historical circumstances that allow the ruler to present himself as a worthy recipient of the gods' favor and support, the highest mark of which is the ability to administer and dispense justice throughout his realm. In return for his able exercise of these powers, he demands absolute loyalty from his subjects.[50]

An individual who identifies herself with the community portrayed in these texts will perceive herself as living out an extension of that story. She will thus see herself as being bound both by the laws and the authority that are established in the story. Some texts conclude with a narrative about the future of the community as well. These include the blessings and curses of the Torah and other ancient Near Eastern texts. In these cases, those who identify with the texts look backwards not only to a narratively constructed past but also to a future defined by the laws and authority system established in the text.[51]

Those who see anecdotes as inherently adverse to the work of framing stories argue that the anecdote's extreme specificity, focusing on a single incident and generally involving only a few individuals, cannot be reconciled with the all-encompassing nature of framing stories.[52] But this is not so. Although individual anecdotes may indeed portray unique events, as we read a group of anecdotes, we often notice that despite the differences, these stories tend to become repetitive in one way or another. When we overlay these stories on each other, a pattern emerges. This consistent structure describes not a single incident but a chain of incidents. It defines a rule, asserting something about the nature of the world and the way in which events unfold in it.[53]

In the previous chapter we saw how a series of similar cases can collectively express a legal rule or principle. Legal anecdotes have the potential to go even farther. As a group, these anecdotes portray the legal system as a whole. In the course of his studies, the reader of such legal texts will repeatedly encounter anecdotes that portray the overall functioning of the legal system in a consistent manner. The stories collectively assert certain principles and patterns of behavior as normative to the system as a whole.

The common denominator of the anecdotes in the Mishnah is that they all portray rabbis, either as individuals or in groups, playing central roles in the adjudication of the halakhah. Rabbinic authority stands at the center of the ideological concerns of the Mishnah story. These stories chart the ways in which the halakhic system described in the Mishnah is fundamentally dependant on rabbis holding absolute authority within the community of practitioners as interpreters, legislators, and, ultimately, embodiments of the law.

The three basic forms of Mishnaic stories that I described in chapter 3, the exemplum, the case story, and the etiological story, represent three different ways in which the halakhah can relate to a concrete event in the past. In turn, these genres each also present a paradigm for a different aspect of the workings of rabbinic authority.

Perhaps the most straightforward of these forms is the exemplum. In citing an individual exemplum with regard to a specific case, the Mishnah asserts that the actions of a given rabbi at a specific time and place are of legal significance in deciding a broader case. The collective impact of the Mishnah repeatedly citing exempla about different rabbis in the context of different situations is to assert that rabbis are, at least in principle, embodiments of the law whose actions can be used to determine appropriate action in other situations.

Along similar lines, each case story presents an incident in which a rabbi or group of rabbis issues a ruling with regard to an incident or situation whose legal status is unclear. Implicit in these stories is that the rabbis in question have the authority to rule on the case at hand. Once again, the repetition of such stories in the Mishnah suggests that this process of consulting rabbis should be applied in any situation in which the law is in question. Case stories thereby establish rabbis as the empowered interpreters of the halakhic tradition.

Etiological tales do not fit so neatly in this schema of framing story versus anecdotes. Unlike case stories and exempla, which generally portray events within a limited time frame of a few days or less, etiological stories have a much broader narrative sweep which often covers generations. Like the framing narrative of ancient legal texts, etiological stories are tales of origins and transformation. However, these stories deal not with an entire legal corpus but with a single ruling. Etiological stories can be described as micro- framing stories which root a particular halakhic practice in the historical experience of the Jewish people.

To the extent that etiological stories deal with only a single law or practice, they function as anecdotes. Each story tells how, in response to some crisis, the rabbis alter a particular practice so that it will remain viable or relevant in particular circumstances. Etiological stories thus portray rabbis not merely as interpreters or practitioners of the law but as true legal innovators. Noting that all of the etiological stories in the Mishnah refer either to the Temple era or to the period immediately following the Destruction, Martin Jaffee argues that the collective message of these texts is that

> while the Temple stood, we appear to be told, qualified authorities intervened into the common practice to preserve or protect [from] threats to Israel's efficacy as a transformer of divine power into worldly blessing; after its destruction, their successors preside over the transformation of the Temple-centered institutions.... By dotting their corpus of halakhic tradition here and there with reports of early patriarchal intervention into customary Israelite usage, the editors of the Mishnah project an image of authority which, while perhaps absent in their own day, can be held out, through nostalgia, as a model of future reconstruction.[54]

Alternatively, we might see these stories as having a more conservative message. These stories can be viewed not as paradigms of halakhic change but as exceptions meant to prove the rule. In this reading, these stories limit the halakhic innovations to minor adjustments in a few special cases, suggesting that all other laws remain free from rabbinic tampering. Both of these readings serve to reinforce the idea of the continuity of the halakhic tradition of the legitimacy of the rabbis as stewards of that tradition.

By interspersing their work with exempla and case and etiological stories, the editors of the Mishnah establish a framework for the workings of halakhah within the community. The picture that is presented is essentially that of the narrative approach to law described in the previous chapter. The law emerges from individual circumstances and events. The authority of the law is based not on received principles but on the wisdom and judgment of the rabbis in each generation. The rabbis are the sole source of halakhic teaching. Not only are they responsible for transmitting the halakhic traditions, it is they who are responsible for interpreting and applying these traditions. They alone have the authority to alter halakhic practice in extraordinary circumstances. Finally, they are themselves embodiments of the law, so that their very actions in their day-to-day lives are sources of legal precedent.

We might similarly account for the case stories scattered throughout the *Digest* and its source documents as making an implicit case for the central authority of the Roman jurists as adjudicators and interpreters of Roman law. Once again, however, final conclusions on this matter await a more in-depth literary and stylistic study of the sources of Roman law.

The relationship between framing stories and anecdotes might thus be compared to the similarities and differences between an exoskeleton, like the shell of a beetle, and an endoskeleton like our own interior skeletons. Whereas framing stories create an envelope that surrounds the law and the legal community, defining its boundaries and locating it in time and place, anecdotes form an interior support structure that spreads throughout the law and the legal community, giving them form and definition from within. Both types of stories create master narratives that root the law in a common communal experience. Both types of master narrative thus seek to use narrative as an all encompassing structure to give form to the law and its community. However, whereas the historical narratives in other ancient legal works are stories that seek to create a historical structure for the law and the community, the Mishnah's anecdotes operate largely outside of any linear historical narrative. When read collectively, these narratives repeat themselves in different iterations, over and over again. They supply a paradigm for the day-to-day functioning of the legal community in which rabbinic authority lies at the center of the transmission, development, and interpretation of the law.

The Mishnah's Framing Narrative

All of this does not mean that Mishnah functions without a historical framing narrative. Indeed, the Mishnah is an excellent example supporting Cover's claim that all legal systems and texts function in the context of such a narrative, even if it is not explicitly articulated. The Mishnah only makes sense if we understand that it is based on the narrative presented in the Torah and the rest of the Hebrew Bible.[55] The Mishnah takes for granted that the members of the community to whom it speaks are the physical and spiritual descendants of the biblical Children of Israel and are bound by the covenant between God and Israel that is the central theme of so much of Hebrew scriptures. The laws presented in the Mishnah are meant to be understood as elaborations and continuations of the laws revealed to Moses at Sinai. The Mishnah implicitly links itself to the text of the Torah through its occasional but consistent citing of biblical proof texts as sources for its laws.[56] What distinguishes the Mishnah from its ancient counterparts is the fact that this narrative is not explicitly articulated at the beginning of the text. Rather, the Mishnah assumes that the reader knows and accepts this narrative before engaging the text.

The closest that the Mishnah comes to formulating its framing narrative is in the famous open lines of tractate *Avot*:

מֹשֶׁה קִיבֵּל תּוֹרָה מִסִּינַי
וּמְסָרָהּ לִיהוֹשֻׁעַ
וִיהוֹשֻׁעַ לִזְקֵנִים
וּזְקֵנִים לִנְבִיאִים
וּנְבִיאִים מְסָרוּהָ לְאַנְשֵׁי כְנֶסֶת הַגְּדוֹלָה

> Moses received the Torah at Sinai
> and transmitted to it Joshua,
> and Joshua to the elders
> and the elders to the prophets
> and the prophets transmitted it to the Men of the Great Assembly.

Avot goes on to list the succession of Second Temple–era sages who continued this transmission of the Torah until it reached Hillel and Shammai, the putative founders of the rabbinic movement.[57] The compilers of the Mishnah chose to place this laconic chronicle not at the beginning of the Mishnah but in its middle, at the head of the only tractate that is not devoted to explicating the law. This only emphasizes the fact that the explicit articulation of the historical background of the halakhah is not an integral part of the Mishnah's rhetorical strategy in presenting its laws. *Avot* is the exception that proves the rule. The one tractate with its own distinctive content and style is also the only one to present a genealogy of the tradition.

The implications of this decision not to formulate a historical master narrative at the outset of the text of the Mishnah need to be understood in the wider context both of the development of biblical interpretation in antiquity and of rabbinic strategies of reading and storytelling. The creation of a link between a contemporary community and the mythic community of a framing story is never straightforward. By what claim does a group establish continuity with a series of events in the past? This is particularly difficult in the case of the biblical narrative, which tapers off hundreds of years before the emergence of the rabbis and their communities in the first and second centuries CE. More significantly, in the intervening years, other groups had also emerged to claim the mantle of biblical Israel. Each of these groups also had to establish their own claim to the biblical master narratives.

Most other groups in the Second Temple and post-Destruction period established their claim as the true inheritors of God's covenant with Israel by rewriting the biblical master narrative, producing a new text to supplement or even replace the text of the Bible. These reworked narratives establish this claim using one of two possible strategies, or both. The first is to reformulate the biblical narrative in such a way that it clearly embodies the distinguishing values and ethos of the group in question.[58] Two prominent and very different examples of this strategy are Philo's *Exposition of the Law* and the Samaritan version of the biblical text. Philo transformed the narratives of the Torah into a philosophical work compatible with his Neoplatonic worldview. If we accept Philo's version of the master narrative, only a group that pursues speculative philosophy can possibly claim to be followers of the God of Israel. The Samaritans, on the other hand, altered the text of the Torah so that it would make the establishment of the sacrificial cult on Mount Gerizim central to God's service. If we start with their text, the Samaritans are of the only candidates for the bearers of the covenant at Sinai. No Jews need apply.

The other strategy is to extend the master narrative so that it continues until the time of the group in question. For example, the Damascus Document integrates the story of the origins of the Qumran sect with the ongoing biblical narrative of God embracing those who are loyal to him and rejecting those who sin against him. Along similar lines, we might see the New Testament Gospels as attempts to extend the biblical narrative up until the time of Jesus, establishing him as the true culmination of the covenantal history. In both cases, the group in question puts forth a genealogy which establishes their followers as the direct descendants, either spiritual or physical, of the prophets and holy nation of the Bible.

Rabbinic literature tends to reject both of these strategies. As Jonah Fraenkel notes, "The rabbis clearly abandoned the broad canvas of the original (biblical) narrative"[59] for what we might call an anecdotal approach to storytelling. In the case of rabbinic versions of biblical narratives, the rabbis certainly reshape biblical tales so that they reflect their own values. However, they almost never reconstruct broad swathes of the biblical master narrative to create a new, revised master narrative as we find in the cases of the book of Jubilees, Josephus's *Antiquities*, and other non-rabbinic works which retell biblical history from a new perspective. Rather, Midrashic stories tend to be anecdotal retellings of individual episodes in the Bible.[60] These stories are essentially exegetical in nature, rooted in explicit acts of interpretation of particular biblical verses. So too the rabbis make no real effort to create a narrative that connects the post-Destruction rabbinic community with the prophetic world of the Bible.[61] Rather, they merely present anecdotes about individual events, usually in the lives of prominent people. These stories tend to assume an unbroken chain of tradition stretching from the last of the prophets to rabbinic times. However, short of the first lines of *Avot*, this narrative is almost never recounted explicitly.[62]

One possible explanation of these differences between rabbinic storytelling and its Second Temple–era predecessors has been suggested by Joshua Levinson. He argues that the differences are rooted in the essentially different worldviews of the rabbis and the authors of the Second Temple period. The latter saw themselves as living in a world that was fundamentally the same as that of ancient Israel and as continuing the work of the biblical authors. The biblical text itself remained fluid in this period.[63] The rabbis, in contrast, saw the "current era," following both the end of prophesy in the early Second Temple period and the more recent destruction of the Temple, as one in which direct access to divine favor was far more limited than it had been in the past.[64] The ultimate source of access to the divine was through the revelations that had been passed down from the biblical period. In the case of retelling of biblical stories, Levinson argues that the rabbis thus felt that they lacked the authority to reformulate biblical history outside of an explicitly exegetical context.[65]

Levinson's approach might be taken even further. The rabbis may have felt that they lacked the authority to create new scripture, or in other words, to create new texts that narrate master narratives of the sort found in the Bible. If so, the rabbis would have hesitated to rework the biblical texts into new independent stories or to create accounts of postbiblical history that would fill in the gap between the Bible and their own time.

Still, the rabbinic decision not to explicitly articulate a particular version of the biblical framing story needs to be viewed not just as reflecting an abstract aesthetic or metaphysical preference but as a part of a concrete rhetorical strategy. By not retelling or expanding the biblical narrative, the rabbis are in effect declaring that their version of events is the obvious and only possible one. The need to articulate a framing story suggests that there is some sort of interpretive crisis in which varying versions of the narrative are vying for supremacy. By not formulating a framing story for their key legal text, the rabbis effectively deny that any crisis has occurred. They deal with the existence of other claims to the mantle of biblical Israel not so much through polemic as through solipsism.[66] They simply ignore the existence of any form of Judaism other than their own.

This is especially so in the case of the Mishnah. In contrast to other rabbinic works, the Mishnah's relationship to its biblically based master narrative remains vague. Both the classical Midrash and the Talmuds make systematic efforts to trace the roots and origins of each and every law that they present. Relative to this, the laws of the Mishnah and its sister work, the Tosefta, appear to be almost entirely autonomous. They only sporadically cite biblical proof texts.[67] In most cases, the Mishnah implicitly asserts that its laws represent the will of the God of Abraham, Isaac, and Jacob, without filling in the details or refuting other possibilities.

Such an approach has its risks. It assumes that the reader will be aware of the rabbis' version of history and will be open to a mindset that rejects other possibilities as irrelevant. If this is the case, suppressing the master narrative can be a powerful approach for instilling a particular worldview. However, if these conditions cease to hold, a text such as the Mishnah risks being rejected as incoherent or irrelevant.

We might also see this failure to explicitly formulate a framing narrative as a mechanism for allowing a certain degree of pluralism within the rabbinic community. The rabbis never canonized a single text as their official framing narrative linking their community and its teachings back to the biblical covenants. Multiple versions of this narrative are thus possible, provided that they fall within the general outlines of the narrative implied in the Mishnah and other rabbinic works. Somewhat different conceptions of rabbinic Judaism could thus live side by side without having to compete for the claim of authenticity.

This discussion takes us full circle, back to a consideration of the question of the topography of the Mishnah. In the previous chapter, I rejected Neusner's notion of the Mishnah as a "flat" ideological text whose goal is to transmit a cohesive set of values and ideas. I argued that the Mishnah needs to be viewed as a dialogical text in which different opinions and voices are given expression. Now I argue that the stories of the Mishnah, when taken as a group, appear to make an unequivocal "statement" arguing for rabbinic authority and the authenticity of their transmission of the law.

The Mishnah, then, does in fact have a strong ideological aspect to it. Its use of anecdotal stories collectively serves to reinforce rabbinic authority and, indirectly, the rabbis' claims to be the true inheritors of biblical Israel. I would go further to suggest that this ideological element may be among the most historically significant aspects of the Mishnah. It is quite possible that the Mishnah played a role in consolidating and spreading rabbinic ideology in the centuries following its redaction, a period when rabbinic Judaism was apparently transformed from a relatively marginal sect to the basis of belief and practice for most Jews in the Land of Israel and, by the dawn of the Middle Ages, throughout the world.[68]

All of the above analysis is based on a broad formal and generic examination of narrative forms in the Mishnah. In the upcoming chapters we will shift gears and engage in close analyses of individual Mishnaic stories. These readings will demonstrate that even the apparently ideological aspects of the Mishnah are in fact multivocal, simultaneously constructing and deconstructing the notion of centralized rabbinic authority rooted in biblical tradition. As we shall discover, the Mishnah's stories constitute as much an argument for rabbinic authority as a discourse about the nature and extent of that authority.

Conclusion

An examination of the formal characteristics of cuneiform, biblical, Qumranic, and Roman legal texts reveals that the Mishnah reflects a radical break from its Near Eastern predecessors. These works are marked by a relatively low range of narrativity making use almost exclusively of either apodictic or casuistic formulations. Stories and related forms almost never appear in these legal collections. The Mishnah's stylistic heterogeneity is much more similar to the roughly contemporaneous Roman legal collections, especially Justinian's *Digest*, which similarly make use of a wide range of narrative forms including stories not unlike those found in the Mishnah.

From a different narrative perspective, the Mishnah stands alone among the legal works we have examined. All of the other works we have examined open with a framing story, a narrative that places the laws that follow into a historical context. This creates a master narrative that endows the laws with legitimacy and authority. The Mishnah's lack of a framing narrative does not mean that its laws are not rooted in a master narrative. I have identified two ways that the Mishnah's laws are dependent on a narrative support structure. First, the anecdotes spread throughout the Mishnah collectively serve to present Mishnaic law as rooted in the authority of the rabbis, both individually and as a group. They alone are the authorized transmitters, interpreters, legislators, and, ultimately, embodiments of the law. Second, the Mishnah operates on the basis of an implicit framing story in which the rabbis are the sole inheritors of the scribal and prophetic tradition that goes back to Moses himself. The reader is expected to know and accept this narrative. The Mishnah's refusal to articulate its version of history can be explained alternatively as reflecting a rabbinic hesitancy to rewrite scripture or as a rhetorical move designed to deny the legitimacy of competing historical narratives.

PART TWO

THE MISHNAIC STORY

6

Transmission, Redaction, and Rhetoric

"Tell all the Truth but tell it slant—"
                        Emily Dickinson, *Poem 1129*

Introduction

The remainder of the book will focus on the analysis of individual Mishnaic *ma'asim*. As I explained in chapter 3, our use of the category *ma'aseh* reflects the Mishnah's own use of this term to categorize texts. Technically, this term introduces a text that describes an event that happened in the past which has halakhic implications or ramifications of one sort or another. I use the term to refer to the entire passage in which such an event is described, even in cases in which the term *ma'aseh* is not actually used. The *ma'aseh* is thus a narrative format that allows the concreteness, complexity, and authority of real-life events to engage the more abstract and theoretical world of halakhic discourse.

Thus defined, *ma'asim* generally fall into the category of stories, i.e., texts that portray at least two interrelated events that occurred once and only once in the past. Of the three genres of *ma'aseh*—the exemplum, the case story, and the etiological story—only the exempla is not by definition a story. It can also be formulated using other high-narrativity forms such as repeated and onetime events. For the most part, we shall examine *ma'asim* that are stories. For the sake of simplicity I will refer to the texts under consideration as "stories" and make note of instances when the *ma'asim* under consideration are not true stories according to our definition.

Thus far we have seen two key roles for stories in the Mishnah. First, they anchor the high-narrativity end of the spectrum of literary forms found in the Mishnah; in the dialog between these forms that takes place in the Mishnah, stories represent the voice of narrative approaches to law and rabbinic authority.

Second, stories collectively create the framework of the master narrative that defines how the halakhah of the Mishnah is meant to function within a social and political community. In both roles, stories are presented as speaking collectively in a univocal manner. This voice may exist in dialog with other voices in the Mishnah, but in and of themselves the stories reflect a consistent and confident vision of the nature of halakhah and halakhic authority.

To a degree, this image of the Mishnah's stories as a unifying ideological force is a result of the methods used in the first part of the book. There, we focused on categorizing the various literary forms in the Mishnah and examining their collective roles within the Mishnah. This approach by definition emphasizes the commonality among the stories and within the various subgenres. As we shift now to examining individual stories, a different picture emerges. Very few Mishnaic stories actually fully conform to the straightforward formal and thematic categories that we outlined when considering Mishnaic stories as a whole. Furthermore, individual stories consistently contain elements that complicate or even undermine the ideas about the functioning of halakhah and rabbinic authority that I attributed to the Mishnaic stories as a whole in the previous chapter.

As a genre, Mishnaic stories reflect a notion of law as a flexible system focused on addressing the contingencies of time and place. This system is held together by the authority of the rabbis, both individually and collectively, who apply the law in individual cases. Yet this focus on the fluid and idiosyncratic nature of reality ultimately impacts on the status of the rabbis themselves. The more developed stories in the Mishnah consistently raise questions about the identity of the rabbis and the nature, extent, and justification of their authority as transmitters, adjudicators, and, ultimately, creators of the law.

The Mishnah's stories attempt to bridge the gap between events in the empirical, historical world and the theoretical-hypothetical discourse of halakhah. Yet a careful reading of these stories will reveal their incompleteness and ambiguity. Such a reading calls attention to the fact that these stories do not always bridge this gap and indeed emphasize the shortcomings both of narrative and of law as tools for organizing and regulating social, cultural, and political realities.

From this perspective the Mishnah, and Mishnaic stories in particular, appear not so much as an *authoritative discourse*, which establishes rabbinic norms, as a *discourse of authority*. These texts represent a space in which rabbis are portrayed and discussed from a variety of perspectives, presenting an opportunity to explore the complex and at times problematic nature of the rabbis and their authority.

On the one hand, then, the Mishnah and its stories establish an authoritative framework in which the rabbis and their laws function. On the other hand, they consistently question this framework by testing its boundaries and exposing its limitations. I do not seek here to resolve the apparent contradiction between these two approaches to reading the Mishnah and its stories. I see each approach as reflecting an authentic voice of the Mishnah elicited by legitimate reading practices. In the concluding chapter of this book we shall consider some of the possible implications of the Mishnah's multivocality with regard to the question of rabbinic authority.

In this chapter we will begin our investigation of the Mishnaic story with a consideration of some of the larger methodological issues and poetic features that relate to the nature and study of these stories. In the first section of the chapter we will present two alternative approaches to the question of how the Mishnah was redacted and demonstrate how these different methods shed light on key stylistic elements of rabbinic narrative art. In the second part we will examine various issues and phenomena related to the question of narrative point of view in the Mishnah's stories.

Strategies of Reading, Strategies of Telling: Theories of Mishnaic Redaction and Transmission

No less than four books that treat the question of the transmission and redaction of the Mishnah have appeared in recent years: Elizabeth Shanks Alexander's *Transmitting Mishnah*, Shamma Friedman's *Tosefta 'atikt'a*,[1] Judith Hauptman's *Rereading the Mishnah*,[2] and Martin Jaffee's *Torah in the Mouth*.[3] All these studies focus on the relationship between the Mishnah and parallel passages in other Tannaitic works, especially the Tosefta, the Mishnah's sister compendium. The use of parallel texts to study rabbinic and ancient literature in general is, of course, not new. However, these recent studies have generated fresh insights into this method.

These scholars agree that the Mishnah does not simply transmit received traditions in a relatively unaltered form. They all see Mishnaic texts as carefully crafted works, shaped to fit the needs, interests, and agendas of the creators of the Mishnah. Accordingly, Mishnaic stories need to be read as intentionally formed works, designed to fit their contexts. They differ in the way they envision the method and process by which the Mishnah and its sources were transmitted and shaped. Shamma Friedman and Judith Hauptman adopt what we might call a "textual" approach, whereas Martin Jaffee and Elizabeth Alexander take what I have dubbed a "performative" approach.

A "textual" approach assumes that texts were transmitted in a fairly stable and fixed form. The existence of parallel texts that have strong textual and conceptual similarities along with significant differences can be explained largely through a process of punctuated evolution, in which editors periodically reworked earlier texts for new ideological, pedagogical, or aesthetic purposes. The result was a new work which subsequently was canonized and transmitted as such. This model would tend to imply a written mode of transmission, as is suggested by our use of terms like "fixed text" and "editor." It is possible, however, that such a process could occur by oral means or, more likely, through a process where oral transmission is aided by written texts.[4] Indeed, Hauptman, a proponent of this textual approach, explicitly declares her belief that the Mishnah was transmitted orally.[5]

In the case of the Mishnah, Friedman and Hauptman both argue that the editors worked from earlier texts, particularly an earlier edition of the Tosefta. This theory rejects traditional views of the Tosefta as a later response to the Mishnah.[6] According to Friedman and Hauptman, the editors of the Mishnah reworked these earlier texts to fit their halakhic, conceptual, and stylistic agendas. Generally speaking, we can reconstruct a clear trajectory from the earlier Tosefta text to the later Mishnah. Charting this relationship gives us insight into the choices and agendas of the Mishnaic editors as they decided what to emphasize and what to delete from earlier texts.

The "performative" paradigm draws on the field of orality studies, which examines the art of oral performance in traditional cultures. These studies, initiated by Parry and Lord in the 1930s in their seminal work on bards in the Balkans, describe the way traditional poets improvise works based on received oral tradition.[7] Each telling is an original reworking of received materials. It is shaped by the particular abilities, influences, and agenda of the performer. Though one performance may have occurred earlier than another and even influenced it in some way, oral performances ultimately emerge from, and dissolve back into, an oral "soup" of verbal and thematic traditions that are passed down from performer to performer.[8] A performative approach does not necessarily suggest an exclusively oral mode of transmission. The performative model might also be applied to instances in which scribes freely rework earlier written material.

For Jaffee and Alexander, parallel texts in Tannaitic works should be viewed in many cases not as successive recensions of a fixed text but as records of alternative oral performances emerging from the same oral tradition. These texts must be read parallel to each other. By understanding the different possible renditions of a particular oral tradition, we can better understand the unique choices and strategies implemented by the individuals who produced the versions that we have in our possession.

These two approaches to the Mishnah not only reflect differing historical reconstructions of how the Mishnah came to be, they also offer two different reading strategies for approaching the Mishnah. Friedman and Hauptman advocate a diachronic approach in which the Mishnah is understood in the context of its place in an evolutionary chain of texts. Jaffee and Alexander, on the other hand, feel that in most cases the prehistory of the Mishnaic text cannot be reconstructed with much precision. They advocate a synchronic approach in which passages from the Mishnah and their parallels are seen as existing independently, without any causal relationship between the two. Each of these approaches has the potential to shed a different light on the Mishnaic passage in question. Indeed, even if one believes that one has reconstructed the history of a text through a diachronic reading, it can still be highly advantageous to reread the text and its parallels in a synchronic manner, focusing on the literary and not the historical relationship between the texts.

A Case Study in Mishnaic Narrative Development: 'Eruvin 4:4 and Bavli 'Eruvin 45a

In this section, I will demonstrate the value of such a two pronged approach through an analysis of two parallel stories, one found in 'Eruvin 4:4 and the other in a baraita found in the Bavli 'Eruvin 45a. First, through a diachronic-textual analysis of these sources I will show how a story that was originally composed in an aggadic context was appropriated by and ultimately assimilated into halakhic discourse. This analysis will illustrate the way in which the editors of the Mishnah carefully reworked their sources to further their halakhic and ideological agendas. Then, employing a synchronic-performative approach, I will show how these two stories illustrate two distinct stylistic and rhetorical options that were available to rabbinic authors who sought to use stories in transmitting halakhah. It is precisely the tension between these differing rhetorical models that generates much of the complexity and ambiguity in Mishnaic stories.

Before proceeding to our texts, a little halakhic background is needed. The fourth chapter of the tractate 'Eruvin deals with the laws of the *tehum shabbat*, "the Sabbath limit." In rabbinic law, each Friday afternoon every Jew "acquires his domicile" at the place where he or she finds him or herself at sundown. For the remainder of the Sabbath, the Jew can travel only two thousand cubits (approximately one kilometer) from that location. The exact definition of the "location" or "place" depends on the circumstances. If a person begins the Sabbath in a city or other settlement, he or she can consider the entire settlement to be his or her "place." The person can then travel at will within the city as well as within a two-thousand-cubit radius beyond the city limits. If, however, one begins the Sabbath on the road or otherwise beyond the reach of human settlement, then one's "place" is defined as the exact point where one began the Sabbath. Such a person may only move within a circle of a two-thousand-cubit radius centered on that point. Furthermore, if a person begins the Sabbath within the two-thousand-cubit perimeter surrounding a city, *intent* to acquire one's domicile in the city is sufficient. What happens, then, in a case where the person was initially unaware that he was within two thousand cubits of a city and hence could not have intended to take up residence there over the Sabbath? In Chart 6.1, in synoptic form, are the texts of the Mishnah and baraita which deal with precisely this issue.

Textual-Diachronic Approach

As is clear from the synoptic presentation of the texts above, the Mishnah and the baraita share a core text, section B, in which R. Judah recounts the story

Baraita, cited in Bavli ʿEruvin 45a	Mishnah ʿEruvin 4:4
A	
	מִי שֶׁיָּשַׁב בַּדֶּרֶךְ וְעָמַד
	וַהֲרֵי הוּא סָמוּךְ לָעִיר
	הוֹאִיל וְלֹא הָיְתָה כַּוָּנָתוֹ לְכָךְ
	לֹא יִכָּנֵס
	כְּדִבְרֵי ר׳ מֵאִיר
	ר׳ יְהוּדָה אוֹמֵ׳ יִכָּנֵס
B	
תניא, אמר רבי יהודה	אָמַ׳ ר׳ יְהוּדָה
מעשה ברבי טרפון	מַעֲשֶׂה הָיָה
שהיה מהלך בדרך, וחשכה לו	
ולן חוץ לעיר	
לשחרית מצאוהו רועי בקר	
אמרו לו	
רבי, הרי העיר לפניך, הכנס!	
ונכנס וישב בבית המדרש, ודרש כל היום כולו	וְנִכְנַס ר׳ טַרְפוֹן בְּלֹא מִתְכַּוֵּון
C	
אמר לו ר׳ יעקב	
משם ראייה?	
שמא בלבו היתה	
או בית המדרש מובלע בתוך תחום שלו	

Chart 6.1

A

If a man sat down by the way and upon rising

he observed that he was near a town,

since it had not been his intention to do so

he may not enter it.

So said R. Meir.

R. Judah ruled: he may enter it.

B

It was taught: R. Judah related,	Said R. Judah,
such a case happened regarding R. Tarfon	such a case once actually happened
who was on a journey when dusk fell	
and he spent the night outside a town.	
In the morning he was found by some herdsman	
who said to him,	
"Master, the town is just in front of you, come in."	
He then entered and sat down in the house of study	that R. Tarfon entered a town without intent.
and delivered discourses all that day.	[to do so prior to the Sabbath].

C

R. Jacob said to him,

Is that incident any proof?

Perhaps he had the town in his mind

or the study house was within his Sabbath limit.

Chart 6.1 (Continued)

of R. Tarfon entering the city on the Sabbath. While the Mishnah presents an extremely concise version of the story, the baraita presents a more expansive one. In the Mishnah, R. Judah's account is preceded by a passage, section A, that quotes a dispute between R. Meir and R. Judah as to the permissibility of entering a city on the Sabbath if one unwittingly began the Sabbath within the two-thousand-cubit perimeter of the city. R. Meir forbids, and R. Judah permits. R. Judah then cites the story of R. Tarfon, section B, as a supporting precedent. The baraita, in contrast, begins with section B, the story, which is followed by section C, a series of questions from R. Jacob, asking whether or not this story supports R. Judah's position.

Originally the baraita also apparently opened with a presentation of the dispute between R. Meir and R. Judah akin, if not identical, to the one found in the Mishnah in section A. R. Jacob's questions presuppose that R. Judah is telling his story in order to support his position with regard to Sabbath limits. Furthermore, the questions that R. Jacob asks are appropriate only to the baraita's version of the story and not the Mishnah's. He asks whether or not R. Tarfon was indeed ignorant of the fact that he was within the limits of the city. The Mishnah, however, explicitly states that R. Tarfon was initially unaware that he was within the limits of the city, making this question superfluous. R. Jacob further notes that there is no indication that the house of study to which Rabbi Tarfon journeyed was more than two thousand cubits from his original position. If the house of study were indeed less than two thousand cubits from R. Tarfon's original encampment, it would then be permissible to go there according to all opinions. The Mishnah, however, unlike the baraita, makes no reference to a house of study, instead suggesting that R. Tarfon traveled throughout the city at will. The baraita must thus be seen as independent of the Mishnah. It must have originally opened with a presentation of the dispute between R. Judah and R. Meir, just like the Mishnah does. In all likelihood, this section was eliminated by the redactors or transmitters of the Bavli when they appended the baraita to the Mishnah.

Having established the original form of the baraita, we must now investigate the initial context of the story as it is recorded there. Clearly, this is a story which relates directly to halakhic issues. R. Tarfon's predicament and its solution assume the existence of halakhot regulating one's movement on the Sabbath. In this sense, we might call it a halakhic story.[9] However, as R. Jacob argues, this story is not compelling proof for R. Judah's particular halakhic position regarding entering cities on the Sabbath. It omits several pieces of information necessary to determine R. Tarfon's position on the debate between R. Judah and R. Meir. Instead, the story is replete with details that are not at all germane to this halakhic dispute. It is difficult, then, to imagine that this story was initially composed for the purpose of transmitting a halakhic ruling.

More likely, the narrative originated as an essentially aggadic product. This is a story about R. Tarfon's escape from a difficult situation. At the beginning of the story, we encounter R. Tarfon lost and alone for the night on a dark road.[10] Furthermore, R. Tarfon considers himself trapped, prohibited from walking more than two thousand cubits in any direction until after the Sabbath.

With sunrise comes R. Tarfon's salvation through the intervention of a group of cattle herders. As is common in both rabbinic and general literature, the herdsmen here have a liminal status, moving back and forth between the worlds of human settlement and that of the open range. They serve as the conduit for R. Tarfon's move from the isolation of the wilderness to the shelter and companionship of the city. They inform R. Tarfon that in fact he was adjacent to a city the whole time. Thereupon R. Tarfon enters the city and spends the Sabbath day in the house of study.

There is no explicit reference to any sort of divine intervention in this story. Nevertheless, it is reasonable to read this story as a providential one, in which the herdsmen are divine agents sent unwittingly to rescue a great and holy sage from a difficult predicament. The lesson is that God provides for his loyal servants.

R. Judah (or redactors acting in his name) appropriated this aggadic narrative for particular halakhic ends, arguing that R. Tarfon's actions implicitly support his position. In applying the story to this case, R. Judah presents a reasonable reading of the story, but not a necessary one. As R. Jacob's questions demonstrate, it is at least possible to read this story so that it does not endorse R. Judah's position. This appropriation by R. Judah represents the first stage of the gradual transformation of this story from an aggadic narrative to a halakhic one.

In order to further trace this transformation, we must resolve yet another philological question. When was this baraita composed? Prima facie, baraitot present themselves as Tannaitic texts, composed in Palestine in the first three centuries CE. As is well known, however, many of the baraitot in the Bavli actually represent reworkings of Tannaitic sources at the hands of later Babylonian rabbis.[11] Furthermore, some of the texts presented as baraitot in the Bavli are "fictitious baraitot" that were composed in the Amoraic academies of Babylonia and attributed to the Tannaim.[12] We thus cannot take for granted that a baraita presented in the Bavli is in fact an early Palestinian text. In this case, we can establish that our baraita reflects the original form of the text as it was known in Palestine by examining the Yerushalmi's discussion of our Mishnah.

The Yerushalmi opens its discussion of our Mishnah by citing the following text:

אמרו
והלא בית מדרשו שלר׳ טרפון
היה בתוך אלפים אמה
או שמא הקנה עצמו לבני עירו [מבעוד יום][13]

They said:
Was not the House of Study of R. Tarfon
within two thousand cubits [of the city]?

Or perhaps he established his residence
with the dwellers of the city [while it was still day]?

This passage is almost exactly parallel to the last section of the baraita in the Bavli. They differ mainly in that the Yerushalmi uses a somewhat more wordy formulation, and it presents the questions anonymously rather than attributing them to R. Jacob.[14] It also reverses the order of the questions. Despite these differences, it is clear that the last section of the baraita was known, in a slightly different form, to the Yerushalmi. The text found in the Bavli is quite possibly a later Babylonian recension; nevertheless, it accurately reflects the essential contents of the original baraita as it was known in the Land of Israel.

The Yerushalmi, as we have seen, does not record the story to which these questions are addressed. Undoubtedly, however, the text cited by the Yerushalmi must have originally included an account of R. Tarfon's adventures that is different from the one in the Mishnah, as we find in the baraita in the Bavli. Without such a context, the questions presented by the Yerushalmi make no sense.[15]

Based on the content of the questions, we can reconstruct the key elements of the story to which they respond. The story tells how R. Tarfon entered a city on the Sabbath and proceeded to the local study house, despite the fact that he encamped just outside the city on Friday afternoon. The story does not explicitly state that R. Tarfon did not initially intend to enter the city when he encamped prior to the Sabbath. Furthermore, the Yerushalmi responds to the questions by citing a line of the story as it had it:

אשכח תני
בשחרית זרחה החמה
אמרו לו
ר' הרי העיר לפניך היכנס[16]

We find in the baraita:
In the morning the sun rose.
They said to him,
"Master, behold the town is just in front of you, come in."

This line parallels the Bavli's version:

In the morning he was discovered by some herdsman
who said to him,
"Master, the town is just in front of you, come in."

The story found in the Bavli differs from that which was in circulation in Palestine only in relatively minor details. These differences may have been introduced in Babylonia by later generations of rabbis, or they may reflect an old Palestinian tradition. One way or another, a text closely approximating the baraita in Bavli was in circulation in the Palestinian academies of the third and fourth centuries, and it was regarded there as an authentic Tannaitic teaching.

Before proceeding to the next stage of our analysis, it is worth noting the Yerushalmi's response to the question regarding R. Tarfon's intentions. The questioner asserts that since the story fails to explicitly state one of the key factors in the case, namely R. Tarfon's intentions on Friday afternoon, it cannot be entered as legitimate evidence in halakhic debate. In the baraita these questions remain unanswered. The Yerushalmi, however, responds by citing the line from the story in which R. Tarfon is found by the herdsmen and is told that the city is right before him. The implication seems to be that prior to this point R. Tarfon was unaware that he was so close to the city and as such had no intention to reside there when the Sabbath began. The Yerushalmi's response represents yet another stage of the assimilation of this aggadic text into halakhic discourse. While this text may be aggadic in origin, the Yerushalmi argues that a careful reading will allow us to derive halakhic conclusions.

Having established that both the Mishnah and the baraita in question reflect early Palestinian sources, what remains for us is to consider the relationship between the two texts. As we have seen, Friedman and Hauptman each argue that the editors of the Mishnah consistently reshape and especially abridge passages from the Tosefta in order to make them better fit the stylistic and halakhic context of a given Mishnaic discussion. Hauptman calls particular attention to the way in which the Mishnah condenses narrative and aggadic materials from the Tosefta. It seems most likely that in our case the editors of the Mishnah similarly reshaped an earlier source in order to advance its halakhic agenda. The Mishnah condensed the bariata's story into a single line: "It once actually happened that R. Tarfon entered a town though this was not his intention [when the Sabbath had begun]." The Mishnah's version of the story was tailored to fit exactly into the context of R. Judah's argument in support of his position on Sabbath limits. The account is not even coherent outside of the context of the Mishnah. Furthermore, this story both eliminates and adds key details from the baraita's account. On the one hand, the Mishnah specifies that R. Tarfon entered the city despite his lack of intent to do so the previous afternoon. On the other hand, it eliminates any references to R. Tarfon going specifically to the beit midrash, in order to make clear that R. Tarfon could have traveled the entire length and breadth of the city. The editors of the Mishnah reworked R. Judah's narrative proof for his position so that it is impervious to the questions raised in the baraita. The story has been stripped of all of the thematic and dramatic elements that characterized its original aggadic form and fashioned into an iron-clad proof for R. Judah's position. The Mishnah thus completes the process of transformation of our originally aggadic story into a purely halakhic text.

In sum, I would like to suggest the following hypothesis as to the development of the story of R. Tarfon and the halakhic discussion surrounding it:

1. Initially, there are two independent traditions:

    a. A story about R. Tarfon, similar to what we find in the baraita, whose purpose is to tell an edifying story about R. Tarfon's rescue from distress
    b. A tradition recording a dispute between R. Meir and R. Judah about the role of conscious intent in determining one's "acquisition of domicile" prior to the Sabbath

2. The story of R. Tarfon is attached to the dispute-tradition as a support for R. Judah's position.
3. The use of this story as a precedent is challenged due to the inexact fit between the story and the hypothetical narrative. (The Yerushalmi responds to this challenge.)
4. Our Mishnah reformulates the story to remove all extraneous details and to match it exactly to R. Judah's position.

This reconstruction suggests a process whereby a story that was not explicitly concerned with halakhah is gradually assimilated into halakhic discourse. First, the story, as it was initially composed, is read for its implied halakhic content and used as proof in a halakhic discussion. However, the fit between the story and the halakhic position is far from perfect; critics argue that it is possible to reinterpret the story so that it does not support any particular ruling. In response to these problems, the redactors of the Mishnah rewrite the story, eliminating all extraneous material and reshaping it as an exact proof for the position in question.[17] Though it will require much further investigation to substantiate, my impression is that such transformations of narrative materials from the realm of aggadah to halakhah happen quite frequently in rabbinic literature.

Performative-Synchronic Analysis

The above diachronic analysis has succeeded in advancing our understanding of the Mishnah and its prehistory. However, with these insights comes the cost of a certain blindness to important aspects of our Mishnah and baraita. Our analysis thus far assumes a basic stylistic distinction between halakhic and aggadic narrative discourse. It presumes that, to be effective, halakhic stories require clarity and concision. Editors of these stories must avoid unnecessary details that may be tolerable, or even desirable, in the richer, more multivalent discourse of aggadah. It is on the basis of this understanding that we have described the baraita as a less well-developed halakhic text that would only reach its ultimate form in the hands of the Mishnah's redactors.

These stylistic assumptions reflect the perspective of the editors of the passage in question. The diachronic method that we have utilized thus far privileges this approach by portraying the Mishnah's stories as the final product of an evolutionary process. But there is another way to think about the relationship between these two versions of the story. If we treat these two texts synchronically, then each text emerges as an equal and independent work. We are no longer in a position to favor one version over the other. From such a perspective, the baraita reflects not a more primitive presentation of the halakhah but rather a different approach to the use of stories in halakhic discourse. In constructing its halakhic argument, the creators of the baraita did not simply neglect to remove the unnecessary and potentially distracting details from the aggadic text they received. Rather, they appropriated these "aggadic" details in order to enrich the overall rhetorical impact of the story and its halakhic argument. Any distinctions between halakhic and aggadic narrative styles are thereby eliminated. Aspects of a narrative which are often viewed as aggadic, and even as impeding the halakhic dimensions of the story, can be seen as playing a crucial role in the halakhic rhetoric of the story. Viewed from this perspective, the distinction between halakhic and aggadic narrative becomes even more problematic.

Representational vs. Illustrative Narrative Strategies

The divergent approaches to the use of the R. Tarfon tradition represented by the Mishnah and the baraita correspond to a basic tension confronting all narrative artists who seek to use their stories for didactic or ideological purposes. On the one hand, we have what mid-twentieth-century narrative theorists Scholes and Kellogg term an "illustrative" approach. For this perspective, the author/editor carefully crafts the story for the sake of making a particular argument and eliminates any details that might distract or detract from this purpose. In contrast to the "illustrative" approach, Scholes and Kellogg also outline a "representational" approach to transmitting meaning through narrative. This approach is represented in our case, not atypically, by the baraita. Here the author/editor does not select details purely, or even primarily, for the sake of making a particular argument. Rather, the representational narrator introduces details and information with the goal of constructing a compelling narrative world for the reader.[18]

We will begin with the illustrative approach. Scholes and Kellogg identify this tendency with the creators of didactic narratives. While a story may portray individual characters and specific events, the illustrative story does so in a way that is general enough that the various elements of the story can be seen as representing broader types or categories. A story that portrays people and events that are overly idiosyncratic cannot impart guidance about how other people in different times should act under different circumstances. The illustrative storyteller thus favors sparse narratives with iconic figures that can easily be adapted to new situations. Furthermore, illustrative stories maintain a close and well-defined relationship with an abstract normative structure that the narrator uses to frame his message.

The Mishnah in 'Eruvin and its story represent an example of such a sparse narrative which is carefully linked to an abstract ideological framework. We have already seen how the Mishnah's story was tailored to fit a halakhic argument. In order to better facilitate an even closer reading of the Mishnah, I am re-presenting it, this time broken down into four rather than two sections:

1. If a man sat down by the way and when he rose up he observed that he was near a town
2. he may not enter it, since it had not been his intention to do so; so said R. Meir.
3. R. Judah ruled: he may enter it.
4. R. Judah said, such a case once actually happened that R. Tarfon entered a town though this was not his intention [when the Sabbath had begun].

The first three sections of the paragraph discuss the issue using a casuistic formulation. One of the advantages of using such hypothetical narratives is that they can be manipulated to present multiple, interrelated cases and outcomes. In this case, the Mishnah presents a narrative with two alternative endings, reflecting the opposing rulings of R. Meir and R. Judah.

The first line presents a hypothetical situation in which a person sits down by the road prior to the onset of the Sabbath. The person then arises after the Sabbath has already begun only to discover that he was within the two-thousand-cubit limit of a city. The Mishnah then presents a double end to the narrative in lines 2 and 3, which gives two contrasting evaluations of the case. R. Meir states that the person can only go two thousand cubits from where he stands, just as if he had not stopped near any settlement. R. Judah disagrees. Since, regardless of his intentions, the person began the Sabbath within the city's halakhic boundaries, he is considered to be a resident of that city for the duration of the Sabbath and may travel within the city as he pleases.[19] We thus have two versions of the narrative. Both begin with a person who unwittingly begins the Sabbath just outside a city. In R. Meir's version the person spends the entire Sabbath within a kilometer of his original encampment, whereas in R. Judah's version the person is free to travel throughout the city.

In line 4 the Mishnah now juxtaposes this hypothetical narrative with an actual story. In the story, R. Tarfon begins the Sabbath, unbeknownst to him, within the two-thousand-cubit perimeter of a city. Upon discovering his proximity to the city sometime later, R. Tarfon enters it. Unlike hypothetical narratives, stories can only present a single succession of interrelated events. On the basis of this story, R. Judah argues that there is only one possible conclusion to the hypothetical narrative cited above, namely, that in such a circumstance, entering the city on the Sabbath is permissible. In quoting this story, R. Judah demonstrates that his version of the hypothetical narrative emerges from the deeds of an actual sage of an earlier generation. R. Meir can provide no such grounding for his narrative. His ruling is implicitly rejected.[20]

The interrelationship between the hypothetical narrative and the story is emphasized in this case by the terse wording of the story. The story never explicitly narrates R. Tarfon's initial dilemma. Instead, it opens with the phrase, *ma'aseh hayah* translated here as "such a case once actually happened." In this context, the term *ma'aseh* serves as the narrative equivalent of a pronoun whose antecedent is the hypothetical case at the beginning of the Mishnah. R. Tarfon's situation is not simply parallel to the one formulated in the hypothetical narrative; it is identical to it. In this Mishnah, the theoretical world of halakhic debate and the actual life of R. Tarfon are inextricably linked. R. Tarfon's story is linguistically dependant on the hypothetical formulation at the beginning of the Mishnah, while the resolution of the theoretical debate depends on R. Tarfon's actions in the story. The ease and certainty with which the Mishnah's story can be applied to an entire category of cases, both hypothetical and real, is an example of the efficacy of illustrative storytelling in transmitting general principles.[21]

There exists another side to the art of transmitting meaning through narrative. This is what Scholes and Kellogg call "representational" narrative. According to the principles laid out in the first half of this book, representational narratives strive for maximum specificity. This approach posits that the rhetorical force of stories lies in their ability to draw the reader into a convincing "narrative world" that the reader takes to be coterminous with his or her own. The reader thereby finds it reasonable to apply the information and values presented in the story to his or her own life. In the case of Mishnaic narratives, this form's fundamental advantage over more hypothetical formulations rests in its ability to root a law in historical experience and in the deeds of an individual rabbi. A given practice is no longer presented as a theory or an ideal but as an inevitable fact.[22]

The main device by which an author creates this illusion of the narrative world is the introduction of mimetic detail, especially details that would appear superfluous to the dramatic or ideological needs of the story. These details convey a sense of an immanent reality that encapsulates the characters, events, and ideology of the story. The baraita's version of the story, independent of any context, is anything but representational. It is a brief narrative in which every detail plays a role in the development of the theme or plot. Yet once we read this story as integrated into a halakhic discourse, our evaluation of what constitutes a relevant or irrelevant detail changes. The narrator of the baraita populates his story with characters and events that serve no direct purpose in supporting R. Judah's position about Sabbath limits. It is precisely these details which draw the reader into the world of the narrative and allow him or her to perceive R. Judah's opinion as a narrative fact embodied by R. Tarfon's actions. The narrative world created by the baraita serves as a bridge between halakhic discourse and an integrated experience of the world. In the baraita's story the halakhic content is not in the foreground. Rather, it is embedded in the normative structure which regulates the action of the story. The reader experiences R. Tarfon's concern with the Sabbath limit as a part of R. Tarfon's overall Sabbath and general religious observance. Moreover, these halakhic practices are only a part of a larger human narrative about R. Tarfon's personal journey, his dislocation and eventual return "home" to the beit midrash. Finally, as I have argued, this story can be read not only as a human but also as a divine comedy, in which God's benevolent providence ensures a safe and positive outcome for those who are devoted to his law.

Viewed from this perspective, the baraita's "representational" story is more effective at transmitting and inculcating R. Judah's position than the Mishnah's spartan narrative. The Mishnah's story may be a superior medium through which to bring the "real life" actions of R. Tarfon to bear on theoretical halakhic discourse, but it is not nearly so successful at bringing halakhic discourse to bear on real life situations. In reducing the story to its halakhically significant facts, the Mishnah strips it of all mimetic detail. Far from being "fraught with background," in Erich Auerbach's famous phrase, the Mishnah's story simply lacks all background. It presents halakhically relevant facts devoid of any narrative context. The reader of this story is not drawn into a narrative world which he or she might correlate with his or her own. The reader gets no sense of how halakhic practice might be integrated into a broader life experience.

Furthermore, while literary critics may view mimetic detail as the hallmark of the modern novel, the rabbis, unlike modern critics,[23] had no notion of "realistic fiction" as a positive cultural category. For them, the only stories worth telling were those that actually happened. In this context, the addition of extra detail to a given narrative would have only furthered their claim to the historicity of the account.

Thus, while the baraita may not have the legal precision of the Mishnah, it is far more effective at exploiting the rhetorical potential of stories to transmit values. In this story, the laws of the Sabbath limit appear not as a theory or ideal but a reality of the narrative world of the story, no less than the cattlemen or beit midrash. R. Tarfon's decision to enter the city appears obvious and inevitable not only from a halakhic perspective but also from the perspective of R. Tarfon's unfolding journey and the providential hand which guides it. Viewed in this light, the baraita makes a far more compelling case for R. Judah's position than does the Mishnah.

These two versions of the story of R. Tarfon thus reflect two distinct strategies for using stories in halakhic discourse. The Mishnah's illustrative strategy seeks to integrate the narrative material as seamlessly as possible into the theoretical halakhic discussion that precedes it. The baraita's representational approach, in contrast, integrates halakhic theory into a more complex and variegated narrative world and, by extension, into our own "real" world.

It is not coincidental that a passage of the Mishnah and a baraita provide us with examples of illustrative and representational narrative respectively. The concise and focused style of the Mishnah leans more toward illustrative storytelling, whereas the baraita's tendency toward less tightly woven texts is typical of representational storytelling. However, both of these narrative tendencies are in fact to be found within the Mishnah. While it is true that the Mishnah tends to present stories that are crafted to fit into a particular halakhic argument, very few Mishnaic stories present as close a fit as the case of R. Tarfon. Most Mishnaic stories contain some details that are extraneous to, and even undermine, the halakhic and ideological point they are supposed to make.

Representational vs. Illustrative Narrative Strategies; Further Examples: *Shabbat* 3:4, 16:7, and 22:4

In order to illustrate this tension between illustrative and representational storytelling in the Mishnah, I shall analyze two case stories from *Shabbat*. Each of these stories balances these competing demands in its own way, resulting in differing outcomes for the way they communicate both their halakhic and their ideological messages. The second of the stories actually appears twice in *Shabbat*.

(1) Shabbat 3:4

מַעֲשֶׂה שֶׁעָשׂוּ אַנְשֵׁי טְבֶרְיָיה
הֵבִיאוּ סִילוֹן שֶׁלַּצּוֹנִין לְתוֹךְ אַמָּה שֶׁלַחַמִּים
אָמְרוּ לָהֶם חֲכָמִים
אִם שַׁבָּת[24] כְּחַמִּים שֶׁהוּחַמּוּ בַּשַׁבָּת
אֲסוּרִים בִּרְחִיצָה וּבִשְׁתִיָּיה
אִם בְּיוֹם טוֹב, כְּחַמִּים שֶׁהוּחַמּוּ בְּיוֹם טוֹב
אֲסוּרִין בִּרְחִיצָה וּמוּתָּרִין בִּשְׁתִיָּיה

It happened that the people of Tiberius
placed a cold-water pipe into a channel of hot water.
The sages said to them:
On Shabbat, water heated thus is like any other water heated on Shabbat—
it is forbidden to use it for washing or drinking.
On festivals, it is like any other water heated on festivals—
it is forbidden to use it for washing but permitted for drinking

(2)

Shabbat 22:4	*Shabbat* 16: 7
אֵין נוֹקְבִין	כּוֹפִים קְעָרָה...
מְגוּפָה שֶׁלֶּחָבִית	עַל עָקְרָב שֶׁלֹּא תִישָׁךְ
	דִּבְרֵי ר׳ יְהוּדָה
וְר׳ יוֹסֵה או	

(Continued)

לֹא יְקָבֶינָּה מִצִּידָּה

אִם הָיְתָה נְקוּבָה

לֹא יִתֵּן עָלֶיהָ שַׁעֲוָה

מִפְּנֵי שֶׁהוּא מְמָרֵיחַ

One may not pierce

the body of a barrel.

One may use a dish

to cover a scorpion,

so that it does not bite.

These are the words of R. Judah.

R. Yose says:

Do not open it from its side.

If it is open,

do not put wax on it,

because it constitutes

"smoothing."

Both *Shabbat* 16:7 and 22:4 conclude:

אָמַ' ר' יְהוּדָה
מַעֲשֶׂה בָא לִפְנֵי רַבָּן יוֹחָנָן בֶּן זַכַּאי בַעֲרָב
וְאָמַר חוֹשֵׁשׁ אֲנִי לוֹ מֵחַטָּאת

Rabbi Judah said:
Such a case once came before R. Yohanan ben Zakkai in Arab
and he said, "I suspect that he is liable a sin offering."

First, we will examine these stories from a halakhic perspective. The first story presents a case of a pipe for drinking water that has been placed running through a trough emanating from a hot spring. The question is whether water heated in such a manner may be used on the Sabbath and holidays. The rabbis rule that such water is no different from water heated by conventional means. The case is presented with a fair degree of specificity. The Mishnah describes a distinctive device which is associated with a specific locale, Tiberias and its famous hot springs. The reader can envision the men of Tiberias installing such an apparatus or even inaugurating its use. While this detail draws the reader into the world of this story, making the case more compelling and convincing, it also limits the case's value as a legal text. It is not clear how this case might be applied to other situations. Minimally, we might reasonably apply it to similar mechanisms using water from other geothermal springs, but is there a broader principle underlying this ruling? It is difficult to tell.

The chapter as a whole lists a series of casuistic and apodictic formulations regarding various other cases of cooking through indirect heat on the Sabbath, such as placing food in an oven that is still hot though the coals have been removed. Those cases possess less specificity not only because they are not stories but because they involve what were then presumably more common methods for heating food and water at the time. Given its ambiguity, it is difficult to relate our story to the rules and principles for cooking using indirect heat on the Sabbath that are implicitly established by the cases in the rest of the chapter. Our story thus sacrifices halakhic clarity and utility for the sake of a representational rhetoric that deepens the story's impact on the reader.

The second story adopts at least some aspects of the illustrative approach demonstrated in the Mishnah in 'Eruvin. Similar to the way in which the story in 'Eruvin used the phrase "such a case [ma'aseh] once actually happened," the Mishnah here makes use of the phrase "such a case [ma'aseh] once came before." In both cases the term ma'aseh refers back to a hypothetical case in the previous sentence. Here, hypothetical cases in the laws of the Sabbath involving trapping a scorpion and sealing a punctured vessel with wax are transformed into an actual case brought before R. Yohanan ben Zakkai. The relationship between the specific case and the more general framework of the halakhah is clearly established. This is especially so in the case involving the sealing wax, where the Mishnah explicitly relates the ruling to a more general rule prohibiting "smoothing" on the Sabbath. Here the Mishnaic storyteller opts for minimal detail in order to generate a story whose value as a legal precedent is relatively unambiguous.

Focusing on the rulings presented in these two stories, a different picture emerges. In the first story, an unnamed and disembodied group of rabbis state their ruling using the boilerplate language found in casuistic formulations. The case is evaluated in terms of clear-cut halakhic dichotomies and distinctions: prohibited vs. permitted, Sabbath vs. holidays, drinking vs. washing. Though its wider applicability may be in question, there can be no question as to how the rabbis' ruling locates this particular case within the realm of halakhic categorization.

In the second story, it is precisely in the description of the ruling that we find a shift toward specificity and representational rhetoric. We are told not only the name of the rabbi in question, the illustrious R. Yohanan ben Zakkai, but we are also told the locale where the ruling takes place, the town of Arab. Finally R. Yohanan speaks not through stylized halakhic discourse but with a statement that is more reminiscent of colloquial speech, "I suspect that he may be liable a sin offering." This statement further contextualizes the situation by reminding us of the fact that R. Yohanan, unlike most of the rabbis cited in the Mishnah, was active during the time when the Temple stood, when questions of cultic law remained practical concerns.[25] In the depiction of R. Yohanan's answer, this story comes alive and draws the reader into a miniature narrative world.

This turn toward mimeticism in the second story, while strengthening the Mishnah's rhetorical force, undermines its clarity as a legal text. The Mishnah here does not present R. Yohanan's ruling in the unambiguous terms of prohibited or permitted. Rather, R. Yohanan's words express uncertainty as to the ultimate ruling in this situation. The story neither confirms nor denies the rule laid down in the Mishnah; it merely affirms the case's problematic status.

The broader ideological content of both stories is also affected by the narrator's rhetorical choices. As I have already explained, case stories collectively function to establish the rabbis' authority to interpret and rule on the halakhic ramifications of new and ambiguous situations. They do this by repeatedly citing examples in which individual problematic cases are decided by a rabbi or rabbis. The story of the water pipe is among the few stories in the Mishnah that fits this pattern so exactly. It easily breaks down into two narrative events: (1) the actions of the people of Tiberias, and (2) the rabbis' ruling. The events fit neatly into the structure through which we have defined the case story: an event or situation whose status is halakhically unclear followed by a rabbi or rabbis' response in which they rule on matter at hand. On the surface then, this simple case story paints a picture of the rabbis as authoritative teachers of the law to the entire community.

The water-pipe story further emphasizes this ideal of centralized rabbinic authority by not naming any individual rabbi or group of rabbis. Rather, it was simply "the sages" who issued their ruling to the people of Tiberias. Who is included in "the sages"? By deploying such a vague term, the Mishnah suggests that a ruling cited by "the sages" represents the uncontested opinion of the entire rabbinic class. It is as if "the sages" were a corporate entity speaking with one voice.

Precisely because it adheres so closely to the simple form of the case story, the water-pipe story contains some telling narrative gaps.[26] The story never explicitly establishes the relationship between the people of Tiberias and "the sages." Did the townspeople ask the rabbis' opinion or did the rabbis offer an unsolicited ruling? Similarly, once the rabbis spoke, did the people listen to the ruling or not? It remains possible that people of Tiberias never asked any rabbis about the halakhic status of their water system and did not care when a group rabbis voiced their opinion on the matter. The Mishnah relies on the assumptions of the reader regarding the relationship between Rabbis and laypersons to motivate a sympathetic filling of the narratives gaps.

The ambiguity created by this gap in the story is highlighted by the following debate in the Bavli, in which two Amoraim discuss the outcome of the story:

אמ' עולא
הלכה כאנשי טבריא
אמ' להו רב נחמן
כבר תברינהו אנשי טבריא לסילוניהו[27]

> Ulla said,
> the law is like the people of Tiberias
> R. Nahman said to him,
> the people of Tiberias destroyed their pipe.

According to Ulla, not only did the people of Tiberius not accept the rabbis' ruling, but the people's position was ultimately vindicated as normative law. Ulla's reading radically destabilizes the case story's support of rabbinic authority. Ulla sees the people of Tiberius and the rabbis as two legitimate opposing voices in the halakhic conversation. In this case at least, the rabbis come out on the losing end.[28] According to R. Nahman, on the other hand, the people of Tiberias dutifully accept the rabbis' rulings, going so far as to destroy the offending water pipe. Rabbis indeed appear as the sole legitimate interpreters of the law. The simple form of the case story is thus not optimal for making the argument that I have ascribed to it, as it is open to widely varying interpretations. In the best-case scenario, the narrator would explicitly state that a question was asked of the rabbi and that his ruling was followed.

This narrative gap is partially filled in in the second story, where we are explicitly told that the case was brought before R. Yohanan. Though we do not know who it was that brought the question before him, nor whether his ruling was adhered to, by filling in this added stage of the story, we get a clearer presentation of R. Yohanan as an authoritative expositor of the law.

Indeed, some of the Mishnah's earliest interpreters understood this pair of stories as potentially describing R. Yohanan ben Zakkai as a sage widely consulted by the local populace. In its gloss on *Shabbat* 16:8 the Yerushalmi (81b) records the following account in the name of R. Ulla:

> רבי עולא אמר
> שמונה עשר שנין עביד הוי יהיב בהדא ערב
> ולא אתא קומוי אלא אילין תרין עיבדיא

> R. Ullah said,
> [R. Yohanan ben Zakkai] spent eighteen years in Arab,
> and these are the only two questions that were ever brought before him.

This statement comes to counter the otherwise reasonable assumption that these two stories are evidence that the populace in Arab and the surrounding area frequently consulted with R. Yohanan on halakhic matters during his sojourn there. In fact, we are told, these two cases were the only instances in which people came to R. Yohanan with a question during all his years there. In transforming this story into one that emphasizes R. Yohanan's lack of authority among the local population, the Yerushalmi only emphasizes the fact that in general, case stories implicitly affirm rabbinic authority to answer halakhic questions. In their interpretation, this master narrative of people coming to ask rabbis their questions is demonstrated here not in the observance but in the breach. The ideal, however, of the people turning to rabbinic decisors with halakhic questions remains.

In both stories, to the extent that these stories do use mimetic details, these details serve to draw the reader into a narrative world where the values of rabbinic authority are integrated into everyday life. However, in the case of the story about R. Yohanan ben Zakkai, one of these details undermines the picture of R. Yohanan as an authoritative rabbi. As we have already noted, the fact that R. Yohanan fails to deliver a decisive answer ("I suspect...") limits this story's halakhic value. So, too, the fact that the rabbis are not always sure about their rulings, it would seem, complicates if not calls into question the notion that rabbis have all the answers to halakhic questions.

This tension between illustrative storytelling, with its schematized and abstracted style, and representational storytelling, with its greater specificity, is responsible for much of the complexity that we find Mishnaic stories. It is in part what transforms these texts from assertions of halakhic positions and authority into a site of discourse about halakhah and the nature of halakhic authority.

Narrative Authority and Point of View

This analysis of the above stories raises yet another issue with regard to narrative rhetoric of the Mishnah, that of the narrative voice in which these accounts are related. As has long been understood by students of the modern novel, the author's choice of narrative voice and point of view is essentially a rhetorical maneuver meant to manipulate the reader into a particular perspective on the events described. The voice generally used by the Mishnaic narrator might be described as third person omniscient. Occasionally, the narrator exhibits his omniscience by informing us about a character's inner life and intentions. In general, though, the narrator restricts himself to describing characters' speech and actions. Such an approach to storytelling produces a "quasi-authoritative language," to use a term employed by critics of the modern novel. In such situations, "the reader is commanded to accept the author's statement as unquestionable knowledge about one or the other element of the novelistic world."[29] This strategy is meant to give the reader the sensation of direct, unmediated access to the narrative world the Mishnah describes.

The way in which this narrative strategy functions within Mishnaic stories differs significantly from its role in modern fictional works. In a fictional work, the author seeks to draw the reader into a world that *appears* to be real. Novelists seek only to create a temporary illusion of the existence of a narrative world which is distinct from the world in which we live.[30] Not so the Mishnaic narrator. The rhetoric of the *ma'aseh* is rooted in its claim to deploy an actual historical event in promoting a particular halakhic and ideological position. The reader is meant to believe that there was a real person named R. Tarfon and that he did in fact enter a city one Shabbat morning, having camped outside of it the previous night. The world of the narrative and the world in which the reader lives have the same ontological status. They exist in the same historical and spatial continuum.

In adopting the guise of an omniscient third-person narrator, the Mishnaic storyteller appropriates for himself real authority. He claims not only to be the arbiter of historical truth but, through this knowledge, to have the authority to define normative behavior in the contemporary community.

This use of "quasi-authoritative" narrative language is in many ways similar to Meir Sternberg's understanding of narrative style of the Bible. Sternberg argues that the omniscient narrator of the Bible is intimately connected to the omniscient God who is the implied author of the Bible in the traditional view. For Sternberg, God is the "double author," both of the Bible and of history itself.[31] The Bible's narrative strategy inscribes into the text the Biblical author's most fundamental theological positions. It reinforces the reader's belief both in divine omniscience and in the divine nature of the Bible.

The authors and editors of the Mishnah did not claim to be prophets writing a new scripture. As we have already seen, this fact likely influenced the rabbis' break with the grand narrative tradition of the Bible. Nevertheless, the rabbis still saw their work as being rooted in the work of the prophets and their authority. Their decision to maintain the authoritative narrator similar to that of the Bible would appear to reflect the rabbis' desire that their anecdotes similarly be taken as accurate and unmediated accounts of the events they portray.

Counter-Narratives

If we are to be critical readers, we cannot allow ourselves to be taken in by the narrator's rhetoric. An awareness of the storyteller's rhetorical tools and goals will allow us to expose the gap between the narrative texts and the events they purport to represent. This in turn heightens our appreciation of the constructed nature of these stories and helps us to better understand how these stories functioned in their literary and social contexts.

In the case of the Mishnah, this critical process can be greatly advanced by placing the story at hand in the context of other versions of the events in our possession. These "counter-narratives" demonstrate that there are alternatives to the Mishnah's account, challenging its claim to present the sole, objective version of the story. We have already seen how comparing the story of R. Tarfon in 'Eruvin 4:4 with its parallel in the baraita brings to light the Mishnaic narrator's use of rhetorical strategies to serve his halakhic agenda. According to a diachronic-textual reading of the stories, the Mishnaic storyteller actively reworked an earlier version similar to the baraita to make it clear that the story supports R. Judah's view. If we take a synchronic-oral approach, each storyteller used a different approach to present an effective halakhic story. In either reading, we must read the Mishnah's story as a carefully constructed work of ideological prose rather than an unmediated and objective presentation of historical events.

Counter-Narratives from Extra-Rabbinic Sources: Sukkah 4:9

Most of the counter-narratives for the Mishnah's stories come, as in the case of the story of R. Tarfon, from baraitot, either from the Tosefta or the Talmuds. On rare occasion we are fortunate enough to have a counter-narrative that comes from outside the rabbinic corpus, generally from the works of Josephus. Such counter-narratives are particularly valuable because they tend to offer a totally different perspective on the events. *Sukkah* 4:9 recounts the proper procedure for the ritual of the water libation on Sukkot. The Mishnah concludes:

וְלַמְנַסֵּךְ אוֹמְרִין לוֹ
הַגְבַּהּ אֶת יָדָךְ
שֶׁפַּעַם אַחַת נִיסֵּךְ עַל רַגְלָיו
וּרְגָמוּהוּ כָל הָעָם בְּאֶתְרוֹגֵּיהֶם

> To the one who draws the water libation they say:
> "Raise your hands."
> For once he poured the libation on his feet
> and the entire populace pelted him with their etrogs.

A similar account is recorded in a baraita cited in the Tosefta, the Bavli, and the Yerushalmi.[32] While there are some differences between the two versions of the story, which we shall analyze in a later chapter, the important thing at this point is their similarity. The rabbinic accounts all agree that the incident of the etrog throwing was provoked by the priest's misperformance of the water libation ritual. Proper cultic behavior is at the center of the story.

Josephus, presents a very similar story, with a very different point:

> As to Alexander, his own people were seditious against him; for at the festival which was then celebrated, when he stood upon the altar, the nation rose upon him and pelted him with citrons [which they had in their hands, because] [t]he law of the Jews required, that at the feast of the tabernacles every one should have branches of the palm-tree and the citron-tree; which thing we have elsewhere related. They also reviled him, as derived from a captive and so unworthy of the dignity of sacrificing. At this he was in a rage, and slew of them about six thousand.[33]

Josephus is recounting a story about a political conflict, not a ritual dispute. Alexander was both the high priest and the king at the time. The people took the opportunity of his public appearance in the Temple on Sukkot to vent their rage against the king. Josephus notes that the people also did not think Alexander worthy of the office of high priest at all, due to his questionable lineage. The people's anger is directed against Alexander more generally, and against his action on the altar that day.

This alternative version of the event forces us to reconsider the inevitability of the rabbinic version. Josephus's telling of a story about a high priest being pelted with etrogs significantly raises the chances that this incident actually did occur. However, it also suggests that the idea that this revolt was about the proper way to perform the water libation may well be a product of the ritual-obsessed rabbinic imagination. Ultimately, the evolution of the story and the reclamation of its historical kernel, if any, remain beyond our reconstruction. Several leading scholars are of the opinion that the rabbinic version of this story derives, directly or indirectly, from the Josephean one.[34] Shaye Cohen sees this as an example of the "rabbinization" of historical sources. In his view, the rabbis took a story about an uprising against an unpopular ruler and transformed it into an account concerning a conflict over, and the evolution of, Temple practice. While examples such as this, where we have a parallel to a Mishnaic story in a non-rabbinic source, are not common, they present an important opportunity to read Mishnaic stories in terms of a counter-narrative whose author does not share the same rabbinic values as the Mishnaic story-teller.

Historiographic Counter-Narratives

Our discussion of sources from Josephus and rabbinic accounts of Temple ritual leads us to yet another form of counter-narrative necessary to critique Mishnaic narrative style and agendas. These counter-narratives are found not in other ancient texts but in modern historiographic works. Modern historians, like their ancient predecessors, tell and retell stories about ancient events, in accordance with their own beliefs and values. They provide an alternative narrative framework against which to evaluate the Mishnah's stories. There are fundamental differences between the account of Jewish history in the first centuries CE implicit in the rabbinic texts and the accounts of contemporary historians.

Mishnaic narratives assert that the rabbis were the sole legitimate source of law and religious authority. This claim to represent "normative Judaism" extends not only to the period of the Tannaim from the Destruction in 70 CE till the beginning of the third century but also to the rabbis' predecessors, the Pharisees,[35] who were active in the generations preceding the Destruction. Traditional academic historiography, going back to the nineteenth century, tended to take these assertions at face value, painting a picture of the Pharisees/rabbis as the dominant group in Palestinian Jewry not only religiously but politically as well. In recent decades, however, a growing scholarly consensus has come to reject this picture in favor of a narrative that significantly limits the extent of the rabbis' influence until at least the third century CE.

With regard to the situation pre-70, academic scholars traditionally accepted the Mishnah's view of the Pharisees as by far the most powerful of the groups vying for power in the late Second Temple period. They portrayed the Pharisees as the leaders and opinion makers of the masses as well the dominant force in the Temple cult and Jerusalem politics.[36] These scholars based their view not only on rabbinic sources but on several key passages in Josephus as well.[37] The first important challenge to this version of events was Morton Smith's landmark article, "Palestinian Judaism in the First Century."[38] Smith questioned the reliability of both rabbinic and Josephean claims about the prominence of the Pharisees. He argued that though "the largest and ultimately the most influential of [the sects], the Pharisees, numbered only about 6000 [and] had no real hold either on the government or on the masses of the people."[39] Smith's basic thesis has been adopted with some variants and developments by most contemporary historians. The Pharisees are now widely viewed as an elitist sect whose popular, political, and cultic influence probably varied throughout the century or so leading up to 70 CE. Even at the height of their influence, Pharisaism hardly defined the "normative" Judaism of the era.[40]

The Mishnah's accounts of events preceding the Destruction, especially those describing events in the Temple, must be read in light of this counter-narrative. It is quite telling that rabbinic texts rarely use the term "Pharisees" with regard to the rabbis' predecessors.[41] They refer to them instead as "sages," the same term they use to refer to themselves. This needs to be viewed as part of a broader strategy on the part of the rabbis to portray themselves as the inheritors not of a particular sect but of the leadership of "mainstream" Judaism in pre-Destruction Palestine and especially in Jerusalem and the Temple. The other groups, in contrast, such as the Sadducees or Boethusians, are portrayed as deviant groups who challenged, mostly unsuccessfully, rabbinic hegemony. Challenging the rabbis of the Mishnah reflects a rejection of normative Judaism "as it has always been." The counter-narratives of contemporary historians bring into focus the rhetorical and polemical nature of this portrayal of reality. Though we should not reject the historicity of Mishnaic anecdotes out of hand, these accounts must be read with the awareness that the Mishnah is not simply recording events but shaping a narrative that supports its worldview.

Of particular significance to us is the Mishnah's repeated claim that the rabbis were in full control of the ritual in the Temple. This claim allows the Mishnah to assert that its teachings about the Temple ritual reflect not only the proper practice but actual historical reality. The rabbis of the Mishnah emerge as the inheritors of the Temple and its rituals. Recently, several scholars have argued that there is little historical evidence to suggest that the Temple was run by a council of rabbis according to the rules set down in the Mishnah and other rabbinic sources.[42] As Seth Schwartz writes, "In reality...apart from rare episodes of royal interference reported by Josephus, we know nothing about how decisions regarding temple ritual were made."[43] In light of this finding, we must read rabbinic accounts of Temple ritual with particular care.[44]

The traditional academic historiography of the centuries following 70 CE also by and large accepted the prima facie assertions of the rabbinic materials that the rabbis constituted the religious and political leadership of the Jews in this period as well. These scholars presumed that the rabbis were the preeminent Jewish leaders of the time and that the reconstituted Sanhedrin and the established patriarchate gave them the institutional bases from which to exert their influence on Palestinian Jewry.[45] In recent decades, historians have sought to radically rewrite this story. They have questioned the very existence of a Sanhedrin and of an officially recognized patriarchate during most of the Tannaitic period.[46] The emerging consensus is that the rabbis of this period represented a relatively marginal network of study circles and courts, concentrated in rural areas, which only gradually rose to prominence later in the Talmudic period and after.[47]

Shaye Cohen's work on this issue is of particular interest to us, because it is based in large part on the systematic study of case stories found in Tannaitic literature. Cohen argues that despite the frequent assertions of rabbinic authority in all range of matters both secular and sacred, when the evidence is read carefully, it emerges that the rabbis' power in this period was in fact quite limited. The data shows that the rabbis of this period were largely limited to rural areas, and they were mostly consulted on issues regarding purity and personal status. With regard to normal day-to-day affairs, whether ritual matters or matters of civil law, the rabbis were not viewed as authorities by the people. As Cohen summarizes his findings:

> According to the "traditional" [view], the rabbis were the leaders of the Jews and molders of Judaism. Drawn from all segments of the population they were *the* elite of Jewish society. Their position as judges, teachers and synagogue leaders enabled them to propagate the way of Torah among the masses. In this view rabbinic Judaism is synonymous with Judaism, and rabbinic society is synonymous with Jewish society....
>
> This view is false in almost every detail. The rabbis were not the sole leaders of Jewry. Their status as elites depended as much, if not more, upon their wealth and birth as upon their intellectual and pietistic attainments. They had little inclination and availed themselves of few opportunities to propagate their way of life among their co-religionists. Their judicial authority extended to only a few circumscribed topics. The rabbis were but a small part of Jewish society, an insular group which produced insular literature. They were not synagogue leaders....

> The rabbis claimed judicial authority in all areas of life, but they were consulted most often about the laws of purity and tithing, marriage and divorce, and oaths and vows, least often about the laws of daily prayer, Sabbath and holidays, and commerce and torts. In certain specific matters, then, the Jews recognized the rabbis as authoritative, while in other matters they had no need for them at all.
>
> The gap between theory and practice did not begin to narrow until the tenure of Judah the Patriarch. Rabbinic judicial power now came to include civil cases as well as other concerns of daily life.... These developments probably resulted from the policy of Judah the Patriarch who, unlike his predecessors, enjoyed strong Roman support and attempted to make himself the *de facto* leader not merely of the rabbis but also of Jewish society as a whole.[48]

For Cohen and his colleagues, through much of the Tannaitic period rabbinic authority was more of a theory than a reality. It was only at the end of this era, when the Mishnah was being redacted, that the rabbis began to enjoy real influence in wider Palestinian Jewish society.

When deployed as a counter-narrative against the stories of the Mishnah, the contemporary historiographic narrative about the development of Pharisaic and rabbinic Judaism can shed important light on the narrative techniques and agenda of the Mishnaic storytellers. Read in this context, it becomes clear that though it is very likely rooted in historical memory and data, the Mishnah's storytelling is not a transparent reflection of reality. Rather, it is the product of a strategic use and reworking of historical materials to create an image of consistent rabbinic hegemony dating back centuries. On the one hand, this picture relies on the apparent reality of increasing rabbinic political and religious authority in the third century. The first students of the Mishnah would have found the implicit master narrative underlying the Mishnah's stories to be believable because it was consonant with their own situation. On the other hand, the Mishnah's use of stories also might have served to bolster the new situation of relative rabbinic influence by suggesting that the rabbis had always represented normative Judaism.

An awareness of the nuanced accounts of historians such as Cohen can also sensitize us to complexities within the Mishnah's stories. Despite their overall thrust constructing and arguing for rabbinic authority, the stories of the Mishnah often betray evidence of a more problematic reality. Careful readings of these stories will show that they often depict a world in which rabbinic authority is far from complete or unequivocal. In the readings of individual stories in subsequent chapters, we will pay close attention to the way they both construct and deconstruct an image of total rabbinic hegemony.

Named Narrators and the Mishnah's Internal
Counter-Narratives: Sukkah 3:9, 'Eruvin 10:10,
Betza 2:6, and Sukkah 3:8

Counter-narratives do not always come from sources external to the Mishnah. On rare occasion the Mishnah supplies its own counter-narrative. We have already seen that in Shabbat 16:7 and 22:3, the Mishnah recounts how R. Yohanan ben Zakkai responded to two different questions that he was asked while in the town of Arab with the reply, "I suspect that he is be liable a sin offering." In each case, however, the Mishnah describes a different question posed to R. Yohanan. Clearly, the reader is meant to assume, as does the passage from the Yerushalmi quoted above, that R. Yohanan responded using the exact same words to both. It is certainly possible that this was in fact the case. But the reader must wonder whether in fact the R. Yohanan only uttered these words once (if at all). Perhaps the redactors of the Mishnah reformulated one or both of these accounts so that they would fit into the same stereotypical framework. The fact that certain settings and pieces of dialog repeat themselves in different Mishnaic stories reminds us that our access to the original events is mediated through the redactional activities of authors and editors who potentially shaped the text for their own aesthetic and ideological ends.

Other cases in which the Mishnah suggests the possibility of a counter-narrative involve situations where the Mishnah abandons its usual use of an omniscient third-person narrator. At times, as in the case of the story of R. Tarfon in 'Eruvin 4:4, the account is related in the name of one of the Mishnaic rabbis. The significance of this shift in point of view is less than it might first appear.[49] The narrative voice remains authoritative and objective in its presentation. The narrator rarely interjects himself into the story, and he continues to appear omniscient. Thus R. Judah confidently describes the inner motivations of R. Tarfon in entering the city. Furthermore, the narrator is always a rabbi, whose authority is constantly being reinforced in the Mishnah.

Nevertheless, the very act of identifying the narrator as a historical individual calls our attention to the fact that his story may have been shaped, consciously or not, by his own interests, concerns and shortcomings. In the case of R. Judah's story about R. Tarfon, we cannot escape the fact that R. Judah has a clear bias. His version of the story supports his own position with regard to the laws of city limits on the Sabbath. The possibility exists that there is a suppressed counter-narrative which undermines R. Judah's claims. Indeed, as we have seen, the baraita's version of the story does not present such unequivocal support for R. Judah's position. Furthermore, R. Judah never states how he knows the details of R. Tarfon's solo journey. R. Judah was a student of R. Tarfon,[50] so it is not unreasonable to presume he heard the account from R. Tarfon himself, but this claim is never explicitly made.

The Mishnah does not always obscure its narrator's sources. For example, in *Sukkah* 3:9 we read:

אָמַ' ר' עֲקִיבָה
צוֹפֶה הָיִיתִי בְרַבָּן גַּמְלִיאֵ' וּבִ׳רְ יְהוֹשֻׁעַ
שֶׁכָּל הָעָם מְטַרְפִּים[51] אֶת לוּלַבֵּיהֶם
וְהֵם לֹא נִיעֲנְעוּ אֶלָּא בְאָנָּא ה' הוֹשִׁיעָה נָא בִּלְבָד

R. Aqiba said,
I observed R. Gamliel and R. Joshua.
Whereas the people waved around their lulavs all day,
they only did so at "*anna hashem*."

Here Rabbi Aqiba takes the stance of a first-person narrator, stating that he was present at the events described. This narrative style projects authority differently from the use of a more detached third-person narrator. On the one hand, R. Aqiba tells us how he knows about the events in question: he was an eyewitness. One cannot argue that R. Aqiba speaks without direct knowledge. Furthermore, R. Aqiba speaks with particular authority as he is one of the most prominent sages in the Mishnah. It is R. Aqiba's authority no less than that of R. Gamliel and R. Joshua that underlies the ruling implicit in this story. Yet, by inserting himself into the story, R. Aqiba also emphasizes that he is a subjective observer. Unlike R. Judah in the previous story, R. Aqiba does not know what is going on inside the heads of either the rabbis or the congregation which he describes. He could have erred or perceived things in line with his biases.

In these cases, the suggestion that there may be an alternative way to tell a given story is ultimately speculation, based solely on the fact that the narrator has been identified as an individual human. In some cases, however, the Mishnah actually juxtaposes two conflicting versions of the same events, calling attention to the fact that rabbinic transmission is inherently fallible and perhaps subject to the biases of the transmitters. This is the case in *'Eruvin* 10:10:

נֶגֶר שֶׁיֵּשׁ בְּרֹאשׁוֹ גְלוֹסְטְרָא
ר' אֶלְעָ׳ז' אוֹסֵר
וּרְ' יוֹסֵי מַתִּיר
אָמַ' ר' לְעָ׳ז'
מַעֲשֶׂה בִּכְנֶסֶת הַגְּדוֹלָה[25] שֶׁבִּטְבָּרְיָיה
שֶׁהָיוּ נוֹהֲגִין בּוֹ הֶתֵּר
עַד שֶׁבָּא רַבָּן גַּמְלִיאֵ' וְהַזְּקֵנִים וְאָסְרוּ לָהֶם
ר' יוֹסֵי או'
אִיסּוּר הָיוּ נוֹהֲגִין בּוֹ וְהִיתִּירוּ לָהֶם

A bolt with a knob at the end
R. Eleazar prohibits
and R. Joshua permits.
It happened in the great synagogue of Tiberius
that they were lenient in this regard,
until R. Gamliel and the elders came and prohibited it.
R. Yose said,
they were strict in this regard until they permitted it.

The Mishnah opens with a casuistic formulation. The protasis is a noun phrase of the form "X...that" that posits a bolt with a knob at the end of it. The Mishnah then presents a double apodosis, in which two opposing rulings are put forth. R. Eleazar forbids and R. Yose permits the use of such a door bolt on the Sabbath.[53] In parallel with these two hypothetical positions, the Mishnah now relates two versions of the same story, one in the name of each rabbi. Both agree that R. Gamliel and the elders ruled with regard to just such a door bolt that was used in the synagogue of Tiberias, reversing the previous practice of the congregation. However, whereas according to R. Eleazar the rabbis ruled that it was forbidden to use the bolt on the Sabbath, in Rabbi Yose's version of the case story they rule that it is permitted to use it.

We find here a dialogic tension between the hypothetical casuistic formulation of this debate in the first part of the paragraph and the concrete story version found in part two. The Mishnah never specifies the relationship between the Tannaim's position on the general case of the knobbed bolt and their differing versions of the specific incident involving a particular specimen. It may be that the rabbis' divergent opinions derive from the fact that they have received different versions of the case story. If this is the case, the potential authority of both accounts is undermined, because the stories cannot both be true. At least one of these stories does not represent an accurate account of a genuine historical ruling but rather has been corrupted in the process of transmission. Ultimately, this challenges the authority of all stories used to teach halakhah. The fact that the Mishnah does not always present a conflicting counter-narrative does not mean that in those cases there is not also the potential that the Mishnah's accounts have become corrupted over time.

The alternative possibility is perhaps even more destabilizing. It may be that these rabbis did not derive their ruling from the account that they took to be most historically reliable. Perhaps at least one rabbi adjusted his account based on his preconceived notion about the halakhah. For example, R. Yose may not have received an alternative tradition in which R. Gamliel and his comrades permitted the use of the bolt for the people of Tiberias. Rather, since R. Yose believed he knew for sure that the law permitted such bolts, he presumed that the correct version of the story must portray a lenient ruling. If this is the case, stories and related forms lose their authority entirely as an independent source of law. They can and should be manipulated so that they conform to the apodictic framework of the law.

These two conflicting stories challenge one another on the level of the transmission and ruling of practical halakhah. But as conveyors of broader lessons about rabbinic authority, they in fact reinforce one another. Both stories establish the authority of the rabbis to issue rulings to the community. Indeed, this is one of the few case stories which explicitly portray the people as actually listening to the rabbis' ruling. The fact that the story is repeated twice only reinforces this lesson. Whatever the exact ruling was, lenient or strict, the people listened to the rabbis.

In other situations, the Mishnah presents not two contradictory accounts but two different interpretations of the same events. For example, *Betza* 2:6,

שְׁלוֹשָׁה דְבָרִים רַבַּ' גַּמְלִיאֵ' מַחְמִיר כְּדִבְרֵי בֵית שַׁמַּי׃...
וְאֵין אוֹפִין פִּתָּן גְּרִיצוֹת אֶלָּא רְקִיקִים
אמ' רַבַּ' גַּמְלִיאֵ'
מִימֵיהֶם שֶׁלְבֵית אַבָּא
ל'א הָיוּ אוֹפִין אֶת פִּתָּן גְּרִיצוֹת
אֶלָּא רְקִיקִים
אָמְרוּ לוֹ
מַה נַּעֲשֶׂה לָהֶם לְבֵית אָבִיךְ
שֶׁהָיוּ מַחְמִירִים עַל עַצְמָן וּמְקִלִּים עַל כָּל יִשְׂ'
לִהְיוֹת אוֹפִין אֶת פִּיתָּן גְּרִיצוֹת וְחֲרִי

With regard to three things R. Gamliel was strict like the house of Shammai....
One does not bake thick but rather thin loaves on the holiday.
R. Gamliel said,
"In my father's days,
they only baked thin loaves on the holiday."
They said to him,
"What can we say about your father's house?
They were strict on themselves and lenient on all Israel,
permitting the baking of thick loaves."

The Mishnah opens by presenting a series of three negative apodictic statements grouped under the heading of "cases in which R. Gamliel ruled according to school of Shammai." The Mishnah does not give any rationale for R. Gamliel's decisions. We might suppose that R. Gamliel ruled like house of Shammai in these cases because he found the Shammaite position to be in consonance with his own understanding of the legal principles that underlie the case in question. Then, in the very next line, R. Gamliel is cited as rooting at least one of these positions not in abstract principle but in narrative precedent. He cites an exemplum, a report of a repeated event in his father's household. In the household of the great R. Simeon ben Gamliel they only baked thin loaves on the holiday. It seems that

R. Gamliel holds his position forbidding baking of thick loaves on the festivals at least in part on the authority of his revered father's personal practice.

R. Gamliel's version of events does not go unchallenged. R. Gamliel's authority in presenting this exemplum is his status as an eyewitness observer to events in his father's house. Though this is a privileged position, it does not give R. Gamliel access to all the relevant information in the case. He does not know his father's intent in giving the instructions to produce only flat loaves. This raises a fundamental problem in deriving law from exempla. The fact that a sage behaves stringently in a certain circumstance does not necessarily mean that such behavior is normative. It is possible that the sage in question was merely adopting a personal stringency which does not reflect the black-letter law. In order to distinguish between a stringency and a legal requirement we need access to the inner world of the rabbi in question. We must know his intentions in adopting a particular behavior. R. Gamliel's anonymous interlocutors challenge his account not by suggesting that it is untrue but rather that it is incomplete. They assert that R. Gamliel's extrapolation of a general ruling from his father's actions is erroneous: R. Simeon ben Gamliel's actions reflect not normative law but a personal stringency.

The authority of these anonymous speakers must itself be investigated. How do *they* know R. Simeon ben Gamliel's intentions? They may have an unspecified source of knowledge to which R. Gamliel had no access. Or perhaps they are simply presenting a *possible* interpretation of the events. Given the crucial gap in the account presented by R. Gamliel, his reading of the events as proof for a normative rule with regard to baking on holidays is far from conclusive. Since no definitive reading of the events is possible, this exemplum must be removed from consideration as a source of law.

In either event, the Mishnah here uses a counter-narrative to emphasize that even reliable eyewitnesses do not present complete accounts of the events they see. As a result, these accounts are open to multiple interpretations and may not be as useful as they appear in establishing the law.

A similar case presents itself in *Sukkah* 3:8:

אֵין אוֹגְדִים אֶת הַלּוּלָב
אֶלָּא מִמִּינוֹ
דִּבְ׳ ר׳ יְהוּדָה
ר׳ מאיר או׳
אֲפִילוּ בִמְשִׁיחָה
אָמ׳ ר׳ מֵאִיר
מַעֲשֶׂה בְאַנְשֵׁי יְרוּשָׁ׳
שֶׁהָיוּ אוֹגְדִים אֶת לוּלְבֵּיהֶם
בְּגִימוֹנוֹת שֶׁלְּזָהָב

It is forbidden to bind the lulav
with anything but lulav strands,

said R. Judah.
R. Meir said,
even with cords.
It happened that the people of Jerusalem
bound their lulavs
with gold threads.

The Mishnah here presents, in a pair of apodictic formulations, two opposing opinions as to the appropriate material for binding together the lulav, the palm frond used on the holiday of Sukkot. R. Judah permits the use only of strands derived from a lulav, whereas R. Meir allows cords of any material. R. Meir then backs up his position with an exemplum, a reported event about the people of Jerusalem. They did indeed use non-lulav materials—gold thread, no less—in binding their lulavs.

As presented, this exemplum appears as an unequivocal proof for R. Meir's position. However, the parallel in the Tosefta adds a response to R. Meir's testimony which is quite reminiscent of the response to R. Gamliel in the Mishnah above.

אמרו לו משם ראיה?
אף הם היו אוגדין אותו במינו מלמטה

They answered him, "From there you bring evidence?
They bound it with [strands of] its own species underneath [the strands of gold]."[54]

The anonymous respondents present a counter-narrative which challenges the completeness of R. Meir's account. Just as an outside observer cannot know a person's inner thoughts, neither does he have X-ray vision to peer beneath the surface of the objects he observes. R. Meir's source may well have witnessed gold threads wrapped around the lulavs of the people of Jerusalem, but these threads did not themselves bind the lulav. Rather, they merely covered strands of palm frond that did the binding, in accordance with R. Judah's position. We cannot know if the anonymous respondents speak from actual knowledge or are merely asserting a possible alternative reading which is in line with their convictions. In either event, their alternative explanation of the practice of the people of Jerusalem calls attention to the fact that despite their claims to omniscience and authority, the accounts of the Mishnaic narrators are subject to dispute and reinterpretation.

It is difficult to know in this case which version of the text came first, that of the Mishnah or that of the Tosefta. Friedman and Hauptman argue that in most cases the Mishnah edits earlier Toseftan material. When applied to this case, that would mean that the editors of the Mishnah actively suppressed the counter-narrative found in the Tosefta in order to make R. Meir's position appear normative. However, this counter-narrative was not entirely eliminated from the textual tradition of the Mishnah. The line that claims that there were actually lulav strands underneath the Jerusalemites' gold threads appears in one key textual witness to the Mishnah, the Parma manuscript, as well as in our printed texts. In all likelihood, this reading is merely a later addition by copyists on the basis of the Tosefta and the Bavli.[55] Yet the appearance of this line in important versions of the text still reflects the ultimate failure of the Mishnaic editors to suppress the Tosefta's counter-narrative. The existence of an alternative account had to be noted by scribes and was ultimately incorporated to the printed text, the most disseminated version of the Mishnah.

Conclusion

The Mishnah generally presents its narratives as authoritative, unmediated accounts of events whose halakhic ramifications are clear-cut. The editors of the Mishnah made use of a series of redactional and rhetorical techniques in order to create this effect. According to the "textual" model, the Mishnaic editors carefully reworked earlier materials into a text that conformed with their halakhic, ideological, and rhetorical agendas. According to the "performative" approach, the Mishnah reflects an individual performance of a narrative halakhic tradition which was shaped by the performer's interests and concerns. We have also seen how the Mishnaic narrator makes use of both "illustrative" and "representational" narrative strategies in order to produce a text that is both halakhically precise and believable to the reader.

Our very awareness of these processes and strategies makes us more critical readers, alert to the fact that these narratives are in fact linguistic and ideological constructs whose version of events should not be taken for granted. This critical awareness can be enhanced through the systematic study of alternative accounts found in other ancient sources, rabbinic and otherwise, as well as the historiographic narratives presented by contemporary historians of Judaism in the first centuries CE.

The Mishnaic stories themselves also show evidence and even awareness of the gap between their accounts of past events and "objective" halakhic and historical reality. More importantly, careful reading of these stories show tensions and fissures between the various halakhic, ideological, rhetorical, and redactional interests and agendas that shaped these stories into the form in which they appear in the Mishnah. It is these conflicting trajectories and the inherent shortcomings of narrative as a rhetorical and ideological tool that transform the stories of the Mishnah into a key site for the exploration of the complexities and ambiguities of the halakhah and the rabbinic authority on which it is based.

7

Exempla: Who Is a Rabbi?

"How can we know the dancer from the dance?"
William Butler Yeats, *"Among School Children"*

Underlying much of this book is the argument that the stories of the Mishnah serve to both establish and investigate the authority of the rabbis. This assertion only raises further questions: By what qualifications and characteristics can we identify a rabbi? What is the source of his authority? These questions are most obviously raised by Mishnaic exempla. With regard to case and etiological stories, the halakhic significance of the *ma'aseh*, the event or action which happened in the past, is determined by the rabbis' response to or interpretation of that occurrence. The rabbis either rule on the case at hand or legislate a new norm in response to the changed circumstances. In the exempla, there is no such dichotomy between historical event and authoritative response. Rather, the event is inherently meaningful because it involves the action of a rabbi. More so than in the other genres, in exempla the rabbis appear as living embodiments of the halakhah; their day-to-day behavior, no less than their official pronouncements have normative authority.

This chapter investigates these issues from two different perspectives. In the first part of the chapter we will examine a series of theoretical models for understanding the nature and functioning of the rabbi and his authority. We will also attempt to locate the Mishnaic rabbi among his pagan and Christian colleagues and within modern scholarship on religious leadership in antiquity. This discussion will provide us with a framework in which to interpret individual Mishnaic stories in the remainder of the chapter and in those that follow.

The second part of the chapter presents a series of interpretations of Mishnaic exempla from *Sukkah* 2 and the story of Honi Hame'agel in *Ta'anit* 3:8. Our emphasis will be on demonstrating how these stories challenge conventional understandings of the definition of the rabbi and the nature of his authority.

Constructing Rabbis and Rabbinic Authority

"An" vs. "In" Authority

As we discussed in chapter 5, legal authority in general and rabbinic authority in particular can be profitably thought about in terms of a distinction between being *in* authority and being *an* authority. One who is *in* authority derives power from the position that he holds within a certain social or political structure. In contrast, *an* authority derives his or her power from certain inherent qualities or abilities that he or she displays.[1]

In reality, an individual's authority generally derives from some combination of his or her position within a system and the individual's inherent qualities. For example, a king who comes into his position by virtue of his birth may be deposed if he lacks sufficient leadership abilities. Similarly, in many societies, regardless of his or her talents, a person will not be granted authority on the basis of those abilities unless he or she belongs to the appropriate race, class, and/or gender.

To a degree, the very distinction between *in* authority and *an* authority is illusory. When we say that some individuals hold power due to their personal qualities and abilities, what we mean is that they hold power due to a social consensus that they possess certain desirable qualities and abilities. There are no objective measures of wisdom, valor, or intelligence. What exists in the human soul is not ultimately accessible to the public. In deciding whom to follow, groups and societies rely on certain agreed upon external signals or signs of particular internal qualities. Even a leader who is *an* authority is thus dependent on social and political constructs which allow him to be accepted as worthy of his position.

This observation is particularly important for the study of rabbinic authority as it is presented in Mishnaic stories. The Mishnah does not give us direct access to actual rabbis and certainly not to their inner beings. All that we have are a series of linguistic and literary constructs. Furthermore, the Mishnah rarely argues for the rabbinic status of any individual; the status is self-justifying. The very fact that the Mishnah quotes a sage is itself evidence enough that his opinions and actions have potential normative significance. Our understanding of the rabbis of the Mishnah is always filtered through the perspective and opinions of the Mishnah's editors.

The extent to which we see these rabbis as being *in* authority will depend on the historiographic narrative we adopt when interpreting the Mishnah. Traditionally, historians have understood the rabbis as being in control of an extensive political structure, including the patriarchate, Sanhedrin, and lower courts. These institutions were understood to have enjoyed varying degrees of Roman imperial support. In this view, the rabbis were very much *in* authority. It was the position of being a patriarch, a member of the Sanhedrin, or an official judge that gave many of the rabbis their power.

More recently, historians have come to doubt that the rabbis held such broad and formalized power in the late first and second centuries. By then the Sanhedrin was at best a distant memory, if such a rabbinic institution even existed. The patriarchate, on the other hand, would not reach its full stature until the end of this period. The rabbis at that time were a relatively marginal group and were not recognized as the ultimate religious and spiritual authorities by most Palestinian Jews. Nevertheless, even in this view, the rabbis were not lone rangers but were part of a social network with its own hierarchies and norms. Whatever the precise nature of this arrangement,[2] the rabbis derived at least a certain degree of authority from their position within this network.

On the other hand, to some extent each rabbi was *an* authority. His authority was not entirely rooted in social status or political position but in his personal traits, most importantly his mastery of the rules and principles of the halakhah. In this sense, the rabbi was much like other ritual experts of the ancient world who were seen as controlling a technology necessary to the daily life of the populace.[3] Shaye Cohen, in his study of Tannaitic rabbinic narratives, argues that to the extent that the Tannaim were recognized as halakhic authorities among the broader population, it was due to their reputation for specialized expertise in certain areas of the law.[4]

The difference between being *an* authority and *in* authority might be correlated with the distinction between apodictic and narrative approaches to law that we have identified in the Mishnah. Apodictic approaches to law see law as being fundamentally a system of abstract norms. An individual's legal authority can derive only from a mastery of those principles. It is the law that makes the judge, not the judge that makes the law. In this view then, the jurist is *an* authority, defined by his knowledge of the law. In contrast, a narrative approach to law sees law as constantly changing in order to address new circumstances and situations. Authority cannot rest in preset rules. It must be vested in a social or political structure that grants individuals the power to adjudicate and legislate as they see fit. The tension that we have observed in the Mishnah between these two approaches to law is also reflected in the Mishnah's presentation of these contrasting notions of rabbinic authority.

Rational vs. Supernatural Approaches to Authority

Both the conceptions of the leader as *an* authority and as *in* authority are based on an essentially rational, empirical understanding of the nature of political and social power. In either case, power is derived from preexisting, essentially knowable structures, whether political or conceptual. However, there exists another possible model for authority, one that was quite widespread in religious communities in the ancient world. By considering this alternative we can shed further light on the nature of rabbinic leadership as it is portrayed in the Mishnah.

Scholars of religious leadership in antiquity have argued that the character of the holy man in classical pagan and Christian cultures needs to be divided into two subtypes, the "wise man" and the "miracle worker."[5] The wise man who derives his authority from his intellectual attainments fits into the rational model of the *an/in* authority dichotomy that we have considered thus far. The charismatic miracle worker, in contrast, derives his power neither from his knowledge nor his social position but from a source that is beyond any human attributes or social frameworks. His authority emerges through his perceived direct relationship with the divine, as evidenced by his ability to perform miracles and often by his ascetic behavior as well.

As they appear in the stories of the Mishnah, the rabbis generally fit within the naturalistic "wise man" tradition of the holy man. With the exception of the story of Honi Hame'agel, which we shall examine later in this chapter, and that of Haninah ben Dosa in *Berachot* 5:5, the Mishnah does not present its rabbis as possessing any supernatural powers. Such depictions are quite rare in the rest of Tannaitic literature as well.[6] Similarly, the Mishnah does not portray the rabbis as engaging in the sort of radical ascetic practices common in depictions of Christian saints. Halakhah, which is at the center of the Mishnah's worldview, is fundamentally concerned with establishing norms for the wider community. Behaviors that cannot be imitated by the common people cannot have normative significance and hence have no place in a halakhic exemplum.

One scholar, Henry Fischel, has gone so far as to suggest that the rabbis might be classified as a subset of one of the most prevalent groups of "wise men" in their day, the Greco-Roman rhetoricians. Fischel bases his argument heavily on what he sees as the strong resemblance between the Tannaitic sage story and the *chria*, the predominant narrative genre among the Hellenistic rhetorical and related philosophical schools.[7] A chria is "a saying or act that is well-aimed or apt, expressed concisely, attributed to a person, and regarded as useful for living."[8] Both chriai and Mishnaic stories are brief narratives whose purpose is to prove a particular point in the context of a more abstract discussion of philosophy, ethics, or law. Ancient rhetoricians further divided the chriai into three categories: "saying chriai," which focus on the statement of a sage, "action chriai," which focus on a nonverbal deed, and "mixed chriai," which involve both word and deed.[9] Two of the genres of Mishnaic stories parallel the first two of these categories. Whereas case stories, which center on rabbinic pronouncements, parallel the "saying chriai," Mishnaic exempla correspond to the "action chriai."

On the basis of these literary similarities, Fischel argues that the Pharisees and their successors represented an "elite scholar-bureaucracy,"[10] who adapted the rhetorical tools of the Hellenistic *sophos* for their own purposes. According to Fischel, the rabbis derived their authority both from the mastery of a set of intellectual discipline and from their position within a bureaucratic frame work. The rabbi was both *an* and *in* authority.

Fischel's attempt to reconstruct the social and cultural situation of the actual Pharisees and rabbis who functioned in the first several centuries of the Common Era is quite problematic. Fischel fails to present sufficient evidence that literary and rhetorical aspects of these texts in fact reflect a historical reality, in some cases from centuries before those texts were written or edited. Indeed, Fischel himself emphasizes the difficulty of deriving history from rabbinic narrative texts. Nevertheless, Fischel does present an important analysis of the image of the rabbinic sage as he is constructed in Tannaitic literature in light of literary parallels. The rabbis and rabbinic stories do indeed appear to be in many ways quite similar to the Greco-Roman "wise men" and the literary forms used to portray them.[11]

Of particular interest is the contrast between the Mishnaic story and the chria on the one hand and the dominant literary genre for portraying pagan and Christian charismatic miracle workers on the other, the biography. The latter presents a collection of anecdotes about a single individual, often chronicling the life of the saint from birth to death. We have already discussed the general rabbinic preference for brief anecdotal narratives that are integrated into a wider legal, ideological, or exegetical discourse over self-contained "master narratives." In this case, the alternative literary choices of the rabbinic anecdotalists and Hellenistic biographers may point to a deeper difference in their respective views on the nature and role of their protagonists.[12] In Christian and pagan biography, individual deeds function to illuminate the hero's inner essence or character.[13] The biography is a celebration of the individual holy man, his particular abilities, and his special relationship with God. In Mishnaic stories, the focus is on the deeds themselves and their halakhic significance. These deeds point primarily to the authority of the texts, principles, and institutions from which they emerge rather than on the individual rabbis. As David Levine argues:

> The literature of the rabbis, when presenting its heroes in narrative, is not concerned with the individual sage *per se*, but rather with his role as exemplar. It presents a standard of intellectual achievement and religious behavior which can be attained—at least in principle—by all who aspire.... Each individual is responsible for cultivating his or her own relationship with God.[14]

The editors of the Mishnah thus shy away from presenting their protagonists as epic heroes engaged in national or cosmic struggles. Rather, they are generally prosaic individuals, engaged in the common business of daily life.

Charismatic Authority in the Mishnah

Fundamentally, then, the image of the rabbinic exemplar as it emerges from the Mishnah is an essentially rational one, the rabbis' authority deriving from mastery of a set body of knowledge and affiliation with certain social and political structures rather than from any supernatural factors. This does not mean, however, that the category of the charismatic miracle worker is not relevant to our understanding of the image of the rabbi in Mishnaic stories. Miracle workers assert constant pressure on the margins of Tannaitic storytelling. The occasional references to Honi, Haninah ben Dosa, and generic *hasidim* indicate the Mishnah's awareness of such ascetics and miracle workers at least as literary ideals, if not as actual realities.[15] These figures have the potential to function as exemplars within a rabbinic context. The idea that at least some rabbis draw their authority from their miraculous abilities as well as from their positions and knowledge of the law apparently became quite mainstream not long after the editing of the Mishnah. The Talmuds and Amoraic Midrashim are filled with depictions of both Tannaim and Amoraim performing miracles of various sorts.[16] It is hard to imagine that these attitudes sprang up fully formed in the Amoraic era. Most likely, they developed from notions and traditions that were already in circulation at the beginning of the third century CE. Thus the notion of the rabbi as miracle worker probably existed in the rabbinic culture of the time and was, to one degree or another, actively avoided if not suppressed by the editors of the Mishnah.

Furthermore, in some cases, the Mishnah's portrayals of rabbinic exemplars might betray an attitude toward rabbis not unlike that of some contemporary pagans and Christians toward their charismatic holy men. To be sure, the Mishnah does not portray its rabbis as engaging in radical ascetic behavior that sets them apart from common people. As we have seen, the rabbis' deeds are meant to be normative and attainable by all. However, not everything the rabbi does reflects a halakhic requirement that devolves upon every Jew. In some cases, the Mishnah suggests that a particular rabbinic practice is the product of an individual rabbi's personal stringency. As we have seen previously, in *Betzah* 2:6 an anonymous respondent declares that we cannot learn a prohibition from the deeds of R. Simeon b. Gamliel and his household because they were "stringent toward themselves and lenient to all Israel." Thus the rabbis sometimes accepted for themselves stringent practices that were neither required nor expected of the common people, or even of other rabbis.[17]

The question remains as to why the Mishnah would include exempla that are not of normative value. In its discussion of the exempla about eating outside of the sukkah, which I will discuss later in this chapter, the Bavli remarks that R. Yohanan b. Zakkai and R. Gamliel's behavior teaches us that though it is not necessary to eat snacks in the sukkah, such behavior is permissible and even praiseworthy.[18] Were it not for these exempla, one could argue that such a stringency is forbidden on the grounds that it is a sign of religious arrogance. For the Bavli, exempla that describe personal stringencies have normative significance because they establish the scope of permissible stringency in a given matter.

I would like to suggest an alternative function for this type of exempla. Students were not necessarily meant to always imitate the stringencies of their exemplars. The significance of the stringency was precisely that it was practiced only by the rabbi and not by his followers. In this way, the practice of stringencies is an important deviation from the general principle that I stated at the outset, that the life of Torah modeled by the rabbi is meant to be accessible to all. These stringencies may be the closest parallels in Mishnaic narrative to the practice of asceticism, one of the defining characteristics of ancient pagan and Christian holy men.[19] While the rabbis of the Mishnah certainly did not engage in, nor endorse, the sort of radical mortification of the flesh so familiar to us from pagan and Christian literature, nevertheless, their acts of renunciation beyond the demands of the law established their high degree of commitment to divine service. The sages' extreme behavior is precisely what makes them noteworthy and distinguishes them from the masses. Though individual stringent acts may not be worthy of general emulation, they establish an underlying trait of commitment to halakhah that certainly was meant to be imitated by all who sought to follow a life of Torah, each on his or her own level.

Peter Brown's Model of Charismatic Authority

The model of the holy man whose authority is based on his direct relationship with God has further relevance to the figure of the rabbi in the Mishnah. Peter Brown, in his essay "The Saint as Exemplar in Late Antiquity," suggests yet another model for understanding the authority and influence of the early Christian saints that may have some applicability to rabbis as they appear in the Mishnah. Brown deemphasizes the role of miracle working among early Christian holy men and places them along a continuum of exemplars including Greco-Roman wise men. He locates the emergence of the Christian saint within the larger context of the notion of human exemplars in the late antique Mediterranean world. He describes that world as a "civilization of *paideia*," in which the intensive study of classical texts was seen as the ultimate path toward moral development:

> The Classics, a literary tradition, existed for the sole purpose of "making [people] into classics"; exposure to the classics of Greek and Latin literature was intended to produce exemplary beings, their raw humanity molded and filed away by a double discipline, at once ethical and aesthetic.[20]

Brown goes on to note "the late classical [world's] overwhelming tendency to find what is exemplary in persons rather than general entities."[21] Thus, education in *paideia* took place not in an institutional setting but through intensive personal contact with an individual master of the classical texts. It was through these exemplars that *paideia* was transmitted and applied.

This model might well be applied to the rabbis. When Brown describes "men whose ideal was the ability to recall large chunks of precise and exquisitely shaped material, internalized by memory at an early age, [who] knew only too well what it was like to rummage in the silt of memory for the perfect citation, for the correct word, for the telling rhetorical structure," he could just as well be talking about the rabbis who created and transmitted the teaching of what would come to be known as the Oral Law. This concept of rabbinic authority is quite different from the idea of the rabbi as ritual expert or bureaucrat-rhetor parlaying his technical knowledge and skills into authority over the less educated. In this Brownian model, the rabbi's authority derives from the totality of his mastery and engagement of Torah, which transcends the particular knowledge and skills that he may have acquired along the way. The rabbi himself becomes the embodiment of Torah and his deeds become paradigms for behavior, independent of their relationship to any particular text or principle.

Brown goes on to differentiate the Christian saint from his Hellenistic predecessors in a way that once again may be relevant to the status of the rabbis as they appear in the Mishnah. He writes:

> Judaism, and later Christianity, brought to this Mediterranean-wide system of discipline the unprecedented weight of providential monotheism, which in both cases placed an exceptional weight on the joining points between God and men.... God, and no purely human system of transmission, was now held to play the decisive role in bringing the exemplars of the past alive from age to age.... With this belief, the exemplar ceases to be merely a past human paradigm reactivated, by human means, in the present. The "man of God," the "righteous man," has a revelatory quality about him.[22]

Brown describes the late antique Christian holy man as a "Christ-carrying man" who infuses the community with the "central value system" of the church, not necessarily through dramatic or miraculous activity but through his day-to-day presence. Brown explains the workings of the holy man's charisma to be

> like a water table: the pure water of "central concerns" slowly continues to seep beneath the gravel of daily life.... Charisma, therefore, is seen less in terms of the extraordinary, set aside from society, so much as the convincing concentration... in a person of lingering senses of order and higher purpose.[23]

This notion of the Christian saint, with its emphasis on his day-to-day activities rather than his miraculous deeds, opens up the possibility of describing rabbis via a similar model. Because of their study of Torah and other devotional activities, they may well have been viewed by their followers as having a special relationship with God. In the Tannaitic accounts, this relationship rarely results in supernatural powers. However, this does not negate the possibility that underlying the rabbis' authority presented in the Mishnah lay an assumption of the numinous quality of these individuals and the divinely inspired nature of their acts. The rabbis' very presence in their communities[24] transmitted not only the details of rabbinic halakhah but also an overall commitment to a life devoted to the study and practice of Torah.

Such a theory suggests a radical version of the narrative approach to law. The law is defined by the examples and pronouncements of individuals whose holy qualities ultimately transcend any system of rules and principles and any human authority structure. In its pure form, this approach takes on an antinomian character which can hardly be squared with the worldview of the Mishnah and its creators. However, elements of such a perspective may inform at least certain aspects of the Mishnah and its storytelling. As we have seen, individual Mishnaic exempla at times stand in conflict with the norms and positions that are presented in a given Mishnaic passage. We must at least consider the possibility that these exempla draw their authority at least to some degree from the special status of the individual exemplar, independent of any conceptual or political structure.

Exempla and the Boundaries of Who Is a Rabbi

In the remainder of this chapter we will examine two sets of texts: the exempla found in the second chapter of *Sukkah* and the story of Honi Hame'agel in *Ta'anit* 3:8. We will read both in terms of the various models of rabbinic authority that we have just discussed: being *in* authority versus being *an* authority, and naturalistic versus miraculous or revelatory notions of authority. These stories explore the tensions and ambiguities created by these competing models of authority as they struggle to define the nature and authority of the rabbi as exemplar.

Sukkah 2

The first two chapters of *Sukkah* deal with the commandment to dwell in *sukkot* (singular *sukkah*), temporary dwellings, during the festival of the same name. Chapter 1 focuses on the requirements for the physical structure of the sukkah: the need for walls of the requisite dimensions and for a ceiling made of *sekhakh*—fresh branches and other vegetable matter. Chapter 2 continues some of these discussions but primarily focuses on the requirements of the individual to dwell in the sukkah during the festival, specifically the need to eat and sleep there. Chapter 2 of *Sukkah* contains what is probably the densest concentration of exempla narratives in the entire Mishnah. In each narrative, rabbis display appropriate (and in some cases inappropriate) behavior, both inside and outside of the sukkah.[25]

The exempla in this chapter present instances in which the requirement to eat or sleep in the sukkah is not clear or in which it is fulfilled in dubious manner. The exemplar's behavior helps to determine whether these situations or actions fall within, or beyond, the bounds of the requirements of the laws of the sukkah. As is common in the Mishnah's use of narrative legal forms, the Mishnah here focuses on marginal cases in order to help define the shape of more general categories.[26]

These exempla also explore a different type of borderline case: individuals whose status places them on the margin of the category of rabbis or halakhic exemplars. In some of these stories these individuals and their actions are subjected to scrutiny, in an attempt to define the boundaries of who is and is not a rabbi.

These two definitional agendas coalesce in the question of who is obligated to dwell in the sukkah. This question is crucial for defining the extent of the requirements of the sukkah. It also sets the outside border for the qualifications for the halakhic exemplar by defining the limits of the community of individuals bound by the halakhah. If one is not obligated to follow the commandments, one presumably cannot be a role model for their proper observance to those who are obligated. On several occasions, the exempla in this chapter engage the question of the boundary of obligation as it pertains both to the commandment to dwell in the sukkah and to the identity of the exemplar.

I will not examine these exempla in the order in which they appear in the Mishnah. Rather, I will present them in ascending order of complexity with regard to the various boundary issues that I have outlined. I begin with a group of exempla found in the middle of the chapter, in paragraph 5.

אוֹכְלִים וְשׁוֹתִים עֲרָיֵי חוּץ לַסּוּכָּה

מַעֲשֶׂה שֶׁהֵבִיאוּ לִפְנֵי[27] רַבָּן יוֹחָנָן בֶּן זַכַּאי
לִטְעוֹם אֶת הַתַּבְשִׁיל
וּלְרַבָּן גַּמְלִיאֵ׳ שְׁתֵּי כוֹתָבוֹת וּדְלִי שֶׁלְּמַיִם
אָמְרוּ הַעֲלוּם לַסּוּכָּה
וּכְשֶׁנָּתְנוּ לוֹ לְרִ׳ צָדוֹק
אוֹכֵל פָּחוּת מִכַּבֵּיצָה
נְטָלוֹ בַּמַּפָּא וַאֲכָלוֹ חוּץ לַסּוּכָּה
וְלֹא בֵּירַךְ אַחֲרָיו

Casual eating and drinking are permitted outside the sukkah.

It once happened that they brought before R. Yohanan b. Zakkai
cooked food to taste,
and to R. Gamliel two dates and a pail of water.
They said, "Bring them up to the sukkah."
When they gave to R. Zadok
food less than the bulk of an egg,

he took it in a towel, ate it outside the sukkah,
and did not say the benediction after it.

The paragraph preceding this ends with an apodictic statement of a general principal: it is permissible to eat a "temporary meal," i.e., a snack, outside of the sukkah. This statement establishes the minimum boundary for the requirement to eat in the sukkah as being a "permanent" meal. This rule would in turn appear to be an application of a broader principle, presented at the end of the chapter in paragraph 9: "All seven days (of the holiday) a man makes his sukkah [a] permanent (*qev'a*) abode, and his house [a] temporary (*'arai*) abode."

Section five then presents a series of exempla that relate to this rule. The first two are presented as a unit. The Mishnah uses a single verb phrase "they brought" to present two separate instances in which two different rabbis, R. Yohanan b. Zakkai and R. Gamliel, were presented with various small morsels of food, a taste of a cooked dish in one instance and a pair of dates and a pail of water in the other. Both rabbis are recorded as having the same response: "Bring them up to the sukkah." This distinctive method of formulation creates a hybrid form that combines aspects of the full-fledged exemplum story with that of the repeated narrative. In so doing, the Mishnah achieves the best of both rhetorical worlds. On the one hand, the Mishnah roots the ruling in a concrete, onetime event; on the other hand, it demonstrates the validity of the practice portrayed by showing that it was not an isolated incident but a behavior repeated by several prominent rabbis.

To this pair of exempla the Mishnah then adds a third exemplum involving R. Zadok. This narrative is much more straightforward in that it presents a single chain of events involving only one rabbi. In contrast to R. Yohanan and R. Gamliel, R. Zadok readily eats a small amount of food outside of the sukkah.

As is often the case in reading the Mishnah, the difficult aspect of this passage is establishing the relationship between it parts. Both the opening apodictic statement and closing exempla establish the permissibility of eating a snack outside of the sukkah. How do these statements relate to the middle part of the passage, which records that both R. Gamliel and R. Yohanan insisted on eating even a small amount of food inside the sukkah?

One possibility is the harmonistic reading suggested by the Bavli.[28] The Bavli argues that R. Gamliel and R. Yohanan's actions do not reflect a legal requirement but rather a stringent practice on their part. Thus, there is no conflict between their actions and the law expressed in the lines preceding and following this passage in the Mishnah. The law permitting eating outside the sukkah remains in place. R. Gamliel and R. Yohanan emerge not as exemplars of common practice for all to follow but as members of spiritual and halakhic elite whose "ascetic" behavior testifies to their fitness to possess halakhic authority and inspires others to remain committed to the law.

It is also possible to read the exempla of R. Gamliel and R. Yohanan as challenging the notion that eating snacks outside of the sukkah is permissible.

If this is the case, the Mishnah presents us with two conflicting opinions. The text itself gives us no guidance as to which position is normative. We might argue that R. Yohanan b. Zakkai and R. Gamliel, the two leading figures of the first generation of Tannaim, define the norm in this case. They were *in* authority, and hence their actions define the law despite the fact that they appear to conflict with the Mishnah's apodictic formulation. Alternatively, the case could be made that even the greatest exemplars are not above the law. It is precisely the relatively obscure R. Zadok whose actions define normative practice because they conform to the anonymous rule set down by the Mishnah. In this reading, R. Yohanan and R. Gamliel's deeds need to be interpreted as incorrect and rejected by the Mishnah. R. Zadok's position as *an* authority, who knows the rules and principles which define the law, ultimately triumphs.

The Mishnah provides little guidance as to how evaluate the actions presented in these exempla. Rather it seems more interested bringing these texts into dialog with each other and raising questions than with presenting a conclusive answer either about eating outside of the sukkah or about larger issues of rabbinic authority.

A similar set of issues is raised later on in the chapter in paragraph 8:

נָשִׁים וַעֲבָדִים וּקְטַנִּים[29]
פְּטוּרִים מִן הַסּוּכָּה
וְכָל קָטָן שֶׁאֵינוּ צָרִיךְ לְאִמּוֹ
חַיָּב בַּסּוּכָּה
מַעֲשֶׂה שֶׁיָּלְדָה כַלָּתוֹ שֶׁלְשַׁמַּי הַזָּקֵן
וּפִחַת[30] אֶת הַמַּעֲזֵיבָה
וְסִכֵּךְ עַל גַּבֵּי הַמִּטָּה בִּשְׁבִיל הַקָּטָן

Women, slaves, and minors
are free from the obligation of sukkah.
Any minor who is not dependent on his mother
is bound by the law of sukkah.
It once happened that the daughter-in-law of Shammai the elder gave birth,
and [Shammai] broke away the plaster of the roof
and put sukkah covering over the bed for the sake of the child.

This Mishnah contains three apparently contradictory statements regarding the requirement of a minor to dwell in the sukkah. The first line unequivocally declares that minors, like slaves and women, are exempt from the sukkah. However, the next line states that some minors, those who are independent of their mothers, are in fact obligated to dwell in the sukkah. Finally, we are presented with an exemplum in which Shammai arranges for his newborn grandson to eat and sleep in a sukkah, suggesting that even the smallest infant is obligated to dwell in the sukkah. Once again, the Mishnah leaves us with no guidance regarding the relationship between these positions.[31]

Our primary concern is with last part of the passage, the exemplum, which appears to require even newborns to dwell in the sukkah. The most obvious way to reconcile this conflict with the previous statements in the Mishnah is to presume that Shammai's position expressed in the exemplum is nonnormative. According to conventional understandings of the Mishnah, the reader is expected to know that when confronted with a position attributed to Shammai or his followers that conflicts with another stated ruling, the Shammaite position is to be discounted.[32] If this is the case, Shammai holds a rather marginal, if not paradoxical, position as an exemplar in our Mishnah. On the one hand, Shammai is one of the founding sages of the Pharisaic movement, whose words and deeds are worthy of being recorded in the Mishnah and other rabbinic documents. He is *an* authority whose mastery of the halakhah is undisputed. He further enjoys the aura of authority and even holiness granted to those individuals who are privileged to be cited in the Mishnah. Yet Shammai and his followers are not *in* a position of authority within the larger social and political structure reflected in the Mishnah. Shammaite rulings and actions are not sources of practical law. Indeed, they may function primarily as negative authorities, defining what is *not* the law.

Shammai's marginal status may be reinforced by our exemplum. Shammai is seen cutting a hole in his ceiling in order to create a sukkah for his newborn grandson. It is difficult to know how a reader in the time of the Mishnah would have responded to such a report.[33] However, it seems reasonable to assume that this story presents a rather extreme implementation of an extreme halakhic position. The exemplum may be read as an almost satirical portrayal of Shammai and his followers as extremists who go to absurd lengths to implement their radical views.

It is, however, not necessary to read this passage as rejecting Shammai's actions outright. As in previous cases, Shammai's actions may not reflect the requirements of the law but rather his personal stringency. If this is the case, Shammai's construction work might be seen as casting a positive light on the sage, showing the extent of his commitment to fulfilling the law in the most complete manner possible. According to this reading, the story is akin to accounts of Christian saints who went to great lengths to improve themselves spiritually.

Finally, a compromise reading of the exemplum might see the story as neither ridicule nor hagiography but rather as a sort chria. Cutting a hole in the roof for the sake of a baby might be understood as the eccentric act of a sage, which serves to make his teaching more memorable, just as we find in narratives about Greco-Roman wise men. However we understand this narrative, as satire, hagiography, or memorable rhetoric, Shammai appears as a legitimate sage who is not quite mainstream.

The remaining exemplars and exempla in this chapter might also be considered marginal, in more ways than one. Like the story about Shammai, these narratives portray figures whose status as exemplars is ambiguous. Furthermore, the exempla themselves are structurally heterogeneous. They represent a distinctive genre, combining elements of the exempla with elements of the case story. Because the status of the actors as exemplars in the following narratives is unclear, their actions need to be evaluated by an established rabbinic authority. This makes these texts akin to case stories in which rabbis also evaluate the halakhic status of a situation which is presented to them. By using this hybrid genre, the Mishnah calls attention to the marginal and problematic position of the individuals that it portrays.

Chapter 2 opens with a pair of such quasi-exempla:

הַיָּשֵׁן תַּחַת הַמִּטָּה ל'א יָצָא יְדֵי חוֹבָתוֹ
אָמַ' ר' יְהוּדָה
נוֹהֲגִין הָיִינוּ וִישֵׁנִים תַּחַת הַמִּטּוֹת לִפְנֵי הַזְּקֵנִים[34]
אָמַ' ר' שִׁמְעוֹן
מַעֲשֶׂה בְטָבִי[35] עַבְדּוֹ שֶׁלְּרַבָּן גַּמְלִיאֵ'
שֶׁהָיָה יָשֵׁן תַּחַת הַמִּטָּה
אָמַ' רַבָּן גַּמְלִיאֵ' לַזְּקֵנִים
רְאִיתֶם טָבִי עַבְדִּי שֶׁהוּא תַלְמִיד חֲכָמִ'[36]
וְיוֹדֵעַ שֶׁעֲבָדִים פְּטוּרִים מִן הַסּוּכָּה
וְיָשֵׁן לוֹ תַחַת הַמִּטָּה
לְפִי[37] דַרְכֵּינוּ לָמַדְנוּ
שֶׁהַיָּשֵׁן תַּחַת הַמִּטָּה לֹא יָצָא יְדֵי חוֹבָתוֹ

He who sleeps under a bed in the sukkah has not fulfilled his obligation.
R. Judah stated,
We were accustomed to sleep under a bed in the presence of the elders.
R. Simeon said,
It happened that Tevi, the slave of R. Gamliel,
used to sleep under a bed.
R. Gamliel said to the elders,
Have you seen Tevi my slave, who is a scholar
and knows that slaves are exempt from [the law of] a sukkah,
therefore he sleeps under the bed.
Incidentally we learn [from this story]
that he who sleeps under a bed has not fulfilled his obligation.

The Mishnah begins with a casuistic formulation of general rule: A person does not fulfill his obligation to sleep in the sukkah if he sleeps under a bed.[38] The Mishnah then presents two exempla, one that contradicts this ruling and another that confirms it. Both accounts present individuals who are almost, but not quite, qualified to be an exemplar. These figures appear in a marginal position within the sukkah, physically, socially, and halakhically.

The first exemplum is not a story but a repeated event, in which R. Judah testifies that he and his colleagues regularly slept under beds in the sukkah in the presence of the elders. In some sense, R. Judah is the exemplar in this exemplum. It is on the basis of his actions and those of his fellows that he determines that sleeping under a bed in the sukkah is permitted. R. Judah is a sage whose positions are often cited in the Mishnah. There is no reason per se why his action cannot be exemplary.[39] However, his position as an exemplar in this account is deficient in several ways. First, as narrator, R. Judah cannot point to his own behavior as proof of his own position. He must find support for his opinion in the deeds of others. Second, the fact that R. Judah refers to the "elders" as a distinct group implies that he and his fellows were not themselves elders at the time the events took place. They were apparently students at the time. These not-yet-rabbis inhabit a liminal position in the rabbinic hierarchy, as is exhibited by their social position in the sukkah: they occupy the same sukkah as the elders, yet they sleep in a subservient position under the beds.

As a result of their marginal position, lacking the social status and perhaps the knowledge to serve as exemplars, R. Judah and his colleagues require the approval of the elders in order for their behavior to achieve exemplary status. Unlike in traditional case stories, the rabbis here do not issue a ruling. Rather, R. Judah argues from the silence of the rabbis. The elders' passivity in this narrative serves to highlight R. Judah's actions. Indeed, this entire exemplum is dependent on R. Judah and his marginal status. Though it is permitted according to this opinion, no true rabbi would ever sleep under a bed in a sukkah, as it would be beneath his social status. If there is a bed in a sukkah, the rabbi's place is on the bed, not under it.

The second exemplum similarly features a liminal figure who demonstrates the halakhic status of sleeping in that marginal position in the sukkah, under the bed. Like R. Judah, Tevi is not a member of the rabbinic elite. This is first and foremost because of his social status; he is a slave. It is only after his behavior gains official rabbinic sanction, in this case from R. Gamliel, that his actions are confirmed as exemplary. Tevi's actions demonstrate that sleeping under a bed does not constitute dwelling in the sukkah, a position opposed to that of R. Judah. Thus Tevi serves as an exemplar both because of and despite the fact that he is a slave. By sleeping under the bed in the sukkah, Tevi applies his knowledge of two distinct halakhic rulings: that sleeping under a bed in the sukkah is unacceptable, and that, as a slave, he is exempt from the obligation of the sukkah and it is therefore permissible for him to sleep under the bed. His appropriate behavior is confirmed by R. Gamliel's acclamation.

The Tevi story is far more complex than the exemplum featuring R. Judah. Here is yet another case in which a previously circulating "aggadic" story has been appropriated for use in a halakhic argument. The story is told in the Mishnah by R. Simeon. R. Simeon lived several generations after R. Gamliel and does not claim to have been an eyewitness to the events. He is repeating a story he has heard from others. Unlike most narrators, R. Simeon offers his own commentary at the end of the story. He comments, "Incidentally we learn that he who sleeps under a bed has not fulfilled his obligation."[40] R. Simeon's use of the term "incidentally" emphasizes that this lesson was not the initial point of the story. Indeed, the principle that sleeping under a bed in the sukkah is not permitted is taken for granted in the story and never mentioned explicitly. Like the baraita about R. Tarfon's Sabbath journey, this story was not initially told as a halakhic narrative. Rather, R. Simeon appropriated this story, highlighting its latent halakhic content, in order to use it as a refutation of the position of R. Judah.

The original focus of the narrative was thus apparently more aggadic in nature. The story stresses the tension between Tevi's personal traits and knowledge on the one hand and his social status on the other. It is Tevi's unique and paradoxical position as both a slave and a beloved disciple of R. Gamliel that generates this conflict. Slaves are exempt or disqualified from many of the commandments because they are not full-fledged members of the halakhic community. As such, a slave's social status would normally prevent him from becoming a rabbi or an exemplar of halakhic practice. Furthermore, unlike the baby boy in the story of Shammai and R. Judah in the previous exemplum, Tevi's exclusion from full participation in the world of the rabbis and their halakhah is permanent. Though he might in the future be freed, the expectation is that he will remain a slave for the rest of his life. He is not expected to grow into a halakhic adult or an elder.

Tevi's position within the sukkah emphasizes his problematic status in rabbinic society. An ordinary slave who did not have a special relationship with the rabbis or their teaching would have slept in his usual quarters, outside the sukkah. Tevi desires to be inside the sukkah, celebrating the holiday with the rabbis, yet his commitment to the halakhah is most clearly displayed by his acknowledgment of his inferior position within it. Tevi takes up a position under the bed, emphasizing both his low social position and his ultimate exclusion from the requirement to sleep in the sukkah.[41]

R. Gamliel's response to Tevi's behavior further highlights Tevi's paradoxical status. First, R. Gamliel moves him from the margins of the rabbinic world to its center. R. Gamliel calls on the elders to focus their attention on Tevi, who previously had been hidden under a bed. R. Gamliel expresses his affection and admiration for Tevi by declaring him to be a *talmid hakhamim*, a true member of the rabbinic community. On the one hand, R. Gamliel details Tevi's knowledge and behavior that make him worthy of this accolade. At the same time, R. Gamliel also emphasizes that Tevi's status as a slave. One might conclude that were Tevi not a slave, his knowledge and commitment would not have been worthy of note.

The paradox of Tevi emphasizes the tension between competing demands for knowledge and social status within the rabbinic authoritative framework. Being a slave permanently marginalizes a person in the rabbinic community, even if his knowledge should entitle him to full membership.

The remaining exemplum in this chapter of the Mishnah likewise involves an individual whose exemplary status is unclear and whose actions need the confirmation of other rabbis before they can be considered exemplary. In this story, we encounter an individual whose status would at first appear to be uncomplicated. He is introduced as a full-fledged rabbi, whose conduct might be used as a legal precedent. As the story develops, however, it emerges that this rabbi's actions may be subject to review by other rabbis who appear to be his disciples. Paragraph 7 reads as follows:

מִי שֶׁהָיָה רֹאשׁוֹ וְרוּבּוֹ בַּסּוּכָּה
וְשׁוּלְחָנוֹ בְּתוֹךְ הַבַּיִת
בֵּית שַׁמַּאי פּוֹסְלִין
וּבֵית הִלֵּל מַכְשִׁירִין[42]
אָמְרוּ בֵית הִלֵּל לְבֵית שַׁמַּאי
[43]מַעֲשֶׂה שֶׁהָלְכוּ זִקְנֵי בֵית שַׁמַּאי וְזִקְנֵי בֵית הִלֵּל
לְבַקֵּר אֶת יוֹחָנָן בֶּן הַחוֹרוֹנִי[44] וּמְצָאוּהוּ
רֹאשׁוֹ וְרוּבּוֹ בַּסּוּכָּה
וְשׁוּלְחָנוֹ בְּתוֹךְ הַבַּיִת[45]
אָמְרוּ לָהֶם בֵּית שַׁמַּאי מִשָּׁם רְאָיָה
אַף הֵן אָמְרוּ לוֹ
אִם כָּךְ[46] הָיְתָה נוֹהֵג
לֹא קִיַּימְתָּה מִצְוַת סוּכָּה מִיָּמֶיךָ

> If a man's head and the greater part of his body were within the sukkah
> and his table within the house.
> The school of Shammai declare it invalid
> and the school of Hillel declare it valid.
> The school of Hillel said to the school of Shammai,
> It happened that the elders of the school of Shammai and the elders of the school of Hillel went
> to visit Yohanan b. Hahoroni and found him
> with his head and the greater part of his body within the sukkah
> and his table within the house,
> the school of Shammai answered, is that a proof?
> Indeed, they said to him,
> if you have so conducted yourself,
> you have never in your life fulfilled the law of the sukkah.

The Mishnah opens with a casuistic formulation that has a double apodosis. The protasis establishes a case in which a person sits with his head and the majority of his body in the sukkah, but with his table and the rest of his body inside the house. Once again, the Mishnah presents us with a marginal case. This time the person in question literally sits on the boundary line of the sukkah. The Mishnah presents two alternative endings to the narrative. According to the school of Shammai, the man does not fulfill the requirements for sitting in a sukkah. According to the school of Hillel, he does.

This text now takes a sudden narrative turn as the school of Hillel addresses the school of Shammai, initiating what is presumably a one-time conversation. The school of Hillel presents an exemplum: The elders of both schools once paid a visit to Yohanan ben Hahoroni on Sukkot. They found him "sitting with his head and the majority of his body in his sukkah and his table inside the house." Since this phrase is taken word-for-word from the protasis of the initial casuistic formulation, it is assumed that Yohanan's position precisely fits the criteria established in that case. Since Yohanan is an exemplar, the fact that he was observed in this position implies that it is permissible and that the school of Hillel is correct. The very fact that Yohanan was received a joint visit of the elders of both schools suggests that even the school of Shammai held him in high esteem, further boosting his status as an exemplar.[47] The presence of the elders of the school of Shammai also lends credibility to the account of the school of Hillel, by arguing that representatives of the school of Shammai also witnessed the events.

The school of Shammai responds with a counter-narrative that provides a new context for the events described. According to the Shammaite version, their elders in fact protested Yohanan's actions, declaring that if this was his regular practice, he never fulfilled the obligation to sit in the sukkah in his entire life. The school of Shammai's counter-narrative does not challenge the school of Hillel's description of Yohanan's behavior. Instead, it challenges the underlying assumption of the school of Hillel's account, that Yohanan is an authoritative exemplar whose deeds define normative practice. For the school of Shammai, Yohanan has a rather ambiguous status as a sage. He is worthy of respect as a sage, but his behavior does not define the norm. Indeed, the Shammaites find it perfectly acceptable to publicly berate Yohanan for his practices.

This reading is based on the version found in MS Kaufmann and other manuscripts. Most printed editions add an additional sentence to the school of Hillel's version of the story. In those texts, Hillel concludes by stating that the elders of the school of Shammai "did not say anything to him." In this version, not even the school of Hillel argues that Yohanan is an authoritative exemplar. They too agree that while he is to be respected, his deeds cannot in and of themselves refute the position of the school of Shammai. Like the young R. Judah and Tevi the slave, Yohanan's deeds are only significant because they have been endorsed by established rabbis. It is the tacit endorsement of the elders of the school of Shammai that is of ultimate significance to the Hillelite argument.

In the version of the printed editions, the school of Shammai's counter-narrative does not merely add to the school of Hillel's narrative, it contradicts it outright. They dispute the claim that their elders were silent. The fact that each side presents its own mutually exclusive narrative to support its position raises serious questions about the reliability of these narrators in the first place.

The Mishnah does not explain why it is that Yohanan ben Hahoroni has the status as of a quasi-rabbi, whose behavior is not considered exemplary. However, the Tosefta, in a passage apparently meant to comment on our Mishnah, tells a story about Yohanan ben Hahoroni relating how he once practiced according to the school of Hillel with regard to a problem of ritual impurity. The Tosefta goes on to explain that "even though he was one of the students of the school of Shammai, he acted in accordance with the school of Hillel."[48] The fact that R. Yohanan had a foot in both schools would explain why he was revered by both factions, while his adoption of Hillelite practice would explain why the elders of the school of Shammai did not see his behavior as reflecting a binding norm.

There is one more story in this chapter of *Sukkah*. It does not fit the criteria of the exemplum nor any of the other genres of Mishnaic stories that we have described. Nevertheless, like the other stories in this chapter it directly engages the issue of the authority that underlies the halakhah. It is one of two stories in the Mishnah that can be classified under the category of *mashal* (pl. *meshalim*), or parable. Though the *mashal* is exceedingly rare in the Mishnah, it is one of the most important narrative forms in rabbinic literature in general. The absence of *meshalim* in the Mishnah can be explained by two of the defining features of the *mashal*. First, *meshalim* are generally used as an exegetical tool. The Mishnah, unlike Midrashic works, rarely engages in biblical exegesis and hence has limited opportunities to deploy *meshalim*. Furthermore, *meshalim* are frequently used to discuss theological issues. The relationship between people and God is compared to human relationships such as those between a king and his subjects, a father and his child, and a master and his slave.[49] While in the rabbinic view halakhah is ultimately underwritten by divine command, the details of halakhic discourse do not generally focus on theological issues, focusing instead on more mundane elements of the human relationship with the natural world. For example, the second chapter of *Sukkah* focuses on man's relationship with his environment as structured by the sukkah. Occasionally, however, the Mishnah turns its attention to theological issues, such as in the final paragraph of this chapter:

יָרְדוּ גְשָׁמִים מֵאֵימָתַי וּ[50]מֻתָּר לְפַנּוֹת
מִשֶּׁתִּסְרַח הַמִּקְפָּה
מוֹשְׁלִים אוֹתוֹ מָשָׁל[51] לְמָה הַדָּבָר דּוֹמֶה
לְעֶבֶד שֶׁבָּא לִמְזוֹג[52] לְקוֹנָיו[53]
וְשָׁפַךְ הַקִּיתוֹן עַל פָּנָיו

When rain falls, when is it permitted to leave [the sukkah]?
When the porridge begins to spoil.

A *mashal*. To what may it be compared?
To a slave who comes to mix wine for his master
and he spills the ladle in [the slave's] face.

One last time in this chapter, the Mishnah seeks to identify the line which defines the requirement to sit in the sukkah. This time it is the point at which rain exempts one from sitting in the sukkah. The Mishnah establishes a rule that rain that is severe enough to render the porridge inedible exempts one from sitting in the sukkah.

The Mishnah then presents its *mashal*. It describes a situation in which a slave comes to the dinner table to mix water into the diner's wine, as was the custom in those days. However, instead of allowing the slave to pour his cup, the master takes the ladle and spills it in his face, as if to say, "I have no desire for your services."[54] The *mashal* refers to a situation in which the rain prevents a person from sitting in the sukkah. It argues that such a situation needs to be understood as a rebuke from God, which suggests that we are somehow unworthy of engaging in the divine service.

This *mashal* recontextualizes both the practice of sitting in the sukkah and the notions of rabbinic authority that have been so central to this chapter. In most of the Mishnah, divine authority is present only in the implicit master narrative, which roots the Mishnah's laws in a tradition going back to the theophany at Sinai. On a day-to-day level, this relationship is mediated by the rabbis and their halakhah, which is formulated primarily as regulating an individual's relationships with the human and natural worlds. The Mishnah has described the requirement of sitting in the sukkah in terms of walls and branches and the people who sit inside them. Now the Mishnah considers sitting in the sukkah as a way of serving God. The *mashal* introduces a new authority structure between God and man that bypasses the rabbinic intermediary. This *mashal* emphasizes that each and every Jew has a direct relationship with God through his performance of the divine commands. God communicates directly with his people by sending rain, which, in this case, is a sign of divine displeasure. The *mashal* reminds the reader that rabbinic authority is not an end in and of itself but must be considered as a by-product of the covenantal relationship between God and Israel.

Honi Hameʿagel: *Taanit* 3:8

The story of Honi Hameʿagel, the final text that we shall deal with in this chapter, also deals directly with divine authority and considers its relationship to human rabbinic authority. It too contains a *mashal* and presents God as using rain to communicate with his people.

This story is perhaps the most famous and most analyzed story in the entire Mishnah. Given the volume of critical writing on this story, it is not my purpose here to present a comprehensive reading of the story. Rather, I will focus on the manner in which this story and the character of Honi that it portrays relate to the genre of the exemplum and the figure of the exemplar, respectively. As in the previous readings, I will give special attention to the way in which the Mishnah uses the exemplum form as a tool for exploring the boundaries of rabbinic authority. In particular, I will show how this story directly confronts the tension between what we have called "rational" and "supernatural" conceptions of rabbinic authority. We will then go on to explore the processes whereby this story was transmitted and took the form we find in the Mishnah.

The main part of the story reads as follows:

עַל[55] כָּל צָרָה[56] שֶׁתָּבוֹא עַל הַצִּיבּוּר

מַתְרִיעִים עָלֶיהָ

חוּץ מֵרוֹב גְּשָׁמִים

מַעֲשֶׂה שֶׁאָמְרוּ לְחוּנִי[57] הַמְעַגֵּל

הִתְפַּלֵּל שֶׁיֵּרְדוּ גְשָׁמִים

אָמַ' לָהֶם צְאוּ וְהַכְנִיסוּ תַּנּוּרֵי פְסָחִים

בִּשְׁבִיל שֶׁלֹּא יִמַּקּוּ

וְהִתְפַּלֵּל[58] וְלֹא יָרְדוּ גְשָׁמִים[59]

עָג עוּגָה וְעָמַד בְּתוֹכָהּ

וְאָמַ'

רִבּוֹנוֹ שֶׁלְּעוֹלָם[60]

בָּנֶיךָ שָׂמוּ פְנֵיהֶם עָלַי

שֶׁאֲנִי כְבֶן בַּיִת לְפָנֶיךָ

נִשְׁבָּע אֲנִי בְשִׁמְךָ הַגָּדוֹל שֶׁאֵינִי זָז מִיכָּן

עַל[61] שֶׁתְּרַחֵם עַל בָּנֶיךָ

הִתְחִילוּ הַגְּשָׁמִים מְנַטְּפִים

אָמַ' לֹא כָךְ שָׁאַלְתִּי אֶלָּא

גִּשְׁמֵי בוֹרוֹת שִׁיחִים וּמְעָרוֹת

יָרְדוּ[62] בְזַעַף

אָמַ' לֹא כָךְ שָׁאַלְתִּי

אֶלָּא גִשְׁמֵי רָצוֹן בְּרָכָה וּנְדָבָה

יָרְדוּ כְתִיקְנָן

עַד שֶׁעָלוּ יִשְׂרָאֵ' מִירוּשָׁ' לְהַר הַבַּיִת

מִפְּנֵי הַגְּשָׁמִים

אָמַ' לוֹ

כְּשֵׁם שֶׁהִתְפַּלַּלְתָּה[63] עֲלֵיהֶם שֶׁיֵּרְדוּ

כָּךְ הִתְפַּלֵּל שֶׁיֵּלְכוּ לָהֶם

אָמַ' לָהֶם

צְאוּ וּרְאוּ אִם נִמְחַת אֶבֶן הַ[64]טּוֹעִים

On any calamity that befalls the community,
we cry out,
except for excessive rains

It happened that the people said to Honi the circle drawer,
Pray for rain to fall.
He replied,
Go and brings in the ovens for the paschal offering
so that they do not dissolve.
He prayed and no rain fell.
He drew a circle and stood within it
and exclaimed,
Master of the Universe,
thy children have turned to me
because I am like a member of thy household;
I swear by thy great name that I will not move from here
until thou hast mercy upon thy children.
Rain then began to drip.
He said: It is not for this that I have prayed
but for rain [to fill] cisterns, ditches, and caves.
The rain then began to come down with great force.
He said: It is not for this that I have prayed
but for rain of benevolence, blessing, and bounty.
Rain then fell in the normal way
until the Israelites went up from Jerusalem to the Temple Mount
[for shelter] because of the rain.
They came and said to him:
In the same way as you have prayed for [the rain] to fall,
pray [now] for the rain to cease.
He replied to them:
Go and see if the Stone of Claimants has been washed away.

Until this point, the story reads like an exemplum. The passage opens with a pair of casuistically formulated rules regarding the calling of full-scale fast days.[65] The Mishnah teaches that days of fasting and prayer are to be declared in response to "any distress that may befall the community." The sole exception to this rule is a case of "too much rain." The story that follows illustrates circumstances in which Honi Hameʿagel refused to pray for a cessation of rain in a case of excessive precipitation. However, even at this point, this is clearly not a typical exemplum.

The first unusual aspect is the figure of Honi. He does not fit the standard image of a rabbinic scholar. He is not referred to as a rabbi, and nowhere in rabbinic literature is he quoted as a having an opinion on any halakhic matter.[66] Honi does not belong to the mainstream class of rabbis. He belongs to the group known as *hasidim* or *anshei maʿaseh*.[67] These individuals were not known for their knowledge of rabbinic law; tracing their spiritual lineage back to the biblical prophets, they claimed a special, personal relationship with God based on the wondrous efficacy of their prayers and other miraculous abilities. These *hasidim* are widely viewed as the Jewish expression of the phenomena of charismatic pagan and Christian miracle workers mentioned earlier in this chapter.[68]

Hasidim appear to have had a complex relationship with the Pharisaic and rabbinic establishments of their times. They represented a parallel, and at times competing, moral and spiritual path.[69] *Hasidim* are rarely discussed in the Mishnah. The halakhah's fundamental concern is with individuals' relationships with each other, themselves, and their empirical environments. It does not show much interest in those who claim direct relationships with God and supernatural abilities. An important exception to this tendency is the discussions of the laws regarding prayer. These laws do indeed regulate a Jew's direct relationship with his Creator. To the extent that the rabbis presume that such prayers will at least sometimes be answered, the discussion of prayer also involves God's relationship with his people. It is therefore hardly surprising that it is precisely in tractates *Berakhot* and *Ta'anit*, the two tractates of the Mishnah that deal with prayer, that we find several references to the *hasidim* and their deeds.[70] The editors of the Mishnah may not have viewed the *hasidim* as relevant exemplars in most areas of halakhah, but given the *hasidim*'s virtuosity at prayer, the Mishnaic editors did see the *hasidim*'s prayer practices as worthy of emulation.[71] By portraying Honi as an exemplar for proper prayer procedure, the Mishnah integrates this *hasid*, his activities, and the form of charismatic authority that he represents into a framework of normative rabbinic practices.

This exemplum is also distinguished by its stylistic features. By the standards of Mishnaic stories it is extremely long and well crafted. The narrator carefully builds up suspense through Honi's repeated prayers to God, until Honi finally gets the sort of rain he wants. The level of detail in this story far exceeds that which would be necessary to illustrate the principle of not praying for excessive rain. The Mishnaic narrator here has embraced a representative style, drawing the reader into a developed narrative world that surrounds and ostensibly reinforces the main halakhic point of the story. Given its parenthetical halakhic content, this narrative was likely appropriated from a non-halakhic context. Originally this story was likely meant to celebrate the deeds of this great holy man, and was only later used to teach the law prohibiting prayer for excessive rain.

It is precisely this added detail that potentially undermines the straightforward halakhic message of the story and Honi's status as an exemplar worthy of emulation. The initial ruling at the start of this passage is that excessive rain is the one crisis for which one does not declare fasting and prayer. No reason is given for this ruling. Presumably, it is because rain in its proper time was seen as a sign of unmitigated divine blessing. Furthermore, given the huge effort given to praying for rain during the winter described in detail in *Ta'anit*, it would simply be inappropriate to then turn around and complain to God that he had given too much.[72] Any damage caused by excessive rain would surely be compensated by the benefits of having sufficient water for farming and drinking.[73]

The story of Honi up to this point would appear to be a particularly extreme expression of this principle. After extensive argument with God, Honi finally succeeds in getting God to send exactly the type of rain that the people need, rain that is sufficient to fill the "cisterns, ditches, and caves" and ensure sufficient water supplies for the coming year, but that also comes down gently enough to be "rain of benevolence, blessing, and bounty." Later, as this rain continues, it too proceeds to cause significant damage. The entire city of Jerusalem is flooded, forcing the people to take refuge in the high ground of the Temple Mount. The people quite understandably ask Honi to pray for the rain to stop. Honi refuses without giving a reason. He merely says, "Go and see if the Stone of Claimants has been washed away." (The Stone of Claimants" apparently marked a high point on the local terrain.) Honi is indicating that so long as the flood is not complete, he will not pray for it to stop.

If we read this story as a straightforward exemplum meant to illustrate the principle at the beginning of the Mishnah, it is clear that Honi is saying that he is bound by the prohibition against praying for the cessation of rain.[74] The story comes to teach us just how serious this prohibition is. Nevertheless, it seems reasonable to wonder whether Honi's application of this principle goes too far. Do the rabbis really forbid praying for the cessation of rain in such extreme circumstances? Is rain that floods the entire city of Jerusalem truly a blessing?[75] These questions raise further issues with regard to the nature and extent of Honi's abilities. At first, it seems as if Honi is able to get exactly what he wants from God through dogged determination and sheer chutzpah. But as Honi declines to try and stop the rain, one wonders who has gotten the better of whom. Has Honi successfully argued and cajoled God into acceding to his demands, or has God consistently answered Honi's prayers only in the most literal manner, ensuring that, in any event, disaster will ensue. Perhaps, like the sorcerer's apprentice, Honi is no match for the forces he has unleashed.[76]

These questions about the true nature of Honi and his actions are further developed in the closing scene of the story, in which Simeon ben Shetah responds to the events.

שָׁלַח לוֹ שִׁמְעוֹן בֶּן שָׁטָח אָמַ'[77] לוֹ
צָרִיךְ אַתָּה לְנַדּוֹת[78]
אֲבָל מָה אֶעֱשֶׂה לָךְ
וְאַתָּה[79] מִתְחַטֵּא לִפְנֵי הַמָּקוֹם
כְּבֵן שֶׁהוּא מִתְחַטֵּא לְאָבִיו[80] וְעוֹשֶׂה לוֹ רְצוֹנוֹ
וְעָלֶיךָ הַכָּתוּב אוֹמ'
יִשְׂמַח אָבִיךָ וְאִמֶּךָ וְתָגֵל יוֹלַדְתֶּךָ

Thereupon Simeon b. Shetah sent to him saying:
You should be placed under the ban,
but what can I do unto you?

You who importune God,
as a son that importunes his father and he accedes to his request;
of you scripture says,
"Let thy father and thy mother be glad,
and let her that bore thee rejoice" [Proverbs 23:25].

As in the case of Yohanan ben Hahoroni discussed earlier in the chapter, the actions of Honi, a marginal exemplar, need to be evaluated by a recognized rabbinic authority. Once again, such a rabbinic evaluation transforms the story from an exemplum into a type of case story. The person doing the evaluating in this case is Simeon ben Shetah,[81] who is consistently portrayed in rabbinic literature as the quintessential rabbi of his time.[82] Strikingly, rather than presenting a decisive ruling on Honi's status and actions, Simeon expresses his own ambivalence and frustration with the situation.

At first, Simeon ben Shetah declares his unequivocal opposition to Honi's deeds. He opens by declaring Honi worthy of excommunication. Simeon ben Shetah does not explicitly state what Honi has done to merit this punishment. The nature of Honi's offense has been a subject of much speculation among scholars. Theories range from Honi's improper use of a vow[83] to the arrogant nature of his prayer.[84] Others have argued that Honi's circle drawing and other actions reflected engagement in forbidden magical practices.[85] Finally, it has been argued that Simeon ben Shetah viewed Honi's very practice as a charismatic miracle worker as undermining the authority of the rabbis.[86]

The common denominator between these explanations is that Honi flouts the norms according to which the rabbis and their followers pray to God for rain. Up to this point in the tractate, the Mishnah has outlined the proper procedure for responding to the lack of rain. The rabbinic authorities, represented by the court, organize a series of fasts and other acts of self-mortification and mourning, and there are to be public prayers in which the people are meant to call out to God for mercy. The assumption is that God must be won over through signs of humility and faithfulness to him. In contrast to the fear and trembling that characterizes the rabbinic approach to soliciting God for rain, Honi acts with supreme confidence. He does not beg God but makes demands of him, attempting to force his hand through an oath and perhaps through theurgic activities as well.

Still, Simeon ben Shetah feels he cannot excommunicate Honi. In confronting Honi, Simeon ben Shetah has encountered the limitations of rabbinic authority. In the second part of his speech, Simeon ben Shetah states that Honi, as an authentic miracle worker, has a special relationship with God that places him beyond the reach of the rabbis' ban.

Simeon ben Shetah's message is laced with an irony that reflects his refusal to accept the justice of Honi's status. In making his case, Simeon introduces the second *mashal* in the paragraph. In it, Honi is characterized as a spoiled child. Daube justly draws attention to Simeon's description of the child as *mithate'*

Traditional commentators understand this word as meaning "behaving in spoiled manner" or "nagging."[87] However, the common meaning of the root h-t-' is "to sin." Simeon ben Shetah's choice of a relatively rare usage of a word whose far more common meaning has such negative associations, can hardly be coincidental. Simeon ben Shetah is insinuating that Honi is not just a trouble maker but perhaps a sinner as well.[88] He is outraged to have met his match in such a character. How can such a sinner be favored by God?

Simeon ben Shetah's attack also exploits and undermines Honi's original argument to God. Honi had persuaded God to make it rain by declaring: "Thy children have turned to me because they believe me to be as a member of thy household." Simeon ben Shetah acknowledges Honi's special, "familial" relationship with God, but he argues that this relationship is a dysfunctional one involving a spoiled child and an indulgent parent, hardly one to call attention to in a time of need.

Simeon ben Shetah carries through his complaint against God by citing a verse from Proverbs, "Your father and your mother will rejoice; she who bore you will exult." The citation of this verse in this context can best be understood as bitterly ironic. The verse just previous to the one cited by Simeon ben Shetah reads, "The father of a righteous man will exult; he who begets a wise son will rejoice in him." Parents are meant to rejoice over the righteous and wise child, yet God celebrates Honi, who is spoiled and disrespectful. It is possible that Simeon ben Shetah feels that he is the wise and righteous one who truly deserves God's favor. Simeon ben Shetah here brings a proof text against God's actions, accusing God of not living up to the standards of his own wisdom.

For all of this, Simeon ben Shetah acknowledges that he has met his match. The rabbinic model of halakhic authority rooted in knowledge and practice of halakhah and respect for the rabbinic hierarchy is trumped by the holy man whose authority is charismatic in nature, deriving directly from his relationship with God. Simeon never challenges Honi's status as a legitimate miracle worker.

The story of Honi Hame'agel thus presents a most ambiguous and conflicted picture of the charismatic miracle worker and his place in rabbinic society. This is embodied by the hybrid form of the story. It starts as an exemplum in which Honi is the exemplar. As the story progresses it morphs into a case story in which Honi's actions are subject to rabbinic scrutiny and disapproval. On the one hand, Honi truly has a special relationship with God that he uses to bring rain to the people in time of need. His actions can even be cited in a halakhic context as an illustration of proper behavior. Yet, in the process of bringing rain, he also does great damage, flooding the entire city of Jerusalem. Furthermore, his interactions with God completely flout the protocols set down by the rabbis for dealing with situations in which God withholds rain. Simeon ben Shetah feels that he must condemn Honi's behavior, but he cannot take action against him. The result is a standoff between two models of religious authority and of relating to God: the halakhic and the charismatic.

Conclusion

The Mishnah uses exempla not only to transmit individual rulings but also to construct the rabbis as embodiments of the halakhah, whose very actions are legal precedents. Yet in the exempla we have examined in this chapter, the Mishnah problematizes the very notion of a rabbinic exemplar, primarily by focusing on the difficulty of defining who exactly belongs to this elite class of individuals. The narratives in question weigh competing criteria for the rabbinic sage. Is he an authority whose power is rooted in his social and institutional position or an expert whose power lies in his knowledge? Is he a normative figure whose power lies in his mastery of the law or a wonder worker who claims a direct relationship with God? These questions are never fully resolved. Even as these stories make a case for rabbinic authority, they open up a space for dialog and debate about the exact nature and extent of that authority.

Excursus: The Transmission and Redaction of the Honi Story

Not only is the Honi story among the most commented-upon rabbinic narrative traditions among modern scholars, it is also among the best attested in ancient Jewish sources. Our sources for the story go back to Josephus and extend into Amoraic and post-Amoraic sources.[89] This gives us an opportunity to attempt to reconstruct the process whereby the Honi story of the Mishnah was transmitted and redacted. It is appropriate here to apply both the "performative" and "textual" models of transmission discussed in the previous chapter in order to account for the relationships between the various texts. Unlike the previous cases, where we examined the development of a single oral narrative tradition as it was shaped by various storytellers, in this case, the creators of the Honi story found in the Mishnah drew on a series of independent traditions which they reshaped and wove together to create their own narrative. At some point, probably in the Tannaitic period, the Honi story took on the attributes of a fixed text, of which we have two different recensions, the version found in the Mishnah, and the version presented in the baraita cited in the Bavli. By tracing the development of this narrative tradition we can see how the editors of the Mishnah crafted their story into a complex and ambiguous work, clearly distinguished from other more straightforward versions of the story.

Flavius Josephus

The earliest source that we have for the Honi tradition is found in the works of the first-century CE Jewish historian, Flavius Josephus. Josephus writes in his *Antiquities*, "Now there was one, whose name was Onias, a righteous man he was, and beloved of God, who, in a certain drought, had prayed to God to put an end to the intense heat, and whose prayers God had heard, and had sent them rain."[90] Josephus goes on to describe how during the Jewish civil war of 67–63BCE, the followers of Hyrcanus attempted to force Onias to pray for the failure of Aristobulus and his men. Onias refused to take sides in this war of brothers and died a martyr's death.

Scholars have generally identified Josephus's Onias with the Mishnah's Honi.[91] Such an assumption is strengthened by the fact that Josephus places Onias's death in the 60s of the first century BCE. This would make him a rough contemporary of Simeon ben Shetah, conforming to the Mishnah's account.

Unlike the creators of the Mishnah's Honi story, Josephus does not tell of any circle drawing, dramatic negotiations with God, or flooding of Jerusalem. His account is stripped down to a basic description of a situation, "the people needed rain," which is followed by two interrelated events, "Honi prayed" and "God sent rain." Honi appears as an unambiguously holy and righteous man, whose abilities and qualities are beyond reproach, and he is not shown as having any relations, positive or negative, with the Pharisees of his time. It is possible that Josephus knew the Mishnah's version of the story, or something like it, and, for his own editorial purposes, abridged the story. It seems far more likely, however, that Josephus, writing well over a century before the redaction of the Mishnah, is reporting all that he knows. This simple tale of a holy man who once brought rain in time of need was likely the initial kernel of the Honi tradition, out of which more developed versions later emerged.

The Scholium of *Megilat Ta'anit*

The next set of sources comes from a set of texts known as the scholium of *Megilat Ta'anit* . *Megilat Ta'anit* itself is a list of dates of minor holidays on which fasting and eulogies are prohibited. This work was probably composed sometime in the first century CE, not long before the Destruction.[92] *Megilat Ta'anit* was transmitted with a commentary, or scholium, which elaborated on the events behind the holidays listed in the scroll. This commentary has come down to us in two versions, known as the Oxford and Parma scholia, after the location of the manuscripts in which they are found. Though these texts may have been edited at a fairly late date, Vered Noam argues in the introduction to her critical edition of *Megilat Ta'anit* and its scholium that both the Oxford and the Parma versions contain many authentic historical and literary traditions dating back to the Second Temple period.

The entry in *Megilat Ta'anit* for the twentieth day of the month of Adar reads:[93]

בעשרים ביה צמו עמא על מטרא ונחת להון

On the twentieth thereof, the people fasted for rain and it fell for them.

The Parma scholium on this passage elaborates:

מפני שהיה רעבון ובצורת בארץ ישראל
ולא ירדו להם גשמים ג' שנים זו אחר זו
עד שירד חוני המעגל לפני התיבה
והתפלל(ו) וירדו גשמים
יום שירדו גשמים עשאוהו יום טוב[94]

> Because there was a famine and drought in the land of Israel,
> Rain did not fall for three consecutive years
> Until Honi Hame'agel went down before the ark
> And he prayed and rain fell.
> The day the rain fell they made into a holiday.

Like Josephus, the Parma scholium tells a simple tale of a holy man who successfully prayed for rain. It contains none of the drama or complexity of the Mishnah's account. Indeed, whereas the Mishnah goes out of its way to emphasize the eccentric and nonnormative nature of Honi's prayers, the Parma scholium emphasizes their conventional nature. It uses the phrase *yarad lifnei hateva*, "went down before the ark," to describe Honi's actions. This is a standard phrase used in rabbinic literature to refer to an individual going to lead public prayers.[95] In this account, Honi simply served as a conventional prayer leader, leading the standard prayer prescribed by the rabbis. This would suggest that the account in the Parma scholium is independent of, and likely predates, the account of the Mishnah. Like Josephus, it presents a version of the simple narrative kernel out of which the Mishnah's account grew.

Yet the Parma scholium refers to Honi as "*Hame'agel*," a term that is usually translated as "circle drawer." This would seem to suggest an awareness of Honi's unconventional prayer activities as described in the Mishnah. M. B. Lerner has cogently argued however, that "circle drawer" is not the original meaning of this term.[96] The Mishnah in *Makkot* 2:1 uses the term *me'agel* to describe the act of using a cylinder to flatten the wet plaster on top of a roof.[97] In light of this text, we might suggest that Honi's title indicates that he was a roofer by trade.[98] Identifying Honi as earning his living in this way enhances the story in several ways. First, it emphasizes that Honi was not a member of the elite but a common laborer with unusual spiritual talents. Furthermore, repairing roofs is work that is intrinsically linked with the rainy season. Thus Honi has a special connection to the rain and an understanding of its workings. This makes him a more appropriate candidate to represent the people before God on this matter. If the original meaning of the term *Hame'agel* did in fact refer to Honi's line of work, and not to his activities in the story, then the entire motif of Honi's circle drawing is a later addition. We might describe it as a sort of Midrashic play on Honi's title.

The creators of the Mishnah's version of the Honi story most likely inherited this concise tradition, in which Honi simply prays, or perhaps leads the people in prayer, and is answered. This tradition laid the basic narrative framework for later incarnations of the story. The Mishnah's storytellers also had a tradition that Honi was called "*Hame'agel*." At some stage, storytellers began to interpret this term as "circle drawer" and so the tradition of Honi drawing a circle around himself emerged.

The Oxford scholium on this passage does not mention Honi at all and would at first appear to be unrelated to the Honi tradition. It reads:

שאין הגשמים יורדים
אלא בשביל ישראל
שנ'
יפתח ה' לך את אוצרו הטוב את השמים
וזה היית בימי שמעון הצדיק
ואמר להם
משל למלך שכעס על בנו
ואמר לבן ביתו
אל תתן לבני פרנסה
עד שיבכה ויתחנן לפני[99]

For the rain does not fall
except for the benefit of Israel,
as it is written,
"The Lord will open for you his bounteous store, the heavens."
And this was in the days of Simeon the Just,
and he said to them:
[It is like] a parable in which a king gets angry at his son
and says to his household slave,
"Do not give any sustenance to my son
until he cries and begs before me."

While this text does not mention Honi, it does bear a striking resemblance to the final scene in the Mishnah's account. Here, too, we have an individual by the name of Simeon, who was in the eyes of the later rabbis the leading rabbinic figure of his generation during the Second Temple period. As in the Honi story, he comments on the successful prayer for rain with a parable.[100] Simeon the Just's parable is almost a mirror image of Simeon ben Shetah's. Simeon the Just uses the trope of a father's relationship with his estranged son to portray the proper procedure for praying for rain. The Jews should fast and cry out to God, just as the son must cry and beg to appease his father. Simeon ben Shetah on the other hand uses this trope to illustrate what he deems to be inappropriate behavior in praying for rain. It is not right for the Jews to brazenly demand rain from God as Honi does. Such behavior is like that of a spoiled child before his father. It is almost as if R. Simeon ben Shetah's parable assumes that the listener or reader understands the message, if not the contents, of R. Simeon the Just's parable.

There is an important difference between the fictional worlds portrayed in these two *meshalim*. Simeon ben Shetah portrays a common father and son, whereas Simeon the Just portrays a king and his son. The royal context allows for the introduction of another character, the *ben bayit*, the household slave, or perhaps more accurately, the royal steward,[101] who mediates between the king and his son. Simeon the Just's use of this figure of the *ben bayit* may shed light on yet another element of the Mishnah's story. At the beginning of the story, Honi portrays himself as a *ben bayit* whose job is also to mediate between the king and his son. Whereas Simeon the Just's *ben bayit* represents the interests of the king, Honi sees his role as *ben bayit* as representing the son's interests before the father. Simeon ben Shetah rejects Honi's simile. He insists that Honi's status is not based on his position as God's loyal servant but rather as one of God's children, who has been unjustly rewarded by an indulgent God for his impudent behavior.

Based on these connections between the Oxford scholium's text and the end of the Mishnah's story, it seems most reasonable assume that this scholium also reflects an early tradition which in some way underlies the Mishnah. The creators of the Mishnah's story inherited a tradition in which a certain Simeon from Second Temple days commented on a successful prayer for rain with a parable about a son who needs to appease his father. This tradition was already linked to the events of the 20th of Adar, a date that in other sources was associated with Honi's great feat.[102] The Mishnaic storytellers thus integrated this motif into their account, transforming it from an explanation of the proper way to pray into a conflicted response to a prayer that was at once unacceptable by rabbinic standards yet accepted by God.

Tosefta Ta'anit

There is another brief text that reflects yet another narrative tradition that was incorporated into the Mishnah's tale. This is a story recorded in Tosefta *Ta'anit* 2:13, in a context parallel to that of the Honi story in the Mishnah:[103]

מעשה בחסיד אחד
שאמרו לו
התפלל וירדו גשמים
התפלל וירדו גשמים
אמ' לו
כשם שהתפללת וירדו כך
התפלל וילכו להם
אמ' להם

צאו וראו אם עומד אדם בקרן אפל
ומשקשק את רגלו בנחל קדרון
אנו מתפללין שלא ירדו גשמים
המקום אבל בטוחין שאין
מביא מבול לעולם
שנ'
ולא יהיה עוד מבול וגו'
ואומ'
אשר נשבעתי וגו' כי מי נח זאת לי

> It happened with regard to a certain *hasid*
> that they said to him,
> "Pray, so that might rain."
> He prayed
> and it rained.
> They said to him,
> "Just as you prayed and it rained,
> pray so that [the rain] will go away."
> He said to them,
> "Go and see if a person can stand on the horn of Ofel
> and dip his foot in the Kidron valley,
> then we will pray that it should not rain.
> But we are confident that God will not
> bring [another] flood to the world.
> As it is written,
> "Never again will there be a flood" [Gen. 9:11]
> and it says,
> "For this to me is like the waters of Noah
> as I swore
> [that the waters of Noah nevermore would flood the earth]" [Isaiah 54:9].

This account clearly belongs to the same narrative tradition as one of the key scenes of the Mishnah's Honi story: the people's request that Honi pray that the rain stop and Honi's subsequent refusal. The people's request is formulated using the exact same words in both stories. Similarly, both Honi and the anonymous *hasid* of the Tosefta open their response by saying "go and see" if the water has reached a particular high point in Jerusalem, either the Stone of Claimants or the Horn of Ofel.

There are also important differences between the two accounts. As we have seen, Honi's behavior in this scene raises serious questions as to his character and abilities. Despite the fact that most of the city of Jerusalem has already been overtaken by the flood waters, Honi is either unwilling or unable to attempt to stop the rain. He offers no explanation for his actions. In contrast, in the Tosefta, there is no mention of any serious damage or danger that prompts the people's request of the *hasid* to stop the rain. Thus his refusal does not seem as harsh as Honi's. Similarly, the anonymous *hasid* tells the people that if it were to become necessary, he would pray for them. However, citing the words of the Torah and the Prophets, the *hasid* reassures them that God will never again send a truly catastrophic flood to the earth.

The most likely explanation for the relationship between the Mishnah and the Tosefta here is that the creators of the Mishnah's version had before them a tradition similar to that of the Tosefta which featured an anonymous *hasid* who refuses to pray for the rain to stop in Jerusalem. This tradition had certain fixed phrases, which had to be included regardless of the final form that the story took in the hands of a given storyteller. The creators of the Mishnah's story appropriated this tradition by identifying the anonymous *hasid* with Honi and inserting the story as a scene in a larger Honi narrative. They also reworked the tradition, transforming it from a straightforward portrayal of the *hasid*'s abilities and principles to an ambiguous and ambivalent portrayal of Honi as a questionable exemplar.

In summary, though we cannot reconstruct the exact details of the evolution of the Honi story, the best explanation for the data available to us is that the story of Honi as it appears in the Mishnah is not a simple transmission or redaction of a received texted but a creative "performance" which drew upon, reworked, and wove together a series of interrelated narrative traditions. The plot elements that the creators of the Mishnah's story had at their disposal include:

1. A tradition about a holy man named Honi, who successfully prayed for rain after a long drought (Josephus and Parma scholium)
2. A tradition that this Honi was known as "*Hame'agel*" (Parma scholium)
3. A tradition about a great sage named Simeon, who commented on this successful prayer for rain using a *mashal* about a son asking for his needs from his father. (Oxford scholium)
4. A tradition about a *hasid* who refuses to pray for the rain to stop (Tosefta).

The creators of the Mishnah's story did not simply incorporate these elements into a single story; they transformed them into a significantly different story in at least two key ways. First, they integrated the story into the Mishnah's halakhic discourse. As we have seen, in its context in the Mishnah, the story of Honi takes on the character of a sort of exemplum, meant to illustrate, or at least stimulate discussion about, the rabbinic rule prohibiting prayer for excessive rain. Second, the earlier traditions that we have seen portray Honi and his alter egos in a positive light, as a prayer virtuoso who is distinct from, but does not challenge, the rabbinic establishment. In the Mishnah, Honi is a complex figure. His behavior is unacceptable, yet at the same time he is favored by God.

Bavli Ta'anit

There is yet one more version of the Honi story which is directly related to our Mishnah's. This is the version found in the baraita cited in the Bavli *Ta'anit* 23a. The Yerushalmi apparently had a similar version of this baraita, which it quotes from in its glosses on the Mishnah. The baraita contains the entire text of the Mishnah with slight variations. In addition, it contains numerous other passages interspersed throughout the Mishnah's text. I have numbered and italicized these additional sections in the text and translation below; for the sake of space, I have elided much of the text that is all but identical to the Mishnah.[104]

1) *פעם אחת יצא רוב אדר ולא ירדו גשמים*
שלחו לו לחוני המעגל...
עג עוגה ועמד בתוכה

2) *כדרך שעשה חבקוק הנביא*
שנ' על משמרתי אעמדה ואתיצבה על מצור וג'
אמ' לפניו רבו' של ע' בניך שמו פניהם עלי...
התחילו גשמים מנטפין

3) *אמרו לו*
רבי ראינוך לא נמות
כמדומין אנו שאין הגשמים יורדין
אלא להתר את שבועתך
אמ' להן ראיתוני לא תמותו
אמר לא כך שאלתי אלא גשמי בורות שיחין ומערות
ירדו בזעף

4) *כל טיפה וטיפה כמלא פי חבית*
שיערו חכמ' אין כל טיפה פחותה מלוג.
אמרו לו
רבי ראינוך לא נמות
כמדומין אנו שאין הגשמים יורדין
אלא לשחת את העולם
אמ' להן ראיתוני לא תמותו
אמ' לא כך שאלתי אלא גשמי רצון ברכה ונדבה...
כשם שהתהפללת עליהן וירדו כך התפלל וילכו להן

5) *אמ' להם מקובל אני שאין מתפללין על רוב הטובה אלא אע' פ-כן הביאו לי פר הודאה*
הביאו פר הודאה
סמך שתי ידיו עליו ואמר
ר'ש עמך ישראל שהוצאת ממצרים
אינן יכולין לקבל לא רוב טובה ולא רוב פורענות
השפעת להם טובה אינן יכולין לקבל
כעסת עליהן אינן יכולין לקבל
יהי רצון מלפניך שיהא רוח בעולם
מיד נשבה הרוח ונתפזרו עבים וזרחה חמה

יצאו ומצאו הר-הבית כמהין ופטריות
שלח לו שמעון בן שטח
אלמלא חוני אתה גוזרני עליך נדוי
6) אלו שנים כשני אליהו ומפתחות שמים בידו
לא נמצא שם שמים מתחלל על ידך
אבל מה אעשה שאתה מתחטא לפני המקום ב׳׳ה כבן שמתחטא על אביו ועושה לו רצונו
7) אומר לו הוליכני לחמה מוליכו לחמה
לצונן מוליכו לצונן
תן לי איגוזין הפרסקין שקדים ורמונים
נותן לו
עליך הכת אומר
״ישמח אביך ואמיך ותגל יולדתך״

1. *Once it happened that the greater part of the month of Adar had gone and yet no rain had fallen.*
   The people sent a message to Honi Hameʿagel....
   He drew a circle and stood within it
2. *in the same way as Habakkuk had done, as it is said,*
   "I will stand upon my watch and set me upon the tower" [Habakkuk 2:1].
   He exclaimed before God, Master of the Universe!
   Thy children have turned to me....
   Rain began to drip.
3. They said to him, rabbi! *We look to you to save us from death.*
   We believe that the rain has come down merely to release you from your oath.
   He said to them, You have looked to me and shall not die.
   He said, it is not for this that I prayed
   but for rain [to fill] cisterns, ditches, and caves.
   The rain came down in force,
4. *each drop being as big as the opening of a barrel.*
   The sages estimated that no one drop was less than a log.
   They said to him, We look to you to save us from death.
   We believe that the rain has come down to destroy the world.
   He said to them, you have looked to me and shall not die.
   He said, it is not for this that I prayed....
   They said to him,
   In the same way you have prayed for the rain to fall,
   Pray for the rain to cease.
5. *He said to them, I have it as a tradition that*
   we may not pray on account of an excess of good.
   Despite this bring me a bullock for a thanksgiving offering.
   They brought him a bullock for a thanksgiving offering.
   He laid his two hands upon it and said, Master of the Universe!
   Thy people Israel whom thou hast brought out of Egypt

Exempla: Who Is a Rabbi? 165

cannot endure an excess of good nor an excess of punishment;
when thou showered upon them an excess of good, they could not endure it.
When thou wert angry with them, they could not endure it.
May it be thy will that there be wind in the world.
Immediately the wind began to blow and the clouds were dispersed
and the sun shone and the people went out and found the Temple Mount [full of]
mushrooms and truffles.
Thereupon Simeon ben Shetah sent this message to him,
Were it not that you are Honi, I would have placed you under the ban.

6. *For were the years like the years of [famine in the times of] Elijah,*
and the keys of the heavens were in his hands,
would not the name of heaven be profaned through you?
But what shall I do unto you who act petulantly before the Omnipresent
and he grants your desire,
as a son who acts petulantly before his father and he grants his desires;

7. *he says, "Take me to the warm [bath]," he takes him to the warm [bath].*
"To the cold [bath]." He takes him to the cold [bath].
"Bring me nuts, peaches, almonds, and pomegranates." He gives him.
Of you Scripture says,
"Let they father and they mother be glad, and let her that bore thee rejoice."

Unlike the previous Honi texts, it is unreasonable here to presume that the Mishnah and baraita each emerged from different renditions of a relatively fluid "performative" tradition. Rather, at a certain point the text of the story became fairly fixed. This text was then redacted either through elimination or the addition of the numbered passages. As several recent scholars have noted, in this case it makes the most sense to assume that the baraita represents the later text which contains glosses on the Mishnah's account.[105]

The most significant difference between the two stories is in Honi's response to the request to pray for the rain to stop (5). In the baraita's version, Honi first cites the rule that one may not pray to end excessive rain. He then proceeds to make an exception to this rule and prays for divine mercy in stopping the rain. God accedes to this request and the skies immediately clear. On the one hand, as in the Mishnah, Honi teaches us this important rabbinic rule. However, here in the Talmud, he also shows sympathy for suffering caused to the people by this rule and decides to make a special exception. Honi appears here as both a learned and generous figure.

Honi's image is further bolstered by the fact that the baraita compares Honi's prayer from within the circle to the prayer of the prophet Habakkuk (2), thereby associating Honi with the tradition of the great prophets. Similarly, Honi is repeatedly addressed by the people as "rabbi" (3 and 4), suggesting that he is indeed a part of the religious establishment.

Finally, while the baraita does record Simeon ben Shetah's rebuke of Honi, even expanding on the parable, it also suggests a different reason why Honi deserves to be excommunicated, which is arguably less severe. Simeon ben Shetah argues that Honi had no way of knowing that he would succeed. Had he failed, the result would have been a serious desecration of the divine name. According to this reason, in retrospect, Honi has done nothing wrong. His success to a certain degree makes up for his alleged recklessness. Furthermore, in mentioning the prophet Elijah, Simeon implicitly draws a parallel between Honi's successful calling down of rain from the heavens and Elijah's celebrated deeds.[106]

Summary

The various versions of the Honi story that we have are the product of both performative and textual transmission processes. The rabbis created a distinctively complex rendition of this narrative tradition, drawing on multiple sources to create a story that presents a nuanced and conflicted view of Honi in particular and the role of the holy man as an exemplar in rabbinic society in general. Once this rendition gained a fixed form as a text, it was further edited, producing two versions, the one found in the Mishnah and the one found in the baraita quoted in the Bavli. As is often the case, the Mishnah reflects the more concise of the two versions. Yet it is also the more literarily complex of the two, presenting Honi as a morally ambiguous figure rather than as a simple folk hero.

8

Case Stories: Repetition and Renewal

> A writer once summed the matter up in this way: The sole visible and indubitable law that is imposed upon us is the nobility, and must we ourselves deprive ourselves of that one law?
>
> Franz Kafka, *"The Problem of Our Laws"*

The study of the genre of case stories offers us an opportunity to further investigate some key issues regarding stories, narrativity, and narrative structure. As their name implies, case stories are by definition stories. Unlike exempla, which may contain as little as a single repeated event, case stories always fit the minimal definition of story that we presented in chapter 2. They are defined by a structure of two interrelated events that happened once and only once in the past: (1) an event or situation whose halakhic status is unclear, and (2) a ruling by a rabbi or rabbis determining the proper course of conduct with regard to this event or situation. In this chapter, we shall examine what happens when Mishnaic stories display more complex narrative structures than the simple forms we have used to categorize them thus far. In particular, we will look at a particular type of expanded case story form, which I call the "double-ended" case story.

I will also use this opportunity to examine the place of case stories within the narrative structure of a larger block of Mishnaic text. In this case, the larger text in question will be the first two chapters of *Rosh Hashanah*, which present the procedures for the ritual of the sanctification of the new moon. In this way we will expand our discussion of the complexities of narrative structure beyond case stories to include ritual narratives as well.

Lines and Squiggles

The major features of narrative structure that will concern us in this chapter might best be expressed through a trope first presented by the literary critic and theorist J. Hillis Miller. In an article entitled "Ariadne's Thread: Repetition and the Narrative Line," Miller presents two contrasting metaphors for narrative and narrative structure. The first is that of a straight line. As Miller writes:

> The image of the line tends always to imply the norm of a single continuous unified structure determined by one external organizing principle. This principle holds the whole line together, gives it its law, controls its progressive extension, curving or straight, with some *arché*, *telos*, or ground.[1]

Narrative can always be plotted as a succession of events along a straight line, as reflected by the terms "story line" and "plotline." For Miller, the image of the line suggests more than this temporal ordering of narrative. It also refers to the fact that narratives are unified by underlying principles which control their unfolding and whose illumination is the ultimate purpose of the narration. Miller's notion that each narrative has "its law" is applicable in a most literal manner to Mishnaic stories. These stories are in fact motivated by a desire to impart a particular law to the reader. They seek to draw a straight line between a particular situation or event and a given ruling. The narrative structure of these stories serves to forge an inevitable link between the case and the ruling, marginalizing other possibilities.

The second, contrasting image is that of a tangled and knotted length of twine. For Miller, this image suggests narrative tendency toward repetition: "Repetition might be defined as anything which happens to the line to trouble or even confound its straightforward linearity: returnings, knottings, recrossings, crinklings to and fro, suspensions, interruptions, fictionalizings."[2] Narratives tend to diverge and digress from the straight lines plotted for them at least as often as they hew to them. As we have seen repeatedly, even the simplest stories of the Mishnah often fail to deliver rules and principles in an unequivocal manner. Thus far, we have seen this reflected in tensions between illustrative and representational narrative strategies. These situations generally involved an excess of specificity. Illustrative story telling demands that a story adhere strictly to its "line," supplying only those details which are necessary to make the story's argument. Often, however, even the simplest Mishnaic stories take a representational path, inserting "excess" detail which distracts from and even undermines the story's main point.

Thus far I have sought to resolve these conflicts between the line and the tangled string by arguing that even the "repetitions" found in a given narrative ultimately serve a rhetorical function. They also serve to bring the reader to a certain law or principle in a roundabout, but ultimately more effective, manner. Thus I argued that the "excess" detail in some Tannaitic stories serves to help construct a more engaging "narrative world." This ultimately makes the story's argument more compelling.

In light of Miller's argument, we might suggest another possible understanding as well. Narrativity, and stories in particular, are defined by dynamism and specificity. This does not simply mean that these two qualities help the story achieve its ends. Rather, they are ends in and of themselves. It is in the nature of storytelling to increase a story's narrativity, making the plot more complex and adding mimetic detail. One does not always need to explain these developments in terms of the underlying "line" of the story. Stories naturally tend toward being both unequivocal straight lines and inscrutable tangles.

In this chapter, we will focus on the phenomena of "repetition" at the level of dynamism. Case stories are defined by a simple two-part plot. This structure is designed to optimize the presentation of a halakhic ruling in a given case. The repeated appearance of this narrative structure also collectively makes an argument for rabbis as authoritative interpreters of the law. In order to better make this case, some stories contain one or both of two additional plot elements: (1) a description of the question being asked of the rabbis, and (2) a report of an individual or group actually following the rabbi's ruling once it has been issued. These elements emphasize that the rabbi's ruling is not unilateral but has been solicited and ultimately implemented by non-rabbis who accept the rabbis' authority. Often, however, case stories contain further plot elements. These elements raise the dynamism of the story but do not serve to advance the story's halakhic or ideological agenda. In this chapter, we will deal with one such type of expanded case story. In these stories, the second basic element of the story literally repeats itself. The story offers not one but two halakhic rulings from two different authorities with regard to the situation at hand. On a certain level, we might see such stories as dysfunctional case stories. The stories do not root a particular position in a constructed historical reality. Rather, they grant a voice and legitimacy to two opposing positions.

Similarly, these stories undermine the larger argument that the rabbis are the ultimate arbiters of the law. They show that "the rabbis" are not a monolithic group but are themselves divided on many issues. Following "the rabbis" is insufficient. One also has to know how to choose between conflicting rabbis and their opinions. This issue is of course raised every time the Mishnah cites two opposing positions in apodictic or casuistic forms as well. However, the question becomes even more pressing when it is dramatized as an actual conflict between two individuals acting on the same stage.

Narrative and Narrativity in Rosh Hashanah 1–2: A Narrative in Two Straight Lines

The largest concentration of such "double-ended" case stories in the Mishnah is found in the first two chapters of *Rosh Hashanah*.[3] Before analyzing these individual stories, we will need to consider the narrative elements that underlie this entire section of the Mishnah.[4]

The main subject of the first two chapters of *Rosh Hashanah* is the ritual procedure surrounding the sanctification of the new moon.[5] The rabbinic calendar in the first centuries CE was an intercalated lunar calendar which was based on empirical observation of the moon. The month began with a confirmed citing of the new moon reported by reliable witnesses before the court. The Mishnah here presents a ritual narrative which tells of this process of confirming the appearance of the new moon and the announcing of the beginning of a new month.

This narrative might be conceptualized as a pair of straight lines or vectors: one line terminates at the same point from which the other originates. This central point is the location of the court whose job it is to control and regulate the calendar. The first line traces the path of the witnesses who must make their way from wherever it was that they first observed the new moon to the court where they must report their observation. The second line traces the path of the messengers whom the court sends out to announce the beginning of the new month. The court thus sits at the central point of the narrative. Its rulings motivate all action relevant to the ritual.[6]

One of the primary themes of these chapters is the necessity of completing this narrative despite the obstacles that may present themselves. The law is consistently formulated in such a way as to facilitate the timely arrival of the witnesses and the setting off of the messengers. The Mishnah emphasizes the fact that one may violate the Sabbath in order to travel to the court to report the new moon (1:4–6, 9). It discusses the great length to which the rabbis went to encourage people to come testify (1:6, 2:8) and records how the rabbis overcame attempts at sabotage from their opponents in order to continue receiving witnesses and sending out the announcement of the new month (2:1–2). The lines of this narrative need to be and will be completed at all cost.

The Historical Frame Narrative

Despite this schematic narrative framework, the Mishnah does not present this ritual as a timeless event which repeats itself monthly without change. The Mishnah actually divides its narrative into two distinct iterations: those which occurred "when the Temple stood," when the court for setting the calendar was located on the Temple Mount in Jerusalem, and those conducted in the post-Destruction era, when the court was located outside Jerusalem. In particular, the Mishnah focuses on instances which occurred in the generation following the Destruction when R. Gamliel presided over a court for the sanctification of the new moon at Yavne. The Mishnah repeatedly stops to differentiate between these two eras and to tell stories that take place specifically in one or the other milieus.

By simultaneously narrating these two parallel narrative lines, one set before and the other after the Destruction, the Mishnah implies yet a third narrative line which intersects the first two. This is a story that tells of the continuity between the authority of the court in Jerusalem in Temple times and that of R. Gamliel's court in Yavne. By extension, this narrative also draws a line from

R. Gamliel's court to that of his grandson, R. Judah Hanasi, under whose aegis the Mishnah was likely compiled. The Mishnah thus presents an implicit master narrative, or frame story, which tells of a succession of high calendrical courts starting in Jerusalem at the Temple and continuing after the Destruction in Yavne and other locales under R. Gamliel and his successors. This narrative roots the authority of post-Destruction rabbinic calendrical courts in their position as inheritors of the authority of the court in Jerusalem in Temple times.

In those days, the question of setting the calendar was far more than a matter of chronography; it was deeply political. The issue of whose calendar was correct was central to the sectarian disputes of the Second Temple period.[7] In the rabbinic period, the need for an established calendar was crucial to the ultimate emergence of the rabbis as a relatively united and preeminent force in late antique and early medieval Judaism. As Isaiah Gafni writes:

> Indeed one might argue that control over the calendar indicates, more than any other factor in the social and religious life of the Jewish people, in whose hands lay ultimate authority over the community. It is not surprising, therefore, to find rabbinic literature frequently reverting to issues surrounding the calendar while discussing aspects of the relative authority of different groups or personalities.[8]

One of the reasons why control of the calendar was so crucial to post-Destruction rabbinic authorities was that in Temple times setting the calendar had been one of the powers vested in the central court in Jerusalem. Whoever set the calendar could claim to be the legitimate inheritor of this court and the powers it held. By juxtaposing narratives that center on the Temple with those focusing on R. Gamliel and his court, the Mishnah implicitly establishes continuity between the centralization of Judaism around the Temple Mount and the centralized authority of R. Gamliel and his successors. We might thus see the Mishnah's claims for centralized rabbinic control of the calendar as a sort of metonymy for an argument for centralized rabbinic authority throughout Jewish life.

Such arguments for authority on the basis of institutional continuity almost by definition assert that their beneficiary is *in* authority rather than *an* authority.[9] The Mishnah's frame story makes no claims about the qualifications of those who sit on the court, though a certain level of expertise is no doubt assumed. The Jerusalem court was authoritative ultimately because it was the duly constituted court of the Temple. Subsequent rabbinic courts received their authority as a right of inheritance due to their claim that they were the only legitimate heirs to the court in Jerusalem. As we shall see later on in this chapter, this conception of rabbinic authority exists in tension with the notion that the setting of the calendar is based on the observation of empirical phenomena.

The framing narrative's assertion regarding the continuity between the Temple authorities and rabbinic authorities also needs to be considered in terms of the modern historiographic counter-narrative. As we have already seen, historians today reject the notion that the Temple was necessarily controlled by the rabbis' predecessors, the Pharisees. We don't know how decisions about Temple ritual and the calendar in particular were ultimately made, but it is highly unlikely that they were handed down by a high court which was controlled by the post-Destruction rabbis' spiritual and biological progenitors.[10]

The existence of a centralized rabbinic court that set the calendar for the entire Jewish people in post-Destruction times also needs to be examined. Shaye Cohen and Martin Goodman, historians who generally seek to minimize the authority of the rabbis and the patriarchate in the generations following the Destruction, both accept the notion that a centralized rabbinic authority, originating with R. Gamliel's court at Yavne, took over the job of regulating the calendar from the court that sat in the Temple.[11] Their understanding is apparently based on the assumption that Judaism could not have functioned without a central calendrical authority. Since some group must have filled this role following the demise of the Temple and its institutions, it seems reasonable to attribute this role to the rabbis under R. Gamliel.

However, it is not at all clear that following the Destruction, world Jewry universally recognized the need for a centralized calendar.[12] While the Temple stood, there likely existed a centralized Jewish calendar which was followed by the majority of Jews, at least in the land of Israel. The Temple had a need for its own calendar to regulate its annual ritual observances. Jews around the world identified with the Temple as the heart of Jewish practice. For them, days such as Yom Kippur and Passover would have been defined as the days on which the appropriate rituals took place in the Temple. It would have made no sense to fast on any other day other than the one on which the high priest entered the inner sanctum of the Temple or to remove all leaven from one's house at any other time than the eve of the day on which the paschal sacrifice was offered in Jerusalem. As long as Jews saw their religion as being geographically centered on the Temple in Jerusalem, they likely would have seen it as being chronologically organized by the calendar set in Jerusalem.

After the Destruction, the need for such a unified calendar would not have been as obvious. As far as we know, in the generations following the Destruction, most of the Jews of the land of Israel did not recognize any sort of centralized rabbinic authority. Most historians today agree that it was only in the third century that the masses of Palestinian Jewry began to see the rabbinic class and the patriarchate as the authoritative bodies of Judaism. Until then, Judaism was apparently a local affair governed according to family and regional traditions and authorities. There is no reason to assume that a similar state of affairs did not exist in this period with regard to the calendar. For the majority of Jews, the responsibility for setting the calendar would likely have fallen to local authorities.[13] The exact date of the holidays may have sometimes varied from locale to locale. People did not necessarily see this as a problem. These variations were simply part and parcel of the decentralized nature of post-Destruction Judaism.

The rabbis, on the other hand, sought to maintain a centrally organized Jewish people even in the absence of a Temple. According to the rabbinic accounts, R. Gamliel therefore established a court for setting the calendar.[14] However, in the first generations following the Destruction, the rabbis would not have had sufficient clout with the wider Jewish population to actually implement a centralized calendar. The calendar set by R. Gamliel would likely have been followed at first only by the relatively small group of rabbis and their followers. It was probably only in the later Tannaitic and early Amoraic period when the influence of the rabbis and the patriarchate in particular became quite substantial that the masses of Jews came to accept the rabbinic calendar as authoritative.[15]

The sources in *Rosh Hashanah* never explicitly state that the new months proclaimed by R. Gamliel and his circle were accepted throughout the Jewish world or even in the land of Israel. This is only implied by the way in which these accounts are intertwined with discussion of the court in Jerusalem. Indeed, the aggressiveness with which R. Gamliel is portrayed as promoting this institution would seem to suggest that the position of his court within the wider community was in fact quite tenuous.

The continuity of a centralized calendar under rabbinic auspices from Temple days to the court of R. Gamliel in Yavne and beyond thus cannot be accepted as historical fact. In Temple times the court was not controlled by the Pharisees, and in the generations following the Destruction, the rabbinic apparatus for controlling the calendar probably was not recognized by the masses of Jews. The Mishnah's account reflects an attempt to reshape history into a master narrative which roots the authority of the rabbis and the patriarchate in the second and third centuries CE in the glorious and universally cherished memory of the centralized cult in Jerusalem.

Rosh Hashanah 1–2 thus presents not a single narrative line but a set of parallel and intersecting lines which create a wider halakhic and ideological framework. It establishes the proper procedure for declaring the new month in different historical periods. These differing procedures are held together by a claim of historical continuity and an insistence on centralized rabbinic control of the calendar regardless of the circumstances.

Repetitions and Disruptions

Thus far we have read the Mishnah out of sequence in order to demonstrate the clear narrative and ideological lines that these chapters present. If we read the *Rosh Hashanah* 1–2 in sequence, a very different picture emerges. The narrative does not unfold in a linear, chronological fashion. Rather, the narrator moves back and forth along the narrative line. The account is prone to frequent digressions and irregularities. Indeed, the opening paragraphs of the tractate do not even deal with the unfolding drama of the individual new month but with the larger cycle of the year. The first four paragraphs chart the cardinal points of this annual circle. First the Mishnah notes the four new moons which also signal beginning points of the year for different ritual and legal purposes. Continuing on the theme of important dates during the year, the Mishnah then sets out the four dates on which God annually judges different aspects of his creation.[16] Time here is portrayed in a cyclical rather than a linear, narrative fashion.

It is only after this that we find a direct reference to the ritual of the new moon. The Mishnah lists yet another set of annual events, the months that messengers are sent out from the court to announce the date of the beginning of the month. The Mishnah thus starts its account *in medias res*, in the middle of the ritual. Only in paragraph 4 do we come to the first stage of the ritual, the arrival of the witnesses. The Mishnah discusses those months for which the witness may violate the Sabbath in order to come to the court to testify. Still, the Mishnah portrays the various aspects of this ritual as part of the cycle of the year rather than as part of the unfolding of an individual month. Only in the subsequent paragraphs does the Mishnah finally open the circle and begin to present the procedures for sanctifying the new month in a somewhat linear order.[17]

In chapter two, the Mishnah again digresses from the chronological order of the ritual. Having told a story about how the rabbis had to change their standards for accepting witnesses due to attempted sabotage by sectarians, the Mishnah goes on to tell yet another tale of rabbinic confrontation with sectarian opponents. This story, however, deals with Samaritan interference with the system of flares used to alert the Jewish world of the new month before the system of messengers was adopted. The Mishnah thus leaves behind the arrival of the witnesses in court and skips ahead to the stage in which the new month has already been declared. Now the court must spread the word of their decision to the wider populace. The Mishnah continues its digression devoting two more paragraphs to detailing the procedure for sending of these signals.[18] Only in section five do we pick up where we left off and return to an account of the reception of the witnesses at court. The Mishnah follows the narrative through the point in which the new month is declared by the court. It does not continue to discuss the ways in which the news of this event was disseminated throughout the Jew world. The reader must then fill in the details that have been narrated out of sequence at earlier points.

The Mishnah's lack of a linear narrative style is also demonstrated by the way in which it moves between different forms that together display a full range of narrativity, from stories to apodictic statements. As we have already noted, the Mishnah also moves back and forth between pre- and post Destruction time frames. Furthermore the Mishnah does not relate its narrative by presenting the standard practice. Rather, it presents a series of exceptional cases such as instances where travel on the Sabbath is necessary or where the status of the witnesses is problematic. All of these factors further disrupt the simple sequential presentation of the events involved in the sanctification of the new month.

This tension between the simple lines of the underlying narrative of the new moon ritual and the serpentine path taken by the Mishnah in expounding it might best be thought of in terms of one of the basic dichotomies in modern narrative theory of which Miller's metaphor of the line and the tangled thread is a variant. This distinction was first proposed by the Russian Formalists earlier in the twentieth century using the terms *fabula* and *sjuzhet*.[19] The *fabula* refers to the sequence of events, in chronological order, that make up the story. The *sjuzhet* is the way in which these events are actually presented in the text. This includes a wide range of narrative techniques and strategies that might be employed by the narrator. On the most fundamental level, it refers to the order in which the events are actually narrated. This distinction thus becomes particularly relevant in situations of "out of sequence" narration. These are cases in which the storyteller chooses to narrate the events of his stories in an order other than those in which they take place.

Traditional formalist and structuralist critics tended to give priority to the *fabula*, assuming that it precedes the *sjuzhet* both logically and chronologically. The *fabula* reflects the story's essence as it where, while the *sjuzhet* is merely a representation of this essence. More recently however, students of narrative have begun to understand "*fabula* not as the reality reported by discourse, but as its product."[20] In this view, the *fabula* is only a theoretical construct created by the reader in the process of reading and interpreting the *sjuzhet*. The *sjuzhet* as it is embodied in the text of the story is the only empirical reality that the reader confronts. This newer approach attempts to understand stories without privileging either the *fabula* or the *sjuzhet*, "but rather explores the complex interaction of two modes of determination which both seem necessary to narrative but which do not give rise to harmonious synthesis."[21]

The first chapters of *Rosh Hashanah* show just such a dialogical tension between *fabula* and *syuzhet*. On the one hand, underlying these chapters is the basic narrative of the witnesses' journey to the court and the messengers' journey from the court. The editors of the Mishnah almost certainly presumed that the reader would have prior knowledge of this narrative. Indeed, it is precisely this knowledge that makes the Mishnah's out-of-order presentation comprehensible. Yet the Mishnah fails to adhere to a simple chronological line or to a consistent narrative style. By jumping back and forth, moving between varying degrees of narrativity, and constantly investigating alternative scenarios, the Mishnah emphasizes that in fact no two iterations of the fundamental ritual narrative are the same. They vary based on time and circumstance. Furthermore, in realty, events do not present themselves as having a clearly demarcated beginning, middle, and end. Events often form more of a circle, repeating themselves regularly. Hence the Mishnah can begin its account at the "end" and end its account in the "middle."

This tension between *fabula* and *syuzhet* in the Mishnah reflects the larger tension between "apodictic" and "narrative" approaches to law which underlies much of Mishnaic discourse. The *fabula* of the ritual of the new moon is a type of underlying halakhic structure that is found throughout the Mishnah. It suggests a notion of law which is both systematic and static. The *syuzhet* of the Mishnah's variegated and discursive presentation embodies a narrative approach to law which sees the law as being inherently conditioned by the varying temporal and physical circumstances in which it must be applied. Taken as a whole, these chapters express a rich dialog between divergent voices within the narrative and legal discourse of the Mishnah.

Case Stories in Rosh Hashanah 1–2

The case stories interspersed throughout these two chapters greatly contribute to this interplay of voices and perspectives that pervades the section as a whole. All of the case stories in the first two chapters of *Rosh Hashanah* display the same basic structure that we have called the "double-ended" case story. These stories follow the following pattern:

a) An event or situation whose halakhic status is unclear
b) A ruling by a rabbi or rabbis determining the proper course of conduct with regard to this event or situation
b') A conflicting ruling issued by a different rabbi or group of rabbis

The stories in Rosh Hashanah all deal with cases involving the presentation of witnesses of the new moon. As such, these stories might further be defined by an even more specific common structure:

a) Witnesses whose status and legitimacy are unclear appear before a rabbi or group of rabbis.
b) A rabbi or rabbis rule on the status of the witnesses and his testimony.
b') Another rabbi or rabbis issues a conflicting ruling with regard to the witnesses.

This narrative structure is open to contrasting interpretations. One possibility is to understand the story as truly double ended. The opposing opinions presented in the two endings are both valid. The narrative line forks into two, presenting two viable endings. Such a reading challenges the notion of a centralized halakhic authority which underlies much of these chapters.

The other possibility is to treat the first ending as a false ending. The only authoritative ending is the second answer which concludes the story. The basic integrity of the narrative line remains intact. The first opinion is merely a detour through which the reader must pass in order to arrive at the truth. By presenting another option, the narrative in fact emphasizes the supremacy of the authoritative opinion. The final opinion in these stories reflects the central rabbinic authority, which controls the calendar and, by extension, normative Judaism according to the Mishnah.

It is not possible to fully resolve any of these double-ended stories in favor of one of these readings or the other. Rather, it is the tension between these two possible readings that generates a space for a true discourse of authority. These stories simultaneously argue both for the need for a centralized rabbinic authority and for legitimacy of dissenting viewpoints.

The case stories in *Rosh Hashanah* 1–2 appear in two textual blocks. The first of these is 1:5–7. This section in turn consists of two units, each of which contains a story within it. These two units further share a common literary structure. Each one opens with a pair of casuistic formulations which present opposing halakhic opinions. This is followed by a double-ended case story in which the two hypothetical positions presented above are dramatized as a conflict between two rabbis or groups of rabbis over an actual historical case.[22]

Rosh Hashanah 1:5–6: R. Aqiba v. R. Gamliel

The first of these units is 1:5–6

בֵּין שֶׁנִּרְאָה בַעֲלִיל
וּבֵין שֶׁלֹּא נִרְאָה בַעֲלִיל
מְחַלְּלִים עָלָיו אֶת הַשַּׁבָּת
ר' יוֹסֵי אוֹמֵ'
אִם נִרְאָה בַעֲלִיל
אֵין מְחַלְּלִין עָלָיו אֶת הַשַּׁבָּת

מַעֲשֶׂה שֶׁעָבְרוּ יוֹתֵר מֵאַרְבָּעִים זוּג
וְעִיכְּבָן ר' עֲקִיבָה בְּלוֹד
שָׁלַח לוֹ רַבָּן גַּמְלִיאֵ'
אִם מְעַכֵּב אַתָּה אֶת הָרַבִּים
נִמְצֵאתָה מְכַשְּׁלָן לֶעָתִיד לָבוֹא

Whether [the new moon] has been seen clearly
or has not been seen clearly,
the Sabbath may be profaned on account of it.
R. Yose says,
If it has been seen clearly,
Sabbath is not to be profaned on account of it.

It happened once that more than forty pairs of witnesses were on their way

and R. Aqiba detained them in Lod.
R. Gamliel thereupon sent to him saying:
"If you prevent the multitude [from coming to give evidence]
you will prove to be the cause of their stumbling in the time to come."

The first paragraph utilizes a pair of casuistic clauses to present two different opinions regarding the permissibility of witnesses of the new moon violating the Sabbath. According to the anonymous first opinion, it is always permissible for witnesses to violate the Sabbath whether or not the moon is clearly visible. R. Yose, on the other hand, holds that if the moon is clearly visible, one may not violate the Sabbath on its account. Presumably this is because we can assume, given the high visibility of the moon, that there will be witnesses close to the court who will report their sighting without having to violate the Sabbath. The Mishnah thus presents two alternative rules that govern any situation in which the new moon is sighted on the Sabbath. What the Mishnah does not do is give us any insight into the relationship between these two conflicting rules and the individuals who advocate them. Given the Mishnah's assumption of the necessity of a single, central calendrical court, how is the existence of these two conflicting opinions to be resolved? The fact that the first position is presented anonymously may suggest that it is authoritative. However, this is never stated explicitly. Both positions remain viable options.

The story in the next paragraph places this dispute into a narrative world, giving it a context in time and space. In doing so, it directly confronts the issue of the relationship between authority and dissent in halakhah. First, the story dramatizes the case from the previous paragraph in which the moon can be seen clearly. It tells of an incident in which more than forty pairs of witnesses of the new moon begin to make their way to the court. The fact that so many witnesses came forth implies that the moon could be seen clearly. From the context, it is clear that this takes place on the Sabbath. Next, a rabbi responds to the situation: R. Aqiba waylays the witnesses at Lod. Apparently, R. Aqiba agrees with the opinion of R. Yose; he believes that it is not permissible to violate the Sabbath if the moon is clearly visible. R. Aqiba thus prevents the witnesses from continuing on their journey and violating the Sabbath.[23] R. Aqiba seeks to interrupt the standard narrative line of the new moon ritual in this instance. Rather than allowing the witnesses to make the journey to the court, he cuts them off, preventing the completion of the new moon ritual at court.

If the story were to end here, it would follow a standard case story pattern. However, the story continues with a third section that presents another rabbi's perspective on the same situation. R. Gamliel rebukes R. Aqiba for his actions; he sides with the anonymous first opinion of the previous paragraph, which allows witnesses to violate the Sabbath in all circumstances. R. Gamliel's statement reveals his rationale. He believes that the waylaying of witnesses could have the effect of discouraging witnesses on a future occasion. This could result in the court not having witnesses to sanctify the new moon on a later occasion. As such the witnesses should be allowed to travel on the Sabbath, even though it may not be strictly necessary for the purposes of the upcoming month.

The account of R. Aqiba's actions in this story might be understood as an example of what we have called a false ending. At first, R. Aqiba appears to give an authoritative response to the situation. By the end, this story clearly establishes R. Gamliel as the normative authority to whom R. Aqiba must submit. R. Aqiba is positioned at the periphery, on the way to the court. R. Gamliel sits at the court in Yavne, the central point in new moon narrative, and the ultimate destination of the witnesses. From this central position, he issues his rebuke to R. Aqiba. It is R. Gamliel who has the last word in the story.

The story might also be seen as offering a true double ending in which both R. Aqiba and R. Gamliel offer legitimate, conflicting responses to the problem. The story in fact is hardly so unequivocal in proclaiming R. Gamliel's dominance. In this particular incident, it is R. Aqiba who actually prevails. It seems that R. Gamliel's message arrives too late to have any impact on that month's proceedings. Whereas R. Gamliel is *in* a position of formal authority, R. Aqiba's position on the road to Yavne makes him *an* authority who can actually affect the progress of the witnesses. Furthermore, nowhere is it stated that R. Aqiba accepted R. Gamliel's rebuke. This story can be read as presenting a standoff between two great sages and their conflicting positions regarding this matter. In this reading R. Aqiba's position is no less valid than that of R. Gamliel.

The conflict between R. Gamliel and R. Aqiba apparently goes well beyond this narrow technical dispute. Rather, it reflects a fundamental disagreement about the status of the central calendrical court in Yavne. R. Aqiba does not dispute the court's validity and importance; he agrees that the fixing of the appearance of the new moon is grounds for violating the Sabbath. However, R. Aqiba demands that there be an immediate threat to the completion of the new moon ritual in order to justify the violation of the Sabbath. Cases in which we can assume that other witnesses will arrive without violating the Sabbath do justify such leniency. In contrast, according to R. Gamliel the very existence and viability of the court are concerns for which one can violate the Sabbath. For him the process of sanctifying the new month is not merely an abstract halakhic process. Rather, it exists in the context of a social reality in which people recognize his court and continue to bring testimony to it. Any threat to the long-term functioning of his court is a threat to the sanctification of the new month and hence grounds for the violation of the Sabbath. R. Gamliel emerges as a communal leader whose agenda is much broader than that of R. Aqiba. Like the first paragraphs of the chapter, R. Gamliel is concerned not only with the completion of a single sanctification of the new moon but with its continued iteration within the cycle of the year.

In this debate, R. Gamliel reflects a more institutional, "narrative" view of rabbinic authority. He sees rabbinic authority as being inherently tied up with duly constituted institutions like the calendrical court. These institutions must be preserved and promoted at all costs, even if it involves the violation of the Sabbath. He considers social and political factors in his halakhic decision making, not just abstract rules. R. Aqiba on the other hand, reflects a more apodictic, formalistic approach. For him, the rabbis and their courts are only as legitimate as the laws they enforce. He cannot justify breaking the Sabbath because of social and political concerns about the viability of rabbinic institutions.

The Talmudic Counter-Narrative

Both Talmuds present a very different version of this story. A brief study of this account will give us a greater appreciation of complexity and ambiguity of the Mishnah's version. Below is the text as it appears in the Yerushalmi:[24]

אמ' ר' יהודה הנחתום
חס ושלום
לא נתנדה ר' עקיבה
אלא שזכר ראש גדר היה
ושלח רבן גמליאל והעבירו מראשיתו

> R. Judah the Baker said,
> "God forbid!
> R. Aqiba was not excommunicated.
> Rather it was Shazkhar head of Gader
> and R. Gamliel sent and removed him from his position!"

The Talmuds present their account as a full-fledged counter-narrative whose purpose is to challenge not only the historicity but the very plausibility of the Mishnah's story. R. Judah assumes that whoever challenged R. Gamliel in this manner would certainly have been excommunicated.[25] R. Judah finds it inconceivable that R. Aqiba might have been involved in such an incident. He insists that R. Aqiba played no part in the story. Rather, it was a certain "Shazkhar head of Gader," an otherwise unknown local political leader, who opposed R. Gamliel.

R. Judah's story possesses a very different narrative structure from that of the Mishnah. In the Mishnah, the crisis which demands a halakhic resolution is the surplus of witnesses on the Sabbath. R. Judah never explicitly mentions this event. In his version the crisis that drives the story is the fact that Shazkhar challenged R. Gamliel's authority. This problem contains only a single rabbinic response, R. Gamliel's deposing of Shazkhar. This narrative is thus a standard case story in which R. Gamliel asserts his authority over those who would oppose him. The Talmuds thus seek to suppress the Mishnah's multivocal story with an account that unequivocally portrays R. Gamliel and his ruling as the only authoritative options.[26] This only serves to highlight the nuanced nature of the Mishnah's treatment of R. Gamliel's authority in this case.

Rosh Hashanah 1:7: The Story of Toviah the Physician

The next textual unit follows a similar pattern:

אָב וּבְנוֹ שֶׁרָאוּ אֶת הַחוֹדֶשׁ
יֵלְכוּ
לֹא שֶׁמִּצְטָרְפִים זֶה עִם זֶה
אֶלָּא שֶׁמָּא[27] יִפָּסֵל אֶחָד מֵהֶם
וְיִצְטָרֵף הַשֵּׁנִי עִם אַחֵר
ר' שִׁמְעוֹן או'
אָב וּבְנוֹ וְכָל הַקְּרוֹבִים
כְּשֵׁרִים לְעֵדוּת הַחוֹדֶשׁ
אמ' ר' יוֹסִי
מַעֲשֶׂה בְּטוֹבִיָּה הָרוֹפֵא
שֶׁרָאָה אֶת הַחֹדֶשׁ בִּירוּשָׁלַם
הוּא וּבְנוֹ וְעַבְדּוֹ הַמְשׁוּחְרָר
וְקִיבְּלוּ הַכֹּהֲנִים אוֹתוֹ וְאֶת בְּנוֹ
וּפָסְלוּ אֶת עַבְדּוֹ
וּכְשֶׁבָּאוּ לְבֵית[28] דִּין
קִיבְּלוּ אוֹתוֹ וְאֶת עַבְדּוֹ
וּפָסְלוּ אֶת בְּנוֹ[29]

If a father and son have seen the new moon,
they should both go [to Jerusalem].
Not that they can act as joint witnesses
but so that it one of them is disqualified
the other may join with some other witnesses.
R. Simeon says
that a father and son and all relatives
are eligible to testify to the appearance of the new moon.
R. Yose said:
It happened once with Toviah the physician
that he saw the new moon in Jerusalem
along with his son and his emancipated slave,
and the priests accepted his evidence and that of his son
and disqualified his slave,
but when they appeared before the court
they accepted his evidence and that of his slave
and disqualified his son.

The Mishnah opens with a casuistic statement which rules that a father and son who see the new moon should both go to report their sighting to the court. This is followed by a pair of glosses which offer conflicting interpretations of this ruling. The first, anonymous interpretation states that a father and son are disqualified from testifying together as is the case for all immediate relatives under the normal rules of evidence. Both father and son should go to court because perhaps one of them will have the opportunity to join another, unrelated witness, thus completing the quorum of two witnesses needed for valid testimony. R. Simeon, in contrast, understands the ruling as suggesting that the normal rules of evidence do not apply to sightings of the new moon. In such a case, a father and son can indeed testify together. They should both proceed to court and offer their testimony.

The story which follows is the only case story in *Rosh Hashanah* 1–2 that is set in pre-Destruction Jerusalem.[30] Like the other rabbinic accounts of this era, the story posits the existence of a rabbinically/Pharisaically controlled court sitting on the Temple Mount which had responsibility for matters relating to the calendar. However, this story also introduces another group which also issued rulings with regard to the calendar, the "priests."

Who were these "priests" and what was their relationship with the sages with whom they disagreed? In recent decades, several leading scholars have argued in light of newly published materials from Qumran that the dispute between the Pharisees and their competitors in the late Second Temple period must be seen primarily in halakhic terms.[31] This has led some scholars to hypothesize that there were two competing systems of halakhah extant in the decades surrounding the turn of the Common Era. There was Pharisaic halakhah, which would become the basis for the halakhah of the post-Destruction rabbis, and there was a "priestly" halakhah which was observed, in one form or another, by both the Sadducees and the Essenes of Qumran.[32]

Our story apparently preserves a memory of the struggle for control over the Temple between the ritual representatives of the priestly and the Pharisaic-rabbinic legal systems. The way in which this struggle plays out in the story is hardly straightforward. The most likely understanding of the story is that the account of the priests' ruling is a false ending meant to be rejected in favor of the final ruling of the court. Even this reading grants a certain legitimacy to the priestly position. The Mishnaic storyteller could have easily suppressed any account of the priests and their ruling, giving the impression that the rabbis were the sole authority in Jerusalem. This is the strategy adopted in the rest of this chapter, in which the court in Jerusalem is presented as the unchallenged seat of halakhic authority. By choosing to raise the level of narrativity in this story and including the ruling of the priests, the editors of the Mishnah give voice to the priestly halakhah, albeit with the intent of rejecting it.

Furthermore, this story is presented in the context of a similar dispute between two legitimate rabbis. By juxtaposing the first and second part of the paragraph, the editors imply an identity between the position of R. Simeon and that of the priests. On the one hand, the fact that R. Simeon has sided with the priests over the Pharisaic court demonstrates the nonnormative status of R. Simeon's position. However, the flip side of this is that the dispute between the priests and the rabbis has been assimilated into a dispute between two legitimate Tannaim. The disputes between the Pharisees and the priests are portrayed as internal debates between members of the same community who share basic beliefs and values, rather than as a struggle between two warring factions.

Finally, the story never explicitly states that the Pharisees' position is authoritative. Indeed, in this case, there is no practical distinction between the Pharisaic and priestly positions. In the end, they both found two witnesses to rely upon in order to sanctify the new month that day. The case thus does not lend itself to a decisive rejection of the priestly position. It remains possible to read this as a truly double-ended story, in which both the priests' and Pharisees' responses to the situation are equally legitimate. While this reading remains the less likely one, it cannot be rejected outright. This reading would suggest a fully pluralist approach to the debate between the Pharisees and the priests. The story simply establishes two conflicting opinions on the matter without asserting which position is correct.

The story of Toviah the physician thus presents a significant complication of the basic narrative of a single, centralized authority accepting witnesses and declaring the new month. In the story, there are in fact two loci of authority on the Temple Mount vying for control over the process of setting the calendar. The two groups do not simply make different decisions with regard to particular cases; they operate according to different rules. It is even possible that they had fundamentally different conceptions of the entire process. The Pharisees applied the rules of evidence that apply in civil and criminal cases. They apparently saw the fixing of the new month as an essentially juridical procedure whose purpose was to determine the facts of the case. The appropriate address for such issues was their court, which presumably dealt with other legal issues as well. The priests, on the other hand, rejected the application of the standard rules of evidence to cases concerning the calendar. They accepted witnesses who were related to one another. Their main concern was to eliminate a witness who lacked the proper lineage. It seems that they saw the sanctification of the new moon as a fundamentally cultic procedure which should be under the jurisdiction of the priests and which should take into account their deep concern with lineage and personal status.[33]

The Mishnah suggests that the Pharisaic court held ultimate authority in this debate. However, the priests are never explicitly rejected. They have a vote, even if it can be vetoed. It remains possible to read this story as accepting both positions as equally legitimate. This story opens up a space for considering the sources and extent of Pharisaic and rabbinic centralized authority in the face of their challengers.

Rosh Hashanah 2:8a: In R. Gamliel's Chambers

The second set of case stories in these chapters appears at the very end of chapter 2. Like the previous stories, they too engage the question of the nature and extent of centralized rabbinic control of the calendar. Paragraphs 6 and 7 conclude the ritual narrative of the new moon ritual, recounting the procedure for examining and approving witnesses of the new moon. Paragraph 6 lists a series of technical questions put to the witness to determine that he did in fact see the new moon. In the following section, we move from a generalized discussion of these procedures to a more specific account of the way in which they were carried out by R. Gamliel in Yavne.

Paragraph 8 opens with a description of R. Gamliel's cross-examination methods for witnesses to the new moon:

דְּמוּת צוּרוֹת לְבָנוֹת הָיוּ לוֹ לְרַבָּן גַּמְלִיאֵ׳
בַּעֲלִיָּתוֹ בַּטַּבְלָה וּבַכּוֹתֶל
שֶׁבָּהֶן מַרְאֶה אֶת הַהֶדְיוֹטוֹת
וְאוֹמֵ׳ הֲכָזֶה רְאִיתָה אוֹ כָזֶה.

> R. Gamliel used to have a diagram of phases of the moon
> on a tablet on the wall of his upper chamber;
> he used to show them to the unlearned and say,
> "Did it look like this or this?"

This passage describes a repeated event in which R. Gamliel used visual aids to cross-examine witnesses who did not understand the technical questions laid out previously in paragraph 6.[34] This scene places R. Gamliel at the center of the entire process. He alone undertakes the cross-examination rather than a full panel of judges as suggested previously in the Mishnah. Furthermore, the examination takes place not in a public courtroom but in the privacy of R. Gamliel's upper chambers. R. Gamliel is portrayed as the embodiment of rabbinic calendrical authority.

R. Gamliel's actual methods of examination suggest a certain tension in his approach to the procedure. On the one hand, R. Gamliel makes use of objective, empirical methods to question his witness. His authority appears to be rooted not in his position but in his knowledge of observational astronomy. In theory, a rabbi with greater knowledge could come along and challenge this knowledge, thereby forcing R. Gamliel to concede his supremacy.

Yet previously, in paragraph 6, the generalized ritual narrative makes no mention of the use of visual aids. It lays out specific questions that must be asked of the witnesses in order for the examination to be completed. The witnesses were not shown anything that might jog their memory or help them clarify their testimony. An unlearned witness might thus be turned away because of his inability to articulate what it was that he saw. R. Gamliel deviates from this established practice by offering another option for witnesses who would otherwise have been turned away. He gives them the chance to respond to a series of visual cues. As we have seen, R. Gamliel is portrayed in the Mishnah as concerned not simply with determining the validity of individual witnesses but also with establishing his court as the central authority for the setting of the calendar. The court could only succeed if it was able to regularly declare the new month on the basis of valid witness. This required a steady stream of witnesses. It also required that the court not reject too many witnesses that came before it. Just as he ruled that one should not turn back witnesses on the Sabbath even if their testimony would in the end be unnecessary, so too R. Gamliel expanded the procedure for cross-examining witnesses. R. Gamliel did not see his role as simply one of applying established rules but rather as using his discretion as the head of the court to adjust the rules to fit current circumstances and bolster the court's authority.

Rosh Hashanah 2:8b: R. Yohanan ben Nuri vs. R. Gamliel

The Mishnah then introduces the first of two case stories:

מַעֲשֶׂה שֶׁבָּאוּ שְׁנַיִם וְאָמְרוּ
רְאִינוּהוּ שַׁחֲרִית בַּמִּזְרָח
וְעַרְבִית בַּמַּעֲרָב
אָמַר רַבִּ׳ יוֹחָנָן בֶּן נוּרִי
עֵידֵי שֶׁקֶר הֵם
כְּשֶׁבָּאוּ לְיַוְונָה
קִיבְּלָן רַבִּ׳ גַּמְלִיאֵ׳

On one occasion two witnesses came and said,
"We saw it in the morning in the east
and in the evening in the west."
R. Yohanan ben Nuri thereupon said,
"They are false witnesses."
When they came to Yavne,
Rabban Gamliel accepted them.

In many ways, this story is very similar to the story of R. Aqiba's dispute with R. Gamliel in the previous chapter of the Mishnah. Both R. Yohanan and R. Aqiba are confronted with witnesses whose status is problematic. In both stories, R. Aqiba and R. Yohanan reject the witnesses. Both stories end with R. Gamliel overruling this decision and declaring the witnesses' testimony to be valid.

There are, however, important differences between the two stories. The R. Aqiba story is more of a truly doubly-ended story. Neither R. Aqiba's nor R. Gamliel's position is decisively favored. Each is a viable response to the situation. In this story, R. Yohanan's ruling appears to be a false ending. His decision is clearly overruled by R. Gamliel and has no impact on the outcome of the case. His ruling serves only as a foil for R. Gamliel's view. R. Gamliel clearly emerges as the final authority for all things regarding the calendar.

An examination of the details of R. Yohanan's dispute with R. Gamliel casts a different light on this story. The witnesses claim to have seen the moon in the morning in the east and in the evening in the west. Based on their positions, the morning moon would have to be the last sliver of the waning moon, while the afternoon moon would have to be the first sighting of the new moon. The problem is that it is impossible for there to be such a short interval between the disappearance of the old moon and the appearance of the new moon.[35] One or both of the witnesses' claims must be false. R. Yohanan's position is thus quite clear. The witnesses have presented internally contradictory testimony and hence must be rejected as false witnesses.

The rationale behind R. Gamliel's position accepting the witnesses is hardly as clear. Maimonides presents what seems to me to be the most likely interpretation: R. Gamliel accepted the witnesses' testimony regarding the new moon while rejecting their statements regarding the old moon.[36] In this reading, R. Gamliel is less interested in getting to the objective truth than he is in using his judicial discretion to arrive at the desired outcome. For our purposes, the most important thing is that the Mishnah itself offers no reasoning for R. Gamliel's curious ruling. This gives the impression that in fact it is R. Yohanan's position that is rooted in common sense and empirical understanding, while R. Gamliel's position remains unexplained and is perhaps inexplicable. The fact that it is R. Gamliel's ruling that carries the day would appear to be a result of his position as head of the court rather than the inherent merit of his arguments.

Rosh Hashanah 2:8c–9: R. Joshua vs. R. Gamliel

The next story similarly portrays R. Gamliel as presenting his authority as rooted in his political position while his opponents advocate a law that is governed by objective, empirical rules that can be applied by anyone regardless of their stature. The story opens with a by now familiar pattern:

וְעוֹד בָּאוּ שְׁנַיִם וְאָמְרוּ
רְאִינוּהוּ בִזְמַנּוֹ
וּבַלַּיְלָה בְעִיבּוּרוֹ[37] לֹא נִרְאָה
וְקִיבְּלָן רַבָּן גַּמְלִיאֵ'
אָמַ' ר' דּוֹסָא בֶן אַרְכִּינָס
עֵידֵי שֶׁקֶר הֵם
וְהֵיאָךְ מְעִידִין עַל הָאִשָּׁה שֶׁיָּלְדָה
וּלְמָחָר[38] כְּרֵיסָהּ בֵּין שִׁינֶּיהָ
אָמַ' לוֹ ר' יְהוֹשֻׁעַ
רוֹאֶה אֲנִי אֶת דְּבָרֶיךָ

On another occasion two witnesses came and said,
"We saw it at its proper time,
but on the next night it was not seen,"

and Rabban Gamliel accepted their evidence.
Rabbi Dosa ben Harkinas said,
"They are false witnesses.
How can one testify that a woman has borne a child
when on the next day
her belly is still between her teeth?"
Said R. Joshua to him:
I see [the force of] your argument.

Once again we have a double-ended case story in which R. Gamliel and his disputant each give their rulings with regard to a pair of witnesses to the new moon whose testimony is problematic. Predictably, it is R. Gamliel who accepts the witnesses and his opponents who reject them.

Yet this story is quite different from its predecessors on several levels. First, R. Gamliel's position is even more radical in this case than in the previous one. Witnesses come and claim that they saw the new moon on the night of the thirtieth day of the month. The next evening, however, the new moon is not visible.[39] If the new moon was visible on the night of the thirtieth, it should be visible on the night of the thirty-first.[40] It is highly unlikely that the witnesses saw the moon as they claimed. R. Dosa's response is therefore most logical. The sanctification of the new moon must be retroactively canceled. It is R. Gamliel's insistence on not overturning his court's original ruling that requires explanation. As R. Dosa argues, it is no more likely that the new moon appeared on one night and disappeared on the next than it is that a woman whose belly is huge gave birth to a baby the night before. There seems to be no way of reinterpreting the witnesses' testimony in way that would make it admissible evidence.

What then is the basis of R. Gamliel's ruling? R. Gamliel apparently shares the opinion found elsewhere in Tannaitic literature that sanctification done on the basis of false witnesses remains valid even once the witnesses have been exposed.[41] Once again, R. Gamliel's chief concern is the integrity and authority of the court at whose head he stands, even at the expense of the empirical validity of the ruling. For R. Gamliel, the authority of his court ultimately rests not in the accuracy of its rulings but in its divine mandate to regulate the calendar. As Justice Jackson noted about the supremacy of his own court in Washington, DC, "We are not final because we are infallible, we are infallible only because we are final."[42] R. Dosa, in contrast, tenaciously insists that no jurist can claim the right to exceed the bounds of common sense. Any law worth its name must follow some basic rules and principles.

The story thus far also presents a significant formal difference from its predecessors. Here R. Gamliel does not get the last word. His ruling is rejected by R. Dosa. R. Dosa follows up his challenge with an earthy metaphor about a pregnant woman to suggest that R. Gamliel's position defies common sense. Next, R. Joshua offers his support for R. Dosa's challenge. R. Gamliel finds himself under aggressive attack from two of his colleagues. This story is now truly double ended in a way that the stories involving R. Aqiba and R. Yohanan are not. In those stories, R. Gamliel's right to issue authoritative rulings on matters of the calendar is asserted. Here both R. Gamliel and R. Dosa's rulings remain in play not only in theory but in practice. We do not yet know whose ruling will carry the day—R. Gamliel's, which is rooted in his position of authority, or R. Dosa's, which is rooted in his claim to the empirical truth.[43]

At this juncture, the story is transformed into a very different type of case story. Now the halakhic crisis which demands resolution is not the problematic nature of the witnesses but the refusal of R. Dosa and R. Joshua to accept R. Gamliel's ruling. We thus have yet another form of narrative repetition, as the case-story genre doubles over on itself, generating a case story within a case story. This situation demands yet another ruling from R. Gamliel, which will establish a precedent for conduct in such cases. R. Gamliel's response is unequivocal:

שָׁלַח לוֹ רַבָּ׳ גַּמְלִיאֵ׳
גּוֹזֵר אֲנִי עָלֶיךָ
שֶׁתָּבוֹא אֶצְלִי בְּמַקֶּלְךָ וּבִמְעוֹתֶיךָ
בְּיוֹם שֶׁחָל יוֹם הַכִּיפּוּרִים
לִהְיוֹת בְּחֶשְׁבּוֹנָךְ

Rabban Gamliel sent to him to say,
"I enjoin upon you
to appear before me with your staff and your money
on the day on which the Day of Atonement should be
according to your reckoning."

R. Gamliel quickly moves to quash the incipient rebellion on his hands. We now learn that the month in question was Tishrei. As such, the rejection of the court's decision poses more than a theoretical threat to R. Gamliel's authority. It has serious practical ramifications as well. The dissenters are threatening to celebrate the holidays of the month, including the holiest of holidays, Yom Kippur, on different days than R. Gamliel and his followers. The result would be a factionalization of rabbinic circles that would undermine R. Gamliel's drive for centralized rabbinic authority. R. Gamliel responds to this threat by ordering R. Joshua to publicly profane the day that he holds to be Yom Kippur. Carrying on in the public domain is prohibited on Yom Kippur as is the handling money. R. Joshua would thus be forced to concede the supreme authority of R. Gamliel.

While R. Gamliel's actions are portrayed as justified and perhaps even necessary, the story's depiction of R. Gamliel up to this point can hardly be called sympathetic. R. Dosa's and R. Joshua's original complaints seem more than reasonable. They speak with strong conviction against what they see as a travesty of God's law.

R. Gamliel, in contrast, never justifies his position. He does not attempt to convince R. Joshua of the justice of his behavior, as others will later in the story. Rather, R. Gamliel responds with naked power, demanding R. Joshua's public humiliation.

The story now departs entirely from the pattern of the case story. The section that follows presents a pair of exchanges between several of the main characters in the story. From a formal perspective, these scenes are most akin to the Mishnaic dialogs described in chapter 3 of this book. These stylized conversations are used by the Mishnah to explicate the underlying rationales behind the opposing positions in Tannaitic disputes. Here the Mishnaic narrator makes use of a similar device to explain both R. Gamliel's rationale and R. Joshua's motivations for his actions at the end of the story:

הָלַךְ וּמְצָאוֹ ר' עֲקִיבָה מֵיצֵיר
אָמַ' לוֹ יֶשׁ לִי לִלְמוֹד
שֶׁכָּל מַה שֶּׁעָשָׂה רַבָּ' גַּמְלִיאֵ' עָשׂוּי
שֶׁנֶּ'
אֵלֶּה מוֹעֲדֵי ה' מִקְרָאֵי קוֹדֶשׁ
אֲשֶׁר תִּקְרְאוּ אוֹתָם
בֵּין בִּזְמַנָּן בֵּין שֶׁלֹּא בִזְמַנָּן
אֵין לִי מוֹעֲדוֹת אֶלָּא אֵלּוּ
בָּא לוֹ אֵצֶל ר' דּוֹסָא בֶן אַרְכִינָס
אָמַ' לוֹ
אִם בָּאִים אָנוּ לָדִין⁴⁴ אַחַר [בֵּית דִּינוֹ שֶׁלְּרַבָּן גַּמְלִיאֵ'
צְרִיכִין אָנוּ לָדִין⁴⁵ אַחַר]⁴⁶ כָּל בֵּית דִּין וְדִין
שֶׁעָמַד מִימוֹת מֹשֶׁה וְעַד עַכְשָׁיו
שֶׁנֶּ'
וַיַּעַל מֹשֶׁה וְאַהֲרֹן
נָדָב וַאֲבִיהוּא וְשִׁבְעִים מִזִּקְנֵי יִשְׂרָאֵ'
וְלָמָּה לֹא נִתְפָּרְשׁוּ שְׁמוֹתָן שֶׁלַּזְּקֵנִים
אֶלָּא לְלַמְּדָךְ שֶׁכָּל שְׁלוֹשָׁה וּשְׁלוֹשָׁה
שֶׁעָמְדוּ בֵית דִּין עַל יִשְׂרָאֵ'
הֲרֵי הֵן כְּבֵית דִּינוֹ שֶׁלְּמֹשֶׁה

R. Aqiba went [to R. Joshua] and found him in great distress.
He said to him, "I can bring proof [from Scripture]
that whatever Rabban Gamliel has done is valid,
because it says,
'These are the appointed seasons of the Lord, holy convocations,
which ye shall proclaim in their appointed seasons' [Lev. 23:4]
[which means that whether they are proclaimed]
at their proper time or not at their proper time,
I have no appointed seasons save these.
He then went to R. Dosa ben Harkinas.

He said to him:
If we call into question [the decisions of] the court of Rabban Gamliel,
we must call into question the decisions of every court
which has existed since the days of Moses up to the present time.
For it says,
"'Then went up Moses and Aaron,
Nadab and Abihu and seventy of the elders of Israel' [Ex. 24:9].
Why were not the names of the elders mentioned?
To show that every group of three
which has acted as a court over Israel
is on a level with the court of Moses."

The identity of the speakers in these two speeches remains ambiguous. Traditionally, as reflected in the translation above, both speeches have been understood as being directed at R. Joshua, the first spoken by R. Aqiba and the second by R. Dosa. However, Daniel Schwartz has pointed out that the phrase "he said to him," introducing the second speaker, does not clearly delineate the identities of the speaker and the listener of this speech. Following the lead of Danby's translation, Daniel Schwartz argues that in fact it makes more sense to assign this speech to R. Joshua.[47] David Henshke has gone one step further and argued that the first speech as well should be attributed to R. Joshua.[48]

Regardless of how one resolves these issues, all agree that this section portrays a transformation of R. Joshua from an ardent opponent of R. Gamliel's ruling to someone willing to submit to R. Gamliel's authority. The only question is when this transformation takes place. According to the traditional reading, it only occurs after R. Joshua has heard both R. Aqiba's and R. Dosa's arguments. In Schwartz's reading, R. Joshua is convinced by R. Aqiba and then goes off to rebuke R. Dosa. Henshke argues that this transformation takes place even before R. Joshua has learned of R. Gamliel's decree.

Our main concern is to understand how these two speeches make the case for submitting to R. Gamliel regardless of their authors and audiences. The opening proposition of the first speech makes a broad claim, "All that R. Gamliel does is valid." The support for this statement, however, focuses exclusively on R. Gamliel's powers concerning the calendar. The speaker cites as his proof text Leviticus 23:4: "These are the appointed festivals of the Lord…that you shall proclaim as holy convocations."[49] The emphasis here is on the fact that "*you* shall proclaim." The times of the holidays are not predetermined. Rather, they happen when the court proclaims them, even if that date deviates from astronomical reality.

As Avraham Walfish has noted, this is not the first time this verse is cited in *Rosh Hashanah*.[50] In 1:9, the Mishnah cites this verse for the opposite purpose: there the emphasis is on the final words of the verse, which are elided in our story: "in their times."[51] According to the Mishnah in chapter 1, the holidays must take place at their preset times. Hence it is permissible for witnesses to violate the Sabbath in order to insure that the court's declaration of the new month coincides with the actual empirical citing of the new moon.

These two readings of the verse emphasize the fundamental tension within the laws of the new month and in Mishnaic halakhah in general. On the one hand, the calendar is subject to fixed rules. It is tied to objective phenomena that are not subject to human interference. On the other hand, the calendar is set by a human court whose judgment is subjective and fallible. By citing this verse to argue for R. Gamliel's authority, the speaker implicitly recalls the alternative reading suggested previously, reminding the reader that R. Gamliel's claim to absolute power is hardly so clear-cut.

The second speech deals with R. Gamliel's authority more broadly considered. It focuses on the juxtaposition of Moses with the seventy anonymous sages at Mt. Sinai in the verse from Exodus, seeing this as implying parity between Moses and all other judges. According to this position, a judge's authority is in no way rooted in his personal qualities or abilities. All judges, including Moses, draw their authority from the fact that they are members of a duly constituted halakhic court. It is the position that makes the judge, and not vice versa.

The passage also significantly expands the framing narrative of these chapters that we discussed earlier. Previously we saw how the Mishnah roots the authority of R. Gamliel's and other post-Destruction rabbinic courts in the authority of the central court of the Temple in Jerusalem. This speech traces R. Gamliel's authority all the way back to Moses himself. This is one of the few direct references in the Mishnah to the biblical master narrative that underlies all rabbinic halakhic discourse. R. Gamliel is no different from Moses because he is part of the same chain of tradition that has its roots in the covenant with God at Mt. Sinai. Both men's actions are divinely sanctioned and beyond challenge.

While this speech may present an unassailable argument for the power of R. Gamliel's office, it is hardly a resounding recommendation of R. Gamliel's character and abilities. The implication is that R. Gamliel may well have erred in this case and that indeed he may not be a great leader or scholar by any standard. All that matters is that he holds power.[52]

Following the conclusions of these arguments, R. Joshua decides to submit to R. Gamliel's demands:

נָטַל מַקְלוֹ וּמְעוֹתָיו בְּיָדוֹ
וְהָלַךְ לְיַוְונֶה אֵצֶל רַבַּן גַּמְלִיאֵ'
בְּיוֹם שֶׁחָל יוֹם הַכִּפּוּרִים
לִהְיוֹת בְּחֶשְׁבּוֹנוּ

He [R. Joshua] thereupon took his staff and his money
and went to Yavne to Rabban Gamliel
on the day on which the Day of Atonement
fell according to his reckoning.

With this line, the story returns to the model of the case story. As we have seen in previous chapters, some case stories include a final stage which describes an individual or group as complying with the rabbis' ruling. This serves to reinforce the claim for rabbinic authority implicit in the case story. Here R. Joshua confirms R. Gamliel's claims to authority by complying with his demand. Even those who initially opposed R. Gamliel ultimately recognize the need to submit to his will.

In some textual witnesses, favored by Epstein, the story ends with these words.[53] In this reading, the narrative point of view remains fixed on R. Joshua, almost from the time he appears on the stage until the curtain falls. While R. Gamliel and his authority may be the thematic focus of the story, R. Gamliel the character remains at the periphery. The story gives us good reason to respect him, but our sympathies remain with R. Joshua. The story thus establishes a tension between the need for centralized authority and a concern for those who are on the peripheries of this system.

All of the major textual witnesses, however, conclude the story with a final scene describing R. Gamliel's reaction to R. Joshua's appearance:

עָמַד רַבָּן גַּמְלִיאֵ' וּנְשָׁקוֹ בְּר אשׁוֹ
אָמַ' לוֹ
בּוֹא בְּשָׁלוֹם רַבִּי וְתַלְמִידִי
רַ' בַּחָכְמָה
וְתַלְמִידִי שֶׁקִּיבַּלְתָּהּ עָלֶיךָ אֶת דְּבָרַיי

> Rabban Gamliel rose and kissed him on his head.
> He said to him:
> Come in peace, my teacher and my disciple—
> my teacher in wisdom
> and my disciple because you have accepted my decision.

R. Gamliel now appears as a benevolent father figure embracing his prodigal son. R. Gamliel goes so far as to acknowledge that in fact R. Joshua is the greater scholar. This statement can be seen as a final synthesis of the conflicting modes of authority represent by R. Gamliel and R. Joshua. On the theoretical plane, knowledge and understanding of the principles that underlie the law are to be respected and valued. However, in practice, the law must be determined by those who hold institutional power in light of the needs of the day. Failure to do so will lead to chaos and the collapse of halakhic authority in any form.

In this passage, R. Gamliel himself acknowledges his scholarly inferiority and implies that he may in fact be mistaken on this matter. The story does not make R. Gamliel out to be an ideal leader. Optimally, a leader will be both *in* and *an* authority. Yet, R. Gamliel lacks scholarly supremacy over his colleagues. Furthermore, the story does not portray him as consulting with his wiser fellow rabbis. Rather, he acts unilaterally, demanding compliance from the other members of his court. R. Gamliel may be the ultimate authority, but he is hardly the ideal authority.

Conclusion

The first two chapters of Mishnah *Rosh Hashanah* are characterized by a series of interrelated formal, thematic, and ideological tensions. On the formal level there is the tension between the conception of the story as a "line" and as a "tangle" as well as the related distinction between *fabula* and *syuzhet*. The tension between the underlying narrative structure of the new-moon ritual and the discursive and dialectical manner in which it is presented underlie these chapters and reflect a dialog about the very nature of the law and its implementation.

The double-ended case stories in these chapters reflect these tensions. These stories can be read as simply possessing a more complex structure meant to achieve the same end as simple case stories. In this reading, it is the final ruling that is meant to be authoritative. The first ruling presented needs to be viewed as a momentary detour, not a complete divergence, on the path to a final ruling. This detour can serve several functions. Like all nonessential mimetic detail, this presentation of the rejected position helps to create a richer and more convincing narrative world, which ultimately enhances the stories' rhetorical force. It also creates a foil for the authoritative answer, highlighting the distinctiveness of the ruling.

Alternatively, the double endings can also be seen as irreparably disrupting the simple line of the conventional case story. Rather than giving an unequivocal ruling in a given situation, they present two alternative possibilities. They thus challenge the notion of a single uncontested ruling for any given situation. The tension between these two possible readings remains unresolved.

On the thematic and ideological levels, the Mishnah presents the struggle to establish a centralized rabbinic calendrical court. Underlying this conflict are competing views of the nature of rabbinic authority and of the halakhah itself. Is the head of the court *in* authority or *an* authority? Is the new month declared based on objective rules and fact or on the interpretive discretion of the court? The conflicting positions in the various case stories reflect these differing positions. Ultimately, there can be no question that Mishnah *Rosh Hashanah* and its case stories in particular advocate a centralized rabbinic court, whose head is empowered to set the calendar according to his judgments. Yet the dissenting voices which the Mishnah records show a clear awareness of the shortcomings of such a system and an unwillingness to give up on the idea that a rabbi's authority must ultimately be grounded in his knowledge and proper application of the rules and principles of halakhah.

9

Etiological Stories: Original Nightmares

"History, Stephen said, is a nightmare from which I am trying to awake."

James Joyce, *Ulysses*

"If Woody had gone right to the police, this would never have happened."

"Bunco Busters"

Etiological stories tell of the origins of a particular halakhic practice. They explain how, as a result of some sort of crisis, an initial practice was discontinued and a new one was instituted to take its place. They are, in many ways, the odd man out of the three genres that we are studying. From a formal perspective, etiological stories enter this book only on a technicality. They are included as one of the forms of the *ma'aseh* on the basis of only a single instance in which the word *ma'aseh* is used to refer to an element of an etiological story. These stories also diverge from the anecdotal style of case stories and exempla. Unlike these other genres, etiological stories do not generally portray a limited number of characters involved in a few closely linked events. Rather, their plots are painted on a much broader canvas portraying the changing practices of the entire Jewish people in response to historical events of national significance. Etiological stories are a type of framing narrative that gives authority to current practices by rooting them in the past. When considered collectively, etiological stories contribute to the shaping of the larger implicit framing story that underlies the Mishnah as a whole. They add in details to the covenantal history of the Jewish people, explaining how this relationship with God has remained steadfast despite changes in practice. Yet by emphasizing change and discontinuity, the stories also call attention to the ruptures in the metahistorical fabric in which the rabbis seek to wrap the Jewish national experience.

Despite these differences, etiological stories do share certain key similarities with the other forms of the *ma'aseh*. They too grow out of a an event in the past involving a particular halakhic practice. Furthermore, when taken as a whole, they also aid in establishing the authority of the rabbis. Case stories and exempla demonstrate the authority of the rabbis to transmit and interpret the law. Etiological stories go one step further, asserting the rabbis' rights to actually create the law through legislation. Thus in these stories rabbinic authority is all but merged with the law itself. Etiological stories also present an opportunity to reexamine and shed new light on some of the key issues of this book: the relationship between the stories, master narratives, and ritual narratives of the Mishnah, and the complexities of interconnection between law and narrative in both rabbinic and general culture.

A Case Study in the Form and Function of the Etiological Story: The Evolution of the Lulav Ritual, *Sukkah* 3:12/*Rosh Hashanah* 4:3

In order to illustrate the basic workings of the etiological story, I will focus on a single text, the story of R. Yohanan ben Zakkai's transformation of the lulav ritual which appears twice in the Mishnah, in *Sukkah* 3:12 and in *Rosh Hashanah* 4:3:

בָּרִאשׁוֹנָה
הָיָה¹ הַלּוּלָב נִטָּל
בַּמִּקְדָּשׁ שִׁבְעָה
וּבַמְּדִינָה יוֹם אֶחָד
מִשֶּׁחָרַב בֵּית הַמִּקְדָּשׁ
הִתְקִין
רַבָּן יוֹחָנָן בֶּן זַכַּיי
שֶׁיְּהֵא הַלּוּלָב נִטָּל בַּמִּקְדָּשׁ שִׁבְעָה
זֵכֶר לַמִּקְדָּשׁ

Originally
the lulav was taken
in the sanctuary
during the seven days [of Sukkot]
and in the country only one day.
When the Temple was destroyed,
it was ordained by
R. Yohanan ben Zakkai
that the lulav should be taken in the country seven days
in remembrance of the sanctuary.

This story clearly illustrates the basic tripartite structure of the Mishnaic etiological story. First, there is a description of a previously observed practice, generally introduced with the phrase *barishonah*, "originally." Here we are told that initially the lulav was taken in the Temple all seven days of Sukkot; outside of the Temple, it was taken only on the first day of the holiday.[2] Next, a crisis occurs that disrupts the execution of the established practice. As in many other cases, that crisis is the destruction of the Temple, which made the lulav ritual in the sanctuary impossible. Finally, the rabbis, collectively or represented by an individual, legislate a *taqqanah*, an enactment which establishes a new practice that is suitable to current circumstances.[3] In our story, R. Yohanan ben Zakkai declares that the lulav is to be taken all seven days of the holiday in all locales in order to preserve the memory of the original Temple practice.[4]

We will begin our analysis of this story with a consideration of the dynamics of the halakhic practices in question. Martin Jaffee argues for the "artificiality" of many Tannaitic reports of *taqqanot*.[5] Jaffee points to the fact that many *taqqanot* are represented in other sources as simple legal opinions or as being rulings based on scriptural argument. In other cases, a pair of practices that are presented in one source as reflecting a dispute between tradents are presented in another source as the pre- and post-*taqqanah* stages of an etiological story.[6] This evidence points to the fact that, "far from being ancient legislative acts which later receive literary preservation, there can be no doubt that at least some early rabbinic 'legislation' is the creation of rabbinic tradents and jurisprudents reflecting upon earlier materials."[7]

The development of the lulav ritual would appear to be a case in point. Contemporary historians argue that rabbinic authority was quite limited in the generations following the Destruction. This makes the claim that R. Yohanan ben Zakkai transformed Jewish practice immediately following the Destruction most improbable. Furthermore, the story claims that before the Destruction the lulav was taken outside of the Temple on the first day of the holiday. It is most unlikely that this reflects general practice in the days of the Temple. Several scholars have noted that in the literature of the Second Temple period, the taking of the lulav and other species used in the Sukkot ritual is associated exclusively with the Temple cult.[8] If indeed the practice of taking the lulav outside of the Temple predates the Destruction, it probably emerged gradually in the generations preceding the Destruction as part of an overall tendency among the Pharisees to adapt Temple related laws and rituals to broader practice.[9] In all likelihood, in the period immediately preceding and following the Destruction, there was a range of practices regarding taking the lulav outside of the Temple. The current practice of taking the lulav all seven days of Sukkot in all locales probably emerged as the normative practice as the result of a gradual process and not of a onetime decree.

The Mishnah's portrayal of the shift in practice regarding the lulav represents an example of the rabbinic "construction...of a usable historical memory."[10] The authors of the Mishnah were confronted with a general awareness that the "normative" lulav practice was but one of many options that existed in the past and perhaps even in their day. They dealt with this challenge by acknowledging that there were indeed other legitimate practices. However, they maintained that these practices represented the norms of a bygone era. Etiological stories thus uphold the theoretical legitimacy of multiple opposing views while allowing for only one acceptable practice.

If indeed the notion of a requirement to take the lulav only on the first day did not necessarily reflect practice during the Temple era, what then was the rabbis' source for this ruling? It seems that in this case the rabbis faced not only divergent practices but a problematic scriptural text as well. Leviticus 23:40 reads:

וּלְקַחְתֶּם לָכֶם בַּיּוֹם הָרִאשׁוֹן
פְּרִי עֵץ הָדָר כַּפֹּת תְּמָרִים
וַעֲנַף עֵץ־עָבֹת וְעַרְבֵי־נָחַל
וּשְׂמַחְתֶּם לִפְנֵי ה' אֱלֹהֵיכֶם—שִׁבְעַת יָמִים

On the first day you shall take
the product of the *hadar* trees, branches of palm trees,
boughs of leafy trees, and willows of the brook,
and you shall rejoice before the Lord your God for seven days.

The first half of the verse states that the lulav and the other species are to be taken on the first day of Sukkot.[11] Rabbinic exegetical methods would have directed the rabbis to read this to mean that the lulav should be taken on the first day, and *only* the first day. However, the final part of the verse suggests that one should celebrate with the lulav for all seven days of the holiday. The rabbis resolve this contradiction by localizing the implications of the term "before the Lord," which is understood to refer to the Tabernacle/Temple, to the second part of the verse. The result is that the verse describes two distinct rituals: the first part mandates the taking of the lulav by all Jews in all places on the first day of the holiday; the second part calls for it to be taken as part of the Temple ritual throughout the holiday.[12] While this reading may reconcile the two halves of the verse, it provides no basis for the accepted practice of taking the lulav in all places on all days of Sukkot. The story told in the Mishnah resolves this problem by positing two stages in the development of the practice. The practices referred to in the biblical verse pertain to the time of the Temple, while the current practice was adopted only after the Destruction.

The Mishnah thus resolves the competing claims of scripture, tradition, and practice by narrative means. When viewed from a broader perspective, this story and others like it make a case for centralized rabbinic authority and its capacity to maintain the integrity of the halakhic system in the face of historical change. Circumstances and day-to-day practice may change over time. However, the halakhah is not left to drift along like so much flotsam and jetsam on the river of history. Rabbinic authority remains a constant. It is the only legitimate mechanism for halakhic change, and it assures the authenticity of Jewish practice.

As with exempla and case stories, etiological stories collectively present a model for the workings of rabbinic authority.

Martin Jaffee has come to very similar conclusions about the role of etiological stories in the Mishnah. Noting that all of the etiological stories in the Mishnah refer either to the Temple era or to the period immediately following the Destruction, he argues that the collective message of these texts is that

> while the Temple stood, we appear to be told, qualified authorities intervened into the common practice to preserve or protect [from] threats to Israel's efficacy as a transformer of divine power into worldly blessing; after its destruction, their successors preside over the transformation of the Temple-centered institutions.... By dotting their corpus of Halakhic tradition here and there with reports of early patriarchal intervention into customary Israelite usage, the editors of the Mishnah project an image of authority which, while perhaps absent in their own day, can be held out, through nostalgia, as a model for future reconstruction.[13]

Etiological stories thus have important implications for the relationship between the narrative and non-narrative conceptions of law represented in the Mishnah. On the one hand, they clearly represent a narrative conception of law. They portray the halakhah as a changing system under the guidance of human authority figures. Yet etiological stories also reflect an essentially conservative viewpoint reflecting the apodictic conception of law as essentially unchanging. Such a conservative approach toward legal change was the dominant one in the premodern world. The legal historian Fritz Kern explains this view of legal change in a discussion of medieval legal theory:

> There is, in the Middle Ages, no such thing as "the first application of a legal rule." Law is old; new law is a contradiction in terms; for either new law is derived explicitly or implicitly from the old, or it conflicts with the old, in which case it is not lawful. The fundamental idea remains the same: the old law is the true law, and true law is the old law. According to mediaeval ideas, therefore, the enactment of new law is not possible at all; and all legislation and legal reform is conceived of as the restoration of the good old law which has been violated.[14]

Etiological stories respond to this problem of legal change. These stories may be seen as limiting halakhic change to a relatively limited set of cases, suggesting that in all other instances the law remains as it was. Furthermore, etiological stories emphasize the restorative nature of rabbinic *taqqanot*, making them compatible, at least to a certain extent, with the non-narrative tendencies in Mishnaic law. *Taqqanot* are not innovations but attempts to preserve at least some aspect of an old law or practice that has been rendered unfeasible by practical circumstances. Etiological stories thus generate a common ground where narrative and non-narrative approaches to the law can both function. The law emerges as at once static and dynamic.

Etiological Stories as Covenantal Narratives

In a similar manner, etiological stories such as the one above can be seen as helping to strengthen and supplement the biblical framing narrative which underlies the Mishnaic discourse. As we have seen, the key event in this historical narrative is the covenant between God and Israel at Sinai. This established the central place of the law in mediating the relationship between God and his people. Fundamentally, Sinai is the only truly significant historical event in this scheme. Israel's fate throughout history is regulated by its loyalty to the law given at Sinai. In the rabbinic view, nothing can ultimately break this relationship or change its rules. Between Sinai and the Messianic era, Jewish history is an extended middle game which plays itself out according to covenantal procedures.

Nevertheless, a large percentage of the law revealed to Moses in the Torah is centered on the Temple cult. The Temple was the linchpin of the Jews' continued relationship with their God. Its destruction must be viewed on some level as a disruption of the grand covenantal narrative in which the rabbis situated themselves. The story about R. Yohanan ben Zakkai is one of a series of etiological stories that note changes in the ritual observances of the holidays and other practices which were instituted, in many cases by R. Yohanan, as a result of the destruction of the Temple.[15]

In many other rabbinic sources, the loss of the Temple is portrayed as far more than a disruption of ritual and social life. It is seen as the only event in postbiblical history of true covenantal significance. The Destruction seriously ruptured the framing narrative in terms of which the rabbis understood Israel's relationship with God. Along with the Temple, Israel lost the primary nexus of their relationship with God. All future existence is in some way one step removed from the divine.[16]

The etiological stories of the Mishnah present a different perspective. They serve to integrate the Destruction into the rabbinic framing story. While the Destruction had a huge impact on Jewish practice, continuity was ultimately maintained. In this view, the rabbis remained in charge and their enactments ensured that the Jewish people's relationship with God through the halakhah was maintained.

Similarly, this focus on the Destruction also served to streamline the complexities of the history of Jewish practice. As in the case of the taking of the lulav, Shmuel Safrai argues that that virtually all of the major rituals of the Temple that were not strictly cultic migrated to the synagogue. He sees this as a gradual process that had already begun in the days of the Temple.[17] The Mishnah, in contrast, consolidates these changes around a single event: the Destruction of the Temple.

Yet, for all of their efforts to emphasize the continuity between pre- and post-Destruction Jewish practice, the stories inevitably call attention to the very significance of the events of 70 CE. The etiological stories concerning the Temple project an essentially tragic vision of Jewish history and of halakhic practice. Jews today live in a postlapsarian state in which their practices are at best a pale memory of those of Temple days (*zekher lamiqdash*). These stories do not offer any explicit hope of returning to the previous state of grace.[18] They exhibit rather a stoic acceptance of reality. While halakhic change is acknowledged, it is viewed as an unfortunate consequence of Israel's tragic fall, not as an ideal state of affairs.

The "Steady Decline" Approach: *Sheqalim* 1:2

Other etiological stories describe other crises in addition to the Destruction of the Temple that lead to revisions of the halakhah. These stories suggest a somewhat different interpretation of the rabbinic master narrative of Jewish history. In *Sheqalim* 1:2, R. Judah relates:

בָּרִאשׁוֹנָה הָיוּ עוֹקְרִים
וּמַשְׁלִיכִים לִפְנֵיהֶם
מִשֶּׁרַבּוּ עוֹבְרֵי עֲבֵירָה
עַל הַדְּרָכִים הָיוּ מַשְׁלִיכִים[19]
הִתְקִינוּ
שֶׁיְּהוּ מַבְקִירִים אֶת כָּל הַשָּׂדֶה[20]

Originally they used to pluck up [the diverse kinds of crops]
and cast them before the owners.
[But] when the transgressors increased in number,
they used to cast them on the roads.
[Finally,] they ordained
that the whole field should be declared ownerless property.

This story deals with methods whereby the authorities dealt with violators of the prohibition against *kil'ayim*, the forbidden mixture of different species in agriculture. The initial practice was simply to uproot the offending plants and leave them in their place. This practice had to be altered in response to a crisis. As the number of sinners multiplied, stricter measures were needed to enforce the *kil'ayim* laws. The authorities began to remove the plants that they uprooted and throw them onto the roads, thereby depriving the owners of the use of those crops. Thus far, the story has fit the basic structure of the etiological story that I have outlined above. It describes an original practice, a crisis, and a *taqqanah* enacted to rectify the situation.[21] However, the story continues for one more sentence, relating yet another *taqqanah*. The text does not tell us what precipitated the second *taqqanah*. Either the practice of discarding the offending produce was not sufficient to dissuade people from planting *kil'ayim*, or people became even more sinful with passing years. One way or another, even harsher measures were needed. In response, the rabbis instituted a practice of declaring any fields which contained *kil'ayim* ownerless.[22] This story thus contains an extended structure telling of a second *taqqanah* and implying the occurrence of a continued or second crisis that necessitated it.[23]

The Mishnah contains one other example of a *taqqanah* that was enacted "when the sinners became numerous."[24] The Mishnah also presents several other accounts in which specific violations are named as the cause of a particular *taqqanah*.[25] Collectively, these stories suggest a paradigm of history in which the Jews become increasingly sinful and the rabbis must constantly revise their practices in order to counter the people's backsliding. In this version of history, the Destruction was not an isolated event. It was simply the most prominent incident along a long path of spiritual and moral decline of the Jewish people, resulting in their increasing alienation from God and his law.

This vision of covenantal history is most clearly expressed in the last chapter of Mishnah *Sota* and its parallels in the Tosefta. Starting with 9:9, the Mishnah lists a series of events preceding, including, and following the Destruction and notes their halakhic and spiritual implications. The list begins with a depiction of the cancellation of the biblical cultic rituals for dealing with cases of manslaughter and suspected adultery:

מִשֶּׁרַבּוּ הָרוֹצְחָנִים[26]
בָּטְלָה עֶגְלָה עֲרוּפָה...
מִשֶּׁרַבּוּ הַנּאֲפִים[27]
פָּסְקוּ הַמַּיִם הַמְאָרְרִים[28]

When murderers multiplied,
the ceremony of breaking a heifer's neck was discontinued....
When adulterers multiplied,
the ceremony of the bitter waters was discontinued.

Even before the Destruction, key cultic practices for the maintenance of a just society had already been discontinued. The extreme rise in capital crimes overwhelmed the system, requiring the abandonment of these rituals.

The Mishnah in *Sota* goes on to describe the gradual decline of Jewish society, including the rabbinic establishment. The passing of each of the leadings rabbis the generations before and after the Destruction is described as marking the end of yet another era. Each of these rabbis possessed a unique quality that would not be rivaled in subsequent generations. The Mishnah predicts that this decline will continue until the coming of the Messiah. The Tosefta traces this process of decline all the way back to the period of the wandering in the wilderness following the covenant at Sinai. Taken together, these sources portray Jewish history as having a consistently downward trajectory from Beginning to End. This decline will only be reversed with the coming of the Messiah and the end of history. In this context it is the rabbis' job to continuously adjust the law and adapt it to increasingly non-ideal circumstances.

The Emergence of Sectarianism: Rosh Hashanah 2:1–2

Among the major crises that according to the Mishnah marked the continuous decline of the Jewish people in ancient times was the splintering of Judaism into sects during the Second Temple era. As we have seen, most contemporary historians believe that none of these sects represented "authentic" Judaism, nor did their various laws and rules reflect the practice of the majority of Jews. Similarly, the Temple was not the exclusive domain of any one sect or faction throughout this period.

As far as the rabbis were concerned, however, their predecessors, the Pharisees, represented the "mainstream." The other sects represented a corrupt diversion of this stream. Despite the best efforts of these deviant groups, they remained on the margins. The rabbis maintained control of the central institutions of Jewish life. This narrative is reflected in a pair of etiological stories found in *Rosh Hashanah* 2:1–2:

בָּרִאשׁוֹנָה
הָיוּ מְקַבְּלִים עֵדוּת הַחוֹדֶשׁ מִכָּל אָדָם
מִשֶּׁקִּלְקְלוּ הַמִּינִים[29]
הִתְקִינוּ
שֶׁלֹּא יְהוּ מְקַבְּלִים אֶלָּא מִן הַמַּכִּירִים
בָּרִאשׁוֹנָה הָיוּ מַשִּׂיאִים מַשּׂוּאוֹת
מִשֶּׁקִּלְקְלוּ הַכּוּתִים
הִתְקִינוּ
שֶׁיְּהוּ שְׁלוּחִים יוֹצְאִין

    Originally
    testimony with regard to the new moon was received from anyone.
    When the sectarians became corrupted,
    It was ordained
    that testimony should be received only from persons known [to the court].
    Originally,
    they used to light beacons.
    When the Cutheans became corrupted,

It was ordained
that messengers should go forth.

In line with the major themes of the first two chapters of *Rosh Hashanah*, these stories deal with rabbinic/Pharisaic control of the calendar. They portray the Pharisees as possessing centralized authority in Jerusalem and imply that their inheritors, the post-Destruction rabbis, deserve similar powers. However, unlike the other narratives in these chapters, these stories portray a direct challenge to the Jerusalem authorities. In both cases, the narrator is vague about the exact nature of the threat. The crisis is described simply as "when the sectarians/Cutheans became corrupted." The very emergence of these groups is the root of the problem. They presented an immediate threat to centralized Pharisaic authority and to the proper practice of the halakhah. In the first case, the Tosefta[30] plausibly fills in the details of this story relating how the Boethusians once attempted to hire false witnesses in order to mislead the court in Jerusalem. In the second case, we can only presume that the Cutheans, better known as the Samaritans, lit signal fires on the wrong night in order to disrupt the Pharisees' communications system.

The Mishnah portrays both of these groups entirely in terms of their deviation from, and attacks on, Pharisaic norms and authority. They reflect the entropic forces of corruption and decline that rabbis struggle to mitigate and weaken. The rabbis succeed in rescuing their calendar and their authority by adopting more stringent and tamper-proof methods of fixing and disseminating the date of the new month.

An examination of these stories from a more critical perspective will reveal the counter-narratives that these stories suppress. In the first story, the sectarians in question are best understood as Essenes or a similar such group.[31] This sect did not oppose Pharisaic control of the calendar simply for political reasons; their opposition was based on fundamental differences in their beliefs. They rejected the very notion of the lunar calendar, regardless of who administered it. In their view, the Bible mandates a solar calendar of the type described in the book of Jubilees and elsewhere.

On the other hand, it seems most unlikely that the Samaritans referred to in the second story were interested in actively disrupting the calendrical court in Jerusalem. Very little is known about the calendar used by the Samaritans in antiquity.[32] However, Saul Lieberman, basing his claim on a Tosefta text which deals with divergences between the rabbinic and the Samaritan calendar, argued that the Samaritans used a calendar that was in principle the same as the calendar set by the Jews in Jerusalem and later by rabbinic courts. However, the Samaritans made independent determinations with regard to the date of the new moon and when to intercalate a leap month. As a result, the two calendars were occasionally either a day or month apart.[33]

In light of this, Lieberman argues that in all likelihood the Samaritans did not seek to actively disrupt the Jews' signal fires. Rather, they lit fires to alert their own community as to when they fixed the beginning of the new month. These flares would have originated from the Samarian cultic center at Mount Gerizim in Samaria. The Samaritans' fires could thus easily have been mistaken as a part of the Jews' relay which headed northward from Jerusalem through Samaria.[34] The Mishnah's account, however, suggests that the Samaritans actively and maliciously disrupted the flares originating in Jerusalem in an effort to undermine Pharisaic authority and practice.

The Mishnaic narrator of the two stories suppresses sectarian perspectives in order to give the impression of a Pharisaic establishment that is both in the right and in the might. The other groups appear as calendrical anarchists rather than as communities with beliefs and authority structures of their own. Yet these stories do not completely write out the rabbis' opponents. They acknowledge that both factions succeeded in forcing the rabbis to retreat and adopt less than optimal practices in order to preserve the integrity of their calendar system. The rabbis are not entirely invincible. To some degree they are at the mercy of the ever declining spiritual state of the Jewish people. The stories are caught in a tension between a desire to present the hegemony of Pharisaic-rabbinic halakhah, and the reality of the strong dissenting voices.

Ritual, Violence, and the Law

In the concluding section of this chapter and of the body of this book, I will look at a group of etiological stories that share a set of distinctive features which sets them apart from other etiological stories and, indeed, Mishnaic stories in general. From a structural point of view, these stories are distinguished by the fact that the "crises" that they describe take the form of anecdotes. The crises are presented in a self-contained story portraying a relatively limited number of individuals over a brief period of time. They do not refer directly to national events or developments such as the Destruction of the Temple or the increasing sinfulness of the people at large. The crises which the rabbis must respond to in these are the result of the inevitable instability of human nature and of the human condition.

These stories are all set in the Temple and are interpolated into Mishnaic passages which present ritual narratives.[35] Ritual narratives describe the details of the cult practice as it was meant to unfold on a regular basis. They operate in an almost mythic structure of time and space in which the same events repeat themselves exactly over and over again, presenting the world of the Temple and, to a lesser degree, halakhic practice in general as being insulated from crisis and change. The etiological stories which we will consider rupture the fabric of the ritual narrative by telling of instances in which the normal functioning of the Temple was interrupted by an act of violence. This juxtaposition of genres creates a dialogic tension between the regular and regulated world of ritual narratives and the crisis, violence, and change which characterizes etiological stories.

In all of these cases, order is ultimately restored through a *taqqanah*. These enactments are meant to head off further incidents of the nature described. The relationship between law and narrative presented in these stories is thus quite different from what we have seen thus far. Law and narrative are now in direct conflict with each other. In most of this book, I have argued that law and narrative cannot be directly contrasted because they need to be viewed as two overlapping literary and cultural categories. Some narratives possess legal elements, while some laws are formulated through narrative means. Furthermore, I have attempted to show how in Mishnaic stories, narrative structure and halakhic authority work, each on its own level, to hold together the conflicting demands of narrative and non-narrative tendencies of law. In general, narratives in the Mishnah function much the way Robert Cover imagines them, as helping to forge an organic and harmonious legal community. In these etiological stories, however, law and narrative are directly opposed to each other. These anecdotes embody the sort of chaos and violence that the law is meant to prevent and control. The purpose of law is to prevent stories from occurring and to keep society running smoothly along the pattern of a predictable repeated narrative. When repeated narratives overflow their assigned channels and are transformed into stories, it is the law's job to beat the narrative back into its predicable format and insure that such disruptions do not happen again.

Murder and Mayhem on the Altar: *Yoma* 2:2

We will begin with the well-known story of the priest who fell from the altar ramp while racing to its top. Before turning to the text of this story, I would like to first examine the parallel version of the story presented in a baraita. I believe the Mishnah's version reflects a reworking of this earlier baraita.[36] In turn, this baraita needs to be understood in the context of a passage from Mishnah *Tamid* 2:1–2, which describes the daily morning cleaning of the ashes and remains from the previous day:

רָאוּהוּ אֶחָיו שֶׁיָּרַד
וְהֵם רָצוּ וּבָאוּ
מִיהֲרוּ וְהִקְדִּישׁוּ יְדֵיהֶם וְרַגְלֵיהֶם מִן הַכִּיּוֹר
נָטְלוּ אֶת הַמַּגְרֵפוֹת וְאֶת הַצִּינוֹרוֹת
וְעָלוּ לְרֹאשׁ הַמִּזְבֵּחַ
הָאֵיבָרִים וְהַפְּדָרִים שֶׁלּ׳׳א נִתְאָכְלוּ מִבָּעֶרֶב
סוֹנְקִין[37] אוֹתָן לְצִדְדֵי הַמִּזְבֵּחַ
אִם אֵין הַצְּדָדִין מַחֲזִיקִין
סוֹדְרִין אוֹתָן בַּסּוֹבֵב עַל הַכֶּבֶשׁ
הֶחֱלוּ מַעֲלִין בָּאֵפֶר עַל גַּבֵּי הַ[38]תַּפּוּחַ

וְתַפּוּחַ הָיָה בְאֶמְצַע הַמִּזְבֵּחַ
פְּעָמִים עָלָיו שְׁלֹשׁ מֵאוֹת כּוֹר
וּבָרְגָלִים לֹא הָיוּ מְדַשְּׁנִים אוֹתוֹ
מִפְּנֵי שֶׁהוּא נוֹיִי לַמִּזְבֵּחַ מִיָּמָיו
לֹא נִתְעַצֵּל כֹּהֵן מִלְּהוֹצִיא אֶת הַדֶּשֶׁן

> When his brethren saw that he had descended,
> they came running
> and hastened to wash their hands and feet at the laver.
> They then took the shovels and the forks
> and went to the top of the altar.
> Such limbs and pieces of fat as had not been consumed since the evening
> they removed to the sides of the altar.
> If there was not room on the sides,
> they arranged them on the ledge and on the ramp.
> They began to throw ashes onto the heap.
> This heap was in the middle of the altar,
> and sometimes there was as much as three hundred *kor* on it.
> On festivals they would not clear away the ash
> because it was reckoned as an ornament to the altar.
> It never happened that a priest was tardy in taking out the ashes.

The Mishnah here emphasizes the haste with which the assembled priests undertook this job.

They "came running" and "hastened," and we are told that they were "never tardy"[39] in their zeal to clean the ashes off the altar. This depiction contrasts sharply with the solemn order that generally pervades ritual narrative descriptions of the Temple service. As we shall see, the Mishnah in *Yoma* seeks to suppress this element of the daily service apparently in order to maintain a more dignified image of the Temple.

This scramble up the altar described here in *Tamid* would appear to be the original context of the following story which appears numerous times, with slight variations, throughout rabbinic literature.[40] Here is the text as it appears in the Tosefta *Yoma* 1:12:

מעשה בשנים כהנים שהיו
שווין[41] רצין ועולין בכבש
דחף אחד מהן את חבירו לתוך ארבע אמות
נטל סכין ותקע לו בלבו
בא רבי צדוק ועמד על מעלות האילים[42] ואמר
שמעוני אחינו בית ישראל
הרי הוא אומר
כי ימצא חלל וגו׳

ויצאו זקניך ושופטיך ומדדו
בואו ונמדוד על מי ראוי להביא עגלה
על ההיכל או על העזרות
געו כל העם אחריו בבכיה
ואח"כ בא אביו של תינוק
אמר להם
אחינו אני כפרתכם
עדיין בנו[43] מפרפר
וסכין לא נטמא
ללמדך שטומאת סכין
קשה להם לישראל יותר משפיכות דמים
וכן הוא אומר
וגם דם נקי שפך מנשה הרבה מאוד
עד אשר מלא את ירושלים פה לפה
מכאן אמרו בעון שפיכות דמים
שכינה נעלית ומקדש נטמא.

It once happened that two priest were
even as they ran up the ramp [of the altar].
One came within four cubits of his comrade.
He took a knife and thrust it into his heart.
R. Zadok stood on the steps of the hall [of the Temple]
and said:
Hear me, brethren of the house of Israel.
Behold, it says,
"If one be found slain in the land…
then thy elders and judges shall come forth and measure." [Deut. 21:1].
Come let us measure. On whose behalf should the heifer be brought, the Temple
or its courts?
All the people burst out weeping.
Then the father of the young man came
and said to them:
Brothers! I am your atonement![44]
My son is still in convulsions
and the knife has not yet become unclean.
This teaches us that the uncleanliness of a knife
was more grievous to Israel than the spilling of blood.
As it says,
"Moreover Menasseh shed innocent blood very much,
till he had filled Jerusalem from one end to the other" [2 Kings 16].[45]
From here we learn that the sin of bloodshed
causes the divine presence to ascend and the Temple to be defiled.

This story breaks down into three sections. Its structure might be compared to the double-ended case story discussed in the previous chapter. It presents an event, the murder of a priest on the altar, followed by two contrasting responses to the event, that of R. Zadok and that of the victim's father.

The opening scene describes two priests running up the ramp of the altar. The narrator gives no explanation as to why they are doing so. Based on the description of the daily service in the Temple in *Tamid*, it would seem that the two were among the priests who were running up to clean off the altar following the ritual removal of the ashes. The zealous priests each wanted to get the first crack at cleaning the altar for the day. When one feels the other is about to overtake him, he draws a knife and kills his fellow priest.

Needless to say, such a callous murder at the altar is itself a scandal of the first order. The altar is a place where the use of weapons is prohibited even in its construction, not to mention for nefarious purposes.[46] The crime is compounded by the fact that it was committed ostensibly out of the murderer's desire to better serve God.

The horror of this crime is expressed by R. Zadok in his lament. He ironically compares the situation to the *eglah arufah*, the ritual for atoning for the death of the victim of an unsolved murder in the wilderness. The town which is nearest to the crime scene must be determined and its elders must complete the atonement ritual. In this case, a man has been murdered not in the seclusion of the wilderness but in broad daylight in the Temple court. R. Zadok asks how this ritual will be carried out in this case, emphasizing the impossibility of ever atoning for such a crime. The reader is no doubt meant to identify with the wailing chorus of bystanders that responds to R. Zadok's speech.

Finally, the victim's father appears on the scene. His presence only raises the pathos of the situation, emphasizing the personal and not just communal nature of the tragedy. Yet the father does not eulogize his son or rail at the murderer. He responds with the cool detachment of an outsider. Rather than seeking to be comforted as the chief mourner, he announces that he will comfort the assembled crowd.[47] He observes that his son's heart is still beating. As such, the knife which is lodged in his body has not yet been rendered ritually impure. If the knife is removed immediately, it will not be defiled. Astonishingly, the father is more concerned with the status of the knife than that of his son. He calls for hastening his son's death to preserve the purity of the knife, since removing the knife would almost certainly increase his son's bleeding and hasten his death.[48]

The narrator of the story takes the father to be emblematic of the misplaced values of the Jews of the time; they were more concerned with maintaining the ritual purity of the Temple than with preventing and responding to bloodshed. The narrator compares the people's behavior to the massacres committed by the biblical king Manasseh. Just as Manasseh's sins led to the destruction of the first Temple, the people's sins, as exemplified in this story, were responsible for the destruction of the Second Temple.

Though this is not an etiological story per se, it presents a historical outlook similar to that found in the etiological stories that we examined in the first part of the chapter. The people of Israel are shown as being in a process of moral and spiritual decline which climaxes with the Destruction of the Temple.

The horrific details of the baraita's story completely shatter the image presented in Tannaitic ritual narratives of the Temple as a place of purity and solemn ritual order. The Temple emerges as more of the rough-and-tumble "criminal's lair" described by Jeremiah (7:11).

The Mishnah's version of the story reflects an attempt to get control of the violent and chaotic forces of this narrative tradition. It transforms the story from a melodramatic morality tale into a technical etiological story which is integrated into the ritual narrative depicting the Yom Kippur rites. The story appears in the context of tractate *Yoma*'s account of the Yom Kippur services in the Temple. While this service contains many rituals unique to the holiest day of the year, including the high priest's entry into the Holy of Holies and the sending out of the scapegoat to Azazel, it also includes many of the sacrifices and other rituals that were performed in the Temple every day of the year. These daily rituals are also narrated in more detail in *Tamid*. There are several instances in which there are exact parallels between the accounts in *Tamid* and *Yoma*. Notably, both tractates detail the process whereby the honor of performing various daily rites was awarded through a lottery system.[49] The first among these honors was the removal of the ashes from the altar described in Leviticus 6:3. In the rabbinic understanding, this involved removing only a panful of the ashes of the previous day's sacrifices each morning. In *Tamid* this ritual removal is followed by the description of the priests running up the altar to complete a thorough cleaning of the altar. *Yoma* omits any reference to this event. Rather, it describes the ritual of removing ashes from the altar as follows:

בָּרִאשׁוֹנָה
כָּל מִי שֶׁהוּא רוֹצֶה
לִתְרוֹם אֶת הַמִּזְבֵּחַ תּוֹרֵם
בִּזְמַן שֶׁהֵן מְרוּבִּים
וְ[50]רָצִים וְעוֹלִים בַּכֶּבֶשׁ
וְכָל הַקּוֹדֵם אֶת חֲבֵירוֹ
לְתוֹךְ אַרְבַּע אַמּוֹת זָכָה...
מַעֲשֶׂה שֶׁהָיוּ שְׁנַיִם שָׁוִוין וְ[51]רָצִים וְעוֹלִין בַּכֶּבֶשׁ
דָּחַף אֶחָד מֵהֶן אֶת חֲבֵירוֹ
וְנִשְׁבְּרָה רַגְלוֹ
וּכְשֶׁרָאוּ בֵּית דִּין שֶׁהֵן בָּאִין לִידֵי סַכָּנָה
הִתְקִינוּ
שֶׁלֹּא יְהוּ תּוֹרְמִים אֶת הַמִּזְבֵּחַ אֶלָּא בְּפַיִיס

Originally,
whosoever desired

to remove [the ashes from] the altar did so.
If they were many,
they would run and mount the ramp [of the Altar]
and he that came first
within four cubits obtained the privilege....
It happened once that two were even as they ran up the ramp.
One of them pushed his fellow
who fell and broke his leg.
When the court saw that they incurred danger,
it was ordained
that the altar be cleared only by lottery.

The creators of this passage reworked the traditions found in Mishnah *Tamid* and the baraita in order to limit the images of chaos and bloodshed that pervade these earlier sources. The Mishnah in *Yoma* makes no reference to the scramble to clean off the altar described in *Tamid*. It posits instead the existence of an orderly and regulated footrace that was once used instead of the lottery to determine who got the honor of doing the ritual removal of the ashes. The Mishnah in *Yoma* thus makes use of the etiological narrative structure to deal with a problematic practice. The run up the ramp is transformed from a regular part of the daily service into an occasional practice that was banned due to the danger involved. The existence of this practice is not denied, but it is transformed into a far more orderly exercise which was nevertheless discontinued.

Similarly, the baraita's account of a fatal stabbing is replaced in the Mishnah with a mere shove, possibly accidental, that results only in a broken leg.[52] The race which leads to this injury is discontinued as a result. The horrific and catastrophic nature of the baraita's story is thus reined in by the Mishnah. Whereas the baraita's account ends with the ultimate destruction of the Temple, this story ends with the protorabbinic court restoring order in the Temple.

This story is a prime example of the way in which the rabbis sought to gain control over history by insisting that it be submitted to the twin controls of rabbinic authority and narrative structure. Events are reconstructed as following a familiar pattern in which the rabbis confront limited crises with their wisdom and authority insuring that excessive dynamism that might threaten the practice of the law is kept in check.

Yet, the Mishnah's story still contains strong echoes of the key themes of the baraita that it seeks to suppress: The power of human desire, the call to divine service, and the tragic consequences that can emerge when these two forces coalesce. The court's enactment is only a stopgap measure that addresses the symptoms, but not the cause of the problem. So long as there are humans serving and worshipping in God's Temple, the potential for outbreaks of violence of one sort or another will remain. Rabbinic legislators can have only limited success in preventing more stories from breaking out and disrupting the sacred order of the Temple.

The Madding Crowd: *Sukkah* 4:9 and 4:4

The fourth chapter of *Sukkah* details the procedures for the Temple rituals distinctive to the Sukkot holiday. Each rite is presented as a separate ritual narrative marked off in its own section of the chapter. In two instances, these ritual narratives are interrupted by an etiological story. Both of these stories describe how the proceedings in the Temple were interrupted by an outbreak of violence on the part of the assembled masses. In each case, the narrator deviates from the standard form of the etiological story in a way that emphasizes the threat of violence and chaos to the orderly functioning of the Temple.

The story in *Sukkah* 4:9 comes in the context of the ritual of the water libation which took place annually on the Sukkot holiday. The Mishnah follows the path of this sacred water as it is drawn from the spring of Siloam and is ceremoniously brought into the Temple and to the altar. It then states:

וְלַמְנַסֵּךְ אוֹמְרִין לוֹ
הַגְבַּהּ אֶת יָדְךָ
שֶׁפַּעַם אַחַת
נִיסֵּךְ עַל[53] רַגְלָיו
וּרְגָמוּהוּ כָל הָעָם בְּאֶתְרוֹגֵיהֶם

> To [the priest] who performed the libation, they used to say,
> "Raise thy hand,"
> For on a certain occasion, [a certain priest]
> poured out the water over his feet
> and all the people pelted him with their etrogs.

As in the story in *Yoma* 2:1–2, this story tells of an adjustment made to the Temple ritual as a result of a violent incident. Initially, the priest was not given any instructions about the proper method of performing the libation. Once, however, the priest poured the water at his feet rather than on the appropriate place on the altar. In response, the people pelted him with their etrogs. In order to prevent further outbreaks such as this, the authorities inserted into the ritual explicit instructions to be given to the priest right before he is to pour the water.

The Mishnah does not explain why the priest in the story deviated from the established practice. This Mishnah is generally understood as a conflict between practitioners of the priestly and rabbinic streams of halakhah with regard to the legitimacy of the water libations, which are not mandated by scripture.[54] However, the Mishnah itself does not place this event in a historical context. The priest's objectionable behavior could have been rooted in ignorance or even clumsiness. Once again, the Mishnah presents a rabbinic enactment as an attempt to guard against human failure and the resultant disruption that it produces, while suppressing explicit mention of dissenting views.

The story's attitude toward the people's outburst is ambivalent. Clearly, violence of this sort in the Temple must be avoided if at all possible. Yet the people acted with the best of motivations. They are responding in anger to what was essentially a desecration of the Temple service. As in the case in *Yoma*, the authorities here must grapple with the potential violence inherent in situations in which human nature confronts the demands of the divine service.

This story's efforts to contain stories and violence in the Temple are further highlighted when it is put into the context of its counter-narratives. An alternative version of this story appears in a baraita that is cited, in various forms, numerous times throughout rabbinic literature.[55] Below is the story as it appears in Tosefta *Sukkah* 3:16:

שכבר היה מעשה בביתוסי אחד
שניסך על רגליו
ורגמוהו כל העם באתרוגיהן
ונפגמה קרנו של מזבח
ובטלה עבודה
עד שהביאו גוש אחד של מלח ונתנו עליו
כדי שלא יראה מזבח פגום
שכל מזבח שאין לו
לא קרן ולא יסוד פסול

It once happened that a certain Boethusian
poured the water libation over his feet
and the all the people pelted him with their etrogs
and the horn of the altar became damaged
and the Temple service was halted
until they brought a chunk of salt and put it there
so that the altar would not appear damaged.
For an altar which lacks
a horn or a base is invalid.

This version of the story adds two important details. First, it identifies the priest as a Boethusian. The events are clearly placed in the context of the larger struggles between the Pharisees and their ideological rivals for control of the Temple ritual. In keeping with the overall historical narrative told by the rabbis, in this story the Pharisees enjoy both the support of the masses and ultimate control over the Temple.

The baraita also tells of how the altar itself was damaged in the fray, rendering it unfit for use and temporarily suspending the entire Temple service. Here the threat of violence in the Temple is far more severe than in the Mishnah. Such outbreaks have destructive potential beyond disrupting the peaceful decorum of the services and the injuring of an errant priest. They threaten to damage and disable the centerpiece of the regular Temple rite, the altar.

To use the terminology developed in chapter 6, the relationship between the baraita and the Mishnah in this case is almost certainly of a textual rather than a performative nature. Both versions share a common fixed core. Either the baraita provided a gloss on the Mishnah, adding in the lines about the damaging of the altar, or the Mishnah is in fact a slightly edited version of the baraita. Either way, if we read the Mishnah in light of the baraita, we can see how the Mishnah presents a more restrained account of this incident, just as with the story about the priest running up the ramp. In this case, the Mishnah elides any reference to links between the violent actions of the crowd and a larger ideological conflict. Similarly, the violence is not shown as posing any immediate threat to the Temple itself.

As we have seen in chapter 6, a similar incident is recorded by Josephus in his *Antiquities*.[56] In Josephus's account, the pelting was not provoked by a violation of the Temple rite. Rather, the priest in question was none other than King Alexander Janneus (103–76 BCE). He was attacked not for his conduct in the Temple but as part of an uprising against his reign as king. Josephus's version further raises the stakes with regard to violent outbreaks in the Temple. In the rabbinic accounts, violence in the Temple almost always arises from internal conflicts relating to the Temple rite. Josephus suggests that the Temple was not insulated from the social and political conflicts that shook the Jewish world beyond its holy precincts.

The Temple was an integral part of the turbulent life of the Jewish people at the turn of the era. Chaos and occasional violence stemming from the unstable social and political environment in Roman-occupied Palestine were as much a part of the reality of the Temple as the solemn order of the service. Elsewhere, Josephus relates that the holidays, when large numbers of Jews gathered together at the Temple, were the normal times for insurrections in Jerusalem.[57] In the New Testament as well, the holidays are referred to as a potentially volatile time in Jerusalem, when riots were likely to break out if the people were stirred up.[58] The historian Gedaliah Alon goes so far as to claim, "It appears that it was a daily occurrence for the people to pelt with citrons anyone whom they wished to insult."[59]

The accounts of violent Temple incidents presented in the rabbinic sources, in contrast, tend to suppress any outside factors, portraying the events as internal to the Temple. This gives the appearance of the Temple as insulated from the wider social and political issues of the day. Conflicts in the Temple appear as the result of ideological conflicts, and passions are raised around the Temple service itself. This makes the violence seem like it can be prevented simply by instituting proper reforms in the Temple service.

For all of the efforts of the Mishnaic storyteller to portray the violence in the Temple as something which can ultimately be managed by the authorities through the law, the structure of this story in fact emphasizes the violence over the restoration of order. This story is constructed in a way that places the *fabula* and the *syuzhet* in tension.[60] The order in which the events are narrated is different from the order in which they actually take place. In most etiological stories, events are presented in chronological order. First, a previous state of affairs is described. Then a crisis disrupts this state of affairs. Finally, a rabbinic enactment creates a new social and ritual equilibrium. This story begins at the end, with a description of the revised practice. Only then does it describe the events that led to the institution of this practice. The original state of affairs is never described at all; it is only implied.

As a result of this structure, the anecdote describing the outbreak of violence is removed from the context and control of the wider etiological narrative. The reader must reconstruct the fact that the authorities were ready to regulate and prevent similar incidents. The main focus is on the anecdote itself and the crisis it depicts. The final image with which the reader is left is that of the people pelting the priest on the altar. The order of the ritual and the authority of the rabbis who regulate it recede into the background. In the foreground is the continual threat posed by the unpredictable and unruly behavior of both the priests and masses who attend the Temples services.

The complex interrelationship between ritual narratives, etiological stories, and the disruptive anecdotes they contain is even more strikingly illustrated in *Sukkah* 4:4:

מִצְוַת הַלּוּלָב כֵּיצַד
[61]כָּל הָעָם מוֹלִיכִים אֶת לוּלַבֵיהֶם לְהַר הַבַּיִת
וְהַחַזָּנִים מְקַבְּלִים מִיָּדָם
וְסוֹדְרִים אוֹתָם עַל גַּג הָאִיסְטָוְנָה
וְהַזְּקֵנִים מַנִּיחִים אֶת שֶׁלָּהֶן בַּלִּשְׁכָּה
וּמְלַמְּדִים אוֹתָם לוֹמַר
כָּל מִי שֶׁהִגִּיעַ לוּלָבִי לְיָדוֹ
הֲרֵי הוּא לוֹ מַתָּנָה
וּ[62]לְמָחֳרָת מַשְׁכִּימִים וּבָאִים
וְהַחַזָּנִים מְזַרְקִים לִפְנֵיהֶם
וְהֵן מְחַטְּפִים
וּמַכִּים אִישׁ אֶת חֲבֵירוֹ
וּכְשֶׁרָאוּ בֵית דִּין שֶׁהֵם בָּאִים לִידֵי סַכָּנָה
הִתְקִינוּ
שֶׁיְּהֵא כָל אֶחָד וְאֶחָד נוֹטֵל בְּבֵיתוֹ[63]

How was the ceremony of the Lulav carried out?
All the people brought their lulavs to the Temple Mount.
And the attendants received them
and arranged them in order upon the portico,

while the elders laid theirs in a chamber.
And the people were instructed to say,
"Whosoever gets my lulav in his hand,
let it be as a gift."
On the morrow they arose, and came [to the Temple Mount]
and the attendants threw down [their lulavs] before them,
and they snatched at them.
and so they came to blows with one another.
When the court saw that they reached a state of danger,
it was ordained that
each man should take [his lulav] in his own house.

At first, this text appears to be a fairly standard example of a ritual narrative. It presents a detailed description of how, in years when the first day of Sukkot falls on the Sabbath, the people would bring their lulavs to the Temple on the prior day in order to avoid carrying them on the Sabbath.

The Mishnah here uses the *qotel* verb form, which, as I previously noted, is one of the standard verb forms for ritual narratives.[64] The *qotel* form in these contexts appears to suggest a timeless prescription. However, it also may be a shortened form of *hayah qotel*, which implies a repeated action. This tension between the prescriptive and descriptive aspects of ritual narrative captures the genre's attempt to construct a world that is at once historical and beyond the reach of historical forces.

The Mishnah's account also emphasizes the dignified order and hierarchy that characterized the Temple. The Temple officials would collect the lulavs from the people and arrange them on the roof of the portico while the elders placed theirs in a separate chamber. Finally, the people were taught to grant their lulav as a gift to anyone who should happen to take it the next morning so that no theft or conflict should occur as result of the proceedings.[65]

When the narrative moves on to recount the events of the next day, it continues to use the *qotel* form. However, the content of the events described makes it clear that the narrative has shifted from the staid mode of the ritual narrative to the dynamic and at times brutal world of the anecdote. The *qotel* now refers to the simple past. The Temple officials throw the lulavs in front of the people and the scene quickly dissolves into a melee over whose lulav is whose. This is clearly not the required procedure to be repeated year after year. This is an unanticipated event that happened once or at most a few times. Once again, human selfishness and a lack of foresight on the part of the authorities lead to an eruption of violence at the Temple.

As a result of this scene, the central court realizes the potential danger of the situation. They make a *taqqanah* that the lulav henceforth be taken by individuals at home and not in the Temple.[66] As in previous cases, the law responds belatedly in an attempt to prevent another eruption of violence. The root of the problem lies not in external factors but in the inherent danger when human selfishness is combined with divine service.

Rather than juxtaposing a ritual narrative with an etiological story, here the Mishnah melds the two genres. What begins as a ritual narrative is gradually transformed into an etiological story. The result is a text that demonstrates the complex interplay between these genres and the worldviews they represent. Crisis and chaos emerge almost imperceptibly out of well-planned ritual. Change is eventually instituted in the name of restoring order to the Temple. However, the potential remains for ritual narrative to be transformed into anecdote and for order to dissolve into conflict.

The Lost and Found Ark: *Sheqalim* 6:1–2

The last story in this group is also about violence in the Temple. However, this time the perpetrator is neither an individual nor a group of human beings who give in to their mortal weakness. Here it is God himself who strikes down a priest and brings death into the sanctuary.

וּשְׁלוֹשׁ עֶשְׂרֵה הִשְׁתַּחֲוָיוֹת הָיוּ בַּמִּקְדָּשׁ
שֶׁלְּבֵית רַבָּן גַּמְלִיאֵ'
וְשֶׁלְּבֵית ר' חֲנַנְיָה סְגַן הַכֹּהֲנִים
הָיוּ מִשְׁתַּחֲוִים בְּאַרְבַּע עֶשְׂרֵה
וְאֵיכָן הָיְתָה יְתֵירָה
כְּנֶגֶד דִּיר הָעֵצִים
שֶׁכַּן מְסוֹרֶת בְּיָדָם מֵאֲבוֹתֵיהֶם
שֶׁשָּׁם הָאָרוֹן גָּנוּז
מַעֲשֶׂה בְכֹהֵן אֶחָד שֶׁהָיָה מִתְעַסֵּק
וְרָאָה אֶת הָרִיצְפָּה
שֶׁהִיא מְשׁוּנָּה מֵחַבְרוֹתֶיהָ
בָּא וְאָמַר לַחֲבֵירוֹ
וְלֹא הִסְפִּיק לִגְמוֹר אֶת הַדָּבָר
עַד שֶׁיָּצְתָה[67] נִשְׁמָתוֹ
וְיָדְעוּ בְיֵיחוּד שֶׁשָּׁם הָאָרוֹן גָּנוּז

There were thirteen prostrations in the Temple.
[Members] of the household of R. Gamliel
and of R. Hanniah, chief of priests,
used to prostrate themselves fourteen times.
And where was the additional [prostration]?
In front of the wood storeroom.
For thus they had a tradition
that the Ark was hidden there.
Once it happened that a certain priest who was busy [there]

Noticed that the pavement
was different [there] from the elsewhere.
He went and told his fellow,
But before he had time to finish his words,
his soul had departed.
So they knew for certain that the Ark was hidden there.

This etiological story follows a non-chronological pattern similar to that of the story about the priest who is pelted by the crowd. Here too the Mishnah begins with the current practice followed by an anecdote that explains its origins. The original state of affairs is never explicitly narrated. Rather, the story relates to the practice of prostration at certain locations in the Temple. The Mishnah states that there are thirteen such locations. At this point, it says neither where these points are nor what their significance is.[68]

The Mishnah notes that two of the leading families of Jerusalem had a tradition to prostrate themselves at a fourteenth location as well, the wood storeroom. This is presumably the same as the "chamber of wood" described in Mishnah *Midot* 2:5 as being located in the northeast corner of the Women's Courtyard of the Temple. According to this source, it was here that priests who were unfit for regular service due to physical blemishes checked the wood designated for the altar for worms.

The reason that these families bowed down at this unlikely point is that they had a tradition that it was here the Ark of the Covenant was hidden. The Ark which symbolized God's enduring relationship with the people of Israel was supposed to rest in the Holy of Holies at the very heart of the Temple. However, in the Second Temple there was no Ark, and the Holy of Holies remained empty. The fate of the Ark was a matter of widespread speculation. Tosefta *Sota* 13:1 states that the Ark was hidden by King Josiah in anticipation of the Babylonian conquest of Jerusalem.[69] The Bavli cites an alternative tradition that the Ark was in fact taken to Babylonia.[70] Another tradition first found in 2 Maccabees maintains that the Ark was hidden in a cave or in the ground by Jeremiah not long before the destruction of the first Temple.[71]

In all of these other traditions, the Ark is hidden somewhere far away from the Temple Mount. This serves to emphasize the absence of the Ark from the Second Temple. Despite the existence and operation of the Temple, God's presence was in some way lacking during this period. Only with the coming of the final redemption will the Ark be returned and with it the proper relationship between God and Israel.

Our Mishnah text reflects a very different attitude toward the place of the Ark and the Divine presence it represents in the Second Temple. It records a tradition that the Ark never left the Temple Mount. It continued to imbue the Temple with its holiness. Those who worshipped there were in close proximity to the Ark, though they did not know exactly where it was. A full restoration of the

Ark to the Holy of Holies and of God's close relationship with Israel remained an elusive Messianic hope. But as long as the Temple stood, the Jews remained but a few steps away from this goal.

The Mishnah then goes on to tell the story of the discovery of the fact that the Ark was located somewhere under the wood storehouse and the origins of the practice of bowing at that place. In the course of working in the wood storeroom, one of the priests noticed an irregularity in the floor. He understood this to mark the place where the pavement had been removed in order to bury the Ark. Before he could disclose its exact location, he suddenly died; God had struck him down to prevent the Ark from being discovered prematurely.

This story is part of larger tradition of narratives that tell of people who were struck down as a result of inappropriate behavior in the sanctuary or relating to the Ark. Most prominent among these is the story of the death of Nadab and Abihu in Leviticus 10:1–7. This theme repeats itself throughout the book of Samuel's account of the Ark's journeys, from its removal from Shiloh and capture by the Philistines to its eventual arrival in Jerusalem under King David. Most relevant to our purposes is the story of the death of Uzza in 2 Samuel 6:6–7. As in our story, Uzza did not act maliciously. He was well intentioned in his attempt to prevent the Ark from falling. Nevertheless, he was struck down by God.

These stories emphasize that the Temple is a place of both purity and danger. Though the proper performance of the Temple rituals may be associated with peace and prosperity, the threat of divine wrath is never far away in the Temple. The experience of the Temple is one of constant tension between the order and harmony of the divine service and the constant possibility of an outbreak of violence, be it human or divine.

This story upsets the equilibrium of the Temple in another way as well. The Mishnah initially presents an image of the Temple in which its perimeter is punctuated by thirteen gates, each of which leads ultimately to the Holy of Holies. This story presents a second focus for the Temple. It turns out that the real holiness of the Temple lies beneath the wood storeroom, a location at the far corner of the Temple court, where priests unfit for regular service went about their menial work. God's presence turns up in unexpected places and its exact location can never be known. The Temple turns out to be a place of ultimate uncertainty and tension. The experience of the Temple involves balancing knowledge and ignorance, order and chaos, stasis and dynamism.

Conclusion

Etiological stories embody some of the fundamental tensions between law and narrative in rabbinic culture. In the first group of etiological stories examined, we saw how rabbinic storytellers sought to create a historical narrative that would account for changes in the law while affirming the essential stability of rabbinic authority and the covenantal relationship between God and Israel. Yet these stories also present a fundamentally tragic view of Jewish history, in which it is the rabbis' job to compensate with their legislation for an increasing state of alienation between the Jewish people and God and his law.

The second set of stories dealt not with historical master narratives but with anecdotes that reveal the persistence of human weakness and its particular tendency to flare up into violence when proper conduct of the divine service is at stake. These narratives challenge idealized notions of the Second Temple that are exemplified by the Mishnah's ritual narratives. Even in the Temple there is a constant tension between order and chaos. This is a result not only of the inevitable human factor but also of the very nature of the God of Israel, who demands both intimacy and awe-filled reverence of those who tread in his Sanctuary.

In this scenario, the law of the rabbis works ex post facto, trying to prevent the recurrence of tragic incidents. The rabbis cannot, however, eliminate the instability inherent in the Temple service. Once in a while, harmonious ritual narrative will give way to stories of violence as God and humanity struggle to dwell together in a single house.

10

Conclusion

> The symmetry of form attainable in pure fiction cannot so readily be achieved in a narration essentially having less to do with fable than with fact. Truth uncompromisingly told will always have its ragged edges.
>
> Herman Melville, "Billy Budd, Sailor"

In the course of this book, I have treated an array of issues connected to the nature of narrative, the relationship between law and narrative, and the study of the Mishnah and its stories. In this concluding chapter, I will re-present the central arguments of the book, organized around these central theoretical and methodological questions, to help clarify and highlight the book's major points and contributions.

Narrative as Mode of Discourse

The underlying assumption of my discussion of narrative and narrative theory is that the terms "narrative" and "story" do not refer to clearly defined, self-enclosed genres. Rather, they are part of a spectrum which embraces all forms of texts. Similarly, narratives and stories are not independent discourses but rather are an integral part of virtually all forms of discourse, be it day-to-day conversation or more specialized discourses.

In order to analyze the relationship between narratives and other modes of discourse, we first introduced the concept of *narrativity*. Narrativity refers to a collection of textual attributes. All texts exist along a continuum of greater or lesser narrativity, depending on the number and prominence of the narrative attributes they contain. When we refer to a text as a story, we mean that it contains a critical mass of narrativity.

Most theorists of narrative have defined narrativity purely in terms of "dynamism"—that is, the extent to which a text portrays transition and change. To this I have added the quality of "specificity." Specificity refers to the extent to which a text focuses on a particular time or place, a unique event, or individual people and objects. Many if not most texts contain a certain degree of narrativity. We have established, however, that in order to be considered a story the text must present a sequence of at least two interrelated events that occurred once and only once in the past. In other words, a story must have a certain degree of dynamism in that it portrays the transition from at least one event to another. It must also have specificity at least to the degree that the text narrates events that happened at a fixed time in the past.

This theoretical framework allows us to chart the relationship between different types of texts within a single discourse. It also gives us a vocabulary for discussing different parts of more complex narratives which often contain elements of varying narrativity.

Narrative Structure

One thing the above framework does not account for is the role of structure in narrative. The question of narrative structure has been central to the endeavor of narrative theory going back to the early twentieth century. Traditional narratologists have generally viewed structure as a fixed attribute of the narrative text. In fact, narrative structure is not an objective quality. Virtually any text can be described using a variety of structural models. Rather, identifying structure is a crucial part of the process whereby the reader decodes and finds meaning in the text.[1] Structure is especially valuable to interpretation because stories are frequently understood in the context of other stories. Identifying a common structure is one of the key ways in which we can establish some sort of identity between stories.

Establishing a narrative structure is a process of removing the specificity from a text to a certain degree and leaving behind a series of interrelated events or sets of events. By reducing the specificity of narrative, we potentially reveal its wider significance or meaning. Take for example the following story:

> I was driving on Highway 1 from Jerusalem to Tel Aviv at 160 kilometers per hour. I was stopped by the police and given an 800 shekel ticket and had my license suspended for three months.

This story can be reduced to the following structure: (1) driving from Jerusalem to Tel Aviv, (2) speeding, (3) being stopped by police, and (4) receiving a large fine and a suspended license. This structure establishes a causal relationship between speeding on the Jerusalem–Tel Aviv highway and being stopped by the police and punished. The moral of this story can thus be expressed as "Don't speed on Highway 1 in Israel; you risk being pulled over, getting a hefty ticket, and having your license suspended."

This story could also be translated into a less specific, more abstract structure such as: (1) driving well above the speed limit, (2) being stopped by police, (3) receiving a ticket. Reading the story through this structure, we receive a much broader lesson that applies far beyond a single highway in a particular country: "If you speed, you may be pulled over and fined."

Finally, we can remove all specificity from the story with the following structure: (1) violating the law, (2) getting caught, (3) being punished severely. Now the moral of the story is even broader: "Crime doesn't pay."

A single anecdote has limited ability to convey a broader message. The reader can always say, "Just because it happened to him doesn't mean it will happen to me." But, if a person hears numerous stories, all based on the same narrative structure, he is much more likely to conclude that the advice implicit in those stories is worth heeding. Thus, multiple stories of different people being stopped and ticketed on the Jerusalem–Tel Aviv highway will collectively teach the lesson that the chances of getting caught speeding there are actually quite high. The same would be true for a series of stories about getting caught for speeding in different locales or a set of stories narrating crime and punishment. A large number of stories that all have the same structure suggests that the causal relationship between events portrayed by that structure is, in fact, inevitable.

Repetition and the Rhetoric of Narrative Worlds

Dynamism, narrative structure, and the lessons they teach might be seen as essentially linear. Event follows event in a clear order, leading to an inevitable conclusion. In truth, only the simplest of stories fit this paradigm so neatly. Most stories contain numerous disruptions of this line, which J. Hillis Miller describes collectively as "repetitions."[2] These include not only deviations from and repetitions of the set of events laid out by the narrative structure but also additional details and information that does not serve the story's ultimate message. These are precisely the sort of story elements that get removed in the process of creating a narrative structure. Indeed, these details often distract from, and even undermine, the lesson transmitted by the narrative structure. Yet the pervasiveness of these "repetitions" suggests that they cannot simply be ignored in the analysis of the story. Rather, as we have argued, "repetition" is an end in itself in storytelling. It is in the nature of storytelling to increase the story's narrativity, making the plot more complex and adding in mimetic detail. Not every plot element or detail needs to serve an ideological end. Indeed, these "extra" plot elements often complicate or undermine the straightforward message that the story allegedly advocates through its structure.

In some cases, ostensibly superfluous detail can actually play an important role in a story's rhetorical strategy. It is precisely an abundance of details in a story that allows the text to create the illusion of a complete narrative world in which the characters play out the action of the story. This serves not only an aesthetic function but a rhetorical one as well. The more a reader feels that the story takes place in a recognizable world, the more likely he is to internalize the lessons of the story as reflecting the values and workings of the real world.

Law and Narrative

Narratives do not function in a vacuum. They generally operate in the context of and in juxtaposition to other modes of discourse. One important realm that narrative often finds itself in dialog with is that of law. Contemporary scholarship has tended to view law and narrative as two distinct and even opposing entities. In this book I have attempted to chart a different path. Law and narrative are seen as two potentially complementary frameworks for structuring the world around us. Legal texts can be composed with varying levels of narrativity, ranging from the minimal narrativity of apodictic statements and abstract principles to the high degree of narrativity found in legal stories such as accounts of specific cases and judgments. Narrative and narrativity are thus potential formal attributes of legal texts, and law is a potential subject of narrative texts.

Narrativity and Comparative Legal Studies

The analysis of degrees of narrativity in legal texts can be a valuable tool for the classification of legal works and traditions. Through such analysis, we have identified a formal tradition of legal writing that might be called the ancient Near Eastern tradition. This includes the major legal codes written in cuneiform, including the Code of Hammurabi and the Laws of Eshnunna; the Bible, especially the Torah; and legal texts of the Dead Sea Scrolls as exemplified by the Damascus Document. All of these texts are characterized by a fairly uniform method of presenting laws using either casuistic formulations, apodictic formulations, or occasionally some combination of the two. These texts almost never contain formulations using higher levels of narrativity such as stories.

On the other hand, we have also tentatively identified a formal style of legal composition that we might call "classical Mediterranean." This includes the Mishnah and Roman legal works, notably Justinian's *Digest*. The works present a wide range of forms of differing levels of narrativity. They include several types of stories and accounts of events in addition to casuistic and apodictic formulations.

The study of these various legal works introduces us to another type of relationship between narrative and law. With the exception of the Mishnah, all of these texts open with a "framing story," an account of the events, both human and divine, that led to the formulation of the law at hand, the establishment of the legal tradition to which it belongs, and, in many cases, the formation of the national entity that is bound by those laws.

Apodictic and Narrative Approaches to Law

What then is the significance of the literary form through which the law is formulated? Narrative reflects a tendency toward the dynamic and the specific. Conversely, apodictic formulations, which have little to no narrativity, reflect a tendency toward the static and the general. These two sets of attributes can also be applied to law, producing two opposite poles on the continuum of possible approaches to the legal process. Apodictic approaches see law as an unchanging and universal system of rules and principles, much like a natural science. The law in any given situation emerges from a proper application of the rules to the case at hand. This approach defines the judge as being *an* authority. His power to rule is based on his knowledge of the law and his ability to apply it. Such a judge may be proved wrong by another individual who can demonstrate superior knowledge and understanding of the law on a given point.

In contrast, a narrative approach to law views law as a dynamic process whose ultimate expression is the issuing of a ruling regarding a specific case. General rules and principles are at best only non-binding summaries of earlier rulings. The judge is *in* authority. His power to issue rulings flows from the fact that he is a duly appointed judge. He cannot be challenged by an outsider because there is no such thing as an objective interpretation of the law. The judge combines his knowledge of previous rulings with his own intuition and judgment in order to arrive at a ruling that is appropriate for the circumstances.

In reality, most legal systems adopt some combination of these two approaches. They rely both on case law and on legal codes, and judges are both *an* and *in* authority. What differentiates various legal cultures is the way in which they balance the two approaches. To the extent that a legal text makes use of high-narrativity forms, it implicitly favors a narrative approach to law. To the degree that a legal text uses low- or no-narrativity forms, it implicitly advocates for an apodictic approach to law. Texts that mix high- and low-narrativity forms can be seen as paradoxically embracing both approaches.

Framing Stories and Anecdotes

Another way in which stories can imbue law with meaning can be found by examining the framing stories that introduce and sometimes conclude so many legal texts. These stories give meaning to a body of laws by anchoring them in concrete historical events, political institutions and communities, and the divine will. Individuals who identify themselves with the community, institutions, and god or gods described in the framing story will feel themselves bound by the laws set forth in the subsequent text.

In a slightly different manner, the legal anecdotes that we find sprinkled throughout the Mishnah and Roman law codes also function to establish legal authority. These stories portray actual instances of the working of the legal system. If we abstract a narrative structure from one of these stories, or better, a group of these stories, the result will be a lesson in how the legal system works. In general, these stories reinforce the status of the judges and legal scholars by portraying them as authoritative transmitters, interpreters, and creators of the law.

These anecdotes function as "hegemonic tales" which help to constitute and reinforce the existing power structure. This is a particularly effective strategy for disseminating an ideology, because its underlying assumptions remain unexpressed. As Patricia Ewick and Susan S. Sibley explain:

> [Hegemonic] narratives embody general understandings of the world that by their deployment and repetition come to constitute and sustain the lifeworld. Yet, because narratives depict specific persons existing in particular social, physical and historical locations, those general understandings often remain unacknowledged. By failing to make these manifest, narratives draw on unexamined assumptions and causal claims without displaying these assumptions and claims or laying them open to challenge or testing. Thus as narratives depict understandings of particular persons and events, they reproduce, without exposing, the connections of the specific story and persons to the structure of the relations and institutions that made the story possible.[3]

Hegemonic tales obscure the relationship between the specific and the general. They argue that events of an individual story or set of stories which occur at a specific time and place to particular individuals in fact reflect more universal principles about the way in which the world works. Narrative specificity creates a metonymic effect, rooting general principles in the particular.

Law and Narrative in Opposition

Narratives can also function to challenge and undermine normative law and legal authority. Unlike hegemonic stories, these subversive stories

> do not aggregate to the general, do not collect particulars as examples of a common phenomenon or rule; subversive stories recount particular experiences as *rooted* in and part of an encompassing cultural, political and material world that extends beyond the local.... They shock and enlighten precisely because they juxtapose the particular and private with the legal abstractions that are supposed to contain them.[4]

Subversive narratives present examples of instances where reality does not conform to the paradigms set forth by the law, or in which the legal authorities do not behave as expected. They thereby call into question at least one aspect of the law, if not the system as a whole.

Finally, in some cases the law actually functions to impede the development of narrative. Stories such as these tend to emerge when the law is conceived of in an apodictic manner, as being a static structure whose purpose is to impose order on a disorderly world. The narrative in question on the other hand is particularly dynamic, at times to the point of being chaotic.

Thus the plots of many stories are driven by an event or series of events in which the law is broken. It is precisely this state of transgression that generates a dramatic and dynamic plot. Once the rule of law is restored, the story comes to an end. Had the law never been violated, there would have been no story in the first place. In this context, law exists to prevent stories from taking place. In situations such as these, law and narrative find themselves diametrically opposed.

The Mishnah as Heterogeneous Text

The primary objective of the first part of this book was to apply the categories of narrativity to an analysis of the Mishnah as a whole. Such an endeavor reveals the fundamentally heterogeneous nature of the Mishnah's formal composition. The Mishnah embraces a broad range of literary forms from abstract apodictic statements which contain almost no narrativity to fully developed stories that are rich in narrativity. These forms are constantly juxtaposed with each other. Stories appear in the midst of a series of casuistic formulations, and apodictic statements brush up against repeated events.

The Mishnah's heterogeneity is also apparent in some of its nonformal aspects. Most notably is the Mishnah's policy of recording opposing views concerning the halakhah without giving any indication of which view is authoritative. Further, the Mishnah includes within it an extraordinarily large range of subjects, from civil and criminal law to ritual and cultic rules. No other ancient legal text that we have studied embraces such a wide variety of topics. Generally, these diverse subjects are segregated into *sedarim* and tractates. However, frequently enough, the Mishnah digresses to deal with issues far afield from the tractate's designated topic.

The Mishnah as Dialogic Text

Given the heterogeneous characteristics of the Mishnah, we must determine an interpretive approach that best suits its nature. I have suggested adapting the dialogic approach of Mikhail Bakhtin to the reading of the Mishnah. Bakhtin advocates reading at least some texts as containing differing "voices" rather than as presenting a single unequivocal statement. These voices, which represent different perspectives and worldviews, are juxtaposed with one another, supplementing or contradicting each other. The real meaning of the text is contained not in any one of these voices nor in a synthesis of them but rather in the "dialogic" interactions between these voices and their contrasting worldviews. A thorough reading of the text results in an intensification of the differences and refraction of the voices as they come into contact with one another rather than in the resolution of the tension between its various voices.

The Mishnah's competing voices are represented by its variety of literary forms with their range of narrativity. As we argued above, in a legal context the tension between high- and low- or no-narrativity forms can be seen as reflecting the fundamental split between what we have called apodictic and narrative approaches to law. Most legal texts tend to favor a single literary form or a small set of forms. These texts thus implicitly advocate a single position along the spectrum from narrative to apodictic approaches to law. The Mishnah, on the other hand, is one of the few legal texts that actively and aggressively mixes literary forms. This creates an open dialog between the various approaches to law. The Mishnah insists that law must emerge both from fundamental universal principles and at the same time from the idiosyncratic demands of a particular case relating to specific people and a particular time and place in history.

The Mishnah's dialogic nature is reflected not only in its consideration of larger jurisprudential questions but also in its discussion of particular halakhic issues. It is notoriously difficult to translate the Mishnah's discussions into either unequivocal rulings on specific cases or general underlying principles. One of the key reasons for this is that the Mishnah rarely specifies the relationship between the different parts of its text. Is a story that follows an apodictic ruling meant to oppose the ruling or merely to suggest an exception to the rule? Do casuistic statements simply present a rule of thumb regarding a particular situation or do they point to a more fundamental principle? If the latter, how are we to determine this principle? When presented with opposing views, is one of them meant to be authoritative? If so, how are we to know which view to accept? This open nature of the Mishnah's discourse lays the groundwork for the unique mode of discourse found in the Talmuds.[5] In the process of interpreting and evaluating the Mishnah's often elusive statements and positions, the Talmuds elucidate and often intensify the Mishnah's ambiguities, producing a Talmudic discourse that in some ways is even more open and discursive than that of the Mishnah.

Mishnaic Stories

Mishnaic Stories as Master Narratives

Like most anecdotes, the stories of the Mishnah can be read for the lesson or message that they are supposed to teach. Taken individually, each story's "message" is the halakhic ruling it presents. However, taken collectively, these stories portray the proper functioning of the legal system. They serve as hegemonic tales whose purpose is to implicitly reinforce the notion that the rabbis are the ultimate arbiters of appropriate halakhic behavior.

These stories can be divided into three categories on the basis of their underlying narrative structures. Each group of stories shares a common structure and through this structure teaches a different lesson about the role of the rabbis in the halakhic process.

The first category, the exemplum, need not necessarily be a story, though it often fits that definition. An exemplum is minimally composed of a single event in which a rabbi is portrayed as doing or refraining from doing a particular action of halakhic significance. This teaches us that the action in question is either required, permitted, or prohibited, depending on the case. Taken together, these stories teach that the rabbis are in some sense embodiments of halakhah who transmit the law not simply through oral teachings but through their very actions in their day-to-day lives.

The second category is the case story. Case stories all have the following basic narrative structure: (1) A situation arises whose halakhic implications are not clear. (2) A rabbi or group of rabbis renders a halakhic ruling with regard to the situation. By repeatedly linking a halakhic problem with its resolution by the rabbis, these stories suggest that such a process is normative. That is, the proper response to an unresolved halakhic issue is to present it to a rabbi for adjudication. The rabbis are the sole legitimate arbiters and interpreters of the law. Some stories contain additional elements that further reinforce this message. They present individuals asking the rabbi a question and/or following a ruling after it has been given. This further emphasizes the need to ask rabbis questions and to obey their answers.

The final category is that of the etiological story. These stories fit the following pattern: (1) a description of a ritual as it was originally practiced; (2) a crisis which makes the original practice impossible or problematic; and (3) a rabbinic enactment of a new practice which, while rooted in the old one, is suitable to contemporary conditions. The stories tell of the transformation of halakhic practice. They establish the circumstances in which the law may legitimately be changed. The rabbis have the right and responsibility to change halakhah in cases where a particular practice has been rendered unfeasible by historical circumstances. These stories thus establish limited legislative powers for the rabbis while asserting the overall stability of halakhic practice.

The stories of the Mishnah thus collectively present a picture of the halakhic process in which the rabbis are at the center. They are the sole legitimate transmitters, interpreters, innovators, and embodiments of the law.

Mishnaic Stories as Dialogic Texts

Mishnaic stories can also be read as much more elusive or even subversive texts which do not present a single straightforward message about rabbinic authority. Lurking behind the overt message suggested by the form of the master narrative are often dissonant voices which complicate and undermine this message.

On the most basic level, this occurs when a Mishnaic story itself presents two rabbis advocating two opposing positions, or when a story is juxtaposed with another story or other text which takes a contradictory view of the matter at hand. The Mishnah rarely gives explicit instructions regarding how to adjudicate these conflicts and determine normative practice. The simple notion of the authority of the individual rabbi must thus be reexamined. One cannot simply listen to the rabbis, because the rabbis themselves often disagree. We are left with an unresolved dialog between two different individuals or positions.

On a more sophisticated level, in our study of the exempla of *Sukkah* 2 we saw how these texts problematize the very notion of the rabbinic exemplar who stands distinct from the rest of the community as a living embodiment of religious practice. As these stories demonstrate, it is often difficult to distinguish between a rabbi and a non-rabbi. We meet a lowly slave who sleeps on the ground, yet, as it turns out, is a scholar whose behavior teaches us basic principles of the law. We also meet a revered sage whose behavior is nevertheless not recognized as exemplary but rather is rejected by the students of Shammai as being simply mistaken.

We have also seen stories that present conflicts not simply between two narrow halakhic positions but between two differing conceptions of spiritual and legal authority and of the nature of Jewish religious practice. The story of Honi Hameʻagel presents a confrontation between Honi and R. Simeon ben Shetah. Honi is a charismatic miracle worker whose authority is rooted in his special relationship with God. R. Simeon is the paradigmatic halakhist whose authority comes from his knowledge of the law and his leadership of the rabbinic establishment. The story ends in a stalemate, with neither side showing clear dominance.

Similarly, in the first chapter of *Rosh Hashanah*, there are a series of stories that portray R. Gamliel in conflict with some of the other leading rabbis of the period regarding questions about the calendar. Once again, this debate reflects conflicting notions of halakhah and halakhic leadership. R. Gamliel sees himself as being *in* authority. His power emerges from his position as head of the central court for the setting of the calendar. He takes a narrative view of halakhah, which means that decisions need to be made on the basis of the larger social and political conditions and their implications for the future of the halakhic community and its institutions. The other rabbis, in contrast, see themselves each as *an* authority and have an apodictic approach to halakhah. They see halakhic decisions as being governed by a set of preset rules. Their own authority is based on their knowledge of those rules and their ability to apply them in a consistent and empirical manner. Though R. Gamliel's ruling and his authority ultimately carry the day, the other rabbis are still presented as having a strong and legitimate voice.

Finally, etiological stories are meant to present the ultimate stability and continuity of halakhic practice and particularly Temple ritual over the generations. At the same time, these stories constantly remind the reader of the discontinuities, catastrophes, and chaos that have punctuated life in the Second Temple and so much of Jewish history of the period. The reader is left to wonder whether the rabbis have as much control over Jewish life and practice as it first appears.

Notably, when Ewick and Sibley describe the role of subversive stories in legal contexts, they present texts narrated by "outsiders" to the legal system who need to challenge and critique the law in order to protect their own political or existential interests. In the Mishnah, we find tales which have the potential to destabilize rabbinic and halakhic authority. These texts are are fully intergrated into mainstream halakhic discourse.

Read in this light, Mishnaic stories present a sort of internal critique, portraying an ambiguous world in which the nature and extent of rabbinic authority is unclear and the law itself is never fully resolved.

Mishnah as "Authoritative Discourse" vs. "Discourse of Authority"

These two approaches to reading Mishnaic stories might well reflect different conceptions of Mishnaic discourse as a whole. In a certain sense, this dichotomy is actually a development of the classic debate between Y. N. Epstein and Hanokh Albeck about whether the Mishnah was meant to be a definitive "code" or an academic "collection."[6] Epstein's notion of the Mishnah as a code suggests that the Mishnah is meant to be read as an "authoritative discourse." The Mishnah ultimately speaks with a single voice meant to impose uniform halakhic jurisprudence and practice within its community of readers. Albeck's idea of the "collection" suggests more of a "discourse of authority." In this view, the Mishnah is multivocal, placing opposing views into dialog with each other without privileging any one voice.

If we look at the Mishnah as not just a narrow halakhic text but an ideological one, these tensions between the Mishnah as authoritative discourse or discourse of authority take on wider implications. From this perspective, in addition to its discussion of individual rules and cases, the Mishnah is engaged in a broader discussion about the nature and functioning of halakhah and rabbinic authority as a whole. The question is what sort of discussion it is.

As an authoritative discourse, the purpose of the Mishnah is to expound a set of master narratives that establish the authority of the rabbis. The Mishnah's stories need to be read collectively so that the differences drop out and what remains is a series of basic narrative structures which argue for the inevitability of rabbinic authority over all aspects of halakhah. Along similar lines, the Mishnah also consistently reinforces its implicit framing story in which the rabbis are the sole inheritors of Moses and the prophets by way of the Pharisees, who in the rabbis' view controlled the Temple and were the leaders of "mainstream" Judaism in the Second Temple period.

On the other hand, the notion of the Mishnah as a discourse of authority suggests that the Mishnah engages in an ongoing and open-ended conversation about the workings of rabbinic authority. Despite their brevity, the Mishnah's stories demonstrate a fairly high level of complexity and ambiguity that allows them to become sites for the exploration of tensions and inconsistencies within the rabbinic power structure.

The question remains: what are we to do with these two different approaches to the Mishnah and its portrayal of rabbinic authority? My inclinations and biases lead me to favor letting the two models stand without reconciliation. The tension between "authoritative discourse" and "discourse of authority" would then represent a sort of metadialog that cuts across the Mishnah and its stories. The student of the Mishnah is meant to embrace both of these readings and all their implications without resolving the contradictions between them, just as he or she is meant to embrace both apodictic and narrative understandings of the law without fully working out the relationship between the two. This is the approach I have implicitly taken throughout the book.

Nevertheless, the dissonance between these two aspects of the Mishnah should not be overstated. Even within the discourse-of-authority model, rabbinic authority as a broader concept is never challenged and indeed is presumed throughout. Rather, the discourse of authority raises the difficulties and problems inherent in applying this notion to actual situations. Ultimately, such challenges could bring the entire system down by showing that it is not workable. The Mishnah never goes that far. The system continues to function despite disagreements and the messiness of day-to-day reality, which does not conform to simple patterns and principles.

The Mishnah might thus be seen as more than just a halakhic text around which rabbinic practice and study would coalesce in the Amoraic period. The Mishnah is also an ideological document which laid out an aggressive yet nuanced and self-critical argument for the rabbis, both individually and collectively as the central authorities of what was quickly becoming the dominant form of Judaism in the land of Israel, Babylonia, and ultimately the entire Jewish world.

Appendix

LIST OF STORIES IN THE MISHNAH

Below is a list of stories in the Mishnah based on the definition of "story" set forth in chapters 2 and 3. Stories are identified as case stories (C), exempla (Ex), etiological stories (Et), beit midrash stories (B), or other (O). Additionally, I have also marked stories in which the dialog form (D) plays a significant part. In some exempla and case stories the designation is followed by "+D." This indicates that the standard forms of these stories are followed by a dialog between the rabbi who is the subject of the story and an individual or group who observed the rabbi's actions. This represents a subgenre of Mishnaic narrative which deserves further study. Some beit midrash stories have the designation "B/D." These stories are essentially dialogs that meet the criteria for being a full-fledged story. This list is preliminary and is not meant to be an exhaustive catalog of stories in the Mishnah.

Zera'im
Berakhot 1:1 (C); 1:3 (C); 1:5 (B); 2:5 (Ex+D); 2:6 (Ex+D); 2:7 (Ex+D); 4:2 (Ex+D); 5:5 (Ex+D)
Kil'ayim 4:9 (C); 6:4 (C); 7:5 (C)
Shevi'it 4:1 (Et); 8:9 (B/D); 8:10 (B/D); 10:3 (Et)
Terumot 4:13 (C)
Ma'aser Sheni 5:2 (Et); 5:8 (Et); 5:9 (Ex)
Hallah 4:7 (B/D); 4:10–11 (C) [Multiple Stories]
'*Orlah* 2:12 (O)
Bikkurim 1:3 (C); 3:7 (Et)

Mo'ed
Shabbat 1:4 (B); 3:4 (C); 16:7 (C); 16:8 (Ex); 22:3 (C)
'*Eruvin* 1:2 (B/D); 2:6 (B); 4:1 (Ex); 4:2 (C); 4:4 (Ex); 6:2 (Ex); 10:10 (C)
Pesahim 4:8 (C)
Sheqalim 1:2 (Et); 1:4 (B/D); 2:4 (Et); 6:2 (Et); 7:5 (Et)
Yoma 2:1 (Et); 3:2 (Et)

Sukkah 2:1 (Ex); 2:5 (Ex) [Multiple Stories]; 2:7 (Ex.); 2:8 (Ex); 2:9 (O);
   3:12 (Et); 4:4 (Et); 4:9 (Et)
Betzah 3:2 (C); 3:5 (C)
Rosh Hashanah 1:6 (C); 1:7 (C); 2:1 (Et); 2:2 (Et); 2:5 (Et); 2:8 (C); 2:8–9 (C);
   4:1 (Et); 4:3 (Et); 4:4 (Et)
Ta'anit 2:5 (C); 3:6 (C); 3:8 (Ex); 3:9 (C); 4:4 (B)
Hagigah 2:2 (B)

Nashim
Yevamot 6:4 (Ex); 12:5 (C); 12:6 (Ex); 15:2 (B); 16:4 (C) [Multiple Stories];
   16:6 (C) [Multiple Stories]; 16:7 (B); 16:7 (Ex)
Ketubbot 1:10 (C); 7:10 (C)
Nedarim 5:6 (C); 6:6 (C); 9:5 (C); 9:8 (C); 9:10 (C)
Nazir 1:7 (O); 3:6 (C); 5:4 (C); 6:11 (C); 7:4 (B)
Sotah 1:8–9 (O) [Multiple Stories]; 7:8 (C); 8:1 (O); 9:9 (Et) [Multiple Stories];
   9:12 (Et) [Multiple Stories]; 9:14 (Et) [Multiple Stories]; 9:15 (Et)
Gittin 1:5 (C); 3:4 (B); 4:2 (Et) [Multiple Stories]; 4:3 (Et); 6:5 (Et); 6:6 (C); 7:5(C)
Qiddushin 2:7(C)

Neziqin
Bava Qamma 8:6 (C)
Bava Metsi'a 4:3 (O); 7:1 (C)
Bava Batra 8:3 (Ex); 9:7 (C); 10:8 (C)
Sanhedrin 7:2 (Ex)
'Eduyot 2:3 (C); 2:5 (B); 5:6–7 (B); 7:3 (C); 7:4 (C); 7:6 (Ex); 7:7 (C)
'Avodah Zarah 2:5 (B/D); 3:4 (Ex+D); 3:7 (C); 4:7 (B/D); 4:10 (C); 4:12 (C); 5:2 (C)

Qodashim
Zevahim 14:4–8 (Et)
Menahot 10:2 (Ex); 10:5 (Et)
Bekhorot 1:7 (Et); 4:4 (C); 5:3 (C) [Multiple Stories]; 6:6 (C); 6:9 (C)
Arakhin 5:1 (C); 8:1 (C); 9:4 (Et)
Temurah 3:1 (Ex)
Keritot 1:7 (Et); 3:7 (B/D); 6:3 (Ex)
Middot 1:2 (C); 1:6 (O); 2:3 (Et); 3:1 (Et)

Teharot
'Ohalot 5:3 (B); 17:5 (C)
Nega'im 7:4 (B/D); 9:3 (B/D)
Miqva'ot 4:1 (B)
Niddah 8:3 (C+D); 10:6 (Et)
Makhshirin 1:6 (C)
Tevul Yom 4:5 (Et) [Multiple Stories]
Yadayim 3:1 (C); 4:3 (B/D); 4:4 (C+D)

NOTES

Chapter 1

1. Indeed, the story can be read as having an open ending. It is never explicitly stated that the dawn in fact had not arrived. We never find out for sure if they were able to say the Shema or not.
2. The Mishnah was most likely transmitted orally. Nevertheless, for the sake of clarity and convenience I will use the terms "reader" and "read" to refer to the implied student of the Mishnaic text.
3. For a more general discussion of this term see Shmuel Safrai, "Halakha," in *The Literature of the Sages*, ed. Shmuel Safrai (Assen, the Netherlands: Van Gorcum, 1987), 121–22.
4. This definition of aggadah was first explicitly formulated in the post-Talmudic period. For a discussion of the meaning and status of the term within classical rabbinic literature itself, see Berachyahu Lifshitz, "'Aggadah' and its Place in the History of the Oral Law," *Shenaton Ha-Mishpat Ha-Ivri* 22 (2003) [Hebrew]. An abridged translation of this article appears as Berachyahu Lifshitz, "Aggadah versus Haggadah: Towards a More Precise Understanding of the Distinction," *Diné Yisrael* 24 (2007): *11–*29 (English section). See also Jonah Fraenkel, "The Aggadah in Talmudic Literature," *Netuim* 11–12 (2004): 63–79 [Hebrew].
5. There was a wide range of opinions among Jewish scholars as to the exact nature of aggadah's special status, as well as regarding the tools needed to explicate it. The most extensive treatment of medieval and early modern approaches to aggadah is Jacob Elbaum, *Le-havin divre hakhamim: Mivhar divre mavo le-agadah ule-midrash, mi-shel hakhme yeme ha-benayim* (Jerusalem: Bialik Institute, 2000). For a brief overview of the medieval sources see Marc Saperstein, *Decoding the Rabbis: A Thirteenth-Century Commentary on the Aggadah*, Harvard Judaic Monographs 3 (Cambridge, MA: Harvard University Press, 1980), 1–20. It should be noted that the Tosafists of medieval France and Germany did not accept such a clear distinction between halakhah and aggadah. They tended to attribute the same status and apply the same reading techniques to all types of rabbinic literature. See ibid., 7–8.
6. For a survey of Geonic discussions on aggadah, see Elbaum, *Le-havin divre hakhamim*, 47–64. It should be clear that the Geonic position is in fact more nuanced and diverse than I portray it in this brief survey. See David E. Sklare, *Samuel ben Hofni Gaon and his Cultural World: Texts and Studies* (Leiden, the Netherlands: Brill, 1996), 42–48.
7. Cited in Abraham ben Isaac of Narbonne, *Ha-Eshkol* (Jerusalem: Magnes, 1935), 157–58. Also cited in Elbaum, *Le-havin divre hakhamim*, 54–55.
8. For a broader consideration of the place of aggadah in Jewish culture, see David Stern, "Aggadah," in *Contemporary Jewish Religious Thought: Original Essays on Critical Concepts, Movements, and Beliefs*, ed. Arthur A. Cohen and Paul Mendes-Flohr (New York: Scribner's, 1987), 7–12.
9. On the former see Joshua Levinson, *Ha-Sipur she-lo supar: Omanut ha-sipur ha-Mikraa'i ha-murkhav be-midreshe Hazal* (Jerusalem: Magnes, 2005). On the latter see David Stern,

Parables in Midrash: Narrative and Exegesis in Rabbinic Literature (Cambridge, MA: Harvard University Press, 1991).
10. Bavli *Bava Metz'ia* 59a–60a. For a bibliography of studies of this story see Jeffrey Rubenstein, *Talmudic Stories: Narrative Art, Composition, and Culture* (Baltimore: Johns Hopkins University Press, 1999), 314n1. To this should be added Rubenstein's own sensitive reading of the story, ibid. 34–63, as well as Devora Steinmetz, "Agada Unbound: Inter-Agadic Characterization of Sages in the Bavli and Implications for Reading Agada," in *Creation and Composition: The Contribution of the Bavli Redactors (Stammaim) to the Aggada*, ed. Jeffrey L. Rubenstein (Tübingen, Germany: Mohr Siebeck, 2005), 293–337; Charlotte Elisheva Fonrobert, "When the Rabbi Weeps: On Reading Gender in Talmudic Aggadah," *Nashim* 4 (2001): 56–83.
11. Abraham ben Moses ben Maimon, *Milhamot ha-Shem* (Jerusalem: Mosad Harav Kook, 1963), 93.
12. Ibid.
13. Cited in Elbaum, *Le-havin divre hakhamim*, 169.
14. Azariah dei Rossi, *Me'or 'enayim* (Vilna, Lithuania: 1866). On dei Rossi's approach see Salo W. Baron, "Azariah de' Rossi's Historical Method," in *History and Jewish Historians: Essays and Addresses by Salo W. Baron*, ed. Arthur Hertzberg and Leon Feldman (Philadelphia: Jewish Publication Society of America, 1964), 205–39; Robert Bonfils, "Some Reflections on the Place of Azariah de Rossi's *Meor Enayim* in the Cultural Milieu of Italian Renaissance Jewry," in *Jewish Thought in the Sixteenth Century*, ed. Bernard Dov Cooperman (Cambridge, MA: Harvard University Press, 1983), 23–48; Levinson, "Literary Approaches to Midrash," 199–202. Though Levinson agrees that dei Rossi was primarily a historian, he sees him as the father of modern literary approaches to aggadah as well.
15. Both these scholars wrote numerous articles. The primary syntheses of their work are Gedaliah Alon, *The Jews in Their Land in the Talmudic Age*, trans. Gershon Levi, 2 vols. (Jerusalem: Magnes, 1980); Ephraim E. Urbach, *The Sages: Their Concepts and Beliefs*, trans. Israel Abrahams (Jerusalem: Magnes, 1975).
16. Joshua Levinson, "Literary Approaches to Midrash," in *Current Trends in the Study of Aggadah*, ed. Carol Bakhos (Leiden, the Netherlands: Brill, 2006), 202. See also Shmuel Safrai, "Tales of the Sages in the Palestinian Tradition and the Babylonian Talmud," in *Studies in Aggadic and Folk Literature*, ed. Joseph Heinemann and Dov Noy, Scripta Hierosolymitana 22 (Jerusalem: Magnes, 1971), 210.
17. See, inter alia, Jacob Neusner, "Story and Tradition in Ancient Judaism," in *Judaism: The Evidence of the Mishnah* (Chicago: University of Chicago Press, 1981); Neusner, *Development of a Legend: Studies on the Traditions Concerning Yohanan ben Zakkai* (Leiden, the Netherlands: Brill, 1970); Neusner, "The Rabbinic Traditions about the Pharisees before 70 in Modern Historiography," in *Method and Meaning in Ancient Judaism, Third Series* (Chico, CA: Scholars Press, 1981), 185–213; William Scott Green, "What's in a Name? The Problematic of Rabbinic 'Biography,'" in *Approaches to Ancient Judaism: Theory and Practice*, ed. William Scott Green (Missoula, MT: Scholars Press for Brown University, 1978), 77–96. Neusner was preceded in several key elements of his critique by Fischel, whose work I will discuss later in this book. See Henry A. Fischel, "Studies in Cynicism and the Ancient Near East: The Transformation of a Chria," in *Religions in Antiquity: Essays in Memory of Erwin Ramsdell Goodenough*, ed. Jacob Neusner (Leiden, the Netherlands: Brill, 1968), 372–411; "Story and History: Observations on Greco-Roman Rhetoric and Pharisaism," in *Essays in Greco-Roman and Related Talmudic Literature*, ed. Henry A. Fischel (New York: Ktav, 1977), 59–88. Also important is Shamma Friedman's critique of traditional historical methods from the perspective of Talmudic source and form criticism. For an English summary of these views see, Shamma Friedman, "Literary Development and Historicity in the Aggadic Narrative of the Babylonian Talmud: A Study Based upon B.M. 83b–86a," in *Community and Culture: Essays in Jewish Studies in honor of the Ninetieth Anniversary of the Founding of Graetz College*, ed. Nahum M. Waldman (Philadelphia: Graetz College, 1987), 67–80.

18. Neusner, "Story and Tradition," 322.
19. Fraenkel's most important articles on the subject have recently been collected into a single volume: Jonah Fraenkel, *Sipur ha-agadah, ahdut shel tokhen ve-tsurah: Kovets mehkarim* (Tel Aviv: Hakibbutz Hameuchad, 2001). Fraenkel also published a more popular volume on the subject, *'Iyunim be-'olamo ha-ruhani shel sipur ha-agadah* (Tel Aviv: Hakibbutz Hameuchad, 1981). He summarized his conclusions on this topic in *Darkhe ha-agadah veha-midrash*, 2 vols. ([Givataim, Israel]: Yad La-Talmud, 1991), 235–86. Unfortunately, very little of Fraenkel's work has thus far been translated into English. For discussions of Fraenkel's method see Joshua Levinson, "From Parable to Invention: The Development of Fiction as a Cultural Category," in *Higayon le-Yonah: Hebetim hadashim be-heker sifrut ha-Midrash, ha-Agadah veha-piyut, kovets mehkarim li-khevodo shel profesor Yonah Frenkel bi-melot lo shiv'im ve-'amesh shanah*, ed. Joshua Levinson, Jacob Elbaum, and Galit Hasan-Rokem (Jerusalem: Magnes, 2007), 1–32 [Hebrew]; Rubenstein, *Talmudic Stories*, 8–10. Around the same time that Fraenkel was formulating his approach, his colleague at the Hebrew University, Dov Noy, was working on a parallel approach to rabbinic literature using the tools of folklore studies. In particular Noy's student Dan Ben-Amos applied these techniques to rabbinic stories. Dan Ben-Amos, "Narrative Forms in the Haggadah: Structural Analysis" (Ph.D. diss., Indiana University, 1967). See also Eli Yassif, *The Hebrew Folktale: History, Genre, Meaning*, (Bloomington: Indiana University Press, 1999), 70–243. For a survey of the development of this school, see Galit Hasan-Rokem, *Web of Life: Folklore and Midrash in Rabbinic Literature*, trans. Batya Stein (Palo Alto, CA: Stanford University Press, 2000), 1–7. On Fraenkel's debate with the folklorists, see Levinson, "From Parable to Invention," 31.
20. See Cleanth Brooks, "New Criticism," in *Princeton Encyclopedia of Poetry and Poetics*, ed. Alex Preminger (Princeton, NJ: Princeton University Press, 1974), 567–68.
21. Fraenkel, *Sipur ha-agadah*, 27–39.
22. Ibid., 15–23.
23. Ibid., 23n34.
24. Ibid., 366.
25. Fraenkel, *Sipur ha-agadah*, 220–35. See also Jonah Fraenkel, "The Aggadah in the Mishnah," in *Mehqerei Talmud 3: Talmudic Studies Dedicated to the Memory of Professor Ephraim E. Urbach*, ed. Yaakov Sussman and David Rosenthal (Jerusalem: Magnes, 2005), 655–83 [Hebrew].
26. On the trend among literary critics to question the value of classifying texts as either "literary" or "nonliterary," see Jonathan Culler, *On Deconstruction: Theory and Criticism after Structuralism* (Ithaca, NY: Cornell University Press, 1982), 180–84; Terry Eagleton, *Literary Theory: An Introduction* (Minneapolis: University of Minnesota Press, 1983), 1–16; Catherine Gallagher and Stephen Greenblatt, *Practicing New Historicism* (Chicago: University of Chicago Press, 2000), 1–19.
27. This claim is made most explicitly by Rubenstein, *Talmudic Stories*, 8.
28. In addition to the writers noted below, see the work of Ofra Meir, "The Acting Character in the Stories of the Talmud and Midrash (A Sample)" (Ph.D. diss., Hebrew University, 1977) [Hebrew]; Meir, *Sugyot ba-po'etikah shel sipure Hazal* (Tel Aviv: Sifriat Poalim, 1993); Meir, *Rabi Judah ha-Nasi: Deyokno shel manhig be-masorot Erets-Yisra'el u-Vavel* (Tel Aviv: Hakibbutz Hameuchad, 1999); as well as that of Alon Goshen-Gottstein, *The Sinner and the Amnesiac: The Rabbinic Invention of Elisha ben Abuya and Eleazar ben Arach* (Palo Alto, CA: Stanford University Press, 2000).
29. Rubenstein, *Talmudic Stories*; Shulamit Valler, *Women and Womanhood in the Talmud*, trans. Betty Sigler Rozen, Brown Judaica Studies (Atlanta: Scholars Press, 1999); Barry Wimpfheimer, "'But It Is Not So': Toward a Poetics of Legal Narrative in the Babylonian Talmud," *Prooftexts* 24(2004), 51–86; Wimpfheimer, "Talmudic Legal Narrative: Broadening the Discourse of Jewish Law," *Diné Yisrael* 24 (2007): *157–196. See also Moshe Simon, review of *Talmudic Stories: Narrative Art, Composition, and Culture* by Jeffrey L. Rubenstein and *Woman and Womanhood in the Talmud* by Shulamit Valler, trans. Betty Sigler Rozen, *AJS Review* 26, no. 1 (2002): 129–131.

30. This critique is perhaps least true with regard to Wimpfheimer, whose approach to the relationship between law and narrative is most similar to my own.
31. Robert Cover, "Nomos and Narrative," in *Narrative, Violence, and the Law: The Essays of Robert Cover*, ed. Martha Minow, Michael Ryan, and Austin Sarat (Ann Arbor: University of Michigan Press, 1992), 95–171.
32. See for example the articles collected in Peter Brooks and Paul Gewirtz, *Law's Stories: Narrative and Rhetoric in the Law* (New Haven, CT: Yale University Press, 1996).
33. Peter Brooks, "Narrativity of the Law," *Cardozo Studies in Law and Literature* 14 (2002): 1–10; Peter Brooks, "Narrative Transactions—Does the Law Need a Narratology?," *Yale Journal of Law and the Humanities* 18, no. 1 (2006): 1–28.
34. Peter Brooks, "Narrativity of the Law," 2.
35. E. Z. Melammed, "The 'Case' in the Mishnah as a Source of Halakha," *Sinai* 23 (1960): 152–66 [Hebrew]; Melammed, "Collections of Tanaitic Stories," in *Essays in Talmudic Literature* (Jerusalem: Magnes, 1986), 168–82 [Hebrew]; Arnold Goldberg, "Form und Funktion des Ma'ase in der Mischna," *Frankfurter Judaistische Beiträge* 2 (1974): 1–38.
36. Catherine Hezser, *Form, Function, and Historical Significance of the Rabbinic Story in Yerushalmi Neziqin* (Tübingen, Germany: Mohr Siebeck, 1993).
37. Daniel Boyarin, *Carnal Israel: Reading Sex in Talmudic Culture* (Berkeley: University of California Press, 1993). See especially 14–15. Galit Hasan Rokem's contribution to the application of cultural studies methodologies to rabbinic literature also deserves mention. However, she does not generally deal with halakhic texts or issues. See Hasan-Rokem, *Web of Life*.
38. Charlotte Elisheva Fonrobert, *Menstrual Purity: Rabbinic and Christian Reconstructions of Biblical Gender* (Palo Alto, CA: Palo Alto University Press, 2000).
39. Beth A. Berkowitz, *Execution and Invention: Death Penalty Discourse in Early Rabbinic and Christian Cultures* (New York: Oxford University Press, 2006); Ishay Rosen-Zvi, *Ha-Tekes she-lo hayah: Mikdash, midrash u-migdar ba-masekhet Sotah* (Jerusalem: Magnes, 2008).

Chapter 2

1. William Labov, "Some Further Steps in Narrative Analysis," *Journal of Narrative and Life History* 7 (1997): 396.
2. Jerome Bruner, *Making Stories: Law, Literature, Life* (Cambridge, MA: Harvard University Press, 2002), 96–97.
3. E. M. Forster, *Aspects of the Novel*, (London,: Edward Arnold and Company, 1927), 116. Forster makes use of a different set of terms than I do. Forster calls this text a "plot," in contrast to a "story," which for him refers to a set of events that lack causality. For the sake of clarity, I have replaced Forster's terms with my own.
4. Ibid.
5. Aristotle already declared that "the plot is the mimesis of the action—for I use 'plot' to denote the construction of events." Aristotle, *Poetics*, trans. Stephen Halliwell, Loeb Classical Library L199 (Cambridge, MA: Harvard University Press, 1995), 39.
6. Suzanne Fleischman presents a useful survey of the critical discussion surrounding the question of "events" in narrative. Fleischman, *Tense and Narrativity: From Medieval Performance to Modern Fiction* (Austin: University of Texas Press, 1990), 97–100.
7. See Gerald Prince, *A Grammar of Stories* (The Hague: Mouton, 1973), 17.
8. Aristotle anticipates the need for causality at the end of Book 9 of his *Poetics*.
9. Guyora Binder and Robert Weisberg, "Narrative Criticism of Law," in *Literary Criticisms of Law* (Princeton, NJ: Princeton University Press, 2000), 221. The authors make this statement in explicating the position of Arthur Danto.
10. See for example, Roman Jakobson, "On Realism in Art," in *Language in Literature*, ed. Krystyna Pomorska and Stephen Rudy (Cambridge, MA: Belknap Press of Harvard University Press, 1987), 19–27, and Roland Barthes, "The Reality Effect," in *French Literary Theory Today: A Reader*, ed. Tzvetan Todorov (Cambridge, UK: Cambridge University Press, 1982), 11–17.

11. Gerald Prince, "Narrativity," in *Axia: Davis Symposium on Literary Evaluation*, ed. Karl Menges and Daniel Rancour-Laferriere (Stuttgart: Akademischer Verlag Hans-Dieter Heinz, 1981), 61–76; Wendy Steiner, *Pictures of Romance: Form against Content in Painting and Literature* (Chicago: University of Chicago Press, 1988).
12. G. A. Gaballa, *Narrative in Egyptian Art* (Mainz, Germany: Verlag Philipp von Zabern, 1976), 5.
13. Perhaps the earliest systematic attempt to demonstrate the integral relationship between the past tense and narrative was undertaken by Emile Benveniste with regard to the French language in "The Correlation of Tense in the French Verb," in *Problems in General Linguistics*, trans. Mary Elizabeth Meek, Miami Linguistics Series 8 (Coral Gables, FL: University of Miami, 1971). Fleischman offers a more thorough, cross-linguistic study of the role of tense in narrative and the past tense in particular. See Fleischman, *Tense and Narrativity*. See also Roland Barthes' comments on the French *passé simple* in *Writing Degree Zero*, trans. Annette Lavers and Colin Smith (New York: Hill & Wang, 1968), 34. Barthes emphasizes the role of the past tense in what I have called the dynamic nature of narrative.
14. See Labov, "Some Further Steps," 400.
15. See Paul Ricoeur, *Time and Narrative*, trans. Kathleen McLaughlin and David Pellauer, vol. 2 (Chicago: University of Chicago Press, 1985), 98–99.
16. Fleischman, *Tense and Narrativity*, 104.
17. Fleischman presents two similar definitions of a story which compliment my own. First she defines narrative in strictly linguistic terms. She defines the "constituent properties" of narrative as being "*past* time reference, *perfective* aspect, and a *distanced, objective* perspective on events that are *realis, semelfactive* (unique occurrence), and *sequentially ordered*." (ibid., 55). Later, Fleischman quotes Susan Herring's previously unpublished description of a "prototypical narrative":

> The prototypical past tense narrative is concerned with *events* rather than static description, and the events are not narrated in random order but rather in a *sequence* which is iconic with the temporal order in which they actually occurred.... Further, the completion of one event is implied by the inception of that which follows, a fact, which may give rise to an interpretation of aspectual *perfectivity* for the (simple) past tense where no other value is specifically indicated.... The prototypical narrative is *factual* and *time-bound*, in that it chronicles a *unique set of events*, which took place at a specific point (or over a specific bounded interval) in time. There is also a sense in which the ideal narrator is *objective*, maintaining distance between him or herself and the events narrated in order to relate them as they actually occurred, in linear order with minimum of personal evaluation or digression. It is this complex of features which, in the absence of indications to contrary, the "narrative past" typically evokes (101).

Both Fleischman and Herring add an additional narrative attribute to the two I propose, namely, that the events be narrated in an objective manner. This opens up the possibility of a third general category of narrative attributes, namely, that narratives are *narrated*. See also Barbara Herrnstein Smith, "Narrative Versions, Narrative Theories," in *On Narrative*, ed. W. J. T. Mitchell (Chicago: University of Chicago Press, 1980), 209–32. I will deal with the question of the narrator later on in this book.
18. Leo Tolstoy, *Anna Karenina*, trans. Joel Carmichael (New York: Bantam, 1960).

Chapter 3

1. On exegesis in the Mishnah see Alexander Samely, *Rabbinic Interpretation of Scripture in the Mishnah* (New York: Oxford University Press, 2002).
2. Moshe Azar, *Tahbir leshon ha-Mishnah* (Jerusalem: Academy of Hebrew Language, 1995), 71–79.

3. Printed editions read מנפץ.
4. Printed editions and a genizah fragment (T-S E.2.39, Cambridge University Library) end the line with הם.
5. Outside of this passage, this halakhic category appears twice in the Mishnah (*Berakhot* 1:9 and *Shabbat* 6:9). It appears in a halakhic context in only one other time in Tannaitic sources (Mekhilta, Shirah 2) and has no independent usages in the Talmuds.
6. Benjamin De Vries, *Toldot ha-halakhah ha-Talmudit: Perakim nivharim* (Tel Aviv: Avraham Zioni, 1962), 142–56. Ephraim E. Urbach, *The Halakhah: Its Sources and Development*, trans. Raphael Posner ([Jerusalem?]: Yad la-Talmud, 1986), 177–205.
7. Leib Moscovitz, *Talmudic Reasoning: From Casuistics to Conceptualization* (Tübingen, Germany: Mohr Siebeck, 2002), 6.
8. Ibid., 5.
9. Ibid., 59.
10. Ibid., 55.
11. Since the distinction between morphology and syntax is crucial to this discussion, I make use of the morphologically descriptive terms based on the root *q-t-l* favored by linguists writing in Modern Hebrew.
12. Printed editions read סכין שמן ורד על מכותיהן.
13. I have translated the modal *qotlim* as "[We] may" in order to capture the plural nature of the verb and convey the structure of the sentence, both of which are crucial to our discussion. Overall it may not be the best translation possible for these formulations.
14. Aba Bendavid, *Leshon mikra u-leshon hakhamim* (Tel Aviv: Devir, 1967), 535–37; Shimon Sharvit, "The Tense System in the Language of the Mishna," in *Mehkarim b'Ivrit uvi-leshonot Shemiyot: Mukdashim le-zikhro shel Prof. Yehezkel Kutsher*, ed. Gad B. Sarfatti (Ramat Gan, Israel: Bar-Ilan University Press, 1980), 115–17 [Hebrew]; Mordechay Mishor, "The Tense System in Tannaitic Hebrew" (Ph.D. diss., Hebrew University, 1983), 272–304 [Hebrew]; Azar, *Tahbir leshon ha-Mishnah*, 20–22.
15. Sharvit, "Tense System in the Mishna," 111.
16. Azar, *Tahbir leshon ha-Mishnah*, 15–18.
17. M. H. Segal, *Dikduk leshon ha-Mishnah* (Tel Aviv: Devir, 1936), 129.
18. Dwight L. Bolinger, "More on the Present Tense in English," *Language* 23 (1947), 434. Bolinger makes this statement specifically with regard to the English language. However, Suzanne Fleischman cites this passage in the context of her own cross-linguistic discussion of tense (*Tense and Narrativity*, 34). For a similar analysis of the use of the present tense in nineteenth century English case reports see Ayelet Ben-Yishai, "Victorian Precedents: Narrative Form, Law Reports and *Stare Decisis*," *Law, Culture and the Humanities* 4 (2008): 395.
19. On this form see David Daube, *The New Testament and Rabbinic Judaism* (London: Athlone, 1956), 90–105.
20. Sharvit, "Tense System in the Mishna," 116.
21. Mishor, "Tense System in Tannaitic Hebrew," vi.
22. Printed texts read שגרופה.
23. A *muliar* and an *antiki* are two different types of pots that contain compartments for coals to heat water.
24. For a treatment of word order in Biblical Hebrew see Katsuomi Shimasaki, *Focus Structure in Biblical Hebrew: A Study of Word Order and Information Structure* (Baltimore: CDL, 2002).
25. This word is inserted above the line in MS Kaufmann.
26. MS Parma reads השבת.
27. An *'eruv* is a legal device that increases one's range of motion or ability to transport objects on the Sabbath.
28. The last two letters of this word are inserted above the lines in MS Kaufmann and are absent from MS Parma.
29. For a thorough treatment of this use of *qotel* see Mishor, "Tense System in Tannaitic Hebrew," 164, 66–69.

30. See also Danby's translation. Herbert Danby, *The Mishnah* (Oxford: Clarendon Press, 1967).
31. Printed editions and MS Parma add here גוי.
32. Azar, *Tahbir leshon ha-Mishnah*, 3.
33. Mishor, "Tense System in Tannaitic Hebrew," v.
34. M. H. Segal, *Dikduk leshon ha-Mishnah*, 126.
35. Printed editions and MS Parma read ונעל.
36. Printed editions and MS Parma read ונעל.
37. Printed editions and MS Parma add here גוי.
38. Printed editions read יורד.
39. I have found no examples of independent prescriptive statements using *yiqtol* in *Shabbat*. Neither Mishor nor Azar list such a usage in their surveys of the uses of *yiqtol*. Mishor, "Tense System in Tannaitic Hebrew," 103–11, esp. 105; and Azar, *Tahbir leshon ha-Mishnah*, 8–12, esp. 11, #17.
40. The vocalization in MS Kaufmann here is problematic. We have presented here the text as it appears in the printed editions, which is nearly identical to MS Parma. Abraham Goldberg suggests an alternative vocalization for MS Kaufmann which would yield essentially the same meaning for this phrase as that found in other witnesses. See Abraham Goldberg, *Perush la-Mishnah, masekhet Shabat* (Jerusalem: Jewish Theological Seminary of America, 1976), 330.
41. This letter is found in the margins in MS Kaufmann.
42. This letter is found in the margins in MS Kaufmann. It does not appear in MS Parma.
43. Borges, *Labyrinths*, 19–29.
44. Seymour Chatman, *Story and Discourse: Narrative Structure in Fiction and Film* (Ithaca, NY: Cornell University Press, 1978), 56–57.
45. Mishor, "Tense System in Tannaitic Hebrew," 532.
46. This word is missing from MS Parma.
47. These last two words are missing from printed editions.
48. This letter is inserted above the line in MS Kaufmann.
49. This letter is crossed out in MS Kaufmann and is missing from MS Parma and the printed editions.
50. Yochanan Breuer, "Perfect and Participle in Descriptions of Ritual in the Mishna," *Tarbits* 56, no. 3 (1987) [Hebrew].
51. Ibid., 303.
52. Ibid., 326.
53. Printed editions read אמר ר' צדוק.
54. For previous attempts to define and classify the use of *ma'aseh* in the Mishnah see Melammed, "The 'Case' in the Mishnah as a Source of Halakha."; Goldberg, "Form und Function des Ma'ase in der Mishna." My argument is in many ways similar to that of Goldberg. See also Shimon Sharvit, "The Opening 'Ma'aseh She' and Its Relatives in the Language of the Tana'im," in *Segulah le-Ari'elah: ma'asaf divre mehkar ve-sifrut le-zikhrah shel Ari'elah Dim-Goldberg*, ed. Moshe Idel, et al. (Jerusalem: private imprint, 1990), 159–71 [Hebrew].
55. Technically, these texts should probably be called "*halakhic* exempla", as the term "exempla" generally has a much broader meaning in the study of both rabbinic and general narrative. For the sake of simplicity however, I have chosen to use the single word "exempla." For examples of the use of the term exempla in its more usual, broader sense see Yassif, *The Hebrew Folktale*, 120–30; Susan Rubin Suleiman, *Authoritarian Fictions: The Ideological Novel as a Literary Genre* (Princeton, NJ: Princeton University Press, 1993), 25–62.
56. Printed editions and MS Parma add here גוי.
57. Printed editions read יורד.
58. This letter added, presumably by the vocalizer, in MS Kaufmann.
59. This word is inserted above the line in MS Kaufmann.
60. Printed editions and MS Parma read בשבת.

61. See Arnold Goldberg, "Form und Funktion des Ma'ase," 8.
62. Arnold Goldberg, ibid., suggests a similar structure for the case narrative.
63. *Yoma* 2:1.
64. MS Munich and other Talmudic MSS read here בייתוסים. See *Dikdukei Soferim*, ad. loc.
65. Goldberg similarly counts "*das ätiologische Ma'ase*" in his typology of the *ma'aseh*. He argues that despite the fact the *Yoma* 2:1 is the only example in the Mishnah, such a usage occurs more frequently in *baraitot*. He gives only two examples from the Bavli, and of these only in *Berakhot* 23a does the term *ma'aseh* actually appear in a baraita in the context of an etiological tale. Arnold Goldberg, "Form und Funktion des Ma'ase," 18.
66. Rivka Shemesh conducted a thorough linguistic study of verbs of saying and speech acts in the Mishnah. She counts 5,475 appearances of the root '-m-r in the Mishnah, which she classifies under twenty-four distinct usages. Rivkah Shemesh, "Verbs of Saying in Mishnaic Hebrew: A Syntactic, Semantic and Pragmatic Analysis" (Ph.D. diss., Bar-Ilan University, 1998), 359–65 [Hebrew].
67. One usage of *'amar* that does not fit this pattern is the phrase *kellal 'amar*, which appears in *Shabbat* three times: 15:2, 19:1, and 23:3.
68. Printed editions add here חייב ואם ראויין הן. MS Parma reads ואם ראויין הן. The printed version appears to be the best reading and is reflected in the translation.
69. This word appears in the margin in MS Kaufmann.
70. This letter added, presumably by a different hand, in MS Kaufmann.
71. *Yevamot* 15:2; *'Eduyyot* 1:12 (twice), 13, 14; *Kelim* 9:2; *Ohalot* 5:3, 4.
72. Printed editions read גוריון.
73. MS Parma reads ונמנו.
74. Scholars since the Middle Ages have debated the reason for the placement of *Shabbat* 1:1 at the head of the chapter. See Pinhas Kehati, *Mishnayot mevo'arot* (Jerusalem: Hekhal Shelomoh, 1966–67) for a survey of the traditional solutions to this problem. For other possibilities see Jacob N. Epstein, *Mevo'ot le-sifrut ha-Tana'im: Mishnah, Tosefta u-midrashai-halakhah* (Jerusalem: Magnes, 1957), 282; Abraham Goldberg, *Perush la-Mishnah, masekhet Shabat*.
75. Exactly which of the laws stated in sections 1–3 are referred to in section 4 remains a point of debate. See Kehati, *Mishnayot mevo'arot*; Epstein, *Mevo'ot le-sifrut ha-Tana'im*, 282; Hanokh Albeck, *Shisha sidre Mishnah* (Jerusalem: Mosad Bialik, 1952), 2:406; Abraham Goldberg, *Perush la-Mishnah, masekhet Shabat*. The existence of an alternative reading *ve-eilu*, further raises the possibility that this narrative refers to the rulings that follow, rather than those that precede it. See *Tiferet Yisrael*; Jacob N. Epstein, *Mavo le-nusah ha-Mishnah*, 3rd ed. (Jerusalem: Magnes, 2000), 426.

Chapter 4

1. Zacharias Frankel, *Darkhe ha-Mishnah* (Leipzig: Hunger, 1859); David Zvi Hoffmann, *Ha-Mishnah ha-rishona u-felugta de-tana'e* (Berlin: Gruenberg, 1914); Epstein, *Mevo'ot le-sifrut ha-Tana'im*; Hanokh Albeck, *Mavo la-Mishnah* (Jerusalem: Bialik, 1959); Abraham Goldberg, "The Mishnah—A Studybook of Halacha," in *The Literature of the Sages*, ed. Shmuel Safrai, Compendia Rerum Iudaicarum ad Novum Testamentum (Assen, the Netherlands: Van Gorcum, 1987), 211–51.
2. The idea that some sections of the Mishnah date from Second Temple times has been a mainstay of critical scholarship of the Mishnah since the days of David Zvi Hoffmann. For a discussion and critique of this concept see Rosen-Zvi, *Ha-Tekes she-lo hayah*, 161–64.
3. Jacob Neusner, "The Mishnah Viewed Whole," in *The Mishnah in Contemporary Perspective*, ed. Alan J. Avery-Peck and Jacob Neusner (Leiden, the Netherlands: Brill, 2002), 10.
4. Jacob Neusner, *Judaism Without Christianity: An Introduction to the System of the Mishnah* (Hoboken, NJ: Ktav, 1991), 99.
5. Neusner, "Mishnah Viewed Whole," 21.
6. See Jacob Neusner, *Judaism as Philosophy: The Method and Message of the Mishnah* (Columbia: University of South Carolina Press, 1991), 12.

7. Neusner outlines the methods and conclusions of his approach to the historical study of the Mishnah in Jacob Neusner, *Judaism: The Evidence of the Mishnah*, 2nd ed. (Atlanta, GA: Scholars Press, 1988). He has reaffirmed his commitment to these theories as recently as 2006, in "Why We Cannot Assume the Historical Reliability of Attributions: The Case of the Houses in the Mishnah-Tosefta," in *The Mishnah in Contemporary Perspective*, vol. 2, ed. Alan J. Avery-Peck and Jacob Neusner (Leiden, the Netherlands: Brill, 2006).
8. For example, Jacob Neusner, "Method and Meaning in Mishnah," in *Method and Meaning in Judaism: Third Series* (Chico, CA: Scholars Press, 1981); Neusner, *The Mishnah: An Introduction* (Northvale, NJ: Aronson, 1989); Neusner, *Judaism as Philosophy*; Neusner, "Mishnah Viewed Whole"; Neusner, *Making God's Word Work: A Guide to the Mishnah* (New York: Continuum, 2004).
9. Indeed, on some occasions Neusner appears to deny that the Mishnah has any history, stating that it was "formulated all at once." Neusner, *The Mishnah: An Introduction*, 25. See also Neusner, "Method and Meaning in Mishnah," 25.
10. For a far more nuanced and sophisticated attempt to demonstrate the literary and thematic unity of the Mishnah, see the work of Avraham Walfish. Walfish convincingly argues for the existence of chiastic and other literary structures organizing the Mishnah. Avraham Walfish, "Literary Method of Redaction in the Mishnah Based on Tractate Rosh Hashana" (Ph.D. diss., Hebrew University, 2001) [Hebrew]; Walfish, "The Poetics of the Mishnah," in *The Mishnah in Contemporary Perspective*, ed. Alan J. Avery-Peck and Jacob Neusner, Handbuch der Orientalistik Abt. 1, Der Nahe und der Mittlere Osten (Leiden, the Netherlands: Brill, 2006), 153–89.
11. It should be noted that several critical scholars have made use of formal literary tools similar to those that I employ as part of their attempts to uncover the history of the Mishnaic text. David Halivni claims that the apodictic material represents the Mishnah's earliest historical stratum; J. N. Epstein may have held a similar opinion. On the other hand, Ben Zion Wacholder hypothesizes that the various stories about R. Gamliel scattered throughout the Mishnah have their origins in a single, preexisting compendium of stories. David Weiss Halivni, *Midrash, Mishnah, and Gemara: The Jewish Predilection for Justified Law* (Cambridge, MA: Harvard University Press, 1986), 57; Epstein, *Mevo'ot le-sifrut ha-Tana'im*, 414; Ben Zion Wacholder, "Tales about R. Gamliel in the Mishnah and Tosefta," in *Fourth World Congress of Jewish Studies: Papers*, vol. 1 (Jerusalem: World Union of Jewish Studies, 1967) 143–44 [Hebrew].
12. M. M. Bakhtin, "Discourse in the Novel," in *The Dialogic Imagination: Four Essays*, ed. Michael Holquist (Austin: University of Texas Press, 1981), 271–72.
13. Ibid., 292. For a lucid exposition of Bakhtin's concept of "heteroglossia," see Gary Saul Morson and Caryl Emerson, *Mikhail Bakhtin: Creation of a Prosaics* (Stanford, CA: Stanford University Press, 1990), 259–422.
14. Cover, "Nomos and Narrative."
15. See Peter Stein, *Roman Law in European History* (Cambridge, UK: Cambridge University Press, 1999); Alan Watson, *The Making of the Civil Law* (Cambridge, MA: Harvard University Press, 1981).
16. See Gerald Postema, "Classical Common Law Jurisprudence (Part 1)," *Oxford University Commonwealth Law Journal* 2, no. 2 (2002): 155–80; Gerald Postema, "Classical Common Law Jurisprudence (Part 2)," *Oxford University Commonwealth Law Journal* 3, no. 1 (2003): 1–28. On the narrativity of British common law reports see Ben-Yishai, "Victorian Precedents," 382–402. For an application of a similar set of categories based on Anglo-American jurisprudence to rabbinic texts, see Suzanne Last Stone, "On the Interplay of Rules, 'Cases' and Concepts in Rabbinic Legal Literature: Another Look at the Aggadot of Honi the Circle-Drawer," *Diné Yisrael* 24 (2006): 125–56.
17. Perhaps the most extreme case of this empowering of academic legal scholars occured in sixteenth-century Germany, where law faculties gained an official role in the adjudication of cases. Stein, *Roman Law in European History*, 90.

18. On the distinction between law as thing and law as activity see Richard A. Posner, "What Is Law and Why Ask?," in *The Problems of Jurisprudence* (Cambridge, MA: Harvard University Press, 1990), 220–44.
19. The distinction between an individual being *an* authority or *in* authority was first proposed by R. S. Peters and extensively applied to the question of rabbinic authority by Michael Berger. R. S. Peters, "Symposium on Authority," *Aristotelian Society Supplement* 32 (1958): 204–24; Michael S. Berger, *Rabbinic Authority* (New York: Oxford University Press, 1998).
20. Postema, "Classical Common Law Jurisprudence (Part 1)," 158. One of the strongest formulations of this view of judges is to be found in the thought of the American Legal Realist school with its notion of judges as legislators. See Brian Leiter, "American Legal Realism," in *The Blackwell Guide to the Philosophy of Law and Legal Theory*, ed. Martin Golding and William Edmundson (Oxford: Blackwell, 2005), 50–66.
21. Peter Brooks, "Narrative Transactions," 2. For a partial bibliography of this approach to the relationship between law and narrative, see Paul Gewirtz, "Victims and Voyeurs: Two Narrative Problems at the Criminal Trial " in *Law's Stories: Narrative and Rhetoric in the Law*, ed. Peter Brooks and Paul Gewirtz (New Haven, CT: Yale University Press, 1996), 259n2. This approach is also advocated in Bruner, *Making Stories*. Barry S. Wimpfheimer similarly seeks to retrieve suppressed "voices" from the narratives of the legal narrative Talmud. Barry S. Wimpfheimer, *Narrating the Law: A Poetics of Talmudic Legal Stories* (Philadelphia: University of Pennsylvania Press, 2011).
22. For a historical example of the dynamics of this relationship, see Arthur J. Jacobson, "Death of the Hypothetical," *Stanford Literature Review* 9, no. 2 (1992): 125–38. For a more theoretical consideration, see Frederick Schauer, "Rules and the Rule of Law," *Harvard Journal of Law and Public Policy* 14, no. 3 (1991): 645–94.
23. Duncan Kennedy, "Form and Substance in Private Law Adjudication," *Harvard Law Review* 89 (1976): 1685–1778.
24. Elizabeth Shanks Alexander and Leib Moscovitz both argue for such implicit conceptualization in the Mishnah's presentation of casuistic laws. Elizabeth Shanks Alexander, *Transmitting Mishnah*, 117–67; Moscovitz, *Talmudic Reasoning*, 47–50. The classic study of the creation of a conceptual rubric to organize a previously amorphous body of halakhah is Yitshak D. Gilat's analysis of the emergence of the thirty-nine categories of Sabbath labor. Yitshak D. Gilat, *Perakim be-hishtalshelut ha-halakhah* (Ramat-Gan, Israel: Bar-Ilan University Press, 1992), 32–62.
25. Printed texts read מביאין שפוד.
26. Printed texts and MS Parma read ר' יוסה הגלילי.
27. Printed editions read אמר ר' צדוק.
28. This principle is almost certainly based on the rabbis' reading of Exodus 12:8–9. These verses relate the requirement that the paschal sacrifice be roasted over a fire. They explicitly exclude boiling. As is clear from numerous other sources, many rabbis took these requirements very seriously. See especially the formulation in Bavli *Pesahim* 74a, "'roast with fire' and not roast through something else." Such readings of these verses trace back to Tannaitic times, as can be seen from the interpretations of the Mechilta on the verse.
29. In the Mishnah, these terms are assumed to refer to metal implements unless otherwise specified. See *Avodah Zarah* 5:12 and *Ohalot* 1:3.
30. Note that Alon argues that this account refers to R. Gamliel II and describes events that took place *after* the Destruction. Alon, *The Jews in Their Land in the Talmudic Age*, 263.
31. *Pesahim* 7:2, 34b.
32. *Pesahim* 75a.
33. It is difficult to know whether both texts refer to the same R. Gamliel.
34. Printed editions and MS Parma add here גוי.
35. Printed editions read יורד.
36. This letter added, presumably by the vocalizer, in MS Kaufmann.
37. This word is inserted above the line in MS Kaufmann.

38. In the parallel version of this story in Tosefta *Shabbat* 13:14, R. Gamliel explains that disembarking is only permitted "since he did not make it in front of us." This condition is similar, but not necessarily identical, to the Mishnah's requirement that the work not be done for the benefit of a Jew. The Yerushalmi cites this line from the baraita as a gloss on the Mishnah. This may reflect an attempt on the part of the Yerushalmi to resolve the ambiguity inherent in the Mishnah's version of the story. On the relationship between the Mishnah and baraita here, see Shamma Friedman, "The Primacy of Tosefta to Mishnah in Synoptic Parallels," in *Introducing Tosefta: Textual, Intratextual and Intertextual Studies*, ed. Harry Fox and Tirzah Meacham (Hoboken, NJ: Ktav, 1999).
39. Bavli *Shabbat* 122a implicitly raises these issues.

Chapter 5

1. Stephen J. Lieberman, "A Mesopotamian Background for the So-Called 'Measures' of Biblical Hermeneutics?," *Hebrew Union College Annual* 58 (1987): 157–225; Markham J. Geller, "The Influence of Ancient Mesopotamia on Hellenistic Judaism," in *Civilizations of the Ancient Near East*, ed. Jack M. Sasson (New York: 1995), 43–54; Shalom E. Holtz, "'To Go and Marry Any Man That You Please': A Study of the Formulaic Antecedents of the Rabbinic Writ of Divorce," *Journal of Near Eastern Studies* 69, no. 4 (2001): 241–58.
2. Martha T. Roth, *Law Collections from Mesopotamia and Asia Minor* (Atlanta, GA: Scholars Press, 1995), 214.
3. Indeed, Albrecht Alt claimed that the cuneiform law collections make exclusive use of the casuistic formulations to the total exclusion of apodictic statements. Alt, "The Origins of Israelite Law," in *Essays on Old Testament History and Religion* (Garden City, NY: Doubleday, 1967), 101–72.
4. R. A. F. Mackenzie lists five such cases in the laws of Hammurabi and one each in the Hittite laws and the Middle Assyrian laws. Mackenzie, "The Formal Aspect of Ancient Near Eastern Law," in *The Seed of Wisdom*, ed. W. S. McCullough (Toronto: University of Toronto Press, 1964), 41–42. See also Reuven Yaron, *The Laws of Eshnunna* (Jerusalem: Magnes, 1969), 65.
5. Roth, *Law Collections from Mesopotamia and Asia Minor*, 3.
6. David Daube, *Forms of Roman Legislation* (Westport, CT: Greenwood, 1956), 6. Yaron was the first to apply Daube's work on this subject to Mesopotamian law. Yaron, *Laws of Eshnunna*, 67.
7. Yaron claims that there are five such examples, but does not list them. Yaron, *Laws of Eshnunna*, 65. See also Mackenzie, "Formal Aspect," 40.
8. Remko Jas, *Neo-Assyrian Judicial Procedures*, State Archives of Assyria Studies 5 (Helsinki: Neo-Assyrian Text Corpus Project, 1996); William W. Hallo, *The Context of Scripture*, vol. 2 (Leiden, the Netherlands: Brill, 2000), 267–71.
9. James B. Pritchard, *Ancient Near Eastern Texts Relating to the Old Testament* (Princeton, NJ: Princeton University Press, 1969), 331–64.
10. Baruch A. Levine, "The Descriptive Ritual Texts from Ugarit: Some Formal and Functional Features of the Genre," in *The Word of the Lord Shall Go Forth: Essays in Honor of David Noel Freedman in Celebration of his Sixtieth Birthday*, ed. Carol L. Meyers and M. O'Connor (Winona Lake, IN: Eisenbrauns, 1983), 467–75.
11. Tosefta *Eduyot* does, however, open with a story, which recounts the circumstances of its composition.
12. Shalom Paul, *Studies in the Book of the Covenant in Light of Cuneiform and Biblical Law*, ed. G. W. Anderson, Supplements to Vetus Testamentum 18 (Leiden, the Netherlands: Brill, 1970), 1.
13. Ibid., 12–13.
14. Delbert R. Hillers, *Covenant: The History of a Biblical Idea* (Baltimore: Johns Hopkins Press, 1969), 24–45; Hallo, *Context of Scripture*, 93–106.

15. For discussions of the issue of law and narrative in the Torah, see Jonathan Magonet, "'Halacha' and 'Aggadah' in the Bible," in *The Bible in Light of Its Interpreters: Sarah Kamin Memorial Volume*, ed. Sara Japhet (Jerusalem: Magnes, 1994), 651–70 [Hebrew]; James W. Watts, "Rhetorical Strategy in the Composition of the Pentateuch," *Journal for the Study of the Old Testament* 68 (1995): 3–22.
16. Hillers, *Covenant*; Paul, *Studies in the Book of the Covenant*, 27–43; Watts, "Rhetorical Strategy."
17. Alt, "Origins of Israelite Law"; M. Weinfeld, "The Origin of the Apodictic Law," *Vetus Testamentum* 23, no. 1 (1973): 63–75.
18. Mackenzie, "Formal Aspect ," 35, 37.
19. Three of the most useful works on the topic are B. Gemser, "The Importance of the Motive Clause in Old Testament Law," in *Congress Volume: Copenhagen, 1953*, Supplements to Vetus Testamentum 1 (Leiden, the Netherlands: Brill, 1953), 50–66; Rifat Sonsino, "Motive Clauses in Hebrew Law Biblical Forms and Near Eastern Parallels" (Ph.D. diss., University of Pennsylvania, 1975); Pinchas Doron, "Motive Clauses in the Laws of Deuteronomy: Their Forms, Functions and Contents," *Hebrew Annual Review* 2 (1978): 61–78.
20. Sonsino, "Motive Clauses in Hebrew Law," 112.
21. Ex. 22:20, 23:9 and Lev. 19:33–34.
22. Ex. 34:18 ; cf. Ex. 12:17, 23:15; and Deut. 16:1, 3.
23. Arguable exceptions to this rule are Gen. 32:32 and Deut. 23:5.
24. Robert Alter, *The Art of Biblical Narrative* (New York: Basic Books, 1981), 47–62.
25. For more on these passages and their interrelationship, see Michael Fishbane, *Biblical Interpretation in Ancient Israel* (Oxford: Clarendon, 1985), 98–106. More recently, Simeon Chavel has placed these narratives into the larger context of the question of law and narrative in the Bible. See Chavel, "'Oracular Novellae' and Biblical Historiography through the Lens of Law and Narrative," *Clio* 39, no. 1 (2009): 1–27.
26. Steven Fraade, "Ancient Jewish Law and Narrative in Comparative Perspective: The Damascus Document and the Mishnah," *Diné Yisrael* 24 (2007) 65*–99*.
27. Ibid., 76*.
28. On the sources found in the *Digest*, see Olivia F. Robinson, *The Sources of Roman Law: Problems and Methods for Ancient Historians*, Approaching the Ancient World (London: Routledge, 1997), 105–15.
29. Ibid., 62.
30. Yaakov Elman, "Order, Sequence, and Selection: The Mishnah's Anthological Choices," in *The Anthology in Jewish Literature*, ed. David Stern (Oxford: Oxford University Press, 2004), 53–80; Catherine Hezser, "The Codification of Legal Knowledge in Late Antiquity: The Talmud Yerushalmi and Roman Law Codes," in *The Talmud Yerushalmi and Graeco-Roman Culture*, vol. 1, ed. Peter Schaefer (Tübingen, Germany: Mohr Siebeck, 1998), 581–641.
31. Hezser, "Codification of Legal Knowledge."
32. *Institutes* 1.3; translation from Gaius, *The Institutes of Gaius*, trans. W. M. Gordon and O. F. Robinson (Ithaca, NY: Cornell University Press, 1988).
33. Elman, "Order, Sequence, and Selection."
34. E.g., *Digest* 1.11.1, 1.13.1.
35. *Digest* 19.2.61.1; translation from Hezser, "Codification of Legal Knowledge," 588.
36. *Digest* 1.10.11; translation from Justinian, *The Digest of Justinian*, trans. Alan Watson, vol. 1 (Philadelphia: University of Pennsylvania Press, 1985) 1.
37. Hezser, "Codification of Legal Knowledge," 590–95.
38. Ibid., 602–5.
39. See Elman, "Order, Sequence, and Selection."
40. On methods for treating parallels between Greco-Roman and rabbinic literature, see Catherine Hezser, "Interfaces between Rabbinic Literature and Graeco-Roman Philosophy," in *The Talmud Yerushalmi and Graeco-Roman Culture*, vol. 2, ed. Peter Schäfer and Catherine Hezser (Tübingen, Germany: Mohr Siebeck, 2000), 161–87.

41. Fritz Schulz, *History of Roman Legal Science* (Oxford: Clarendon, 1946), 130.
42. Peter Stein, *Regulae Iuris: From Juristic Rules to Legal Maxims* (Edinburgh: Edinburgh University Press, 1966), 45.
43. Ibid., 115.
44. Ibid., 73.
45. Ibid., 94–95.
46. *Digest* 50.17.202. See also Paul's definition of a *regula*, *Digest* 50.17.1.
47. Gallagher and Greenblatt, *Practicing New Historicism*, 49. See also Joel Fineman, "The History of the Anecdote," in *The New Historicism*, ed. H. Aram Vesser (New York: Routledge, 1989), 49–76.
48. Peter Brooks, "Narrativity of the Law."
49. Cover, "Nomos and Narrative," 95–96.
50. Roth, *Law Collections from Mesopotamia*, 2.
51. It should be noted that Cover himself did not accept the hegemonic use of narrative displayed in these ancient texts. Quite to the contrary, he focuses on the way in which multiple narratives and narrative interpretations often compete to explain a given set of laws or legal principles as well as the tensions that often exist between the law and its narrative. Nevertheless, Cover drew on this biblical paradigm in his conception of narrative as a form distinct from law that provides the context for the exercise of legal authority and interpretation.
52. Indeed, I drew on this argument earlier in the chapter when I asserted that anecdotes serve to increase the heterogeneity and dialogic nature of a legal text, whereas master narratives tend to homogenize the text.
53. Much of the modern study of narrative has focused on questions of narrative structure. I do not believe that any given story has an objective structure. Any text can be described using a variety of structural models. But there can be no question that the act of imposing structure both consciously and intuitively is central to the way in which we read stories. No story can be interpreted in a vacuum. It can only be understood in the context of other stories. Abstracting a structure is one of the key ways in which we can establish some sort of identity between stories. See Jonathan Culler, *Structuralist Poetics: Structuralism, Linguistics, and the Study of Language* (Ithaca, NY: Cornell University Press, 1975), 207; Barbara Herrnstein Smith, "Narrative Versions, Narrative Theories," 213. For a brief review of twentieth-century efforts to define narrative structure, see Wallace Martin, *Recent Theories of Narrative* (Ithaca, NY: Cornell University Press, 1986), 107–129.
54. Martin Jaffee, "The *Taqqanah* in Tannaitic Literature: Jurisprudence and the Construction of Rabbinic Memory," *Journal of Jewish Studies* 41, no. 2 (1990): 211, 213.
55. While the Biblical canon may have been in flux to a certain extent during the rabbinic period, there can be no doubt that by that point, the text of the Hebrew Bible had for the most part already taken on the form that we recognize today. See Sid Z. Leiman, *The Canonization of Hebrew Scripture: The Talmudic and Midrashic Evidence* (New Haven: Connecticut Academy of Arts and Sciences, 1991).
56. For a thorough survey of this phenomena see Samely, *Rabbinic Interpretation of Scripture*.
57. On this passage in light of previous scholarship and its potential Hellenistic and Christian contexts see Amram Tropper, *Wisdom, Politics, and Historiography: Tractate Avot in the Context of the Graeco-Roman Near East*, Oxford Oriental Monographs (Oxford: Oxford University Press, 2004), 158–72, 208–39.
58. This group of texts roughly corresponds to the category scholars call "rewritten bible," broadly construed. For two recent discussions of this critical term and its limitations, see Moshe J. Bernstein, "'Rewritten Bible': A Generic Category Which Has Outlived Its Usefulness?" *Textus* 22 (2005): 169–96; and Michael Segal, "Between Bible and Rewritten Bible," in *Biblical Interpretation at Qumran*, ed. Matthias Henze (Grand Rapids, MI: Eerdmans, 2005), 10–28.
59. Fraenkel, *Methods of the Aggadah*, 469.
60. The one exception to this is *Seder Olam Rabba*, which attempts to completely rewrite the Biblical history from the Creation until the time of Alexander. However, *Seder Olam* is so

different from all other Midrashic works that it may be safely bracketed here, awaiting a full-length treatment of its own. See Chaim Milikowsky, "Rabbinic Interpretation of the Bible in the Light of Ancient Hermeneutical Practice: The Question of the Literal Meaning," in *"The Words of a Wise Man's Mouth Are Gracious" (Qoh 10, 12); Festschrift for Günter Stemberger on the Occasion of His 65th Birthday*, ed. Mauro Perani (Berlin: De Gruyter, 2005), 7-28.
61. One of the few examples of a rabbinic story that might be considered a master narrative is the rabbinic account of the destruction of the Temple, especially as found in the Bavli, *Gittin* 55b-56b.
62. An almost complete genealogy, tracing rabbinic transmission back well into the Second Temple period, can be found in *Hagigah* 2:2.
63. Michael Segal, "Between Bible and Rewritten Bible," 12.
64. See Shemaryahu Talmon, "Between Scripture and Mishnah: The World of Qumran from Within," in *Megilot Midbar-Judah, arbaim shenot mehkar*, ed. Magen Broshi et al. (Jerusalem: Mosad Bialik 1992), 10-48 [Hebrew].
65. Levinson, *Ha-Sipur she-lo supar*, 309-12.
66. The notion that solipsism is fundamental to the formation of rabbinic identity was suggested and developed by Sacha Stern, *Jewish Identity in Early Rabbinic Writings* (Leiden, the Netherlands: Brill, 1994). See especially 200-215.
67. On the stylistic uniqueness of the Mishnah among Tannaitic texts, see Halivni, *Midrash, Mishnah and Gemara*, 38-65.
68. For two very different accounts of the rise of rabbinic Judaism in antiquity see Lee I. Levine, *The Rabbinic Class of Roman Palestine in Late Antiquity* (Jerusalem: Yad Ben-Zvi, 1989); Seth Schwartz, *Imperialism and Jewish Society, 200 B.C.E. to 640 C.E.* (Princeton, NJ: Princeton University Press, 2001).

Chapter 6

1. Shamma Friedman, *Tosefta 'atikt'a: Masekhet Pesah rishon, makbilot ha-Mishnah veha-Tosefta, perush u-mavo* (Ramat-Gan, Israel: Bar-Ilan University Press, 2002). For an English summary of Friedman's positions see, Friedman, "The Primacy of Tosefta to Mishnah."
2. Judith Hauptman, *Rereading the Mishnah: A New Approach to Ancient Jewish Texts* (Tübingen, Germany: Mohr Siebeck, 2005).
3. Martin S. Jaffee, *Torah in the Mouth: Writing and Oral Tradition in Palestinian Judaism, 200 B.C.E.-400 C.E.* (New York: Oxford University Press, 2001).
4. Shelomo Naeh suggests one such possibility of oral transmission, in which memorization of rabbinic materials was accomplished through the visualization of "virtual" texts. It may have been possible for memorizers to edit and manipulate such texts in a manner similar to written texts. Shelomo Naeh, "The Art of Memory, Structures of Memory and the Organization of Texts in Rabbinic Literature," in *Mehqerei Talmud III: Talmudic Studies Dedicated in Memory of Professor Ephraim E. Urbach*, ed. Yaakov Sussman and David Rosenthal (Jerusalem: Magnes, 2005), 543-89 [Hebrew].
5. Hauptman, *Rereading the Mishnah*, 2n4. The case for an entirely oral transmission of the Mishnah has recently been made most forcefully by Yaakov Sussman, "'Oral Law' Taken Literally: The Power of the Point of a Yod," in *Mehqerei Talmud III: Talmudic Studies Dedicated in Memory of Professor Ephraim E. Urbach*, ed. Yaakov Sussman and David Rosenthal (Jerusalem: Magnes, 2005), 209-384.
6. For a review of scholarly positions on the relationship between the Mishnah and the Tosefta, see Friedman, *Tosefta 'atikt'a*, 9-71.
7. Albert Bates Lord, *The Singer of Tales*, ed. Stephen A. Mitchell and Gregory Nagy, 2nd ed. (Cambridge, MA: Harvard University Press, 2000).
8. For a more detailed introduction of this body of scholarship as it relates to the study of the Mishnah, see Elizabeth Shanks Alexander, *Transmitting Mishnah*, 9-17.

9. Given the fact that the story itself makes no explicit reference to the Sabbath, it is possible that the original story was not set on the Sabbath and hence had no halakhic context at all. This reading cannot be absolutely refuted. However, in all of the other instances of the phrase "*hashkhah le*" in classical rabbinic literature, the term is used only with reference to the beginning of the Sabbath or holidays. Similarly, the term "*baderekh vehashkhah*" consistently appears within the Sabbath-related context of the laws of the '*eruv*. Finally, in all contexts, the word "*hashkhah*" overwhelmingly refers to the onset or termination of the Sabbath and holidays, which have similar proscriptions. It seems most likely that our story is implicitly set on the Sabbath as well.
10. This is not the only case in which it is reported that R. Tarfon found himself in a halakhic quandary due to his nocturnal travels; see *Berakhot* 1:3.
11. See Shamma Friedman, "The Baraitot in the Babylonian Talmud and Their Relationship to Their Parallels in the Tosefta" in *Atara L'haim: Studies in the Talmud and Medieval Rabbinic Literature in Honor of Professor Haim Zalman Dimitrovsky*, ed. Daniel Boyarin et al. (Jerusalem: Hebrew University Magnes Press, 2000), 163–201 [Hebrew]; Friedman, "Towards a Characterization of Babylonian Baraitot: 'Ben Tema' and 'Ben Dortai,'" in *Neti'ot Ledavid: Jubilee Volume for David Weiss Halivni*, ed. Yaakov Elman, Ephraim Bezalel Halivni, and Zvi Arie Stienfeld (Jerusalem: Orhot, 2004), 195–274 [Hebrew].
12. Louis Jacobs, "Are There Fictitious Baraitot in the Babylonian Talmud?," *Hebrew Union College Annual* 42 (1971): 185–96.
13. Words in brackets were added to the manuscript by a later hand.
14. Note that this parallels the reading found in the printed editions of the Bavli. These editions may in fact reflect the Palestinian transmission rather than a corrupt text.
15. For more on such "missing baraitot" in the Yerushalmi, see Leib Moscovitz, "More on the 'Missing Baraitot' of the Yerushalmi," *Proceedings of the American Academy of Jewish Research* 61 (1995) [Hebrew].
16. Yerushalmi *Eruvin* 4:4, 22a.
17. This reconstruction remains hypothetical. I believe it to be the most likely, but not the only, possible account of the development of this narrative and legal tradition. Regardless of the model that one proposes, there is no escaping the conclusion that in this case an aggadic narrative was appropriated for use in a halakhic argument, at least to some extent, at some stage of the process.
18. Robert E. Scholes and Robert Kellogg, *The Nature of Narrative* (New York,: Oxford University Press, 1966), 82–159.
19. This paraphrase is based on Maimonides' commentary. For a different reading, see the commentary of R. Hannanel in the standard printed editions of the Bavli.
20. So rules Maimonides in his commentary on this passage.
21. For a similar argument regarding the low level of narrativity in nineteenth-century British case reports see Ben-Yishai, "Victorian Precedents," 382–402.
22. This understanding of representational narratives is developed in Richard J. Gerrig, *Experiencing Narrative Worlds: On the Psychological Activities of Reading* (New Haven, CT: Yale University Press, 1993).
23. Roman Jakobson, "On Realism in Art," in *Language in Literature*, edited by Krystyna Pomorska and Stephen Rudy (Cambridge, MA.: Belknap Press of Harvard University Press, 1987), 19–27; Barthes, "The Reality Effect."
24. Printed editions and MS Parma read בשבת.
25. Though it seems probable that this story took place before the Destruction, it is also possible it happened afterwards, but that R. Yohanan continued to think within a cultic frame work.
26. On the role of gaps in classical Hebrew narrative, see Meir Sternberg, *Poetics of Biblical Narrative: Ideological Literature and the Drama of Reading* (Bloomington: Indiana University Press, 1985).
27. Text from MS Munich 95. Note that Oxford Opp. Add. Fol. 23 reads באנשי טבריא.
28. See also Yerushalmi *Shabbat* 3:3, 6a.

29. Michał Głowiński, "On the First-Person Novel," *New Literary History* 9, no. 1 (1977): 103. The classic discussion of the rhetoric of narrative strategies is Wayne C. Booth, *The Rhetoric of Fiction* (Chicago: University of Chicago Press, 1961).
30. The question of the ontological status of fictional worlds had been dealt with extensively by contemporary narrative theorists. See especially, Thomas G. Pavel, *Fictional Worlds* (Cambridge, MA: Harvard University Press, 1986).
31. Sternberg, Poetics of Biblical Narrative, 82.
32. Tosefta *Sukkah*, 3:16, Yerushalmi *Sukkah* 4:6, 20b, Bavli *Sukkah* 48b.
33. Flavius Josephus, *Antiquities* 13.14.5, translation from *The Works of Josephus: Complete and unabridged in one volume,* translated by William Whitson, (Peabody, NH: Hendrikson Publishers, 1987).
34. Shaye J. D. Cohen, "Parallel Historical Tradition in Josephus and Rabbinic Literature," *Proceedings of the World Congress of Jewish Studies* 9, no. B/1 (1986): 7–147; Seth Schwartz, *Imperialism and Jewish Society*, 97.
35. On the essential continuity of Pharisees and the post-Destruction rabbis see E. P. Sanders, *Judaism: Practice and Belief, 63 B.C.E.–66 C.E.* (London: SCM, 1992), 413; Isaiah Gafni, "The Historical Background," in *The Literature of the Sages,* ed. Shmuel Safrai (Philadelphia: Fortress, 1987), 8.
36. Heinrich Graetz, *History of the Jews*, vol. 2 (Philadelphia: Jewish Publication Society of America, 1956), 17–22; Salo Wittmayer Baron, *A Social and Religious History of the Jews*, 2d ed. (New York: Columbia University Press, 1952), 35–38; Alon, *The Jews in Their Land*, 21–22; Shmuel Safrai, "Jewish Self Government," in *The Jewish People in the First Century: Historical Geography, Political History, Social, Cultural and Religious Life and Institutions* (Assen, the Netherlands: Van Gorcum, 1974), 384; R. Travers Herford, *Pharisaism, Its Aim and Its Method* (London: Williams & Norgate, 1912), 1–57. George Foot Moore, *Judaism in the First Centuries of the Christian Era, the Age of the Tannaim* (Cambridge, MA: Harvard University Press, 1944), vol. 1: 56–71.
37. For a survey of the key Josephean passages and the scholarly discussion of them up to that point see David Goodblatt, "The Place of the Pharisees in First Century Judaism: The State of the Debate," *Journal for the Study of Judaism* 20, no. 1 (1989): 12–30; Seth Schwartz, *Josephus and Judean Politics*, Columbia Studies in the Classical Tradition 18 (Leiden, the Netherlands: Brill, 1990), 170–200.
38. Morton Smith, "Palestinian Judaism in the First Century," in *Israel: Its Role in Civilization*, ed. Moshe Davis (New York: Seminary Israel Institute of the Jewish Theological Seminary of America, 1956), 67–81.
39. Ibid., 81.
40. Jacob Neusner, *From Politics to Piety: The Emergence of Pharisaic Judaism* (Englewood Cliffs, NJ,: Prentice-Hall, 1972); Shaye J. D. Cohen, *From the Maccabees to the Mishnah* (Philadelphia: Westminster, 1987), 160–64; Goodblatt, "Place of the Pharisees"; Sanders, *Judaism: Practice and Belief*, 380–412, 58–543; Albert I. Baumgarten, *The Flourishing of Jewish Sects in the Maccabean Era: An Interpretation*, Supplements to the Journal for the Study of Judaism 55 (Leiden, the Netherlands: Brill, 1997), 42–123; Seth Schwartz, *Imperialism and Jewish Society*, 91–99; Daniel R. Schwartz, "MMT, Josephus and the Pharisees," in *Reading 4QMMT: New Perspectives on Qumran Law and History*, ed. John Kampen and Moshe J. Bernstein (Atlanta: Scholars Press, 1996), 67–79. Finally, while accepting Smith's basic thesis, Goodman maintains that the Pharisees were "highly influential" with regard to religious matters. Martin Goodman, *The Ruling Class of Judaea: The Origins of the Jewish Revolt against Rome, A.D. 66–70* (Cambridge, UK: Cambridge University Press, 1987), 74.
41. See Moshe D. Herr, "Who Were the Boethusians? *Proceedings of the Seventh World Congress of Jewish Studies* 3 (1981): 13–14 [Hebrew].
42. Sanders, *Judaism: Practice and Belief* 63, 458–90; Seth Schwartz, *Imperialism and Jewish Society*, 97.
43. Seth Schwartz, *Imperialism and Jewish Society*, 97.

44. This argument about the ideological rather than the historical nature of the Mishnaic accounts of the Temple cult has most recently been made with regard to the Sotah ritual in Rosen-Zvi, *Ha-Tekes she-lo hayah*.
45. Graetz, *History of the Jews*, 360–64, Moore, *Judaism in the First Centuries*, 83–92; Michael Avi-Yonah, *The Jews under Roman and Byzantine Rule: A Political History of Palestine from the Bar Kokhba War to the Arab Conquest* (New York: Schocken Books, 1984), 54–57; Alon, *The Jews in Their Land*; Safrai, "Jewish Self Government," 406–7; Ephraim E. Urbach, *Collected Writings in Jewish Studies*, ed. Robert Brody and Moshe D. Herr (Jerusalem: Hebrew University Magnes Press, 1999), 404–72.
46. Joshua Efron, "The Great Sanhedrin in Vision and Reality," in *Studies on the Hasmonean Period* (Leiden, the Netherlands: Brill, 1987), 287–338; Martin Goodman, *State and Society in Roman Galilee*, Oxford Centre for Postgraduate Hebrew Studies Series (Totowa, NJ: Rowman & Allanheld, 1983), 93–98. Goodblatt similarly rejects a post-Destruction Sanhedrin, but has a more traditional view with regard to rise of patriarchate. See David Goodblatt, *The Monarchic Principle: Studies in Jewish Self-Government in Antiquity* (Tübingen, Germany: Mohr Siebeck, 1994), 170–278.
47. Lee I. Levine, *Rabbinic Class of Roman Palestine*; Catherine Hezser, *The Social Structure of the Rabbinic Movement in Roman Palestine* (Tübingen, Germany: Mohr Siebeck, 1997); Shaye J. D. Cohen, "The Rabbi in Second Century Jewish Society," in *The Cambridge History of Judaism*, ed. William Horbury, W. D. Davies, and John Sturdy (Cambridge, UK: Cambridge University Press, 1999); Seth Schwartz, *Imperialism and Jewish Society*, 103–28; Goodman, *State and Society in Roman Galilee*, 93–98. For survey of the historiography on rabbinic Judaism in the century or so following the Destruction, see Hezser, *Social Structure of the Rabbinic Movement*, 1–36.
48. Cohen, "The Rabbi in Second Century Jewish Society," 975–76.
49. As Wayne Booth argues, "Perhaps the most overworked distinction [in the description of point of view] is that of person. To say that a story is told in the first or the third person will tell us nothing of importance unless we become more precise and describe how the particular qualities of the narrators relate to specific effects." Booth, *The Rhetoric of Fiction*, 150.
50. See Tosefta *Nega'im* 8:3.
51. Printed editions read היו מנענין. See Epstein, *Mavo le-nusah ha-Mishnah*, 359.
52. MS Parma and printed editions lack this word.
53. The reason why the status of this object on the Sabbath is problematic is debated by the Talmuds and commentators and need not concern us here. For a survey of interpretations see Kehati, *Mishnayot mevo'arot*.
54. Tosefta *Sukkah* 2:10 See also Bavli *Sukkah* 37a.
55. See Epstein, *Mavo le-nusah ha-Mishnah*, 960.

Chapter 7

1. Berger, *Rabbinic Authority*. Berger lays out these categories on pp. 10–12.
2. The most ambitious attempt at a reconstruction of the social structure in which the rabbis operated is probably Hezser, *Social Structure of the Rabbinic Movement*.
3. See David Frankfurter, "Dynamics of Ritual Expertise in Antiquity and Beyond: Towards a New Taxonomy of 'Magicians,'" in *Magic and Ritual in the Ancient World*, ed. Paul Mirecki and Marvin Meyer (Leiden, the Netherlands: Brill, 2002), 159–78. Rabbis would appear to fit best into the category Frankfurter defines as "quasi-institutional *literati*." Note that in his description of the group, Frankfurter carefully balances the social and the knowledge-based sources of their authority.
4. Cohen, "The Rabbi in Second Century Jewish Society," 969.
5. David Lenz Tiede, *The Charismatic Figure as Miracle Worker*, SBL Dissertation Series (Missoula, MT: Society of Biblical Literature, 1972), 1–100. Moses Hadas suggested a similar dichotomy several years earlier in Moses Hadas and Morton Smith, *Heroes and Gods*

(New York: Harper & Row, 1963), 63. Morton Smith strongly critiqued Tiede's contention that these two categories of holy man were at one point clearly distinct in the ancient literature. Nevertheless, Smith does not challenge the basic utility of these categories for understanding the figure of the holy man in ancient literature. Morton Smith, "On the History of the Divine Man," in *Paganisme, judaïsme, christianisme: Influences et affrontements dans le monde antique: Mélanges offerts à Marcel Simon* (Paris: De Boccard, 1978), 335–45. See also Morton Smith, "Prolegomena to a Discussion of Aretalogies, Divine Men, the Gospels and Jesus," *Journal of Biblical Literature* 90 (1971): 174–99. Also important is Cox's critique of Tiede's classification. Patricia Cox, *Biography in Late Antiquity: A Quest for the Holy Man* (Berkeley: University of California Press, 1983), 30–44. See especially p. 43. Once again, I do not think Cox's arguments undermine the utility of these categories in our case.

6. See Morton Smith, *Tannaitic Parallels to the Gospels*, Journal of Biblical Literature Monograph Series (Philadelphia: Society for Biblical Literature, 1951), 80–85.
7. Fischel, "Story and History"; "Studies in Cynicism."
8. Fischel, "Studies in Cynicism." See also Ronald F. Hock and Edward N. O'Neil, *The Chreia in Ancient Rhetoric*, vol. 1, *The Progymnasmata* (Atlanta: Scholars Press, 1985), 23–27.
9. Hock and O'Neil, *Chreia in Ancient Rhetoric*, 27; Vernon K. Robbins, "The Chreia," in *Greco-Roman Literature and the New Testament: Selected Forms and Genres*, ed. David E. Aune (Atlanta: Scholars Press, 1988), 4.
10. Fischel, "Story and History," 81.
11. On the place of chria in the "wise man" tradition of the ancient holy man, see Tiede, *Charismatic Figure as Miracle Worker*, 43–44.
12. Hellenistic biographers were also anecdotalists in that the anecdote was one of the fundamental building blocks of their biographies. However, these anecdotes were integrated into a larger narrative structure, whereas the rabbinic anecdote is an independent narrative form. See Cox, *Biography in Late Antiquity*, 58–62.
13. Ibid., xi, 9, 57, 65. The closest approximation of such biographies in Tannaitic literature would be the hypothetical collections of narratives about individual sages whose existence is hypothesized by several twentieth-century scholars. Melammed, "Collections of Tanaitic Stories"; Ben Zion Wacholder, "Tales about R. Gamliel"; Arnold Goldberg, "Form und Funktion des Ma'ase," 25–26. The editors of the Mishnah would have used these collections as sources for the Mishnah in much the same way as rhetoricians used biographies as sources for their chriai, as described in Hock and O'Neil, *Chreia in Ancient Rhetoric*, 8.
14. David Levine, "Holy Men and Rabbis in Talmudic Antiquity," in *Saints and Role Models in Judaism and Christianity*, ed. Marcel Poorthuis and Joshua Schwartz, Jewish and Christian Perspectives Series (Leiden, the Netherlands: Brill, 2004), 52.
15. See Baruch M. Bokser, "Wonder-Working and the Rabbinic Tradition: The Case of Hanina ben Dosa," *Journal for the Study of Judaism* 16, no. 1 (1985), 42–92; Chana Safrai and Zeev Safrai, "Rabbinic Holy Men," in *Saints and Role Models in Judaism and Christianity*, ed. Marcel Poorthuis and Joshua Schwartz (Leiden, the Netherlands: Brill, 2004), 59–78 and the sources cited therein.
16. Morton Smith, *Tannaitic Parallels to the Gospels*, 80–85; David Levine, "Holy Men and Rabbis," 48.
17. See *'Eruvin* 4:1, in which not all of the rabbis presented in the story partake in the stringency. Another example of a rabbinic action defined as a stringency, once again connected to the house of R. Gamliel, is to be found in *Baba Metzi'a* 5:8. Finally, see *Mo'ed Qatan* 2:5, in which a stringency is attributed to a group of laypeople.
18. *Sukkah* 26b.
19. On these practices see Cox, *Biography in Late Antiquity*, 25–30; Robert Browning, "The 'Low Level' Saint's Life in the Early Byzantine World," in *The Byzantine Saint: University of Birmingham Fourteenth Spring Symposium of Byzantine Studies*, ed. Sergei Hackel, Studies Supplementary to Sobornost 5 (London: Fellowship of St. Alban and St. Sergius, 1981), 117–27. On the extent to which asceticism was a part of rabbinic culture, see most

recently Eliezer Diamond, *Holy Men and Hunger Artists: Fasting and Asceticism in Rabbinic Culture* (Oxford: Oxford University Press, 2004).
20. Peter Brown, "The Saint as Exemplar in Late Antiquity," *Representations* 1, no. 2 (1983): 1.
21. Ibid., 2.
22. Ibid., 6.
23. Ibid., 9.
24. Once again, we cannot know the exact extent or makeup of these communities, but the evidence suggests that as time went on these communities grew from small circles of students to large congregations in major population centers.
25. The significance of this concentration of etiological stories is difficult to determine. It is tempting to argue, based on Avraham Walfish's work on the literary structure of the Mishnah, that the editors of the Mishnah consciously placed these stories throughout this chapter with the intent of inserting a discussion about the nature of rabbis and their authority. However, it is also possible that this chapter took its current shape as a result of a more gradual and less self-conscious redactional process, whose exact contours and trajectories remain beyond our recovery. If this is the case, the complexity and ambiguity that I identify in these stories reflect not the original intent of an individual author/editor or cadre of such individuals but rather the final product of a range of forces and processes that shaped the text as it presents itself to us.
26. See Elizabeth Shanks Alexander, *Transmitting Mishnah*, 155–67.
27. Printed editions read והביאו לו. MS Parma reads שהביאו ל.
28. *Sukkah* 26b.
29. This word is missing from MS Munich 6, as noted in Epstein, *Mavo le-nusah ha-Mishnah*, 723.
30. MS Parma reads פָּחָת.
31. The Bavli, *Sukkah* 28b, attempts to reconcile these two lines by suggesting that the first line refers only to the biblical requirement to sit in the sukkah, which exempts minors, while the second line refers to a rabbinic requirement which includes older minors. This is likely an anachronistic solution, since the Tannaim do not seem to have recognized this distinction between biblical and rabbinic requirements. Epstein sought to solve this problem by emending the text of the Mishnah in light of MS Munich 6, which lacks the reference to minors in the first line. Epstein, *Mavo le-nusah ha-Mishnah*, 723.
32. The Talmuds report that at some time in the early Tannaitic period, the law was decided decisively in favor of the school of Hillel over the school of Shammai, rendering Shammaite positions beyond the pale of normative practice. However, as numerous scholars have pointed out, Tannaitic material does not support such an account. Current scholarly consensus repudiates the notion of a specific decision to reject the ruling of the school of Shammai en bloc. Rather, the rejection of the school of Shammai was a gradual process that took place over the course of generations. Nevertheless, there is a general consensus among scholars that the editors of the Mishnah clearly favored the house of Hillel and its rulings. See Shmuel Safrai, "The Ruling in Favor of Beit Hillel in Yavne," in *Proceedings of the Seventh World Congress of Jewish Studies: Studies in Talmud, Halacha and Midrash* (Jerusalem: World Union of Jewish Studies, 1981), 21–44 [Hebrew]; Avigdor Bitman, "On the Nature of the Rule 'The Halakhah is According to Beit Hillel,'" *Sinai* 82 (1978): 185–96 [Hebrew]; Abraham Goldberg, "The Mishnah," 213, 217. For a survey of the literature on this topic see Aryeh Y. Hayoun, "The Schools of Shammai and Hillel: A Study of Their Halakhic and Ideological Theories" (Ph.D. diss., Bar-Ilan University, 2003), 28–42 [Hebrew]; Mordechai Sabato, "The Recital of *Shema* by R. Yishmael and Elazar b. Azaria and the Decision that the *Halakha* Follows the School of Hillel," *Sidra* 22 (2007) [Hebrew].
33. On ceiling construction in Roman Palestine, see Yizhar Hirschfeld, *The Palestinian Dwelling in the Roman-Byzantine Period* (Jerusalem: Franciscan Printing Press, 1995), 237–48. Notably, Hirschfeld describes the tendency of this sort of plaster and wood ceiling to collapse and the need to annually replaster these roofs before the rainy season.
34. Printed editions add ולא אמרו דבר.

35. MS Parma reads טָבְי. Printed editions read טָבִי.
36. MS Parma and printed editions read חכם.
37. MS Parma and printed editions read ולפי.
38. The structure of the bed is seen as intervening between the individual and the sukkah. Such a person therefore cannot be seen as dwelling in the sukkah.
39. Yet, as far as I have found, the Mishnah does not cite any exempla involving rabbis later than R. Aqiba.
40. See the baraita quoted in the Bavli *ad loc.* 21b. Here this comment is explicitly attributed to R. Simeon.
41. The Yerushalmi, *Sukkah* 2:1, 53a, further emphasizes Tevi's liminal position in the sukkah by asking why, even if Tevi was exempt from the sukkah, he could not sleep in the sukkah without being covered by a bed. They answer that Tevi refused to take the place of one of the rabbis in the sukkah. The Yerushalmi responds by asking why, if so, given the limited space in the sukkah, he was not sent out altogether, and answers that Tevi wanted to hear the scholarly discussions of Torah of the rabbis.
42. On this formulation see Epstein, *Mavo le-nusah ha-Mishnah*, 630–31.
43. Printed editions read לא כך היה.
44. Some printed editions read רבי יחנן בן החורני. See Melech Shachter, *Ha-Mishnah ba-Bavli uva-Yerushalmi: Hashva'ot nusha'oteha* (Jerusalem: Mosad Harav Kook, 1959), 91.
45. Most printed editions read ולא אמרו לו דבר. See Raphael Nathan Rabinowitz, *Dikduke sofrim* (New York: M.P., 1976), *ad loc*.
46. Printed editions read כן.
47. Perhaps this visit was meant to fulfill the custom of visiting one's teacher on the holiday. This custom, however, is recorded only in the Bavli, *Rosh HaShannah* 16b and *Sukkah* 27b.
48. Tosefta *Sukkah* 2:4.
49. For more on the *mashal* see David Stern, *Parables in Midrash*.
50. On this apparently extraneous "ו" in MS Kaufmann, see Epstein, *Mavo le-nusah ha-Mishnah*, 1087. For a full discussion of the textual variants in this passage, see ibid., 420–21.
51. Printed editions read משלו משל.
52. Printed editions insert here כוס.
53. Printed editions read רבו. Shamma Friedman has suggested to me in conversation that the manuscript's reading of the plural reflects a sort of "plurality of ownership" as in the use of the term *ba'alim* in *Sanhedrin* 1:4. Plural forms of the word *qoneh* are at times used in the liturgy to refer to God. In our case, this plural form apparently takes a singular verb. See also Epstein, *Mavo le-nusah ha-Mishnah*, 420–21.
54. Bavli *Sukka* 29a.
55. MS Parma reads ועל.
56. MS Parma has the word אלש here. It has been crossed out and the reading is corrected to match MS Kaufmann. Printed editions conform to the original reading in MS Parma.
57. Printed editions read חוני. We have followed this common pronunciation in our transliteration.
58. The ה in this word appears to have been added by another hand, in place of a letter that has been erased. MS Parma reads ונתפלל.
59. Printed editions add מה עשה.
60. This word appears as an insertion between the lines of the manuscript. MS Parma reads רַבּוֹנִי Printed editions read רבונו שלעולם.
61. MS Parma and printed editions read עד. Presumably, this is the correct reading.
62. Printed editions read התחילו לירד.
63. MS Parma reads שנתפללתה.
64. This letter appears as an insertion between the lines of the manuscript.
65. The term *matri'im* serves as a synecdoche for the highest level of fast prescribed by the Mishnah. See *Ta'anit* 1:6.
66. Bavli *Ta'anit* 23a does portray him as being an expert expositor of Torah. This is clearly a later source.

67. On *hasidim* and *anshei ma'aseh* see G. B. Sarfatti, "Pious Men, Men of Deeds and the Early Prophets," *Tarbiz* 26 (1957): 126–53 [Hebrew]; Shmuel Safrai, "Teaching of Pietists in Mishnaic Literature," *Journal of Jewish Studies* 16 (1965): 15–33; Bokser, "Wonder-Working and the Rabbinic Tradition"; Safrai and Safrai, "Rabbinic Holy Men."
68. See for example Marc Hirshman, "Changing Loci of Holiness: Honi and his Grandchildren," in *Tura: Studies in Jewish Thought; Simon Greenberg Jubilee Volume* (Tel Aviv: Hakibbutz Hameuchad, 1989), 109–18 [Hebrew]; and Geza Vermes, *Jesus the Jew* (New York: Macmillan, 1973), 69–82.
69. See Safrai, "Teaching of Pietists," and Vermes, *Jesus the Jew*.
70. *Berakhot* 5:1, 5:5.
71. On the use of *hasidic* exempla in prayer and the tension between *hasidic* and normative modes of prayer in the Mishnah see Shelomo Naeh, "'Creates the Fruit of Lips': A Phenomenological Study of Prayer According to Mishnah *Berakhot* 4:3, 5:5," *Tarbiz* 63, no. 2 (1994): 185–218 [Hebrew].
72. See Bavli *Ta'anit* 22b and traditional commentators on the Mishnah.
73. See Bavli *Berakhot* 60a.
74. See M. B. Lerner, *Honi Ha-Me'aggel and Simeon b. Shetah*, ed. Isaac B. Gottlieb, World of the Sages 2 (Tel Aviv: Everyman's University, 1983), 8.
75. Bertinoro seeks to limit this rule to cases where there is not excessive damage. Maimonides appears to agree. See also R. Yosef Karo's ruling on this matter in *Shulhan arukh, Orah hayyim* 578:11.
76. See Hirshman, "Changing Loci of Holiness," 111.
77. MS Parma reads ואמר.
78. MS Parma reads להתנדות. Printed editions lack this entire phrase; instead they read חוני אתה גוזרני עליך נידוי אלמלא.
79. MS Parma and printed editions read שאתה.
80. Printed editions read על אביו.
81. I have followed scholarly convention of transliterating this name as *Shetah*, in accordance with the popular pronunciation, rather than *Shatah*, as it appears in the text.
82. Green goes so far as to argue that "the post-70 rabbis...regarded Simeon as a founding father." William Scott Green, "Palestinian Holy Men: Charismatic Leadership and Rabbinic Tradition," in *Aufstieg und Niedergang der römischen Welt*, ed. Wolfgang Haase (Berlin: De Gruyter, 1979), 637. For a review and synthesis of the rabbinic sources on Simeon ben Shetah see Lerner, *Honi Ha-Me'aggel*, 33–66.
83. Gideon Leibson, "Determining Factors in Herem and Nidui (Ban and Excommunication) During the Tannaitic and Amoraic Periods," *Shenaton Ha-Mishpat Ha-Ivri* 2 (1975): 299–30 [Hebrew]. See also Saul Lieberman, "On Adjurations among the Jews," *Tarbiz* 27 (1958) [Hebrew].
84. Judah Goldin, "On Honi the Circle-Maker: A Demanding Prayer," in *Studies in Midrash and Related Literature*, ed. Barry Eichler and Jeffrey Tigay (Philadelphia: Jewish Publication Society, 1988), 331–35; David Daube, "Enfant Terrible," *Harvard Theological Review* 68 (1975): 371–76. This position is perhaps closest to those expressed by the rabbinic commentators on the story. For a survey of these sources, see Leibson, "Determining Factors in Herem."
85. Green, "Palestinian Holy Men," 133–34 and literature cited therein. Goldin, in the article cited above, argues vigorously against this position.
86. Vermes, *Jesus the Jew*, 69–82; Alon, *Jews in Their Land*, 199–200. On the threat posed to the religious establishment by holy men in a somewhat different milieu, see Peter Brown, "The Rise and Function of the Holy Man in Late Antiquity," *Journal of Roman Studies* 61 (1971): 80–101.
87. See Rashi, Maimonides, Bertinoro, and *Melekhet Shlomo*. See also Bavli *Ta'anit* 23a.
88. Daube goes so far as to argue that "sin" is the primary meaning of the word even in this case. Daube, "Enfant Terrible."
89. The late Midrashic versions of the Honi story are not relevant our discussion. See Tanhuma Buber *Va'era* 22 and Tanhuma *Ki tavo* 4.

90. Josephus, *Antiquities* 14.2.
91. Green, "Palestinian Holy Men," 639; Goldin, "On Honi the Circle-Maker," 331; Vermes, *Jesus the Jew*, 69; Albeck, *Shisha sidre Mishnah*, 2:494.
92. Vered Noam, *Megilat Ta'anit: Ha-nusahim, pesharam, toldotehem; Be-tseruf mahadurah bikortit* (Jerusalem: Yad Ben-Zvi, 2003), 21.
93. Ibid., 309.
94. Ibid.
95. The Mishnah generally uses a similar phrase, *'over lifnei hateva*. On these terms see Ze'ev Weiss, "The Location of the *Sheliah Tzibbur* during Prayer," *Cathedra* 55 (1990): 8–21 [Hebrew].
96. Lerner, *Honi Ha-Me'aggel*, 28–29. Lerner is not the first to make such a suggestion. See his citations of previous scholarship.
97. On ceiling techniques in Roman Palestine see Hirschfeld, *Palestinian*, 237–48.
98. Mishna *Ma'aserot* 1:8 uses this same verb to describe the act of pressing figs into a circle. It seems much less likely that anyone would have made a living from such work.
99. Noam, *Megilat Ta'anit*.
100. Ory Amitai has similarly argued for the identity of the Simeons in these two accounts. He argues that Simeon the Just was in fact a mythic figure who reflects a conflation of several different prominent individuals of that name. Ory Amitay, "Shim'on ha-Ṣadiq in His Historical Contexts," *Journal of Jewish Studies* 58, no. 2 (2007): 236–49.
101. For similar usages of this term see, for example, *Vayikra Rabba* 12:1, *Pesikta de Rav Kahanah* 11:22, *Shemot Rabba* 15:18. See also Gen. 15:2.
102. In addition to the Parma scholium, the Yerushalmi also connects the holiday of the 20th of Adar with Honi. Yerushalmi *Ta'anit* 3:10, 66d.
103. Saul Lieberman, *Tosefta ki-feshutah: Be'ur arokh la-Tosefta*, (New York: Jewish Theological Seminary, 1992), vol. 5:1096.
104. Text according to MS Yad Ha-Rav Herzog.
105. Green, "Palestinian Holy Men," 641–47; Stone, "On the Interplay of Rules."
106. Some versions of *Bereshit Rabba* 13:7, including MS Vatican 60, include an explicit comparison between Elijah and Honi, identifying the two individuals whose spiritual efforts were capable of bringing rain to the world. For further attestations of this reading see the Theodor-Albeck edition of Bereshit Rabba on 13:7.

Chapter 8

1. J Hillis Miller, "Ariadne's Thread: Repetition and the Narrative Line," *Critical Inquiry* 3 (1976): 69–70.
2. Ibid., 68. For a different development of the metaphor of the straight line and the tangled scribble, see Chuck Jones, dir., *The Dot and the Line: A Romance in Lower Mathematics* (Hollywood, CA: Metro-Goldwyn-Mayer, 1965), film.
3. The other examples of this form in the Mishnah that I am aware of are *Nazir* 5:4, *Bekhorot* 6:6, and *Yadayim* 4:4.
4. Avraham Walfish presents an in-depth literary analysis of these chapters, which he uses in order to demonstrate his approach to the Mishnah and its redaction. He offers an important complimentary perspective to these texts. Walfish, "Literary Method of Redaction," 37–104.
5. This discussion in fact continues to 3:1. For explanations of the decisions to place this paragraph in a different chapter that deals with a totally different topic, see ibid., 38–40.
6. Walfish uses a similar metaphor of centrifugal and centripetal forces to describe these two movements. He also notes that the Mishnah's account stresses the importance of a centralized court. Ibid., 71, 73.
7. See Shemaryahu Talmon, "Calendars and Mishmarot," in *Encyclopedia of the Dead Sea Scrolls*, ed. Lawrence H. Shiffman and James C. VanderKam (New York: Oxford University Press, 2000). For a history of the Jewish calendar in antiquity see Sacha Stern, *Calendar*

and Community: A History of the Jewish Calendar Second Century B.C.E.–Tenth Century C.E. (Oxford: Oxford University Press, 2001).

8. Isaiah M. Gafni, *Land, Center and Diaspora: Jewish Constructs in Late Antiquity*, Journal for the Study of the Pseudepigrapha Supplement Series 21 (Sheffield, UK: Sheffield Academic Press, 1997), 103.
9. See Berger, *Rabbinic Authority*, 27–29.
10. See for example Seth Schwartz, *Imperialism and Jewish Society*; Sanders, *Judaism: Practice and Belief*, 458–90.
11. Goodman, *State and Society in Roman Galilee*, 108–13. Cohen, *Maccabees to the Mishnah*, 222.
12. Baumgarten goes so far as to make the case that the arguments over the calendar may not have been any more or less divisive than other legal and ritual disputes. See Albert I. Baumgarten, "'But Touch the Law and the Sect Will Split': Legal Dispute as the Cause of Sectarian Schism," *Review of Rabbinic Judaism* 5, no. 3 (2002): 301–15. See also Sacha Stern, *Calendar and Community*, which argues that throughout antiquity there was significant diversity in the ways in which different Jewish communities reckoned the calendar.
13. Stern notes that just such a situation existed in ancient Greece, where each local magistrate set the calendar for his locale. Sacha Stern, *Calendar and Community*, 99n1. On the authority of local councils in the Land of Israel during this period, see Seth Schwartz, *Imperialism and Jewish Society*, 112.
14. Stern emphasizes the distinctiveness of this rabbinic insistence on a unified calendar. "Only after studying the diversity of non-rabbinic Jewish calendars in late antiquity does one appreciate how peculiar, in this context, the rabbinic concept of calendrical unanimity would have been" Sacha Stern, *Calendar and Community*, 156.
15. See ibid., esp. 163–64.
16. For various explanations of the placement of these paragraphs at the beginning of the tractate see Epstein, *Mevo'ot le-sifrut ha-Tana'im*, 364; Albeck, *Shisha sidre Mishnah*, 2:307; Walfish, "Literary Method of Redaction," 43–49.
17. See Walfish, "Literary Method of Redaction," 43, 63–64.
18. Ibid., 84–85.
19. Later French and American theorists adopted this distinction for their own purposes, replacing the Russian terms *fabula* and *syuzhet* with their equivalents in their respective languages such as *histoire* and *récit* or "story" and "discourse." Gerard Genette, *Narrative Discourse: An Essay in Method* (Ithaca, NY: Cornell University Press, 1980); Chatman, *Story and Discourse*.
20. Jonathan Culler, "Fabula and Sjuzhet in the Analysis of Narrative: Some American Discussions," *Poetics Today* 1, no. 3 (1980): 29.
21. Ibid., 35. See also Peter Brooks, *Reading for the Plot: Design and Intention in Narrative* (New York: Knopf, 1984), 3–36.
22. This structure is noted in Walfish, "Literary Method of Redaction," 74.
23. This is the position of Melammed, "The 'Case' in the Mishnah," 158. See also, Walfish, "Literary Method of Redaction," 74. He notes the close parallel between the two positions.
24. Yerushalmi *Rosh Hashanah* 1:6, 57b. The Bavli version is found in *Rosh Hashanah* 22a.
25. Note that in the Bavli this detail is not mentioned.
26. From a historical perspective, the Talmuds' story may preserve some valuable data. Given the consensus that R. Gamliel lacked real political power over Palestinian Jewry, it is difficult for us to accept R. Judah's claim that R. Gamliel deposed a local leader. Rather, this would seem to be a retrojection of the circumstances of R. Gamliel's descendants who, as patriarchs, most likely did possess such power. However, the memory of R. Gamliel having a confrontation with a local leader may in fact reflect actual events. Early in this chapter, I argued that at the time of R. Gamliel most Jews probably would not have recognized his claims to hegemony over the calendar. Rather, they would have followed the calendar set by their local authorities. If this is correct, it would make sense that R. Gamliel would have found himself in conflict with the local leadership over his attempts to establish a universal Jewish calendar.

27. Printed editions read שאם.
28. Printed editions read לפני בית.
29. This sentence appears in the margin of the manuscript.
30. Several scholars have suggested that this story in fact occurred after the Destruction. See Seth Schwartz, *Josephus and Judean Politics*, 106; Hezser, *Social Structure of the Rabbinic Movement*, 483. See also Walfish, "Literary Method of Redaction," 75n126. I find this reading quite unlikely.
31. Yaakov Sussman, "The History of Halacha and the Dead Sea Scrolls: Preliminary Observations on *Miqsat Ma 'ase Ha-Torah* (4QMMT)," *Tarbiz* 59: 11–76 (1990) [Hebrew]; Lawrence H. Schiffman, "The Battle for the Scrolls: Recent Developments in the Study of the Dead Sea Scrolls," *Cathedra* 61 (1991): 3–23 [Hebrew]; Daniel Schwartz, "Between Sages and Priests in the Second Temple Period," *Migvan De'ot ve-Hashkafot be-Tarbut Yisra'el* 2(1992) [Hebrew]. For a critique of this position see Baumgarten, "But Touch the Law."
32. I am following Sussman's identification of the Essenes of Hellenistic literature with the Boethusians of rabbinic literature and the members of the Qumran sect. Dissenting views on this matter do not materially impact my reading of this story. Among the followers of this "priestly" halakhah, there was apparently an internal spit with regard to the calendar. Whereas the Essenes used a strictly solar calendar, the Sadducees, at least those who were active in the Temple in Jerusalem, used a lunisolar calendar similar to that of the Pharisees. See Albert Baumgarten, "Who Were the Sadducees? The Sadducees of Jerusalem and Qumran," in *The Jews in the Hellenistic and Roman World: Studies in Memory of Menahem Stern*, ed. Isaiah M. Gafni, Aharon Oppenheimer, and Daniel R. Schwartz (Jerusalem: Zalman Shazar Center for Jewish History, 1996), 393–411 [Hebrew]. Daniel Schwartz has proposed a more theoretical distinction between the halakhah of the priests and of the rabbis/Pharisees, arguing that the former were legal "realists" while the later were "nominalists."
33. See Walfish, "Literary Method of Redaction," 76.
34. See Albeck, *Shisha sidre Mishnah*.
35. See Yerushalmi *Rosh Hashanah* 2:7, 58b. On the positions of the moon at the beginning and end of the month, see Sacha Stern, *Calendar and Community*, 99.
36. See Maimonides and Bertinoro. The interpretation presented in the Talmuds (Bavli 24a; Yerushalmi 2:7, 48b) is that R. Gamliel thought that such a short interval was actually possible.
37. Printed editions read ובליל עיבורו.
38. MS Parma inserts here הרי.
39. On the meaning of the terms *bezemano* and *leyl 'iburo*, see Saul Lieberman, *Tosefta: 'A.p. ketav yad Vinah ve-shinuye nusha'ot mi-ketav yad 'Erfurt, keta'im min ha-Genizah u-defus Venetsi'ah 281 be-tseruf masoret ha-Tosefta u-ferush katsar*, 2nd ed., 5 vols. (New York: Jewish Theological Seminary of America, 1992), 312n2. Rashi apparently had a different reading of this part of the Mishnah. See Rashi 25a s.v. *bezmeano* and *leyl sheloshim*. I am reading the term *lo nir'eh* (not seen) as referring to the general population rather than the witnesses, following Rashi and *Tiferet Yisrael*.
40. *Tiferet Yisrael*, contra Maimonides, sensibly presumes that weather conditions were clear on the night in question. However, as Sacha Stern has informed me, it would still be theoretically possible for the new moon to be invisible due to largely imperceptible atmospheric conditions.
41. Tosefta *Rosh Hashanah* 2:1 and Sifra *Emor* 10:2. Note that the interpretation of Leviticus 23:2 in the *Sifra* parallels R. Aqiba's interpretation of the same verse later in our story. For further sources and discussion, see Saul Lieberman, *Tosefta ki-feshutah*, 1036n1 and Louis Finkelstein, *Sifra on Leviticus*, vol. 1 (New York: Jewish Theological Seminary of America, 1989), 126.
42. Brown v. Allen, Warden, 344 U.S. 443 (1953). See Robert M. Cover, "Nomos and Narrative," in *Narrative, Violence, and the Law: The Essays of Robert Cover*, ed. Martha Minow, Michael Ryan, and Austin Sarat (Ann Arbor: University of Michigan Press, 1992), 141.

43. Schwartz understands R. Dosa's position in terms of his priestly lineage. He seeks to place this debate into a larger conflict between priestly and Pharisaic halakhah, which he understands as being "realist" and "nominalist," respectively. Daniel Schwartz, "Law and Truth." These categories parallel but do not exactly correspond to our distinctions between "apodictic" and "narrative" approaches to law, as well as between the conceptions of a jurist being *an* or *in* authority. It is noteworthy that Schwartz understands R. Dosa's debate with R. Gamliel as reflecting such a deeper debate. His argument is similar to our claim that R. Dosa and R. Gamliel's debate reflects a fundamental disagreement about the nature of halakhah and halakhic authority. See also Jeffrey L. Rubenstein, "Nominalism and Realism in Qumranic and Rabbinic Law," *Dead Sea Discoveries* 6, no. 2 (1999): 157–83."
44. Printed editions read לדון.
45. Printed editions read לדון.
46. Text in brackets inserted in bottom margin of MS Kaufmann by different hand. It was probably omitted from the original text due to haplography.
47. Daniel Schwartz, "From Priests to their Left to Christians on their Right? On the Interpretation and Development of a Mishnaic Story (Rosh Hashannah 2:8–9)," *Tarbiz* 74, no. 1 (2005): 21–41 [Hebrew].
48. David Henshke, "R. Joshua's Acceptance of the Authority of R. Gamliel II: A Study of Two Versions of the Same Event," *Tarbiz* 76, nos. 1–2 (2007): 81–104 [Hebrew].
49. NRSV translation.
50. Walfish, "Literary Method of Redaction," 103.
51. My translation.
52. The parallel passages in the Tosefta (2:18) and in the Bavli (25a) invoke the names of Samson, Jephthah, and Gideon as representative of the worst leaders in Jewish history.
53. Epstein, *Mevo'ot le-sifrut ha-Tana'im*, 370. Henshke notes that this reading is found in two genizah fragments (Cambridge University Library T-S A.S. 78.16 and Oxford Bodleian Heb.e.77 [2851]) as well as in Maimonides' text of the Mishnah and in the Pisaro edition of the Mishnah. Henshke, "R. Joshua's Acceptance," n23. Epstein apparently based his argument on the claim that since the Bavli cites these lines from a baraita (*Rosh Hashana* 25b), we can conclude that they were not in the Bavli's version of the Mishnah. Rather, these lines were added by later scribes on the basis of this baraita. See also Yerushalmi *Rosh Hashana* 2:8, 58b.

Chapter 9

1. MS Kaufmann on *Sukkah* 3:12 reads הָיָה.
2. For the sake of simplicity, I am interpreting the term *beit hamiqdash* in this passage according to the straightforward interpretation of Rashi and Bertinoro, as referring only to the Temple itself. However, I do not mean to reject Maimonides' opinion that the lulav was taken all seven days throughout Jerusalem. See Albeck, *Shisha sidre Mishnah*, 2:476.
3. As Jaffee points out, the term *taqqanah* itself is never used in the Mishnah to refer to an act of legislation. The current usage of the term seems to have originated with the Amoraim. Jaffee, "*Taqqanah* in Tannaitic Literature," 206–7. Nevertheless, I am using the term for convenience's sake as the noun form of *hitqin*, the standard term used in the Mishnah's etiological stories to refer to the rabbis' enactments. On the use of the root *t-q-n* in rabbinic Hebrew, see ibid., 207n7.
4. On R. Yohanan b. Zakkai and his legislation see Shmuel Safrai, "New Perspectives on the Problem of R. Yohanan b. Zakkai's Status and Deeds after the Destruction," in *Bi-yeme ha-bayit ha-sheni uvi-yeme ha-Mishnah: Mehkarim be-toldot Yisra'el* (Jerusalem: Magnes, 1994), 341–64.
5. Jaffee himself is hesitant to extend this claim to the Mishnah, focusing instead on the Tosefta and halakhic Midrashim. This is based on his assumption regarding the historical

primacy of the Mishnah. However, the recent work of Friedman, Hauptman and others argues that in many cases, the Mishnah in fact represents a revised form of the Tosefta. In light of these conclusions, there is no reason not to apply Jaffee's conclusions to the Mishnah as well. Friedman, *Tosefta 'atikt'a*; Judith Hauptman, "Mishnah as a Response to 'Tosefta'," in *The Synoptic Problem in Rabbinic Literature*, ed. Shaye J. D. Cohen (Providence, RI: Brown Judaica Studies, 2000), 13–34.

6. Jaffee, "Taqqanah in Tannaitic Literature," 215–21.
7. Ibid., 221.
8. Jeffrey Rubenstein, *The History of Sukkot in the Second Temple and Rabbinic Periods*, Brown Judaica Studies (Atlanta: Scholars Press, 1995), 101, 182–86; Shmuel Safrai, "Temple and Synagogue," in *Bi-yeme ha-bayit ha-sheni uvi-yeme ha-Mishnah: Mehkarim be-toldot Yisra'el* (Jerusalem: Magnes, 1994), 142–43 [Hebrew]; Gedaliah Alon, "On Philo's Halacha," in *Jews, Judaism and the Classical World* (Jerusalem: Magnes, 1977), 131–33.
9. Rubenstein, *History of Sukkot*, 187.
10. Jaffee, "Taqqanah in Tannaitic Literature," 206.
11. I am using the rabbinic terms for the four species mentioned in the verse. On earlier interpretations of the verse, see Rubenstein, *History of Sukkot*, 25–30.
12. This reading of the verses is assumed by virtually all of the traditional commentaries on the Mishnah. See *Sifra* on this verse and Yerushalmi *Sukkah* 3:13, 54a.
13. Jaffee, "Taqqanah in Tannaitic Literature," 211, 213.
14. Fritz Kern, *Kingship and Law in the Middle Ages*, trans. S. B. Chrimes (New York: Praeger, 1956), 151.
15. *Ma'aser Sheni* 2:5, *Rosh Hashanah* 4:1, 4:4, *Mo'ed Qatan* 4:6, *Menahot* 10:5.
16. For discussions of the place of the Destruction in rabbinic thought see Moshe Beer, "The Destruction of the Second Temple in Early Jewish Thought," in *The Jews in the Hellenistic-Roman World: Studies in Memory of Menahem Stern*, ed. Isaiah M. Gafni, Aharon Oppenheimer, and Daniel R. Schwartz (Jerusalem: Zalman Shazar Center for Jewish History, 1996), 437–450 [Hebrew]; Robert Goldenberg, "Early Rabbinic Explanations of the Destruction of Jerusalem," *Journal of Jewish Studies* 33 (1982): 517–25; Goldenberg, "The Broken Axis: Rabbinic Judaism and the Fall of Jerusalem," *Journal of the American Academy of Religion* 45 (1977): 353–60.
17. Safrai, "Temple and Synagogue."
18. But see Tosefta *Rosh Hashanah* 2:9, which ends, "When the Temple is rebuilt, speedily in our days, these things will return to their original status."
19. Printed text reads עוקרין ומשליכין.
20. Printed text adds כולה.
21. The Mishnah does not use the term *taqqanah* at this stage of the story. I am not sure of the significance of this fact.
22. The Mishnah does not state whether or not this harsh penalty was in any way effective in curbing the planting of *kil'ayim*.
23. For a slightly different interpretation of the Mishnah see the baraita quoted in Yerushalmi *Sheqalim* 1:2, 46a.
24. *Shevi'it* 4:1. See also Tosefta *Shabbat* 3:3.
25. See the texts cited in the next several pages.
26. Printed editions read רצחנים.
27. Printed editions read מנאפים.
28. Printed editions read מרים.
29. MS Munich and other Talmudic MSS read here בייתוסים. See *Dikdukei Soferim*.
30. *Rosh Hashanah* 1:15.
31. This is in line with Sussman's identification of the Boethusians with the Essenes. Sussman, "History of Halacha."
32. T. C. G. Thornton, "The Samaritan Calendar: A Source of Friction in New Testament Times," *Journal of Theological Studies*, n.s., 42, no. 2 (1991): 577–80.

33. Saul Lieberman, *Tosefta ki-feshutah* 4:486.
34. Ibid., 5:1029. This appears to be the simple reading of the Yerushalmi's explanation, "They would signal on one day and they would signal on the next day," (*Rosh Hashanah* 2:1, 58a). The exact path of the Jewish signal fires remains open to speculation. See ibid., 5:1031.
35. Goldberg argues that in the case of the *Yoma* stories, these texts were indeed actively inserted by a Tannaitic editor. He argues that much of *Yoma* functions as a sort of "tosefta" to *Tamid*. Abraham Goldberg, "The Tosefta—Companion to the Mishnah," in *The Literature of the Sages*, ed. Shmuel Safrai (Assen, the Netherlands: Van Gorcum, 1987), 287. In *Tamid*, the descriptions of the *terumat hadeshen* (1:2) and the identification of the first sunlight appear without any accompanying etiological stories.
36. Until this point, I have endeavored to consider the full range of possibilities regarding the way in which a given story tradition evolved. In this instance, a full treatment of the relationship between the various sources and their manuscript variants is not feasible. I am presenting the single theory that I find most likely here and that has been advocated by several leading scholars; this does not preclude other possibilities. I hope to present a full discussion of the development of this narrative tradition in a separate study. On the primacy of the baraita version of the story over the Mishnah's, see Melammed, "'Case' in the Mishnah," 157; Friedman, *Tosefta 'atikt'a*, 44–45. On the primacy of *Tamid*'s account of the daily service over that found in *Yoma*, see Epstein, *Mevo'ot le-sifrut ha-Tana'im*, 28–30; Abraham Goldberg, "Tosefta—Companion to the Mishnah," 287.
37. On this word, see Epstein, *Mavo le-nusah ha-Mishnah*, 1228.
38. This letter is inserted above the line in the manuscript.
39. See *Menahot* 10:5.
40. Tosefta *Shevu'ot* 1:4, Sifrei, end of *Seder Ma'asei*, Yerushalmi *Yoma* 2:2, 39d, Bavli *Yoma* 23a.
41. This word is missing from the printed edition and from MS London. There is significant variation of the word order in the various manuscripts of the different versions of the story. Furthermore, the Yerushalmi reads מעשה באחד שקדם את חבירו בתוך ארבע אמות של מזבח. The Yerushalmi also has a significantly different formulation later on in the story as well. For our purposes, however, these differences are not significant.
42. Other MSS and witnesses read האולם. I have translated accordingly. See Saul Lieberman, *Tosefta ki-feshutah* 4:753.
43. MSS London, Erfurt, and printed editions read בני. This would appear to be the proper reading, and I have translated accordingly.
44. A traditional formula for comforting mourners. See Yerushalmi *Sanhedrin* 2:2, 19d.
45. This translation is based on the Soncino translation of Bavli *Yoma* 23a.
46. Ex. 20:22.
47. See note 45 above. We can only wonder if this father's actions are meant in some way to recall those of another father, who, over a millennium earlier, stood ready to slaughter his own son at the very same spot.
48. This was first pointed out to me by a physician whose identity I do not know. It has been confirmed by my brother, Jeremy Rosenbaum Simon, M.D., Ph.D, of the Division of Emergency Medicine and the Center for Medical Ethics at the Columbia University College of Physicians and Surgeons.
49. This is how the term *payyis* is generally translated. However, in this case it seems that the method used was more akin to "eeny, meeny, miny, moe" or "the twenty-first finger is it," protocols employed by children today. See Tosefta *Yoma* 1:10 and Rashi's comments on Bavli *Yoma* 22a, s.v. *hatsbi'u*.
50. Missing from MS Parma and printed editions.
51. Missing from MS Parma.
52. Note, however, that such an injury would permanently disqualify the priest from service in the Temple. See Lev. 21:18–19.
53. Printed editions read על גבי.

54. Tosefta *Sukkah* 3:16 explicitly identifies the priest in question as a "Boethusian." Bavli *Sukkah* 48b refers to him as a "Sadducee." Scholars generally assume that these sects rejected the practice of water libations altogether. However, Rubenstein argues that the dispute was of a more technical nature, either about where to pour the libation or whether or not to perform the rite on the Sabbath. Jeffrey Rubenstein, "The Sadducees and the Water Libation," *Jewish Quarterly Review* 84, no. 4 (1994), 417–44.
55. Yerushalmi *Sukkah* 4:8, 54d; *Yoma* 1:5, 39a; Bavli *Sukkah* 48b; *Zevahim* 62a.
56. 13.14.5.
57. *Wars* 1.4.3. See Josephus's accounts of the Passover riot against the procurator Cummanus (48–52 CE) *Wars* 2.12.1, *Antiquities* 20.5.3.
58. Mk. 14:1–2.
59. Gedaliah Alon, "The Attitude of the Pharisees to Roman Rule and the House of Herod," in *Jews, Judaism and the Classical World* (Jerusalem: Magnes, 1977), 33n34.
60. On these terms see the previous chapter.
61. Printed editions add יום טוב הראשון שלחג שחל להיות בשבת.
62. This letter is inserted above the line in MS Kaufmann. It does not appear in printed editions.
63. For further documentation and discussion of the variants in this text, see Epstein, *Mavo le-nusah ha-Mishnah*, 326.
64. See Breuer, "Perfect and Participle."
65. The story refers to the beginning of the previous chapter of the Mishnah, which invalidates the use of a stolen lulav.
66. Once again, we find an account of a *taqqanah* which expands the practice of taking the lulav beyond the Temple. As I argued previously, such developments may have been the result of a larger process of widening Jewish ritual practice beyond the Temple, rather than an ad hoc response to this event.
67. MS Kaufmann had the word בצפון following this word. It has been crossed out and is apparently a mistake.
68. However, in paragraph 3 of this chapter, immediately following our story, the Mishnah explains that one is obligated to bow down when one comes to one of the thirteen gates to the Temple complex and proceeds to list the names and locations of these gates. This corresponds to the position of Abba Yosi b. Hanan in Mishnah *Midot* 2:6. It contradicts *Midot* 1:4, which lists only seven gates, as well as *Midot* 2:3, which states that the locations for prostration correspond to places where the "Greek kings" made breaks in the partition known as the *soreg*. The breaks were subsequently repaired. On the gates of the Temple see Josephus, *Wars* 5.5.2–3.
69. This is likely based on a reading of 2 Chronicles 35:3. See Yerushalmi *Sota* 8:3, 22c; Bavli *Horayot* 12a, and *Keritot* 5b.
70. *Yoma* 53b.
71. 2 Maccabees 2:4–8. See also 2 Baruch 6:7–9 and 4:3:1–19. For further sources and discussion, see Isaac Kalimi and James D. Purvis, "The Hiding of the Temple Vessels in Jewish and Samaritan Literature," *Catholic Bible Quarterly* 56 (1994): 679–85. I would like to thank Rabbi Dr. David Rothstein for this reference.

Chapter 10

1. See Culler, *Structuralist Poetics, 207*; Smith, "Narrative Versions, Narrative Theories," 213. For a brief review of twentieth-century efforts to define narrative structure, see Martin, *Recent Theories of Narrative*, 107–29.
2. Miller, "Ariadne's Thread."
3. Patricia Ewick and Susan S. Sibley, "Subversive Stories and Hegemonic Tales: Toward a Sociology of Narrative," *Law and Society Review* 29, no. 2 (1995): 214.
4. Ibid., 219.

5. I do not mean to gloss over the significant differences between the discourse of the Yerushalmi and that of the Bavli. On these differences, see Christine Elizabeth Hayes, *Between the Babylonian and Palestinian Talmuds: Accounting for Halakhic Difference in Selected Sugyot from Tractate Avodah Zarah* (New York: Oxford University Press, 1997).
6. Epstein, *Mevo'ot le-sifrut ha-Tana'im*, 224–26; Albeck, *Mavo la-Mishnah*, 99–115. Epstein and Albeck's debate focused fundamentally on the methods of redaction of the Mishnah.

BIBLIOGRAPHY

Abraham ben Isaac of Narbonne. *Ha-Eshkol*. Jerusalem: Mass, 1935.
Albeck, Hanokh. *Mavo la-Mishnah*. Jerusalem: Mosad Bialik, 1959.
———, ed. *Shisha sidre Mishnah*. Jerusalem: Mosad Bialik, 1952.
Alexander, Elizabeth Shanks. *Transmitting Mishnah: The Shaping Influence of Oral Tradition*. New York: Cambridge University Press, 2006.
Alexander, Patrick H., ed. *The SBL Handbook of Style: For Ancient Near Eastern, Biblical, and Early Christian Studies*. Peabody, MA: Hendrickson, 1999.
Alon, Gedaliah. "The Attitude of the Pharisees to Roman Rule and the House of Herod." In *Jews, Judaism and the Classical World*, 18–47. Jerusalem: Magnes, 1977.
———. *The Jews in Their Land in the Talmudic Age*. Translated by Gershon Levi. 2 vols. Jerusalem: Magnes, 1980.
———. "On Philo's Halacha." In *Jews, Judaism and the Classical World*, 89–137. Jerusalem: Magnes, 1977.
Alt, Albrecht. "The Origins of Israelite Law." In *Essays on Old Testament History and Religion*, 101–72. Garden City, NY: Doubleday, 1967.
Alter, Robert. *The Art of Biblical Narrative*. New York: Basic Books, 1981.
Amitay, Ory. "Şhim'on ha-Sadiq in His Historical Contexts." *Journal of Jewish Studies* 58, no. 2 (2007): 236–49.
Aristotle. *Poetics*. Translated by Stephen Halliwell. Loeb Classical Library L199. Cambridge, MA: Harvard University Press, 1995.
Avi-Yonah, Michael. *The Jews under Roman and Byzantine Rule: A Political History of Palestine from the Bar Kokhba War to the Arab Conquest*. New York: Schocken Books, 1984.
Azar, Moshe. *Tahbir leshon ha-Mishnah*. Jerusalem: Academy of Hebrew Language, 1995.
Bakhtin, M. M. "Discourse in the Novel." In *The Dialogic Imagination: Four Essays*, edited by Michael Holquist, 259–422. Austin: University of Texas Press, 1981.
Baron, Salo W. "Azariah de' Rossi's Historical Method." In *History and Jewish Historians: Essays and Addresses by Salo W. Baron*, edited by Arthur Hertzberg and Leon Feldman, 205–39. Philadelphia: Jewish Publication Society of America, 1964.
———. *A Social and Religious History of the Jews*. 2d ed. New York: Columbia University Press, 1952.
Barthes, Roland. "The Reality Effect." In *French Literary Theory Today: A Reader*, edited by Tzvetan Todorov, 11–17. Cambridge, UK: Cambridge University Press, 1982.
———. *Writing Degree Zero*. Translated by Annette Lavers and Colin Smith. New York: Hill & Wang, 1968.
Baumgarten, Albert I. "'But Touch the Law and the Sect Will Split': Legal Dispute as the Cause of Sectarian Schism." *Review of Rabbinic Judaism* 5, no. 3 (2002): 301–15.
———. *The Flourishing of Jewish Sects in the Maccabean Era: An Interpretation*. Supplements to the Journal for the Study of Judaism 55. Leiden, the Netherlands: Brill, 1997.

———. "Who Were the Sadducees? The Sadducees of Jerusalem and Qumran." In *The Jews in the Hellenistic and Roman World: Studies in Memory of Menahem Stern*, edited by Isaiah M. Gafni, Aharon Oppenheimer, and Daniel R. Schwartz, 393–411. Jerusalem: Zalman Shazar Center for Jewish History, 1996 [Hebrew].

Beer, Moshe. "The Destruction of the Second Temple in Early Jewish Thought." In *The Jews in the Hellenistic-Roman World: Studies in Memory of Menahem Stern*, edited by Isaiah M. Gafni, Aharon Oppenheimer, and Daniel R. Schwartz, 437–450. Jerusalem: Zalman Shazar Center for Jewish History, 1996 [Hebrew].

Ben-Amos, Dan. "Narrative Forms in the Haggadah: Structural Analysis." Ph.D. diss., Indiana University, 1967.

Bendavid, Aba. *Leshon mikra u-leshon hakhamim*. Tel Aviv: Devir, 1967.

Ben-Yishai, Ayelet. "Victorian Precedents: Narrative form, Law Reports and Stare Decisis." *Law, Culture and the Humanities* 4 (2008): 382–402.

Benveniste, Emile. "The Correlation of Tense in the French Verb." In *Problems in General Linguistics*. Translated by Mary Elizabeth Meek. Miami Linguistics Series 8. Coral Gables, FL: University of Miami, 1971.

Berger, Michael S. *Rabbinic Authority*. New York: Oxford University Press, 1998.

Berkowitz, Beth A. *Execution and Invention: Death Penalty Discourse in Early Rabbinic and Christian Cultures*. New York: Oxford University Press, 2006.

Bernstein, Moshe J. "'Rewritten Bible': A Generic Category Which Has Outlived Its Usefulness?" *Textus* 22 (2005): 169–96.

Binder, Guyora, and Robert Weisberg. "Narrative Criticism of Law." In *Literary Criticisms of Law*, 201–91. Princeton, NJ: Princeton University Press, 2000.

Bitman, Avigdor. "On the Nature of the Rule 'The Halakhah is According to Beit Hillel.'" *Sinai* 82 (1978): 185–96 [Hebrew].

Bokser, Baruch M. "Wonder-Working and the Rabbinic Tradition: The Case of Hanina ben Dosa." *Journal for the Study of Judaism* 16, no. 1 (1985): 42–92.

Bolinger, Dwight L. "More on the Present Tense in English." *Language* 23 (1947): 434–36.

Bonfils, Robert. "Some Reflections on the Place of Azariah de Rossi's *Meor Enayim* in the Cultural Milieu of Italian Renaissance Jewry." In *Jewish Thought in the Sixteenth Century*, edited by Bernard Dov Cooperman, 23–48. Cambridge, MA: Harvard University Press, 1983.

Booth, Wayne C. *The Rhetoric of Fiction*. Chicago: University of Chicago Press, 1961.

Borges, Jorge Luis. *Labyrinths: Selected Stories and Other Writings*. New York: New Directions Pub. Corp., 1964.

Boyarin, Daniel. *Carnal Israel: Reading Sex in Talmudic Culture*. Berkeley: University of California Press, 1993.

Breuer, Yochanan. "Perfect and Participle in Descriptions of Ritual in the Mishnah." *Tarbiz* 56, no. 3 (1987): 299–326 [Hebrew].

Brooks, Cleanth. "New Criticism." In *The Princeton Encyclopedia of Poetry and Poetics*, edited by Alex Preminger, 567–68. Princeton, NJ: Princeton University Press, 1974.

Brooks, Peter. "Narrative Transactions—Does the Law Need a Narratology?" *Yale Journal of Law and the Humanities* 18, no. 1 (2006): 1–28.

———. "Narrativity of the Law." *Cardozo Studies in Law and Literature* 14 (2002): 1–10.

———. *Reading for the Plot: Design and Intention in Narrative*. New York: Knopf, 1984.

Brooks, Peter, and Paul Gewirtz. *Law's Stories: Narrative and Rhetoric in the Law*. New Haven, CT: Yale University Press, 1996.

Brown, Peter. "The Rise and Function of the Holy Man in Late Antiquity." *Journal of Roman Studies* 61 (1971): 80–101.

———. "The Saint as Exemplar in Late Antiquity." *Representations* 1, no. 2 (1983): 1–25.

Browning, Robert. "The 'Low Level' Saint's Life in the Early Byzantine World." In *The Byzantine Saint: University of Birmingham Fourteenth Spring Symposium of Byzantine Studies*, edited by Sergei Hackel, 117–27. Studies Supplementary to Sobornost 5. London: Fellowship of St. Alban and St. Sergius, 1981.

Bruner, Jerome. *Making Stories: Law, Literature, Life*. Cambridge, MA: Harvard University Press, 2002.
Chatman, Seymour. *Story and Discourse: Narrative Structure in Fiction and Film*. Ithaca, NY: Cornell University Press, 1978.
Chavel, Simeon. "'Oracular Novellae' and Biblical Historiography through the Lens of Law and Narrative." *Clio* 39, no. 1 (2009): 1–27.
Cohen, Shaye J. D. *From the Maccabees to the Mishnah*. Philadelphia: Westminster, 1987.
———. "Parallel Historical Tradition in Josephus and Rabbinic Literature." *Proceedings of the World Congress of Jewish Studies* 9, no. B/1 (1986): 7–14.
———. "The Rabbi in Second Century Jewish Society." In *The Cambridge History of Judaism*, edited by William Horbury, W. D. Davies, and John Sturdy, 922–90. Cambridge, UK: Cambridge University Press, 1999.
Cover, Robert. "Nomos and Narrative." In *Narrative, Violence, and the Law: The Essays of Robert Cover*, edited by Martha Minow, Michael Ryan, and Austin Sarat, 95–171. Ann Arbor: University of Michigan Press, 1992.
Cox, Patricia. *Biography in Late Antiquity: A Quest for the Holy Man*. Berkeley: University of California Press, 1983.
Culler, Jonathan. "Fabula and Sjuzhet in the Analysis of Narrative: Some American Discussions." *Poetics Today* 1, no. 3 (1980): 27–37.
———. *On Deconstruction: Theory and Criticism after Structuralism*. Ithaca, NY: Cornell University Press, 1982.
———. *Structuralist Poetics: Structuralism, Linguistics, and the Study of Language*. Ithaca, NY: Cornell University Press, 1975.
Daube, David. "Enfant Terrible." *Harvard Theological Review* 68 (1975): 371–76.
———. *Forms of Roman Legislation*. Westport, CT: Greenwood, 1956.
———. *The New Testament and Rabbinic Judaism*. London: Athlone, 1956.
De Vries, Benjamin. *Toldot ha-halakhah ha-Talmudit: Perakim nivharim*. Tel Aviv: Zioni, 1962.
Diamond, Eliezer. *Holy Men and Hunger Artists: Fasting and Asceticism in Rabbinic Culture*. Oxford: Oxford University Press, 2004.
Doron, Pinchas. "Motive Clauses in the Laws of Deuteronomy: Their Forms, Functions and Contents." *Hebrew Annual Review* 2 (1978): 61–78.
Eagleton, Terry. *Literary Theory: An Introduction*. Minneapolis: University of Minnesota Press, 1983.
Efron, Joshua. "The Great Sanhedrin in Vision and Reality." In *Studies on the Hasmonean Period*, 287–338. Leiden, the Netherlands: Brill, 1987.
Elbaum, Jacob. *Le-havin divre hakhamim: Mivhar divre mavo le-agadah ule-midrash, mi-shel hakhme yeme ha-benayim*. Jerusalem: Bialik Institute, 2000.
Elman, Yaakov. "Order, Sequence, and Selection: The Mishnah's Anthological Choices." In *The Anthology in Jewish Literature*, edited by David Stern, 53–80. Oxford: Oxford University Press, 2004.
Epstein, Jacob N. *Mavo le-nusah ha-Mishnah*. 3rd ed. Jerusalem: Magnes, 2000.
———. *Mevo'ot le-sifrut ha-Tana'im: Mishnah, Tosefta u-midrashai-halakhah*. Jerusalem: Magnes, 1957.
Ewick, Patricia, and Susan S. Sibley. "Subversive Stories and Hegemonic Tales: Toward a Sociology of Narrative." *Law and Society Review* 29, no. 2 (1995): 197–225.
Fineman, Joel. "The History of the Anecdote." In *The New Historicism*, edited by H. Aram Vesser, 49–76. New York: Routledge, 1989.
Finkelstein, Louis. *Sifra on Leviticus*. Vol. 1. New York: Jewish Theological Seminary of America, 1989.
Fischel, Henry A. "Story and History: Observations on Greco-Roman Rhetoric and Pharisaism." In *Essays in Greco-Roman and Related Talmudic Literature*, edited by Henry A. Fischel, 59–88. New York: Ktav, 1977.
———. "Studies in Cynicism and the Ancient Near East: The Transformation of a Chria." In *Religions in Antiquity: Essays in Memory of Erwin Ramsdell Goodenough*, edited by Jacob Neusner, 372–411. Leiden, the Netherlands: Brill, 1968.

Fishbane, Michael. *Biblical Interpretation in Ancient Israel*. Oxford: Clarendon, 1985.
Fleischman, Suzanne. *Tense and Narrativity: From Medieval Performance to Modern Fiction*. Austin: University of Texas Press, 1990.
Fonrobert, Charlotte Elisheva. *Menstrual Purity: Rabbinic and Christian Reconstructions of Biblical Gender*. Stanford, CA: Stanford University Press, 2000.
———. "When the Rabbi Weeps: On Reading Gender in Talmudic Aggadah." *Nashim* 4 (2001): 56–83.
Forster, E. M. *Aspects of the Novel*. London: Edward Arnold and Company, 1927.
Fraade, Steven. "Ancient Jewish Law and Narrative in Comparative Perspective: The Damascus Document and the Mishnah." *Diné Yisrael* 24 (2007): 65–99.
Fraenkel, Jonah. "The Aggadah in Talmudic Literature." *Netuim* 11–12 (2004): 63–79 [Hebrew].
———. "The Aggadah in the Mishnah" In *Mehqerei Talmud 3: Talmudic Studies Dedicated to the Memory of Professor Ephraim E. Urbach*, edited by Yaakov Sussman and David Rosenthal, 655–83. Jerusalem: Magnes, 2005 [Hebrew].
———. *Darkhe ha-agadah veha-midrash*. 2 vols. [Givataim, Israel]: Yad La-Talmud, 1991.
———. *'Iyunim be-'olamo ha-ruhani shel sipur ha-agadah*. Tel Aviv: Hakibbutz Hameuchad, 1981.
———. *Sipur ha-agadah, ahdut shel tokhen ve-tsurah: Kovets mehkarim* Tel Aviv: Hakibbutz Hameuchad, 2001.
Frankel, Zacharias. *Darkhe ha-Mishnah*. Leipzig: Hunger, 1859.
Frankfurter, David. "Dynamics of Ritual Expertise in Antiquity and Beyond: Towards a New Taxonomy of 'Magicians.'" In *Magic and Ritual in the Ancient World*, edited by Paul Mirecki and Marvin Meyer, 159–78. Leiden, the Netherlands: Brill, 2002.
Friedman, Shamma. "The Baraitot in the Babylonian Talmud and Their Relationship to Their Parallels in the Tosefta." In *Atara L'haim: Studies in the Talmud and Medieval Rabbinic Literature in Honor of Professor Haim Zalman Dimitrovsky*, edited by Daniel Boyarin, Marc G. Hirshman, Menahem Schmelzer, and Israel M. Ta-Shma, 163–201. Jerusalem: Hebrew University Magnes Press, 2000 [Hebrew].
———. "Literary Development and Historicity in the Aggadic Narrative of the Babylonian Talmud: A Study Based Upon B.M. 83b–86a." In *Community and Culture: Essays in Jewish Studies in honor of the Ninetieth Anniversary of the Founding of Graetz College*, edited by Nahum M. Waldman, 67–80. Philadelphia: Graetz College, 1987.
———. "The Primacy of Tosefta to Mishnah in Synoptic Parallels." In *Introducing Tosefta: Textual, Intratextual and Intertextual Studies*, edited by Harry Fox and Tirzah Meacham, 99–121. Hoboken, NJ: Ktav, 1999.
———. *Tosefta 'atikt'a: Masekhet Pesah rishon, makbilot ha-Mishnah veha-Tosefta, perush u-mavo*. Ramat-Gan, Israel: Bar-Ilan University Press, 2002.
———. "Towards a Characterization of Babylonian Baraitot: 'Ben Tema' and 'Ben Dortai.'" In *Neti'ot Ledavid: Jubilee Volume for David Weiss Halivni*, edited by Yaakov Elman, Ephraim Bezalel Halivni, and Zvi Arie Stienfeld, 195–274. Jerusalem: Orhot, 2004 [Hebrew].
Gaballa, G. A. *Narrative in Egyptian Art*. Mainz, Germany: Verlag Philipp von Zabern, 1976.
Gafni, Isaiah. "The Historical Background." In *The Literature of the Sages*, edited by Shmuel Safrai, 1–34. Philadelphia: Fortress, 1987.
———. *Land, Center and Diaspora: Jewish Constructs in Late Antiquity*. Journal for the Study of the Pseudepigrapha Supplement Series 21. Sheffield, UK: Sheffield Academic Press, 1997.
Gallagher, Catherine, and Stephen Greenblatt. *Practicing New Historicism*. Chicago: University of Chicago Press, 2000.
Gaius. *The Institutes of Gaius*. Translated by W. M. Gordon and O. F. Robinson. Ithaca, NY: Cornell University Press, 1988.
Geller, Markham J. "The Influence of Ancient Mesopotamia on Hellenistic Judaism." In *Civilizations of the Ancient Near East*, edited by Jack M. Sasson, 43–54. New York, 1995.
Gemser, B. "The Importance of the Motive Clause in Old Testament Law." In *Congress Volume: Copenhagen, 1953*, 50–66. Supplements to Vetus Testamentum1. Leiden, the Netherlands: Brill, 1953.

Genette, Gerard. *Narrative Discourse: An Essay in Method*. Ithaca, NY: Cornell University Press, 1980.
Gerrig, Richard J. *Experiencing Narrative Worlds: On the Psychological Activities of Reading*. New Haven, CT: Yale University Press, 1993.
Gewirtz, Paul. "Victims and Voyeurs: Two Narrative Problems at the Criminal Trial." In *Law's Stories: Narrative and Rhetoric in the Law*, edited by Peter Brooks and Paul Gewirtz, 135–61. New Haven, CT: Yale University Press, 1996.
Gilat, Yitshak D. *Perakim be-hishtalshelut ha-halakhah*. Ramat-Gan, Israel: Bar-Ilan University Press, 1992.
Głowiński, Michał. "On the First-Person Novel." *New Literary History* 9, no. 1 (1977): 103–14.
Goldberg, Abraham. "The Mishnah—A Studybook of Halacha." In *The Literature of the Sages*, edited by Shmuel Safrai, 211–51. Compendia Rerum Iudaicarum ad Novum Testamentum. Assen, the Netherlands: Van Gorcum, 1987.
———. *Perush la-Mishnah, masekhet Shabat*. Jerusalem: Jewish Theological Seminary of America, 1976.
———. "The Tosefta—Companion to the Mishnah." In *The Literature of the Sages*, edited by Shmuel Safrai, 283–301. Assen, the Netherlands: Van Gorcum, 1987.
Goldberg, Arnold. "Form und Funktion des Ma'ase in der Mischna." *Frankfurter Judaistische Beiträge* 2 (1974): 1–38.
Goldenberg, Robert. "The Broken Axis: Rabbinic Judaism and the Fall of Jerusalem." *Journal of the American Academy of Religion* 45 (1977): 353–60.
———. "Early Rabbinic Explanations of the Destruction of Jerusalem." *Journal of Jewish Studies* 33 (1982): 517–25.
Goldin, Judah. "On Honi the Circle-Maker: A Demanding Prayer." In *Studies in Midrash and Related Literature*, edited by Barry Eichler and Jeffrey Tigay, 331–35. Philadelphia: Jewish Publication Society, 1988.
Goodblatt, David. *The Monarchic Principle: Studies in Jewish Self-Government in Antiquity*. Tübingen, Germany: Mohr Siebeck, 1994.
———. "The Place of the Pharisees in First Century Judaism: The State of the Debate." *Journal for the Study of Judaism* 20, no. 1 (1989): 12–30.
Goodman, Martin. *The Ruling Class of Judaea: The Origins of the Jewish Revolt against Rome, A.D. 66–70*. Cambridge, UK; New York: Cambridge University Press, 1987.
———. *State and Society in Roman Galilee*. Oxford Centre for Postgraduate Hebrew Studies Series. Totowa, NJ: Rowman & Allanheld, 1983.
Goshen-Gottstein, Alon. *The Sinner and the Amnesiac: The Rabbinic Invention of Elisha ben Abuya and Eleazar ben Arach*. Stanford, CA: Stanford University Press, 2000.
Graetz, Heinrich. *History of the Jews*. Vol. 2. Philadelphia: Jewish Publication Society of America, 1956.
Green, William Scott. "Palestinian Holy Men: Charismatic Leadership and Rabbinic Tradition." In *Aufstieg und Niedergang der römischen Welt*, edited by Wolfgang Haase, 519–647. Berlin: De Gruyter, 1979.
———. "What's in a Name? The Problematic of Rabbinic 'Biography.'" In *Approaches to Ancient Judaism: Theory and Practice*, edited by William Scott Green, 77–96. Missoula, MT: Scholars Press for Brown University, 1978.
Hadas, Moses, and Morton Smith. *Heroes and Gods*. New York: Harper & Row, 1963.
Halivni, David Weiss. *Midrash, Mishnah, and Gemara: The Jewish Predilection for Justified Law*. Cambridge, MA: Harvard University Press, 1986.
Hallo, William W. *The Context of Scripture*. Vol. 2. Leiden, the Netherlands: Brill, 2000.
Harrison, Harry, and Brian Aldiss, eds. *The Year's Best Science Fiction No. 6*. London: Sphere 1973.
Hasan-Rokem, Galit. *Web of Life: Folklore and Midrash in Rabbinic Literature*. Translated by Batya Stein. Palo Alto, CA: Stanford University Press, 2000.
Hauptman, Judith. "Mishnah as a Response to 'Tosefta.'" In *The Synoptic Problem in Rabbinic Literature*, edited by Shaye J. D. Cohen, 13–34. Providence, RI: Brown Judaica Studies, 2000.
———. *Rereading the Mishnah: A New Approach to Ancient Jewish Texts*. Tübingen, Germany: Mohr Siebeck, 2005.

Hayes, Christine Elizabeth. *Between the Babylonian and Palestinian Talmuds: Accounting for Halakhic Difference in Selected Sugyot from Tractate Avodah Zarah.* New York: Oxford University Press, 1997.

Hayoun, Aryeh Y. "The Schools of Shammai and Hillel: A Study of Their Halakhic and Ideological Theories." Ph.D. diss., Bar-Ilan, 2003 [Hebrew].

Henshke, David. "R. Yehoshua's Acceptance of the Authority of Rabban Gamliel II: A Study of Two Versions of the Same Event." *Tarbiz* 76, nos. 1–2 (2007): 81–104 [Hebrew].

Herford, R. Travers. *Pharisaism, Its Aim and Its Method.* London: Williams & Norgate, 1912.

Herr, Moshe D. "Who Were the Boethusians?" *Proceedings of the Seventh World Congress of Jewish Studies* 3 (1981): 13–14 [Hebrew].

Hezser, Catherine. "The Codification of Legal Knowledge in Late Antiquity: The Talmud Yerushalmi and Roman Law Codes." In *The Talmud Yerushalmi and Graeco-Roman Culture*, edited by Peter Schaefer, 581–641: Mohr Seibeck, 1998.

Hezser, Catherine. *Form, Function, and Historical Significance of the Rabbinic Story in Yerushalmi Neziqin.* Tubingen: Mohr-Siebeck, 1993.

Hezser, Catherine. "Interfaces Between Rabbinic Literature and Graeco-Roman Philosophy" In *The Talmud Yerushalmi and Graeco-Roman Culture*, edited by Peter Schäfer and Catherine Hezser, 161–187. Tübengen: Mohr Seibeck, 2000.

Hezser, Catherine. *The Social Structure of the Rabbinic Movement in Roman Palestine.* Tubingen: Mohr Seibeck, 1997.

Hillers, Delbert R. *Covenant: The History of a Biblical Idea.* Baltimore: Johns Hopkins Press, 1969.

Hirschfeld, Yizhar. *The Palestinian Dwelling in the Roman-Byzantine period.* Jerusalem: Franciscan Printing Press; Israel Exploration Society, 1995.

Hirshman, Marc. "Changing Loci of Holiness: Honi and his Grandchildren." In *Tura: Studies in Jewish Thought- Simon Greenberg Memorial Volume*, 109–18. Tel-Aviv: Hakibbutz Hameuchad Publishing House, 1989 [Hebrew].

Hock, Ronald F., and Edward N. O'Neil. *The Chreia in Ancient Rhetoric:*. Vol. 1- The *Progymnamata*. Atlanta: Scholars' Press, 1985.

Hoffmann, David Zvi. *ha-Mishnah ha-rishona u-felugta de-tana'e.* Berlin: S. Gruenberg, 1914.

Holtz, Shalom E. "'To Go and Marry Any Man That You Please': A Study of The Formulaic Antecedents of the Rabbinic Writ of Divorce." *Journal of Near Eastern Studies* 69, no. 4 (2001): 241–58.

Jacobs, Louis. "Are There Fictitious Baraitot in the Babylonian Talmud?" *Hebrew Union College Annual* 42 (1971): 185–96.

Jacobson, Arthur J. "Death of the Hypothetical." *Stanford Literature Review* 9, no. 2 (1992): 125–38.

Jaffee, Martin. "The Taqqanah in Tannaitic Literature: Jurisprudence and the Construction of Rabbinic Memory." *Journal of Jewish Studies* 41, no. 2 (1990): 205–23.

Jas, Remko. *Neo-Assyrian Judicial Procedures.* Vol. 5, State Archives of Assyria Studies. Helsinki: The Neo-Assyrian Text Corpus Project, 1996.

The Dot and the Line: A Romance in Lower Mathematics. 10 min. Holywood, Metro-Goldwyn-Mayer, 1965.

Justinian. *The Digest of Justinian.* Translated by Alan Watson. Vol. I. Philadelphia: University of Pennsylvania Press, 1985.

Kafka, Franz. *Complete Stories.* Centennial ed. New York: Schocken Books, 1983.

Kalimi, Isaac, and James D. Purvis. "The Hiding of the Temple Vessels in Jewish and Samaritan Literature." *Catholic Bible Quarterly* 56 (1994): 697–85.

Kehati, Pinhas. *Mishnayot mevo'arot.* Jerusalem: Hekhal Shelomoh, 1966–1967.

Kennedy, Duncan. "Form and Substance in Private Law Adjudication." *Harvard Law Review* 89 (1976): 1685–778.

Kern, Fritz. *Kingship and Law in the Middle Ages.* Translated by S. B. Chrimes. New York: Fredrick A. Praeger, 1956.

Labov, William. "Some Further Steps in Narrative Analysis." *Journal of Narrative and Life History* 7 (1997): 395–415.

Leibson, Gideon. "Determining Factors in Herem and Nidui (Ban and Excommunication) During the Tannaitic and Amoraic Periods." *Shenaton Ha-Mishpat Ha-Ivri* 2 (1975): 7–9 [Hebrew].
Leiman, Sid Z. *The Canonization of Hebrew Scripture: The Talmudic and Midrashic Evidence*. New Haven: Connecticut Academy of Arts and Sciences, 1991.
Leiter, Brian. "American Legal Realism." In *The Blackwell Guide to the Philosophy of Law and Legal Theory*, edited by Martin Golding and William Edmundson, 50–66. Oxford: Blackwell, 2005.
Lerner, M. B. *Honi Ha-Me'aggel and Simeon b. Shetah*. Edited by Issac B. Gottlieb. World of the Sages 2. Tel Aviv: Everyman's University, Israel, 1983.
Levine, Baruch A. "The Descriptive Ritual Texts from Ugarit: Some Formal and Functional Features of the Genre." In *The Word of the Lord Shall Go Forth: Essays in Honor of David Noel Freedman in Celebration of His Sixtieth Birthday*, edited by Carol L. Meyers and M. O'Connor, 467–75. Winona Lake, IN: Eisenbrauns, 1983.
Levine, David. "Holy Men and Rabbis in Talmudic Antiquity." In *Saints and Role Models in Judaism and Christianity*, edited by Marcel Poorthuis and Joshua Schwartz, 45–57. Leiden, the Netherlands: Brill, 2004.
Levine, Lee I. *The Rabbinic Class of Roman Palestine in Late Antiquity*. Jerusalem: Yad Ben-Zvi, 1989.
Levinson, Joshua. "From Parable to Invention: The Development of Fiction as a Cultural Category." In *Higayon le-Yonah: Hebetim hadashim be-heker sifrut ha-Midrash, ha-Agadah veha-piyut, kovets mekharim li-khevodo shel profesor Yonah Frenkel bi-melot lo shiv'im ve-'amesh shanah*, edited by Joshua Levinson, Jacob Elbaum, and Galit Hasan-Rokem, 1–32. Jerusalem: Magnes, 2007 [Hebrew].
———. *Ha-Sipur she-lo supar: Omanut ha-sipur ha-Mikra'i ha-murkhav be-midreshe Hazal*. Jerusalem: Magnes, 2005.
———. "Literary Approaches to Midrash." In *Current Trends in the Study of Aggadah*, edited by Carol Bakhos, 189–226. Leiden, the Netherlands: Brill, 2006.
Lieberman, Saul. "On Adjurations among the Jews." *Tarbiz* 27 (1958): 183–89 [Hebrew].
———. *Tosefta ki-feshutah: Be'ur arokh la-Tosefta*. 10 vols. New York: Jewish Theological Seminary, 1992.
———. *Tosefta: 'A.p. ketav yad Vinah ve-shinuye nusha'ot mi-ketav yad' Erfurt, keta'im min ha-Genizah u-defus Venetsi'ah 281 be-tseruf masoret ha-Tosefta u-ferush katsar*. 2nd ed. 5 vols. New York: Jewish Theological Seminary of America, 1992.
Lieberman, Stephen J. "A Mesopotamian Background for the So-Called 'Measures' of Biblical Hermeneutics?" *Hebrew Union College Annual* 58 (1987): 157–225.
Lifshitz, Berachyahu. "'Aggadah' and its Place in the History of the Oral Law." *Shenaton Ha-Mishpat Ha-Ivri* 22 (2003): 233–328 [Hebrew].
———. "Aggadah versus Haggadah: Towards A More Precise Understanding of the Distinction." *Diné Yisrael* 24 (2007): 11–29*.
Lord, Albert Bates. *The Singer of Tales*. Edited by Stephen A. Mitchell and Gregory Nagy. 2nd ed. Cambridge, MA: Harvard University Press, 2000.
Mackenzie, R. A. F. "The Formal Aspect of Ancient Near Eastern Law." In *The Seed of Wisdom*, edited by W. S. McCullough, 31–44. Toronto: University of Toronto Press, 1964.
Magonet, Jonathan. "'Halacha' and 'Aggadah' in the Bible." In *The Bible in Light of Its Interpreters: Sarah Kamin Memorial Volume*, edited by Sara Japhet, 651–70. Jerusalem: Magnes, 1994 [Hebrew].
Maimon, Abraham ben Moses ben. *Milhamot ha-Shem*. Jerusalem: Mosad Harav Kook, 1963.
Maimonides, Moses. *Mishnah: 'Im pirush Mosheh Ben Maimon*. Jerusalem: Mosad HaRav Kook, 1967.
Martel, Yann. *Life of Pi: A Novel*. New York: Harcourt, 2001.
Martin, Wallace. *Recent Theories of Narrative*. Ithaca, NY: Cornell University Press, 1986.
Meir, Ofra. "The Acting Character in the Stories of the Talmud and Midrash (A Sample)." Ph.D. diss., Hebrew University, 1977 [Hebrew].
———. *Rabi Yehudah ha-Nasi: Deyokno shel manhig be-masorot Erets-Yisra'el u-Vavel*. Tel Aviv: Hakibbutz Hameuchad, 1999.
———. *Sugyot ba-po'etikah shel sipure Hazal*. Tel Aviv: Sifriat Poalim, 1993.

Melammed, E. Z. "The 'Case' in the Mishnah as a Source of Halakhah." *Sinai* 23 (1960): 152–66 [Hebrew].

———. "Collections of Tannaitic Stories." In *Essays in Talmudic Literature*, 168–82. Jerusalem: Magnes, 1986 [Hebrew].

Milikowsky, Chaim. "Rabbinic Interpretation of the Bible in the Light of Ancient Hermeneutical Practice: The Question of the Literal Meaning." In *"The Words of a Wise Man's Mouth Are Gracious" (Qoh 10, 12); Festschrift for Günter Stemberger on the Occasion of His 65th Birthday* edited by Mauro Perani, 7–28. Berlin: De Gruyter, 2005.

Miller, J. Hillis. "Ariadne's Thread: Repetition and the Narrative Line." *Critical Inquiry* 3 (1976): 57–77.

Mishnayot. Vilna: Brothers and Widow Romm, 1908–1910

Mishor, Mordechay. "The Tense System in Tannaitic Hebrew." Ph.D. diss., Hebrew University, 1983 [Hebrew].

Moore, George Foot. *Judaism in the First Centuries of the Christian Era, the Age of the Tannaim*. 2 vols. Cambridge, MA: Harvard University Press, 1944.

Morson, Gary Saul, and Caryl Emerson. *Mikhail Bakhtin: Creation of a Prosaics*. Stanford, CA: Stanford University Press, 1990.

Moscovitz, Leib "More on the 'Missing Baraitot' of the Yerushalmi." *Proceedings of the American Academy of Jewish Research* 61 (1995): 63–75 [Hebrew].

———. *Talmudic Reasoning: From Casuistics to Conceptualization*. Tübingen, Germany: Mohr Siebeck, 2002.

Naeh, Shelomo. "The Art of Memory, Structures of Memory and the Organization of Texts in Rabbinic Literature." In *Mehqerei Talmud III: Talmudic Studies Dedicated in Memory of Professor Ephraim E. Urbach*, edited by Yaakov Sussman and David Rosenthal, 543–89. Jerusalem: Magnes, 2005 [Hebrew].

———. "'Creates the Fruit of Lips': A Phenomenological Study of Prayer According to Mishnah Berakhot 4:3, 5:5." *Tarbiz* 63, no. 2 (1994): 185–218 [Hebrew].

Neusner, Jacob. *Development of a Legend: Studies on the Traditions Concerning Yohanan ben Zakkai*. Leiden, the Netherlands: Brill, 1970.

———. *From Politics to Piety: The Emergence of Pharisaic Judaism*. Englewood Cliffs, NJ: Prentice-Hall, 1972.

———. *Judaism as Philosophy: The Method and Message of the Mishnah*. Columbia: University of South Carolina Press, 1991.

———. *Judaism: The Evidence of the Mishnah*. 1st ed. Atlanta, GA: Scholars Press, 1981

———. *Judaism without Christianity: An Introduction to the System of the Mishnah*. Hoboken, NJ: Ktav, 1991.

———. *Making God's Word Work: A Guide to the Mishnah*. New York: Continuum, 2004.

———. "Method and Meaning in Mishnah." In *Method and Meaning in Judaism: Third Series*, 25–57. Chico, CA: Scholars Press, 1981.

———. *The Mishnah: An Introduction*. Northvale, NJ: Aronson, 1989.

———. "The Mishnah Viewed Whole." In *The Mishnah in Contemporary Perspective*, edited by Alan J. Avery-Peck and Jacob Neusner, 3–38. Leiden, the Netherlands: Brill, 2002.

———. "The Rabbinic Traditions about the Pharasees before 70 in Modern Historiography." In *Method and Meaning in Ancient Judaism, Third Series*, 185–213. Chico, CA: Scholars Press, 1981.

———. "Story and Tradition in Ancient Judaism." In *Judaism: The Evidence of the Mishnah*, 307–26. Chicago: University of Chicago Press, 1981.

———. "Why We Cannot Assume the Historical Reliability of Attributions: The Case of the Houses in the Mishnah-Tosefta." In *The Mishnah in Contemporary Perspective*, vol. 2, edited by Alan J. Avery-Peck and Jacob Neusner, 190–212. Leiden, the Netherlands: Brill, 2006.

Noam, Vered. *Megilat Ta'anit: Ha-nusahim, pesharam, toldotehem; Be-tseruf mahadurah bikortit* Jerusalem: Yad Ben-Zvi, 2003.

Paul, Shalom. *Studies in the Book of the Covenant in Light of Cuneiform and Biblical Law*. Edited by G. W. Anderson. Supplements to Vetus Testamentum 18. Leiden, the Netherlands: Brill, 1970.

Pavel, Thomas G. *Fictional Worlds*. Cambridge, MA: Harvard University Press, 1986.
Peters, R. S. "Symposium on Authority." *Aristotelian Society Supplement* 32 (1958): 204–24.
Posner, Richard A. "What Is Law and Why Ask?" In *The Problems of Jurisprudence*, 220–44. Cambridge, MA: Harvard University Press, 1990.
Postema, Gerald. "Classical Common Law Jurisprudence (Part 1)." *Oxford University Commonwealth Law Journal* 2, no. 2 (2002): 155–80.
———. "Classical Common Law Jurisprudence (Part 2)." *Oxford University Commonwealth Law Journal* 3, no. 1 (2003):1–28.
Prince, Gerald. *A Grammar of Stories*. The Hague: Mouton, 1973.
———. "Narrativity." In *Axia: Davis Symposium on Literary Evaluation*, edited by Karl Menges and Daniel Rancour-Laferriere, 61–76. Stuttgart: Akademischer Verlag Hans-Dieter Heinz, 1981.
Pritchard, James B. *Ancient Near Eastern Texts Relating to the Old Testament*. Princeton, NJ: Princeton University Press, 1969.
Rabinowitz, Raphael Nathan. *Dikduke sofrim*. New York: M.P., 1976.
Ricoeur, Paul. *Time and Narrative*. Translated by Kathleen McLaughlin and David Pellauer. Vol. 2. Chicago: University of Chicago Press, 1985.
Robbins, Vernon K. "The Chreia." In *Greco-Roman Literature and the New Testament: Selected Forms and Genres*, edited by David E. Aune, 1–24. Atlanta: Scholars Press, 1988.
Robinson, Olivia F. *The Sources of Roman Law: Problems and Methods for Ancient Historians*. Approaching the Ancient World. London: Routledge, 1997.
Rosen-Zvi, Ishay. *Ha-Tekes she-lo hayah: Mikdash, midrash u-migdar ba-masekhet Sotah* Jerusalem: Magnes, 2008.
Rossi, Azariah dei. *Me'or 'enayim*. Vilna: 1866.
Roth, Martha T. *Law Collections from Mesopotamia and Asia Minor*. Atlanta, GA: Scholars Press, 1995.
Rubenstein, Jeffrey. *The History of Sukkot in the Second Temple and Rabbinic Periods*. Brown Judaica Studies. Atlanta: Scholars Press, 1995.
———. "Nominalism and Realism in Qumranic and Rabbinic Law." *Dead Sea Discoveries* 6, no. 2 (1999): 157–83.
———. "The Sadducees and the Water Libation." *Jewish Quarterly Review* 84, no. 4 (1994): 417–44.
———. *Talmudic Stories: Narrative Art, Composition, and Culture*. Baltimore: Johns Hopkins University Press, 1999.
Sabato, Mordechai. "The Recital of *Shema* by R. Yishmael and Eleazar b. Azaria and the Decision that the *Halakhah* Follows the School of Hillel." *Sidra* 22 (2007): 41–56 [Hebrew].
Safrai, Chana, and Zeev Safrai. "Rabbinic Holy Men." In *Saints and Role Models in Judaism and Christianity*, edited by Marcel Poorthuis and Joshua Schwartz, 59–78. Leiden, the Netherlands: Brill, 2004.
Safrai, Shmuel. "Halakhah." In *The Literature of the Sages*, edited by Shmuel Safrai, 121–208. Assen, the Netherlands: Van Gorcum, 1987.
———. "Jewish Self Government." In *The Jewish People in the First Century: Historical Geography, Political History, Social, Cultural and Religious Life and Institutions*, 377–419. Assen, the Netherlands: Van Gorcum, 1974.
———. "New Perspectives on the Problem of R. Yohanan b. Zakkai's Status and Deeds after the Destruction." In *Bi-yeme ha-bayit ha-sheni uvi-yeme ha-Mishnah: Mehkarim be-toldot Yisra'el*, 341–64. Jerusalem: Magnes, 1994 [Hebrew].
———. "The Ruling in Favor of Beit Hillel in Yavne." In *Proceedings of the Seventh World Congress of Jewish Studies: Studies in Talmud, Halacha and Midrash*, 21–44. Jerusalem: World Union of Jewish Studies, 1981 [Hebrew].
———. "Tales of the Sages in the Palestinian Tradition and the Babylonian Talmud." In *Studies in Aggadic and Folk Literature*, edited by Joseph Heinemann and Dov Noy. Scripta Hierosolymitana 22. Jerusalem: Magnes, 1971.
———. "Teaching of Pietists in Mishnaic Literature." *Journal of Jewish Studies* 16 (1965): 15–33.

———. "Temple and Synagogue." In *Bi-yeme ha-bayit ha-sheni uvi-yeme ha-Mishnah: Mehkarim be-toldot Yisra'el*, 133–51. Jerusalem: Magnes, 1994 [Hebrew].
Samely, Alexander. *Rabbinic Interpretation of Scripture in the Mishnah*. New York: Oxford University Press, 2002.
Sanders, E. P. *Judaism: Practice and Belief, 63 B.C.E.–66 C.E.* London: SCM, 1992.
Saperstein, Marc. *Decoding the Rabbis: A Thirteenth-Century Commentary on the Aggadah*, Harvard Judaic Monographs 3. Cambridge, MA: Harvard University Press, 1980.
Sarfatti, G. B. "Pious Men, Men of Deeds and the Early Prophets." *Tarbiz* 26 (1957): 126–53 [Hebrew].
Schauer, Frederick. "Rules and the Rule of Law." *Harvard Journal of Law and Public Policy* 14, no. 3 (1991): 645–94.
Schiffman, Lawrence H. "The Battle for the Scrolls: Recent Developments in the Study of the Dead Sea Scrolls." *Cathedra* 61 (1991): 3–23 [Hebrew].
Scholes, Robert E., and Robert Kellogg. *The Nature of Narrative*. New York: Oxford University Press, 1966.
Schulz, Fritz. *History of Roman Legal Science*. Oxford: Clarendon, 1946.
Schwartz, Daniel. "Between Sages and Priests in the Second Temple Period." *Migvan De'ot ve-Hashkafot be-Tarbut Yisra'el* 2 (1992): 63–79 [Hebrew].
———. "From Priests to their Left to Christians on their Right? On the Interpretation and Development of a Mishnaic Story (*Rosh Hashanah* 2:8–9)." *Tarbiz* 74, no. 1 (2005): 21–41 [Hebrew].
———. "Law and Truth: On Qumran-Sadducean and Rabbinic Views of Law." In *The Dead Sea Scrolls: Forty Years of Research*, edited by Devorah Dimant and Uriel Rappaport, 229–31. Studies on the Texts of the Desert of Judah 10. Leiden, the Netherlands: Brill, 1992.
———. "MMT, Josephus and the Pharisees." In *Reading 4QMMT: New Perspectives on Qumran Law and History*, edited by John Kampen and Moshe J. Bernstein, 67–79. Atlanta: Scholars Press, 1996.
Schwartz, Seth. *Imperialism and Jewish Society, 200 B.C.E. to 640 C.E.* Princeton, NJ: Princeton University Press, 2001.
———. *Josephus and Judean Politics*. Columbia Studies in the Classical Tradition 18. Leiden, the Netherlands: Brill, 1990.
Segal, M. H. *Dikduk leshon ha-Mishnah*. Tel Aviv: Devir, 1936.
Segal, Michael. "Between Bible and Rewritten Bible." In *Biblical Interpretation at Qumran*, edited by Matthias Henze, 10–28. Grand Rapids, MI: Eerdmans, 2005.
Shachter, Melech. *Ha-Mishnah ba-Bavli uva-Yerushalmi: Hashva'at nusha'oteha* Jerusalem: Mosad Harav Kook, 1959.
Sharvit, Simeon. "The Opening *Ma'aseh She* and Its Relatives in the Language of the Tannaim." In *Segulah le-Ari'elah: Ma'asaf divre mekhar ve-sifrut le-zikhrah shel Ari'elah Dim-Goldberg*, edited by Moshe Idel, Moshe Bar-Asher, Yosef Tuvi, Harold Fisch, and Nahum Sarna, 159–71. Jerusalem: privately printed, 1990 [Hebrew].
———. "The Tense System in the Language of the Mishnah." In *Mehkarim be-Ivrit uvi-leshonot Shemiyot: Mukdashim le-zikhro shel Prof. Yehezkel Kutsher*, edited by Gad B. Sarfatti, 110–25. Ramat Gan, Israel: Bar-Ilan University Press, 1980 [Hebrew].
Shemesh, Rivkah. "Verbs of Saying in Mishnaic Hebrew: A Syntactic, Semantic and Pragmatic Analysis." Ph.D. diss., Bar-Ilan University, 1998 [Hebrew].
Shimasaki, Katsuomi. *Focus Structure in Biblical Hebrew: A Study of Word Order and Information Structure*. Baltimore: CDL, 2002.
Simon, Moshe. Review of *Talmudic Stories: Narrative Art, Composition, and Culture* by Jeffrey L. Rubenstein and *Woman and Womanhood in the Talmud* by Shulamit Valler, translated by Betty Sigler Rozen, *AJS Review* 26, no. 1 (2002): 129–131.
Sklare, David E. *Samuel ben Hofni Gaon and His Cultural World: Texts and Studies*. Leiden, the Netherlands: Brill, 1996.
Smith, Barbara Herrnstein. "Narrative Versions, Narrative Theories." In *On Narrative*, edited by W. J. T. Mitchell, 209–32. Chicago: University of Chicago Press, 1980.

Smith, Morton. "On the History of the Divine Man." In *Paganisme, judaïsme, christianisme: Influences et affrontements dans le monde antique: Mélanges offerts à Marcel Simon*, 335–45. Paris: De Boccard, 1978.

———. "Palestinian Judaism in the First Century." In *Israel: Its Role in Civilization*. Edited by Moshe Davis, 67–81. New York: Seminary Israel Institute of the Jewish Theological Seminary of America, 1956.

———. "Prolegomena to a Discussion of Aretalogies, Divine Men, the Gospels and Jesus." *Journal of Biblical Literature* 90 (1971): 174–99.

———. *Tannaitic Parallels to the Gospels*. Journal of Biblical Literature Monograph Series. Philadelphia: Society for Biblical Literature, 1951.

Smith, Paul J., dir. "Bunco Busters." *Woody Woodpecker*. Universal City, CA: Universal International, 1955. Film, 6 min.

Soloveitchik, Joseph B. "Majesty and Humility." *Tradition* 17, no. 2 (1978): 25–37.

Sonsino, Rifat. "Motive Clauses in Hebrew Law Biblical Forms and Near Eastern Parallels." Ph.D. diss., University of Pennsylvania, 1975.

Stein, Peter. *Regulae Iuris: From Juristic Rules to Legal Maxims*. Edinburgh: Edinburgh University Press, 1966.

———. *Roman Law in European History*. Cambridge, UK: Cambridge University Press, 1999.

Steiner, Wendy. *Pictures of Romance: Form against Content in Painting and Literature*. Chicago: University of Chicago Press, 1988.

Steinmetz, Devora. "Agada Unbound: Inter-Agadic Characterization of Sages in the Bavli and Implications for Reading Agada." In *Creation and Composition: The Contribution of the Bavli Redactors (Stammaim) to the Aggada*, edited by Jeffrey L. Rubenstein, 293–337. Tübingen, Germany: Mohr Siebeck, 2005.

Stern, David. "Aggadah." In *Contemporary Jewish Religious Thought: Original Essays on Critical Concepts, Movements, and Beliefs*, edited by Arthur A. Cohen and Paul Mendes-Flohr, 7–12. New York: Scribner's, 1987.

———. *Parables in Midrash: Narrative and Exegesis in Rabbinic Literature*. Cambridge, MA: Harvard University Press, 1991.

Stern, Sacha. *Calendar and Community: A History of the Jewish Calendar Second Century B.C.E.– Tenth Century C.E.* Oxford: Oxford University Press, 2001.

———. *Jewish Identity in Early Rabbinic Writings*. Leiden, the Netherlands: Brill, 1994.

Sternberg, Meir. *Poetics of Biblical Narrative: Ideological Literature and the Drama of Reading*. Bloomington: Indiana University Press, 1985.

Stone, Suzanne Last. "On the Interplay of Rules, 'Cases' and Concepts in Rabbinic Legal Literature: Another Look at the Aggadot of Honi the Circle-Drawer." *Diné Yisrael* 24 (2006): *125–56.

Suleiman, Susan Rubin. *Authoritarian Fictions: The Ideological Novel as a Literary Genre*. Princeton, NJ: Princeton University Press, 1993.

Sussman, Yaakov. "The History of Halacha and the Dead Sea Scrolls: Preliminary Observations on Miqsat Ma'ase Ha-Torah (4QMMT)." *Tarbiz* 59 (1990): 11–76 [Hebrew].

———. "'Oral Law' Taken Literally: The Power of the Point of a Yod." In *Mehqerei Talmud III: Talmudic Studies Dedicated in Memory of Professor Ephraim E. Urbach*, edited by Yaakov Sussman and David Rosenthal, 209–384. Jerusalem: Magnes, 2005.

———, ed. *Talmud Yerushalmi According to Ms. Or. 4720 (Scal. 3) of the Leiden University Library with Restorations and Corrections*. Jerusalem: Academy of the Hebrew Language, 2001.

Talmon, Shemaryahu. "Between Scripture and Mishnah: The World of Qumran from Within." In *Megilot Midbar-Yehudah, arbaim shenot mehkar*, edited by Magen Broshi, Shemaryahu Talmon, Sara Japhet, and Daniel Schwartz, 10–48. Jerusalem: Bialik, 1992 [Hebrew].

———. "Calendars and Mishmarot." In *Encyclopedia of the Dead Sea Scrolls*, edited by Lawrence H. Shiffman and James C. VanderKam, 108–16. New York: Oxford University Press, 2000.

Thornton, T. C. G. "The Samaritan Calendar: A Source of Friction in New Testament Times." *Journal of Theological Studies*, n.s., 42, no. 2 (1991): 577–80.

Tiede, David Lenz. *The Charismatic Figure as Miracle Worker*. SBL Dissertation Series. Missoula, MT: Society of Biblical Literature, 1972.

Tolstoy, Leo. *Anna Karenina*. Translated by Joel Carmichael. New York: Bantam, 1960.
Tropper, Amram. *Wisdom, Politics, and Historiography: Tractate Avot in the Context of the Graeco-Roman Near East*. Oxford Oriental Monographs. Oxford: Oxford University Press, 2004.
Urbach, Ephraim E. *Collected Writings in Jewish Studies*. Edited by Robert Brody and Moshe D. Herr. Jerusalem: Hebrew University Magnes Press, 1999.
———. *The Halakhah: Its Sources and Development*. Translated by Raphael Posner. Givataim, Israel: Yad la-Talmud, 1986.
———. *The Sages: Their Concepts and Beliefs*. Translated by Israel Abrahams. Jerusalem: Magnes, 1975.
Valler, Shulamit. *Women and Womanhood in the Talmud*. Translated by Betty Sigler Rozen. Brown Judaica Studies. Atlanta: Scholars Press, 1999.
Vermes, Geza. *Jesus the Jew*. New York: Macmillan, 1973.
Wacholder, Ben Zion. "Tales about Rabban Gamaliel in the Mishnah and Tosefta." In *Fourth World Congress of Jewish Studies: Papers*, vol. 1, 143–44. Jerusalem: World Union of Jewish Studies, 1967 [Hebrew].
Walfish, Avraham. "Literary Method of Redaction in the Mishnah Based on Tractate *Rosh Hashana*." Ph.D. diss., Hebrew University, 2001 [Hebrew].
———. "The Poetics of the Mishnah." In *The Mishnah in Contemporary Perspective*, edited by Alan J. Avery-Peck and Jacob Neusner, 153–89. Handbuch der Orientalistik Abt. 1, Der Nahe und der Mittlere Osten. Leiden, the Netherlands: Brill, 2006.
Watson, Alan. *The Making of the Civil Law*. Cambridge, MA: Harvard University Press, 1981.
Watts, James W. "Rhetorical Strategy in the Composition of the Pentateuch." *Journal for the Study of the Old Testament* 68 (1995): 3–22.
Weinfeld, M. "The Origin of the Apodictic Law." *Vetus Testamentum* 23, no. 1 (1973): 63–75.
Weiss, Ze'ev. "The Location of the *Sheliah Tzibbur* during Prayer." *Cathedra* 55 (1990): 8–21 [Hebrew].
Wimpfheimer, Barry. " 'But It Is Not So': Toward a Poetics of Legal Narrative in the Babylonian Talmud." *Prooftexts* 24 (2004): 51–86.
———. *Narrating the Law: A Poetics of Talmudic Legal Stories*. Philadelphia: University of Pennsylvania Press, 2011.
———. "Talmudic Legal Narrative: Broadening the Discourse of Jewish Law." *Diné Yisrael* 24 (2007): *157–196.
Yaron, Reuven. *The Laws of Eshnunna*. Jerusalem: Magnes, 1969.
Yassif, Eli. *The Hebrew Folktale: History, Genre, Meaning*. Folklore Studies in Translation. Bloomington: Indiana University Press, 1999.

CITATION INDEX: MISHNAH, TOSEFTA, YERUSHALMI AND BAVLI

(for other sources see main index)

Mishnah
Berakhot 1:1, 1, 39
Berakhot 1:3, 249n10
Berakhot 1:9, 240n5
Berakhot 1:11, 54–58
Berakhot 5:1, 255n70
Berakhot 5:5, 133, 255n70
Shevi'it 4:1, 201
Ma'aserot 1:8, 256n98
Ma'aser Sheni 2:5, 260n15
Shabbat 1:1, 36
Shabbat 1:2, 41
Shabbat 1:3, 31
Shabbat 1:4, 53
Shabbat 1:10, 31
Shabbat 1:9, 42
Shabbat 2:4, 34
Shabbat 2:7, 33
Shabbat 3:2, 35
Shabbat 3:4, 32, 47, 111
Shabbat 5:7, 42
Shabbat 6:8, 31
Shabbat 6:9, 240n5
Shabbat 7:2, 28
Shabbat 9:5, 37
Shabbat 12:1, 35
Shabbat 12:4, 35
Shabbat 13:4, 28
Shabbat 13:6, 35, 37
Shabbat 14:2, 31
Shabbat 14:4, 28, 29
Shabbat 15:2, 28, 29, 33, 242n67
Shabbat 16:1, 32
Shabbat 16:2, 29, 35, 37
Shabbat 16:7, 111–112
Shabbat 16:8, 35, 37, 46, 70
Shabbat 17:1, 32
Shabbat 17:2, 31
Shabbat 19:1, 242n67

Shabbat 19:2, 38
Shabbat 21:2, 35, 38
Shabbat 22:3, 33
Shabbat 22:4, 111–112
Shabbat 23:3, 242n67
'Eruvin 10:8, 46
'Eruvin 10:10
'Eruvin 4:1, 252n17
'Eruvin 4:4
Pesahim 5:5–7, 43
Pesahim 6:5, 51
Pesahim 7:1–2, 68
Pesahim 7:2, 45, 46
Sheqalim 1:2, 200
Sheqalim 6:1–2, 216
Yoma 2:1–2, 49, 209
Sukkah 2:1, 143
Sukkah 2:5, 139
Sukkah 2:7, 4, 146
Sukkah 2:8, 141
Sukkah 2:9, 140, 148
Sukkah 3:8, 127
Sukkah 3:9, 124
Sukkah 3:12, 195
Sukkah 4:4, 214
Sukkah 4:9, 11, 211
Betza 2:6, 126
Rosh Hashanah 1–2, 169ff.
Rosh Hashanah 1:5–6, 177
Rosh Hashanah 1:7, 181
Rosh Hashanah 2:1–2, 48, 201
Rosh Hashanah 2:8, 184–186
Rosh Hashanah 2:9, 186–192
Rosh Hashanah 4:1, 256n3
Rosh Hashanah 4:3, 195
Ta'anit 1:6 254n65
Ta'anit 3:8, 5, 150, 153
Mo'ed Qatan 2:5, 252n17
Mo'ed Qatan 4:6, 256n3
Hagigah 2:2, 248n63
Yevamot 15:2, 242n71

Nazir 5:4, 256n3
Sota 9:9, 201
Bava Metzi'a 5:8, 252n17
Sanhedrin 1:4, 254n53
'Eduyot 1:12–14, 242n71
Avodah Zarah 5, 12
Avot 1:1, 88
Menahot 10:5, 256n3, 261n39
Bekhorot 6:6, 256n3
Tamid 2:1–2, 205
Midot 1:4, 262n68
Midot 2:5, 217
Midot 2:6, 262n68
Kelim 5:10, 4
Kelim 9:2, 242n71
'Ohalot 1:3, 244n29
'Ohalot 5:3–4, 242n71
Yadayim 4:4, 256n3

Tosefta
Shabbat 3:3, 260n24
Shabbat 13:14, 245n38
Yoma 1:10, 261n49
Yoma 1:12, 206–207
Sukkah 2:4, 148
Sukkah 2:10, 128
Sukkah 3:16, 212
Sukkah 3:18, 118
Rosh Hashanah 1:5, 203
Rosh Hashanah 2:1, 258n41
Rosh Hashanah 2:9 260n18
Rosh Hashanah 2:18, 259n52
Ta'anit 2:1, 160, 258n41
Sota 13:1, 217
Makot 2:1, 158
Shevu'ot 1:4, 261n40
'Eduyot 1:1, 245n11
Negaim 8:3, 251n50

Yerushalmi
Shabbat 16:18, 81b, 115
'Eruvin 4:4, 21d–22a, 103, 104
Pesahim 7:2, 34b, 69
Sheqalim 1:2, 46a, 26 n23
Yoma 1:5, 39a, 262n55

Yoma 2:2, 39d, 261n40
Sukkah 2:1, 53a, 254n41
Sukkah 3:13, 54a, 260n12
Sukkah 4:6, 20b, 118
Sukkah 4:8, 45d, 262n55
Rosh Hashanah 1:6, 57b, 180
Rosh Hashana 2:1, 58a, 261n34
Rosh Hashanah 2:7, 58b, 258n35, 36
Rosh Hashanah 2:8, 58b, 259n53
Ta'anit 3:10, 66d, 256n102
Sota 8:3, 22c, 262n69
Sanhedrin 2:2, 19d 261n44

Bavli
Berakhot, 23a, 242n65
Berakhot, 60a, 255n72
Shabbat, 39b, 114
Shabbat, 122a, 245n39
'Eruvin 45a, 99–102
Pesachim 74a, 244 n28
Yoma 22a, 261n49
Yoma 23a, 261n45
Yoma 53b, 217
Sukkah 48b, 118
Sukkah 39b, 129
Sukkah 26b, 135n18
Sukkah 21b, 254n40
Sukkah 26b, 140n28
Sukkah 27b, 254n47
Sukkah 28b, 253n31
Sukkah 29a, 149
Sukkah 37a, 251n54
Sukkah 48b, 262n54, n55
Ta'anit 22b, 255n72
Ta'anit 23a, 163, 254n56, 255n87
Rosh Hashanah 16b, 254n47
Rosh Hashanah 22a, 257n24
Rosh Hashanah 24a, 258n36
Rosh Hashanah 25a, 259n52
Gittin 55b–56b 248n61
Bava Metzi'a 59a–60a, 3–4
Zevahim 62a, 262n52
Horayot 12a, 262n69
Keritot 5b, 262n69

SUBJECT INDEX

A
adverbial phrases, 32–33
aggadah 2–3, 235n5, 235n6
  reworking, 99, 105, 144
Albeck, Hanoch, 60, 216–218, 230, 242n75, 263n6
Alexander, Elizabeth Shanks, 97, 98, 244n24
Alon, Gedaliah, 5, 213, 244n30
Alt, Albrecht, 245n3
altar
  cleaning race, 205–207, 210–212
  damage to, 212–213
altar, murder at, 205–210
'amar, 50–51, 242n67
Amitai, Ori, 256n100
Amoraim, xiv, 135
anecdotes, 3, 84–85, 224–225
  and dialog, 247n52
  exegetical, 89
  and frames, 87
  rabbi portrayals, 85, 252n12
anshe ma'aseh, see hasidim (anshei ma'aseh)
apodictic approach to law, *see* law, apodictic approach
apodictic formulations, *see* formulations, apodictic
apodictic statements, *see* statements, apodictic
protasis and apodosis, 34, 36–38, 41
  double-ended, 125, 146
  narrativity chart (Chart 3.1), 26
Aqiba, R., 68, 69, 124, 188
  and R. Gamliel, 177–180, 185
  and R. Joshua, 189, 190
  and R. Judah the Baker, 180
  new moon, 177–180
  Yom Kippur date, 189–190
Aristotle, 82, 238n5, 238n8
Ark of the Covenant, 216–218, 262n69
Auerbach, Erich, 110
authority, 11, 244n19
  charismatic and supernatural, 132–137
  competing models, 138
  divine, 149
  "in" and "an," 65, 171
  judicial, 223–224
  Mishnaic, 230
  negative, 142
authority, rabbinic, 87, 114, 229–231, 244n19, 251n3, 253n25
  calendar court (Yavne), 185–186, 259n43
  and halakhah, priestly, 182–183
  ideology, 90–91
  and learning, 137, 192
  limits of, 154
  and narrative approach, 132
  and power, 192
  rational, 150
  sources of, 71, 191
  and stories, etiological, 194–195
  Tannaitic case stories, 121
Avot, Pirkei, 75–76, 88
Azar, Moshe, 30, 36, 241n39

B
Babylonian Talmud. *see* Bavli
Bakhtin, Mikhail, 62, 63, 226, 243n13
baraita-Mishnah relationship, 213
baraitot, xiv,109–111
  altar fall, 261n36
  counter-narratives, 118
  Sabbath limit story, 99–111
  water libation ritual, 118
Bar Kokhba revolt, 61
Baron, Salo W., 236n14
Barthes, Roland, 239n13
Baumgarten, Albert I, 257n12
Bavli, 129, 252n17
  Aqiba-Gamliel conflict, 180
  discourse, 262n5
  Honi Hame'agel, 163–164
  stringencies, 135
  sukkah dwelling, 253n31
  sukkah stories, eating and drinking, 140

water libation ritual, 118, 261n54
  Yom Kippur date, 259n52
beit midrash stories, 24, 27, 52–54, 56–57
Ben-Amos, Dan, 237n19
Benveniste, Emil, 239n13
Ben-Yishai, Ayelet, 243n16
Bereshit Rabba, 256n106
Berger, Michael, 244n19
Berkowitz, Beth, 11
Bernstein, Moshe J, 247n58
Bertinoro, Obadiah, 255n75, 258n36, 259n2
Bible, 10, 84, 89, 90, 247n55
"Bible, rewritten," 247n58, 261n48
Binder, Guyora, 17
Bitman, Avigdor, 253n32
Boethusians, 120, 212, 260n31
  calendar, 203
  water libation, 212–213, 261n54
Bolinger, Dwight, 30, 240n18
Booth, Wayne, 251n49
Borges, Jorge Louis, 41
Boyarin, Daniel, 11
Breuer, Yohanan, 44
Brooks, Peter, 9
Brown, Peter, 136, 137
Bruner, Jerome 244n21

C
calendar, 171, 257n14, 257n26, 258n32
calendar court (Jerusalem), 170, 171, 181–183, 203
calendar court (Yavne), 170–180, 183–186, 257n26
  divine mandate, 187
  establishment, 193
  R. Joshua vs. R. Gamliel, 186–193
  procedures, 185–186
  witnesses, 183–188
  Yom Kippur date, 188–193
calendar setting, 190, 257n12, 257n13
calendar split, 258n32
calendar threats, 188, 203, 209
case law, 67, 82–83, 224
  see also law, common
cases, hypothetical, 31, 36, 38, 44, 47, 48
  see also irrealis texts
  gangplank story, 54
  Sabbath limit, 71–72
  Sabbath work, 113
case stories, 10–11, 47–48, 75, 176–193, 228
  destabilization, 115
  double-ended, 167, 169–170, 176–179
  patterns, 176–177
  possible readings, 193
  witnesses, 183–187
  halakhic value, 85
  ma'aseh, 46
  pre-Destruction Jerusalem, 180–182
  rabbinic conflicts, 169, 177–180
  repetitions, 169
  structure, 48, 114
  sukkahs, 138, 142
  witness presentation, 176
stories, etiological, 10–11, 48, 194–219, 229, 253n25
casuistic formulations, *see* formulations, casuistic
causality, 17, 238n3, 238n8
chamber of wood, *see* wood storeroom
change, halakhic, 86
change, legal, 195, 198
change, ritual, 262n66
  adultery rituals, 201
  lulav ritual, 201, 262n66
  lulav ritual, Shabbat, 214–216
  new moon sanctification, 170
Chatman, Seymour, 41
Chavel, Simeon, 245n38, 246n25
chriai, 133, 134, 252n13
civil law, *see* law, civil
clauses, if and when, 75
clauses, nonverbal, 25–28, 36, 37, 38, 58
clauses, verbal, 25–27, 29–30, 37
Cohen, Shaye, 119, 121, 122, 132, 172
common law, *see* law, common
continuity, Jewish
  calendar, 171
  and Destruction, 199–200
  halakhah, 86
  and post-Destruction narrative, 198
Corpus Iuris Civilis, *see* Digest, Justinian's
counter-narratives 117–129
  calendar, 171–203
  contemporary historians, 119
  internal sources, 123–124, 129
  Josephus, Flavius, 118
  knobbed bolt, 124, 127
  lulav binding, 128–129
  post-Destruction, 121–122
  rabbinic dominance, 120–122
  Shabbat counter-narratives, 123–124
  signal fires 260n31
  Temple control, 121
  water libation ritual 118, 119
  R. Yohanan ben Hahoroni, 147
covenant at Sinai. *see* Sinai, covenant at
Cover, Robert, 9, 64, 84, 205, 247n51
Cox, Patricia, 251n5, 252n12
crisis narratives, 90, 194, 204
Culler, Jonathan, 237n26
cuneiform legal codes, *see* legal codes, cuneiform
Cutheans, 48, 202, 203

D
Damascus document, 74, 78–80, 89
Daube, David, 74, 75, 255n88
  Honi Hame'agel, 154–155, 255n84, 255n89
Dead Sea Scrolls, 74, 78–80, 223

Subject Index

Destruction, xiii, 44, 86, 90, 119–120, 260n16
   crisis narratives, 204–205
   and master narrative, 89, 198, 199–200
   rabbinic narrative, 120, 248n61
   and ritual crisis, 196
   "spiritual decline," 20, 208–209
DeVries, Benjamin, 28
diachronic approach, 106–107
dialects, 63, 64
dialog, 21–22, 33, 51–52, 67, 226–227, 231
   and anecdotes, 247n52
   gentile Sabbath work, 70–72
   paschal sacrifice, 69–70
   and story, 52
   unresolved, 229
   Yom Kippur date, 189
dialogic texts. *see* texts, dialogic
Digest, Justinian's, 80–81, 87, 92, 223
discourse, aggadic, 106
discourse, authoritative, 96, 177, 230–231
discourse, halakhic, 3–4, 7, 9–11, 176
   in dialog, 49
   and *ma'aseh*, 95
   storytelling complexity, 116
   strategies, 110
discourse, hypothetical, 46
discourse, legal, 65, 82, 134, 176
discourse, Mishnaic, 230
discourse, modes, 9, 11, 161, 223
discourse, narrative, 2, 8, 22, 176, 220
discourse, in Talmuds, 227, 262n5
Discourse on the Dicta of the Sages, 4
Dosa ben Harkinas, R., 187–190, 259n43
dynamism, 16–17, 18, 27, 28, 29, 168, 220
   see also narrativity, specificity
   '*amar*, 51
   formulations, casuistic, 35
   in law, 64
   onetime events, 45
   of prohibitions, 32
   story threshold, 52

E

Eagleton, Terry, 237n26
eglah arufah, 201, 208
Elbaum, Jacob, 235n5, 235n6
Eleazar, 57, 125
Eleazar ben Azariah, 42
Eliezer, 2, 4, 51, 52
Elijah, 164, 165, 166, 256n106
Elman, Yaakov, 80
enactments, rabbinic, 218–219, 228, 259n3, 259n5
   see also taqqanot
ending, false, 179, 185
Epstein, J.N., 60, 242n74, 242n75, 243n11, 253n31, 259n53, 263n6
   R. Gamliel and R. Joshua, 192
   Mishnah as code, 230

Eshnunna, Laws of, 74, 75, 79, 223
Essenes, 182, 203, 258n32, 260n31
etiological stories. *see* stories, etiological
etrog pelting, 118–119, 211–212, 213
events, 17, 127, 222, 238n6, 241n40
events, narrativity, 42
events, one-time, 45
events, repeated, 27, 42–44, 47, 57–58
   exempla, 126, 144, 184
Ewick, Patricia, 225, 230
exempla, 10–11, 95, 228, 241n55
   and apodictic statements, 47
   challenges, 127, 147
   definition, 46
   definitional, 138
   halakhic value, 72, 85
   marginal cases, 138
   narrativity, 47
   as precedents, 126–127
   problematic (quasi-exempla), 143–146
   rabbis, 46–47, 130, 139–142, 140–141
   transition to stories, 71
exemplars, 134–135
   ambiguous, 141–148
   in classical world, 136–137
   hasidim (anshei ma'aseh), 152
   marginal, 144, 147–148, 150–156
   rabbis as, 139–142
   sukkah cases, 143–146

F

fabula and *syuzhet*, 175, 176, 214, 257n19
Fischel, Henry A., 134, 236n17
Fleischman, Suzanne, 238n6, 239n13, 239n15, 239n17
Fonrobert, Charlotte, 11
forms, apodictic, 58
forms, Mishnaic, 226–227
   Chart 3.1, 26
   dominant, 54
   modal, 30
   negative apodictic, 54
   relationships, 25
   typology and examples, 25
formulations, apodictic, 23–24, 44, 54, 72, 113
   Charts 3.1, 3.2, 26–27
   dynamism, 29, 32
   knobbed bolt (Sabbath prohibition) story 125–126
   and law, 223
   lulav binding, 127–129
   and narrative, 75
   prohibitions, 31–32
   Sabbath heating, 112
   specificity, 29, 30–31
   sukkah eating/drinking 140–141
   tendencies 224
   tenses, 30
   Torah law, 77

formulations, casuistic, 25, 34, 48–74, 244n24
  fast days, 151
  gentile Sabbath work, 71–72
  narrativity, 34–35
  post facto case, 41
  Sabbath prohibitions, 58, 125–126
  sukkah dwelling 143
  Torah law, 77
Forster, E.M., 16–17, 18, 22, 238n2, 238n3
Fraade, Steven, 78, 79
Fraenkel, Jonah, 6, 7, 89, 235n4, 237n19
frames and framing stories, 76, 83, 84–85, 97–98
  and anecdotes, 87
  Damascus document, 79
  etiological, 86, 194
  hegemonic, 224–225
  implicit, 90–91, 230
  in Near Eastern law, 84
  Pirkei Avot, 88
  Second Temple period, 90
  Torah, 84
Frankel, Zacharias, 60
Frankfurter, David, 251n3
Friedman, Shamma, 97–98, 105, 128, 236n17, 254n53, 259n5

G
Gaballa, G.A., 19
Gafni, Isaiah, 171
Gaius, 80–81, 83
Gallagher, Catherine, 237n26
Gamliel, R.
  and R. Aqiba, 185
  authority of, 69, 71–72, 229
  Bavli, 252n17
  calendar court (Yavne), 170–171, 173, 184
  descendants, 257n26
  and R. Dosa ben Harkinas, 259n43
  evening Shema narrative, 1
  as exemplar, 69, 124, 135, 139–141, 143–144
  gangplank story, 46–47, 70–72
  R. Joshua vs. R. Gamliel, 186–193
  knobbed bolt story, 125
  new moon, 170–180
  as paradigmatic authority
  paschal sacrifice, 45–46, 68–70
  power, political, 186, 189, 191, 257n26
  precedent, narrative, 126–129
  pre-Sabbath practice, 58
  prostrations, ritual, 216
  sukkah, 140–141, 143, 145
  Tosefta-gangplank story, 245n38
  witnesses, 183–186, 259n43
  and R. Yohanan ben Nuri, 185–186
  Yom Kippur date, 188–193, 259n52
gangplank story, 46–47, 70–72, 245n38

Genette, Gerard, 257n19
Genizah fragments, 259n53
genres, 3, 10, 46, 49, 75
  and *chriae*, 133
  halakhic value, 85–86
  heterogeneous, 215–216
  in law, 66
  ma'asim, 95
  Temple violence narrative, 204
  transformation, 103, 105–106, 249n17
gentile sabbath work, 70–72
Geonim, 3, 235n6
Gilat, Yitshak D., 244n24
Goldberg, Abraham, 60, 241n40, 242n75, 253n32, 261n35
Goldberg, Arnold, 11, 241n54, 242n65
Goldin, Judah, 255n84, 255n85
Goodblatt, David, 251n46
Goodman, Martin, 172, 250n40
Green, William Scott, 255n82
Greenblatt, Stephen, 237n26

H
Habakkuk, 165
Hadas, Moses, 251n5
halakhah
  and aggadah, 2–4
  antinarrative character, 41
  and charisma, 155
  as discourse, 72
  etiology, 194
  formulations, apodictic, 229
  narrative view, 229
  rabbinic, 259n43
  rabbis as embodiment, 130
  realis and irrealis presentation, 45
  and stories, 2, 86
  transmission, 52
halakhah, priestly, 258n32, 259n43, 261n54
  calendar conflict, 182, 258n32
  rules and processes, 183
halakhic agendas, 117
halakhic context, 7–8
halakhic events, 127
halakhic rulings, *see* rulings, halakhic
halakhic thinking, 28
Halivni, David, 243n11
Hallo, William W., 75
Hammurabi, code of, 74, 76, 223, 245n4
  see also law, Near Eastern
Hananiah ben Hezekiah ben Garon, R. 53, 56, 58
Haninah ben Dosa, R. 133, 135
Hannanel, R. 249n19
Hanniah, R. 216
haqotel form (one who...), 35, 54
Hasan Rokem, Galit, 238n37

Subject Index

hasidim (anshei ma'aseh), 135, 151–152
  ambiguities, 155
  narrative difficulties, 155
  Tosefta *Ta'anit*, 160–162
Hauptman, Judith, 97, 98, 105, 128,
  248n5, 259n5
Hayes, Christine, 262n5
hegemonic tales, 225, 227
heifer's neck (*eglah arufah*), 201, 208
Henshke, David, 190, 259n53
Herring, Basil, 239n17
Herring, Susan, 239n17
heteroglossia, 62–63
Hezser, Catherine, 11, 80
Hillel, 4, 88
Hillel, school of, 52, 53, 54, 56, 58, 253n25
  normative practices, 253n32
  sukkah visit, 146–148
  Tannaitic material, 253n32
Hillel of Verona, 5
historical critics, 60
Hittite documents, 76
Hittite laws, 74, 245n4
Hoffman, David Z., 60, 242n2
holy men, 132–133, 134, 136, 251n5
Honi Hame'agel, 130, 229, 255n84,
  256n102
  Bavli *Ta'anit*, 163–166
  and Elijah, 256n106
  text evolution, 150, 156, 162, 165
  and God, 155, 165
  Hillel of Verona, 5
  illustrative exemplum, 149–151
  Josephus, Flavius, 156–157,162
  magic, 255n85
  Megillat Ta'anit, 157–159
  Mishnah *Ta'anit* narrative, 149–156
  performative traditions, 165
  plot elements, 162
  prayer, 165
  rabbinic boundaries, 5,138, 164, 254n65,
    256n95
  in rabbinic commentary, 5, 255n84
  as rabbinic exemplar, 135
  rainmaking, 149–159
    variants, 159, 166
  and sages, 151–152
  scholium of *Megillat Ta'anit*, 157–159, 162
  R. Simeon ben Shetah, 153–154, 165
  R. Simeon the Just, 158–160
  as "sinner," 154–155, 255n89
  Tosefta *Ta'anit* narrative, 161, 162
  wise man depiction, 133
  Yerushalmi *Ta'anit* 163
hypothetical narratives, *see* cases, hypothetical

I
ideology, 230, 231
illustrative approach, 113

Institutes of Gaius, 80
irrealis texts, 20, 23, 25, 41, 113
  Chart 3.1, 26
  qatal forms, 35

J
Jacob, R., 100, 101, 102, 103, 104
Jaffee, Martin, 86, 97, 98, 259n3, 259n5
  lulav ritual, 196, 198
  taqqanot, 259n3, 259n5
Janneus, Alexander, 118–119, 213
Jas, Remko, 75
Javolenus, 83
Jepthah, 259n52
Jerusalem, 128–129, 213
  Ark of the Covenant, 217–218
  calendar, 170–172, 181–182,
    203–204
  rain, 153–157, 161
  Toviah the physician, 181
Josephus, Flavius, 120, 121
  Antiquities, 89, 118, 119
  etrog pelting, 118–119, 213
  Honi Hame'agel, 156–157,162
  Janneus, Alexander, 118–119, 213
  Passover riots, 262n57
  Temple gates, 262n68
Joshua, R, 51, 52, 76, 88, 124–125
  and R. Gamliel, 186–193
  Yom Kippur date, 188–193, 259n52
Josiah, King, 217
Judah, R, 44, 101–111, 117, 123
  as exemplar, 143–144
  and R. Gamliel, 257 n26, 257n26
  kil'ayim (mixed crops), 200
  law, Roman, 57
  lulav binding, 127–128
  Sabbath limit, 101–110
Judah Hanasi, R., xiii, 171
Judah the Baker, R., 180
Justinian's *Digest*, 82, 87, 92, 223

K
Kehati, Pinhas, xv, 242n74, 242n75
Kellog, Robert, 107
Kern, Fritz, 198
Kil'ayim (mixed crops), 200–201, 260n21,
  260n22
knobbed bolt story, 125–127

L
Labov, William, 15
Laebo, 83
law, apodictic approach, 64–65, 66,
  223–224, 225
law, civil, 64–65, 243n17
law, common, 65
  see also case law
law, literary forms and, 67

law, Mesopotamian, 10, 73, 76, 245n6
  see also Eshnunna, Laws of; Hammurabi, code of; law, Near Eastern
law, Mishnaic, 66–67
law, narrativity in, impact, 66
law, Near Eastern, 73, 91–92, 245n4
  contextualization, 76
  cuneiform codes, 74, 75, 79, 223
  frames, 76, 84
  formulations, 79
law, Roman, 10, 73, 91–92
  anecdotes, 84
  case law, 82–83
  case stories, 87
  clause types (if and when), 74–75
  dialogic texts, debates, 82–83
  heterogeneity, 80–81
  juristic principles, 82
  narrative approach, 223–224
  narrativity, 81–83
law, synthetic approach, 66
law, Torah, 73
  and cuneiform codes, 77
  narrativity, 77, 78
  Near Eastern formulations in, 79
  realis texts, 77
law, transmission, 24, 41
law and narrative, 8–9, 64–67, 223, 238n30, 246n25, 247n51
  in conflict, 205
law and order, 226
laws, Hittite, 74, 75, 76, 245n4
Laws of Eshnunna. see Eshnunna, Laws of
Levine, Baruch A., 75
Levine, David, 134
Levinson, Joshua, 5, 90, 235n9, 236n14, 237n19
Lieberman, Saul, xv, 203, 258n36
Lifshitz, Berachyahu, 235n4
Lod, 178, 208, 209
lulav ritual, 214–216, 259n2, 260n12
  taqqanah, 196–197, 262n66

M

Ma'aseh, 24, 95, 113, 241n54
  and beit midrash stories, 53
  case stories, 46
  content, 49
  exempla, 46–47
  forms, 194
  genres, 49, 95
  narrativity, strains of 53
  stories, etiological, 46, 49, 242n65
  use of, 45–46
Mackenzie, R.A.F., 77, 245n4
Maimonides, Abraham, 4, 5
Maimonides, Moses, xv, 5, 249n19, 255n75, 259n53
  aggadah, 3
  Honi Hame'agel, 5, 255n75

lulav ritual, 259n2
new moon, 258n36
  Sabbath limit story, 249n19, 249n20
  witnesses, 186
  Yohanan ben Nuri vs. Gamliel, 186
mashal (parable), 148–149, 162
master narrative, 78, 84, 227–228
  authority for, 90
  collective impact, 230
  competing claims, 88–89
  Destruction, 247n60
  extensions and transformations, 89
  framework, 95–96
  new moon sanctification, 171
  and text, 247n52
Megillat Ta'anit, 157–159
Meir, 68–69, 101–102, 106, 108–109, 128–129
Melammed, E.Z., 11, 241n54
messengers, 174
midrash, 3, 89, 135, 237n19, 247n60, 259n5
Miller, J. Hillis, 165, 166, 175, 222
mimetic detail, 109, 114
miracle workers, 134, 229, 251n5, 252n12
  Christian, 136
  as exemplars, 135
  Honi Hame'agel, 154
  in Talmuds, 135
Mishnah
  characteristics, 79
  contents, 226
  creation, xiii, 243n9
  as dialogic text, 10, 67–72
  forms, 61, 62
  narrative range, 10
  narrativity, 10, 62, 92
  prehistory, 62, 243n11, 252n13
  and Roman law, 80
  structure, xiii, xiv, 243n10
  Torah frame, 87
  and Tosefta, 259n5
Mishnah-baraita comparisons, 102–106
Mishor, Mordehay, 31, 240n29, 241n39
modal forms, see *qatal* forms
Moscovitz, Leib, 28, 29, 244n24
Moses, 75, 78, 88, 191
motive clauses, 77–78

N

Nadab and Abihu, 190, 218
Naeh, Shelomo, 248n4
narrative, 49, 88–89, 107
  see also stories
  Biblical, 88–89
  as construct, 129
  definition, 16, 17, 238n3, 238n5
  hegemonic use, 247n51
  narrators, 239n17
  negative, 34

Subject Index

ordering, 168
  in rulings, 38
  tenses, 239n13, 239n17
  terminology, 257n19
  theoretical framework, 220–221
  as tool, 129
  voice, 116
narrative, didactic, 107–108
narrative, halakhic, 4, 8
narrative, master, *see* master narrative
narrative, ritual, 42–43
  apodictic statements, 44
  and etiological stories, 216
  nature of, 44
  new moon witnesses, 181–184
  paschal sacrifice, 43–44
  use of *qotel* vs. *qatal*, 44
  Temple, 204–219
narrative and law, 247n51
see also law and narrative
narrative approaches, 116
narrative crafting, 107–109, 173–176, 261n36
narrative forms, 54
narratives, actual events, *see* texts, realis
narratives, hypothetical, *see* texts, irrealis
narratives, subversive, 225
  see also counter-narratives
narrative shifts, 215
narrative strategy, *see* strategy, narrative
narrative structure, 36, 47, 247n53
  categories, 227–228
  in law, 64, 224
  theory and methods, 221–222
narrativity, 10, 25, 32, 55–57, 220
  see also dynamism, specificity
  adverbial phrases, 32–33
  axis of, 23
  characteristics, 20–22
  clauses, nonverbal, 37
  clause types (if and when), 75
  definition, 16, 220–221
  events, repeated, 42
  formulations, casuistic, 34
  legal texts, 28, 64, 65–66, 75
  Mishnaic sources, 53
  multiple paths, 38, 38–40
  Near Eastern law, 75
  "Rabbi X" "debates," 50
  range, 23–24, 26
  Shabbat stories, 58
  in Torah, 78
  word order, 32
narrativity, range of, 54–58
narrators, 230, 251n49
Near Eastern law, *see* law, Near Eastern
Neusner, Jacob, 6, 60, 61, 91, 236n17, 243n7, 243n9
new moon, 170, 258n36
  see also calendar; Gamliel
  fabula/sjuzhet tension, 176
  R. Gamliel, 258n36
  master narrative, 171
  narrative path, 174
  Stern, Sacha, on 258n40
  terminology, 258n39
  Tiferet Yisrael, 258n39
Noam, Vered, 157
Noy, Dov, 237n19

O

'omer and *'amar*, 50–51
onetime events, 21, 27, 45–48, 70, 95
Onias and Aristobulus, 157
orality theories, 97, 98
oven of Akhnai, 3–4
Oxford scholium, 157–159, 160

P

paideia, 136–137
Palestinian Talmud, *see* Yerushalmi
parable (*mashal*), 148–149, 152
parallel texts, 97, 98
Parma scholium, 129, 157–158, 256n95, 256n102
paschal sacrifice, 43–44, 45, 51–52, 69–70
paschal sacrifice, roasting, 68–70, 244n28, 244n29, 244n30
Passover observance, 77
paths, multiple, 38, 55, 57, 58, 71
patriarchate, 132, 251n46, 172
Paul, Shalom, 75
performative approach, 97–99, 106, 129, 136, 165–166
Peikta de Rav Kahanah, 256n101
Peters, R.S., 244n19
Pharisees, 133, 133–134, 230, 250n40
  see also Rabbis
  calendar, 173, 182, 203
  counter-narratives, 119–120
  legal system, 182
  as mainstream, 202
  as normative Judaism, 119–120
  and sectarians, 212–213
  water libation, Tosefta, 212
Philo of Alexandria, 89
Pirkei Avot, *see Avot, Pirkei*
post-Destruction period, 244n30
  calendar, 170–172
  counter-narratives, 121–122
  lulav ritual, 195–196
  rabbinic narrative, 121–122
practice, Jewish
  continuity, 198
  and Destruction, 197–199
  migration to synagogue, 198–199

Subject Index

practices, normative, 42
prayer, 151–166
  halakhot on, 152
  Hallel, 165
  hasidim (anshei ma'aseh), 152
  prophetic tradition, 165
prayer times, 1–2
precedent, narrative, 126–129
pre-Sabbath prohibitions, 54–58, 242n74
prescriptive statements, 54, 58
priestly halakhah. *see* halakhah, priestly
priest-Pharisee debates, 182–183
priests
  see also Temple
  altar, 205–209
  Ark of the Covenant, 217
  calendar, 181, 182
  halakhah, priestly, 182, 258n32
  and sects, 212, 261n54
  struck down, 216, 218
  Tosefta *Yoma*, 207–208
  water libation, 211–212
Prince, Gerald, 19
prohibitions, pre-Sabbath, 54, 242n74, 242n75
prohibitions, Sabbath, 54–58, 242n75
proof texts, 190–191
protasis (hypothetical), 34–38, 125, 146–147
  Chart 3.1, 26,
  Chart 3.3, 55
prostrations, ritual, 216–218
protasis and apodosis, 34
pseudostories, 45

Q

qatal, Chart 3.1, 38; 44
qotel, 29–32, 38, 42, 44, 71, 215 240n11
  see also yiqtol; verb forms
  narrativity, Chart 3.1, 26
  narrativity analysis, Chart 3.3, 55–57
  haqotel form (one who...), 34–35, 54
  negative (*qotlim, ein*) 26; 31, 32, 55–57, 240n13
Qumran, 10, 79, 89, 182, 258n32

R

rabbinic authority, *see* authority, rabbinic
rabbinic behavior, 138–166
rabbinic dominance, 120
rabbinic identity, 248n66 rabbinic period, xiii
Rabbis
  see also Pharisees
  in anecdotes, 85
  authority, 131–132, 134–135, 251n31
  congregations, 253n24
  divine inspiration, 137
  as embodiments of law, 86, 130
  exemplars, 135, 139–142, 147–148, 228
    definitional cases, 138
  extreme behaviors, 135–136, 141–143
  halakhic process, 228–229
  historiography, 131
  identifying, 130, 229
  as innovators, 86
  narrative constructs, 131–132
  power, 131–132
  qualities and functions, 130–13,137
  as ritual experts, 132
  Sage stories, 3, 252n13
  and sectarians, 212–213
  stringencies, 135–136, 140–141, 252n17
  as "wise men," 132–135
  world view, 90
"Rabbi X," 50–51
rain, excessive, 151, 152, 255n75
rain, in sukkah, 148–149
rainmaking, 149–166
Rashi, xv, 258n36, 258n39, 259n2
realis forms, 54
realis texts
  frames, 76
  law, Torah, 77
  roles, 76
redaction, 97–99
  of Mishnah, 10, 60–61, 63, 97, 102–103, 106, 123
  conflicting interests, 129
  Honi story, 156–157, 165, 256n4
  techniques, 129
  techniques, 263n6
repetitions, 42, 168, 169, 221–222
representational narrative, 110
rhetorical strategies, 10, 222
  halakhic agendas, 117
Roman law, *see* law, Roman
Rosen-Zvi, Ishai, 11, 242n2, 250n44, 251n45
Rossi, Azariah dei, 5
Roth, Martha, 74, 84
Simeon, R., 145
Rubenstein, Jeffery, 8, 261n54
  water libation ritual, 261n54
rulings, halakhic, 193, 228
  acceptance of, 188
  methods, 53
  presentation, 169
  transmission, 58
rulings, Tannaitic, 187

S

Sabbath limit story, 99–111, 249n9, 249n10
Sabbath rules, 31–34, 38, 112
Sabbath travel, 99, 170, 177–179
sabotage, 78, 174
Sadducees, 120, 261n54
  calendar, 258n32
  water libation, 261n54
Safrai, Samuel, 199, 235n3, 253n32
sage narratives, Tannaitic, 252n13

Subject Index

"Sages, the," *see* Pharisees; rabbis
saints, 135, 137
Samaritans, 89, 174, 203–204
Samely, Alexander, 239n1
Sanhedrin, 132, 251n46
Saperstein, Marc, 235n5
Scholes, Robert E., 107
scholium of *Megillat Ta'anit*, 157–159
Schultz, Fritz, 82
Schwartz, Daniel, 190, 258n32, 259n43
Schwartz, Seth, 121
sectarians, 48, 202–204, 212–213, 260n31, 261n54
  calendar, 203, 205, 258n32
  new moon, 174, 202–203
  Qumran sect, 79
  water libation, 261n54
Seder Olam, 247n60
Segal, M. H., 30, 36
Segal, Michael, 247n58
Shammai, 4, 88, 141–143, 145
  as exemplar, 141–143
  stringency, 142
Shammai, school of, 126, 253n25
  R. Hananiah's chamber rulings, 52–53
  narrativity, 56
  normative practices, 253n32
  rulings formulae, 55–56
  rulings pattern, 54
  sukkah visit, 146–148
  Tannaitic material, 253n32
Sharvit, Shimon, 30, 241n54
Shazkhar head of Gader, 180, 257n26
Shema, evening, 1–2, 57, 235n1
Shemesh, Rivka, 242n66
Shemot Rabba, 256n101
Shimasaki, Katsuomi, 240n24
Sibley, Susan S., 225, 230
Sifra, 258n40, 260n12
Sifrei, 261n40
Simeon, R., 145
  father and son witnesses, 180–181
  as narrator, 143
  new moon witnesses, 182
  priestly position, 182–183
Simeon ben Gamliel, R., 42, 57, 126, 127, 135
Simeon ben Shetah, R., 5, 229, 255n82, 256n100
  Bavli *Ta'anit*, 164, 165, 166
  and Honi Hame'agel, 153–155
  reputation, 255n82
  and Simeon the Just, 158–160
Simeon the Just, R., 158, 159, 256n100
Sinai, covenant at, 87–88, 89, 191, 198, 199
Sklare, David E., 235n6
slaves, 144–146, 181
  see also Tevi the slave
Smith, Morton, 120, 250n40, 251n5
Sonsino, Rifat, 77–78

Sotah ritual, 250n44
specificity, 32–33, 112–113, 168, 220–221, 222
  see also narrativity, dynamism
'amar, 51
  clause types, 27, 75
  and dynamism, 16
  in law, 64
  and narrative, 18–19
  one-time events, 45
  realis texts, 24
  in representational narrative, 109
speech acts, 23, 33, 49–51, 242n66
  beit midrash stories, 24
  clauses, verbal, 58
  form of, 24
  narrativity, 50
statements, anonymous, 50
statements, apodictic, *see* formulations, apodictic
statements, attributed, 50
statements, casuistic (if/then), 23–24
"steady decline" approach, 200, 201, 204, 208
Stein, Peter, 82, 83, 243n17
Steiner, Wendy, 19
Stern, David, 235n8, 235n9
Stern, Sacha, 248n66, 257n12, 257n13, 257n14
  new moon, 258n40
Stone, Suzanne Last, 243n16
stories, 209
  see also narrative
  actual, 36
  case stories, 48
  as community voice, 96
  cuneiform legal codes, 75
  discourse of authority, 96
  exempla as, 47
  frames, 76
  halakhic value, 2
  "message," 227
  roles, 76
stories, definitions, 16, 20, 220, 239n15
stories, didactic, 4
  anecdotes, 86
  concentration, 253n25
  crisis narratives, 204–219
  definitions, 194
  halakhic value, 85–86
  Hittite laws, 75
  Ma'aseh, 46, 242n65
  narrative, ritual, 215–216
  rabbinic history, 86, 218–219
  redaction, 253n25
  "steady decline" approach, 200–202
  structure, 195–196
  and taqqanot, 218–219
  terminology, 48–49
  violence narratives, 204–219
  witness presentation, 167–169
stories, framing, *see* frames and framing stories

Subject Index

story, *see* narrative
story, transition to, 71
storyteller authority, 117
strategy, narrative, 107, 110–111, 168
   Mishnah, 122, 129
   past events, 116–117
strategy, rhetorical, 10, 88–89, 90, 117
stringencies, 142, 252n17
subversive texts, 230. *see* texts, dialogic
sukkah stories, 139–149, 254n47
Suleiman, Susan Rubin, 241n55
Sussman, Yakov, xv, 248n5, 258n32, 260n31
synchronic approach (independent texts), 107, 117

T
Talmud, definitions, xiv
Talmud, Palestinian, *see* Yerushalmi
Talmud, Babylonian, *see* Bavli
Tamid, 261n35
Tanhuma, Midrash, 255n89
Tannaim, xiii, xiv, 98, 121, 135
   specificity, 28–29
   Yoma editing, 261n35
taqqanah
   term, 259n3, 260n21
   water pelting, 211–212
taqqanot, 53, 259n5, 260n21
   see also enactments, rabbinic
   calendar, 204
   crisis narratives, 90, 194, 204, 205
   kil'ayim, 200–201
   law and narrative, 205
   lulav ritual, 196–197, 262n66
   lulav ritual-Shabbat, 215
   reality of, 196–198
   as stopgap, 210
   stories, etiological, 48, 194–219
Tarfon, 100–110, 117, 123, 145, 249n10
Temple
   see also altar, Destruction; altar murder; Destruction
   Ark of the Covenant, 216–218
   disturbance, 218
   etrog pelting, 211–212
   gates, 218, 262n68
   lulav ritual-Shabbat, 214–216
   murder at altar, 206–209
   prostrations, ritual, 216, 217, 262n68
   sudden death, 217, 218
   taqqanot, 210, 211–212, 261n49
   violence, 211–216
   water libation, 211–212
   wood storeroom, 217
Temple control, 120–122
Temple crises, 204, 229
Temple period, 86, 113, 172, 196, 201
Temple ritual, 198, 229, 250n44
Temple violence, 211–216
   Josephus, Flavius, 213
   rabbinic accounts, 212–213
Tevi the slave, 45, 46, 143–145, 229, 254n40, 254n41
texts, diachronic and synchronic, 98–99
texts, dialogic, 10, 63, 67, 91, 226–228, 247n52
texts, irrealis, 20, 23, 25, 36, 41, 71
   beit midrash stories, 53
   narrative, ritual, 44
texts, judicial, 75
texts, legal
   abstraction, 28–29
   anecdotes, 224–225
   framing stories, 224–225
   narrativity, 223–224
   presentations, 223
texts, realis, 20, 23, 42ff
   dynamism, 24
   ma'aseh, 24
   narrative, ritual, 44
   specificity, 24
texts, relationships, 98–99
textual approach, 97–98
Tiberias, 47, 111, 114, 115, 124, 125
Tiede, David Lee, 251n5
Tiferet Yisrael, 258n36
Tolstoy, Lev, 20, 21
topography, historical and textual, 59
Torah law, *see* law, Torah
Tosefta Eduyot 1:1, 245n11
Tosefta, xiv–xv, 212, 217, 245n38, 260n18
   altar murder, 206–209
   counter-narratives, 106, 129
   enactments, rabbinic, 259n5
   Honi Hame'agel, 160–162
   law, Roman, 97
   lulav binding, 128
   and Mishnah, 259n5
   and Mishnah history, 98, 105, 128–129
   redaction, 128–129
   Samaritan calendar, 203–204
   "steady decline" history, 201
   water libation ritual, 118, 261n54
   Yohanan ben Hahoroni, 148
transmission of Mishnah, 2, 10, 98, 235n2, 248n4, 248n5
   performative, textual approaches, 97–98

U
Urbach, Ephraim E., 5, 28

V
Valler, Shulamit, 8
Vayikra Rabba, 256n101
verb forms. 36, 50, 58, 240n18
   see also qotel; yiqtol
   casuistic formulations, 38

and narrativity, 30
preterit, 19
verbs, stative, 17
violence, narrative, 204–219
voices, dissonant, *see* texts, dialogic

W
Wacholder, Ben Zion, 243n11
Walfish, Avraham, 190, 243n10, 253n25, 256n4, 256n6, 257n23
water libation story, 119, 261n54, 211–214
water pipe stories, 111–116, 249n25
waters, bitter, 201
Weisberg, Robert, 17
"when the transgressors increased," 200
Wimpfheimer, Barry, 8, 238n30, 244n21
"wise man" tradition, 133–134
witnesses, 177, 186–193
  examination process, 184–185
  father and son, 181–182
  new moon, 170, 181
  problematic, 185–188
  sectarians, 202
wood storeroom, 216, 217, 218
word order, 32

Y
Yaron, Reuven, 245n6, 245n7
Yassif, Eli, 241n55
Yavne, *see* calendar court (Yavne)
Yehudah, 101
Yerushalmi, 11
  Adar, 20th of, 256n102
  Aqiba-Gamliel counter-narrative, 180
  discourse, 262n5
  Honi Hame'agel, 163, 256n102
  new moon, 180
  paschal sacrifice, 69
  and Roman law, 80
  Sabbath limit counter-narrative, 103–105
  Samaritan fires, 261n34
  Shabbat gangplank story, 245n38
  Tevi the slave, 254n40, 254n41
  water libation ritual, 118
  water pipe stories, 115
  Yohanan ben Zakkai counter-narrative, 115–116
yiqtol form, 31–32, 38, 241n39, *see also qotel*; *qatal*
Yohanan, R., 188
Yohanan ben Hahoroni, R., 4, 146–148, 254n47
Yohanan ben Nuri, R., 185–186
Yohanan ben Zakkai, R., 123, 135, 249n25
  authority questions, 115
  as exemplar, 139–141
  and Jewish practice, 198
  lulav ritual, 195–197, 199
  post-Destruction ritual, 198
  Sabbath cases, 113–116
Yom Kippur date, 188–193, 259n52
Yom Kippur rites, 209–210
Yose, R., 111, 125, 177, 178, 181

Z
Zadok, R., 45, 68, 139, 140–141, 207–208

www.ingramcontent.com/pod-product-compliance
Ingram Content Group UK Ltd.
Pitfield, Milton Keynes, MK11 3LW, UK
UKHW041959230426
12048UKWH00008B/430